SOUL EATER

4

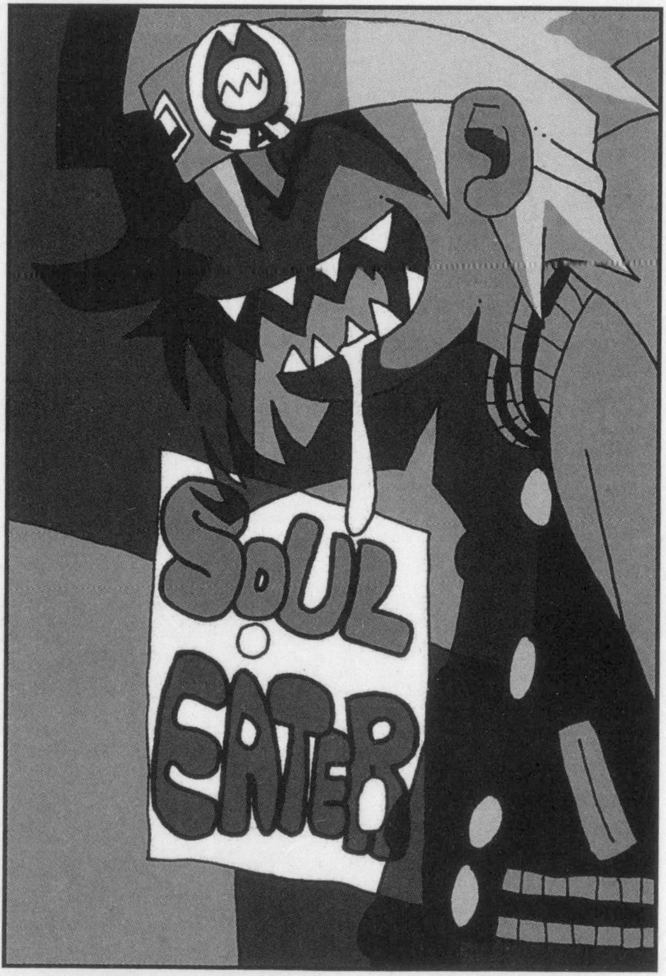
SOUL
EATER

ATSUSHI OHKUBO

DON'T CALL ME...

SOUL EATER

vol. 4
by ATSUSHI OHKUBO

Let us have mercy on the crying SOUL

SOUL EATER 4

CONTENTS

Chapter 10: The Experiment (Part 1) 005

Chapter 11: The Experiment (Part 2) 045

Chapter 12: Ultimate Written Exam 088

Chapter 13: Black Dragon (Part 1) 125

Chapter 14: Black Dragon (Part 2) 161

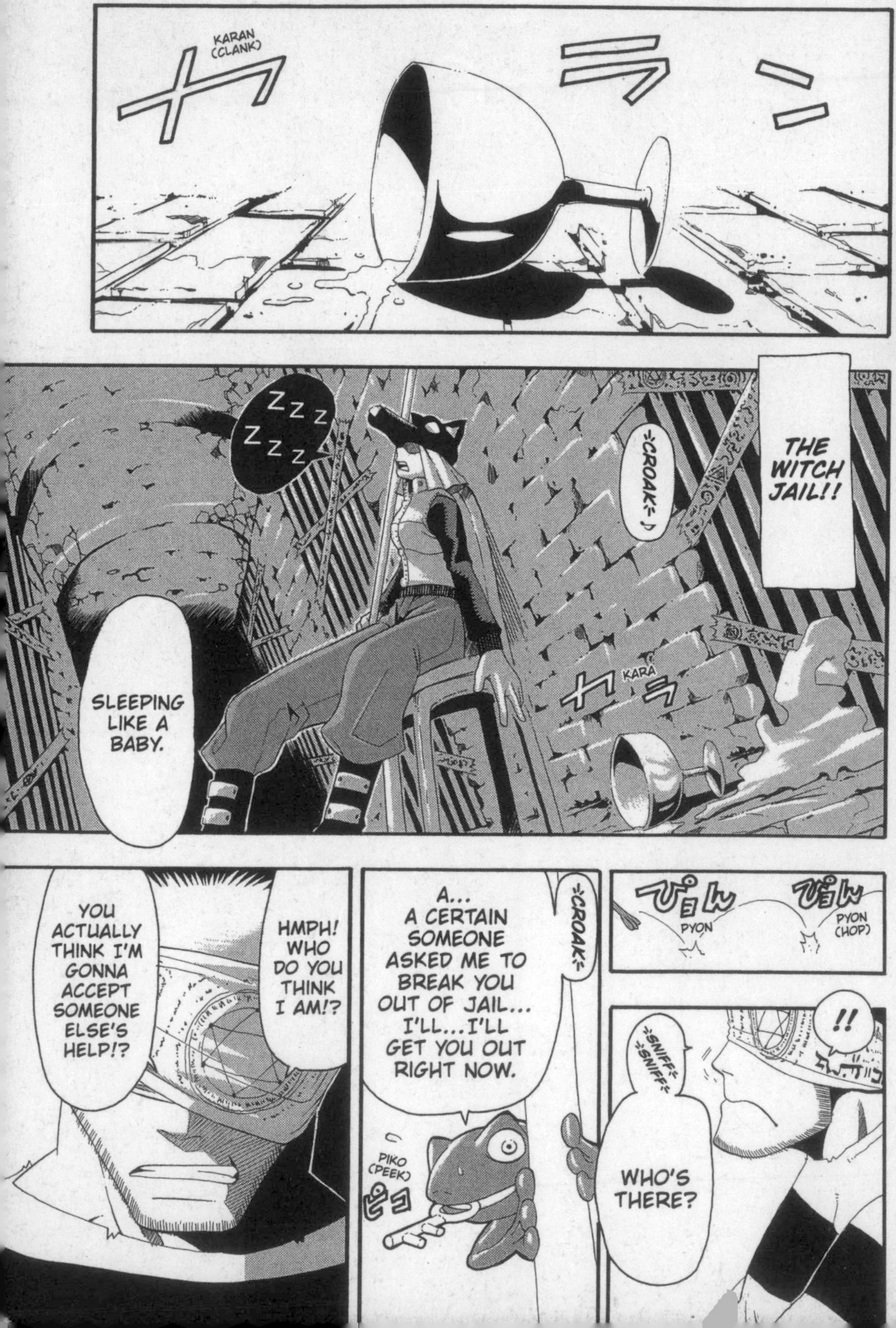
KARAN (CLANK)
THE WITCH JAIL!!
CROAK
ZZZ ZZZ
KARA
SLEEPING LIKE A BABY.
PYON PYON (HOP)
!!
SNIFF SNIFF
WHO'S THERE?
CROAK
A... A CERTAIN SOMEONE ASKED ME TO BREAK YOU OUT OF JAIL... I'LL...I'LL GET YOU OUT RIGHT NOW.
PIKO (PEEK)
HMPH! WHO DO YOU THINK I AM!?
YOU ACTUALLY THINK I'M GONNA ACCEPT SOMEONE ELSE'S HELP!?

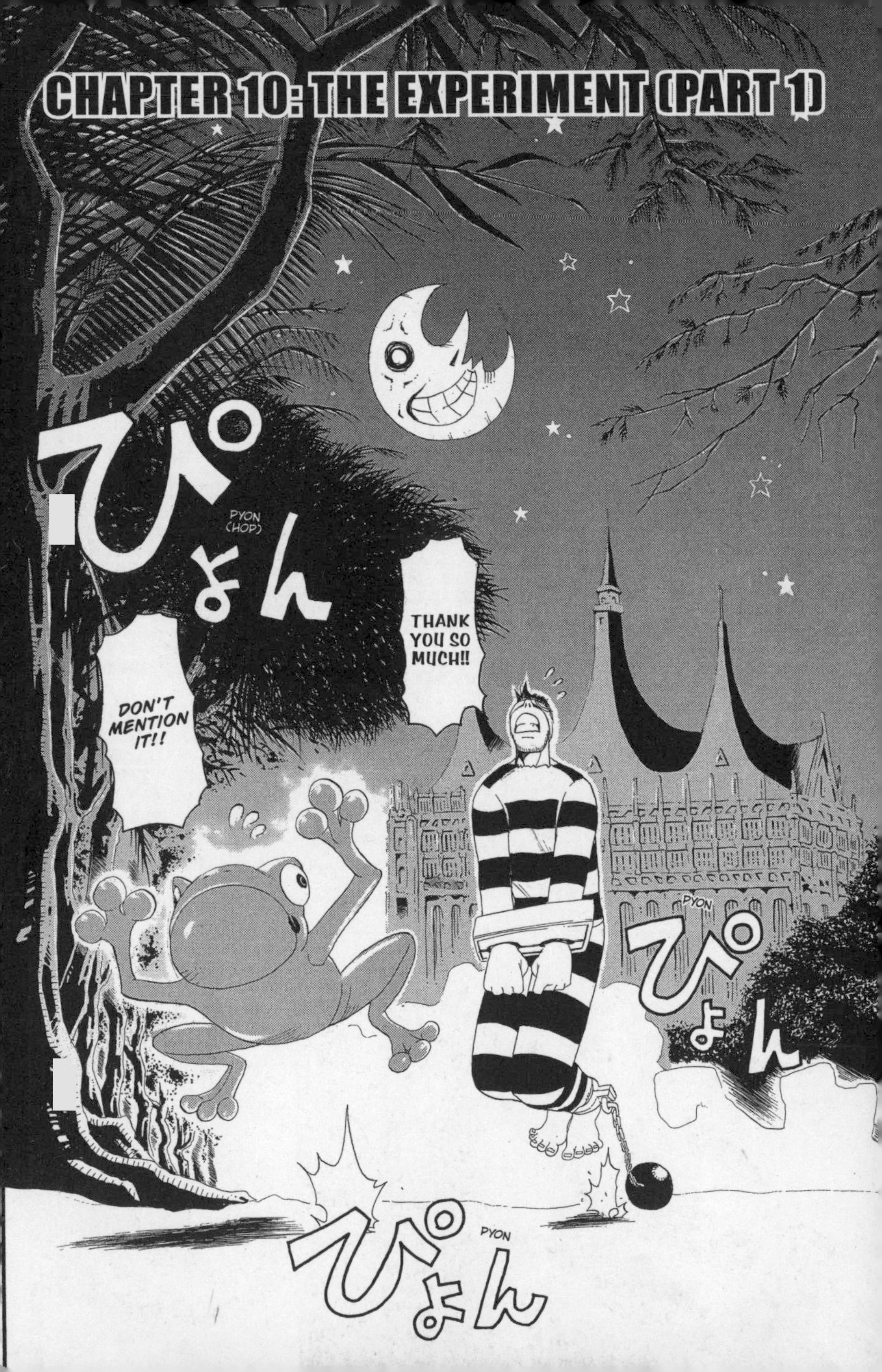
CHAPTER 10: THE EXPERIMENT (PART 1)
ぴょん
PYON (HOP)
THANK YOU SO MUCH!!
DON'T MENTION IT!!
PYON
ぴょん
ぴょん
PYON

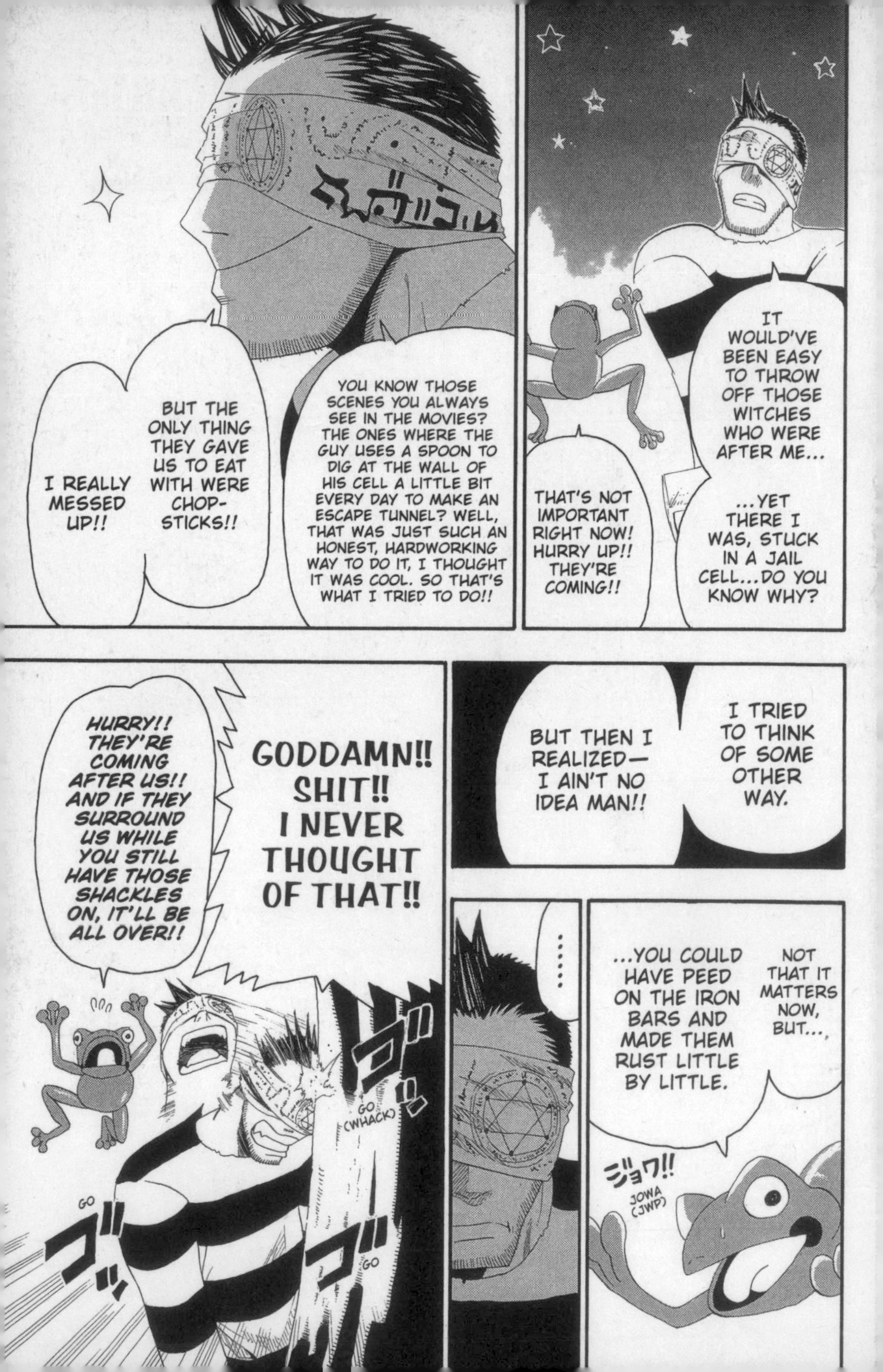
IT WOULD'VE BEEN EASY TO THROW OFF THOSE WITCHES WHO WERE AFTER ME...
...YET THERE I WAS, STUCK IN A JAIL CELL...DO YOU KNOW WHY?
THAT'S NOT IMPORTANT RIGHT NOW! HURRY UP!! THEY'RE COMING!!
YOU KNOW THOSE SCENES YOU ALWAYS SEE IN THE MOVIES? THE ONES WHERE THE GUY USES A SPOON TO DIG AT THE WALL OF HIS CELL A LITTLE BIT EVERY DAY TO MAKE AN ESCAPE TUNNEL? WELL, THAT WAS JUST SUCH AN HONEST, HARDWORKING WAY TO DO IT, I THOUGHT IT WAS COOL. SO THAT'S WHAT I TRIED TO DO!!
BUT THE ONLY THING THEY GAVE US TO EAT WITH WERE CHOP-STICKS!!
I REALLY MESSED UP!!
I TRIED TO THINK OF SOME OTHER WAY.
BUT THEN I REALIZED—I AIN'T NO IDEA MAN!!
NOT THAT IT MATTERS NOW, BUT...,
...YOU COULD HAVE PEED ON THE IRON BARS AND MADE THEM RUST LITTLE BY LITTLE.
ジョワ!!
JOWA (JWP)
......
GODDAMN!! SHIT!! I NEVER THOUGHT OF THAT!!
HURRY!! THEY'RE COMING AFTER US!! AND IF THEY SURROUND US WHILE YOU STILL HAVE THOSE SHACKLES ON, IT'LL BE ALL OVER!!
GO (WHACK)
GO
GO

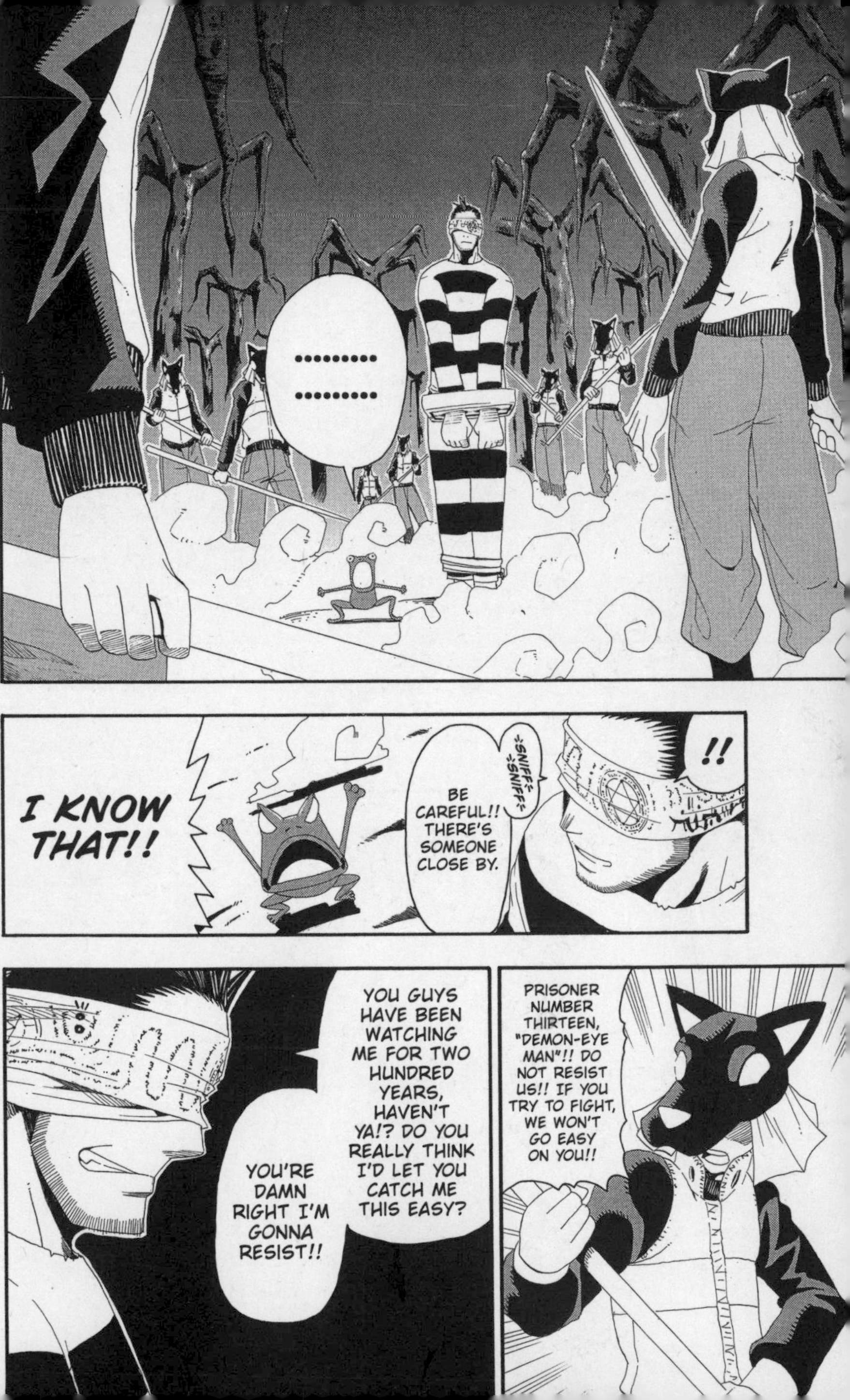
....
....
!!
SNIFF *SNIFF*
BE CAREFUL!! THERE'S SOMEONE CLOSE BY.
I KNOW THAT!!
PRISONER NUMBER THIRTEEN, "DEMON-EYE MAN"!! DO NOT RESIST US!! IF YOU TRY TO FIGHT, WE WON'T GO EASY ON YOU!!
YOU GUYS HAVE BEEN WATCHING ME FOR TWO HUNDRED YEARS, HAVEN'T YA!? DO YOU REALLY THINK I'D LET YOU CATCH ME THIS EASY?
YOU'RE DAMN RIGHT I'M GONNA RESIST!!

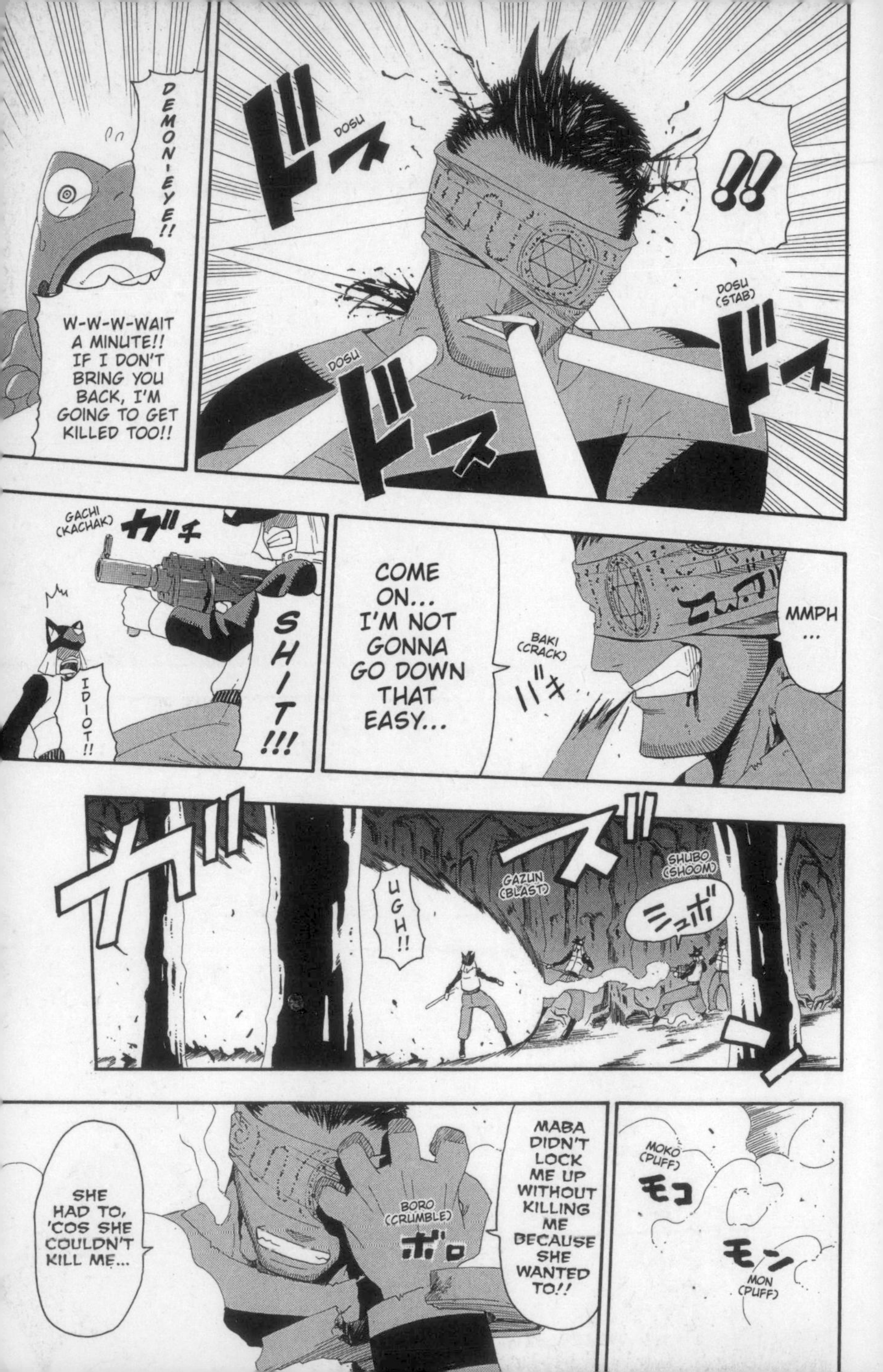

DOSU
!!
DOSU (STAB)
DOSU
DEMON-EYE!!
W-W-W-WAIT A MINUTE!! IF I DON'T BRING YOU BACK, I'M GOING TO GET KILLED TOO!!
MMPH ...
BAKI (CRACK)
COME ON... I'M NOT GONNA GO DOWN THAT EASY...
GACHI (KACHAK)
SHIT!!!
IDIOT!!
SHUBO (SHOOM)
GAZUN (BLAST)
UGH!!
MOKO (PUFF)
MON (PUFF)
MABA DIDN'T LOCK ME UP WITHOUT KILLING ME BECAUSE SHE WANTED TO!!
BORO (CRUMBLE)
SHE HAD TO, 'COS SHE COULDN'T KILL ME...

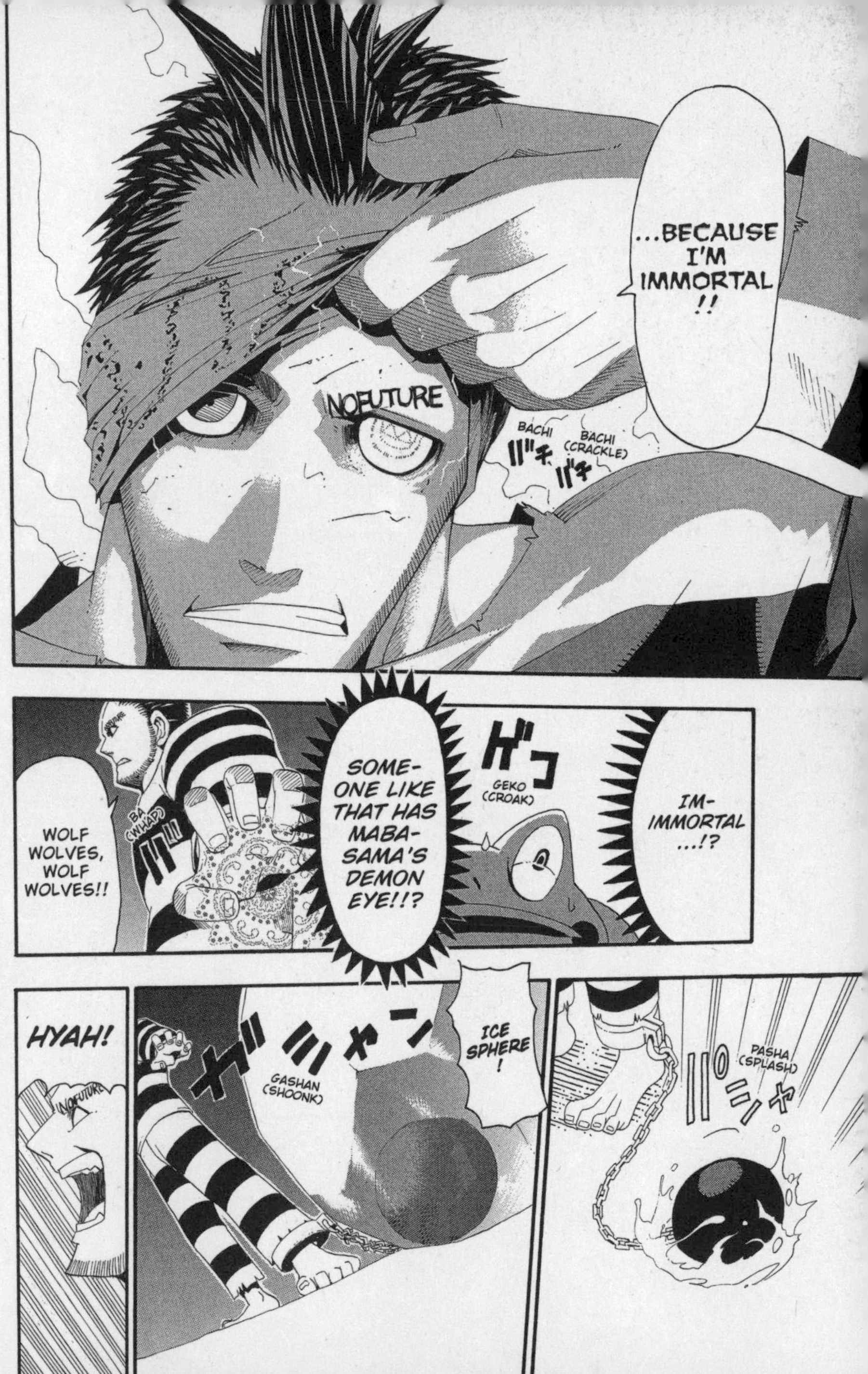
...BECAUSE I'M IMMORTAL!!
NOFUTURE
BACHI BACHI (CRACKLE)
IM-IMMORTAL...!?
GEKO (CROAK)
SOME-ONE LIKE THAT HAS MABA-SAMA'S DEMON EYE!!?
BA (WHAP)
WOLF WOLVES, WOLF WOLVES!!
PASHA (SPLASH)
ICE SPHERE!
GASHAN (SHOONK)
HYAH!
NOFUTURE

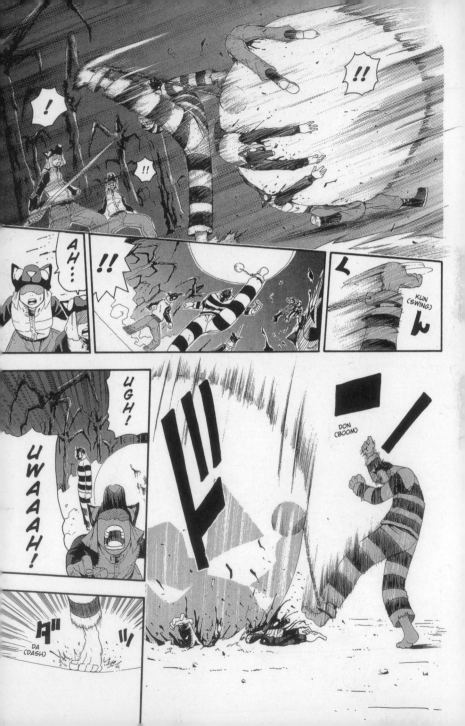

!!

!

!!

AH...

!!

KUN
(SWING)

UGH!

DON
(BOOM)

UWAAAH!

ダ
DA
(DASH)

!!

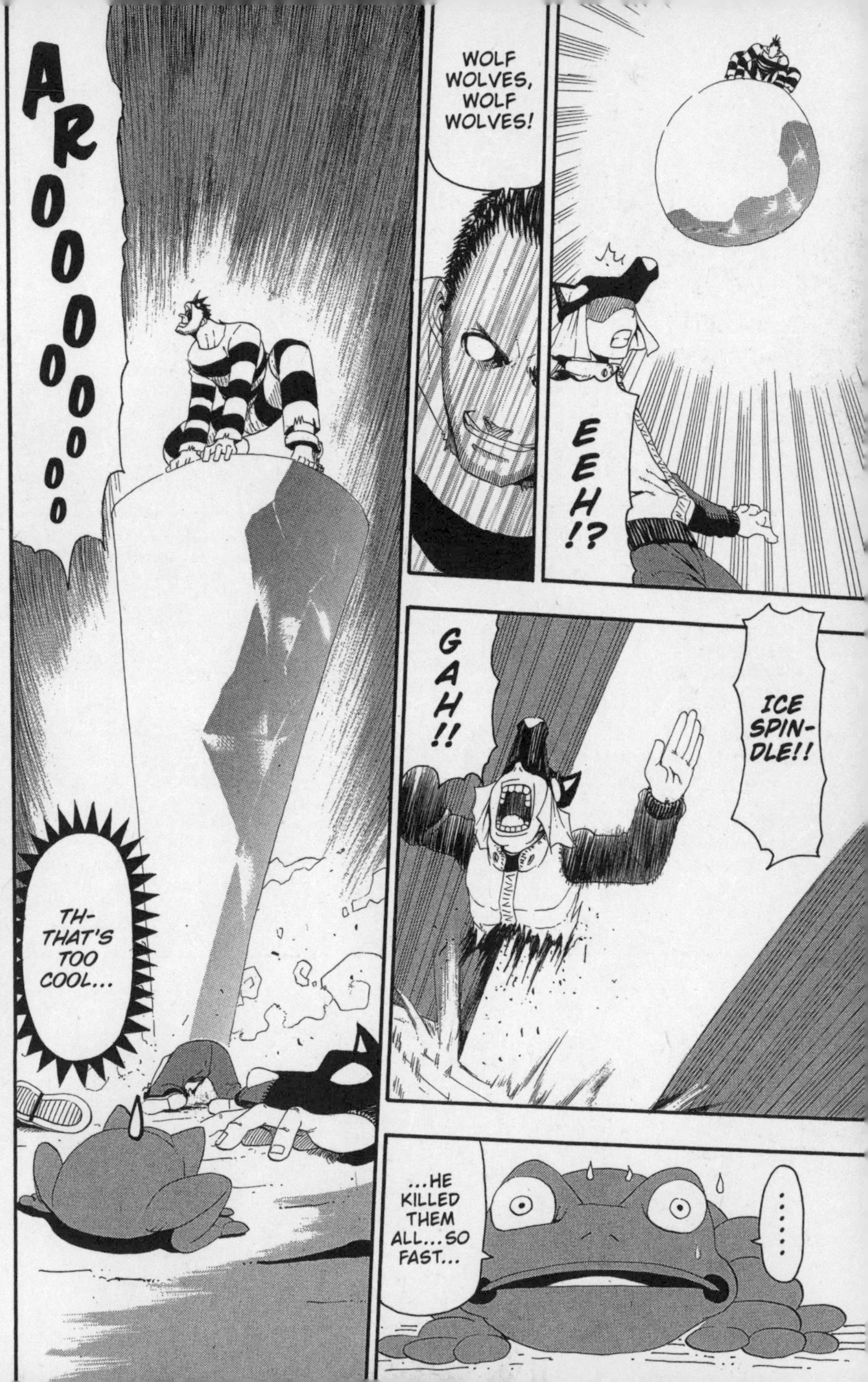
EEH!?
WOLF WOLVES, WOLF WOLVES!
ICE SPIN-DLE!!
GAH!!
......
...HE KILLED THEM ALL...SO FAST...
AROOOOOOOOOO
TH-THAT'S TOO COOL...

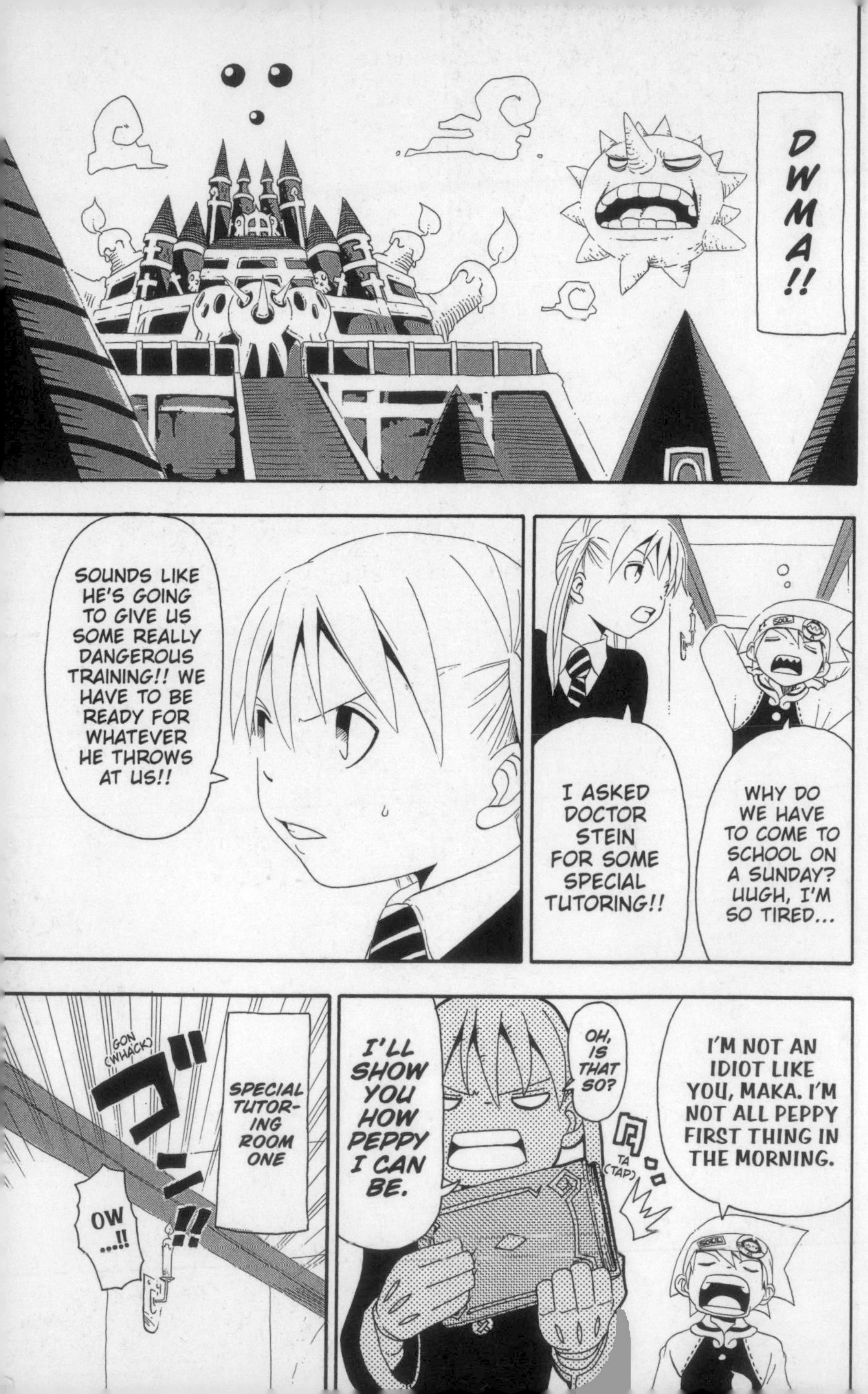
DWMA!!
WHY DO WE HAVE TO COME TO SCHOOL ON A SUNDAY? UUGH, I'M SO TIRED...
I ASKED DOCTOR STEIN FOR SOME SPECIAL TUTORING!!
SOUNDS LIKE HE'S GOING TO GIVE US SOME REALLY DANGEROUS TRAINING!! WE HAVE TO BE READY FOR WHATEVER HE THROWS AT US!!
I'M NOT AN IDIOT LIKE YOU, MAKA. I'M NOT ALL PEPPY FIRST THING IN THE MORNING.
OH, IS THAT SO?
TA (TAP)
I'LL SHOW YOU HOW PEPPY I CAN BE.
SPECIAL TUTORING ROOM ONE
GON (WHACK)
OW ...!!

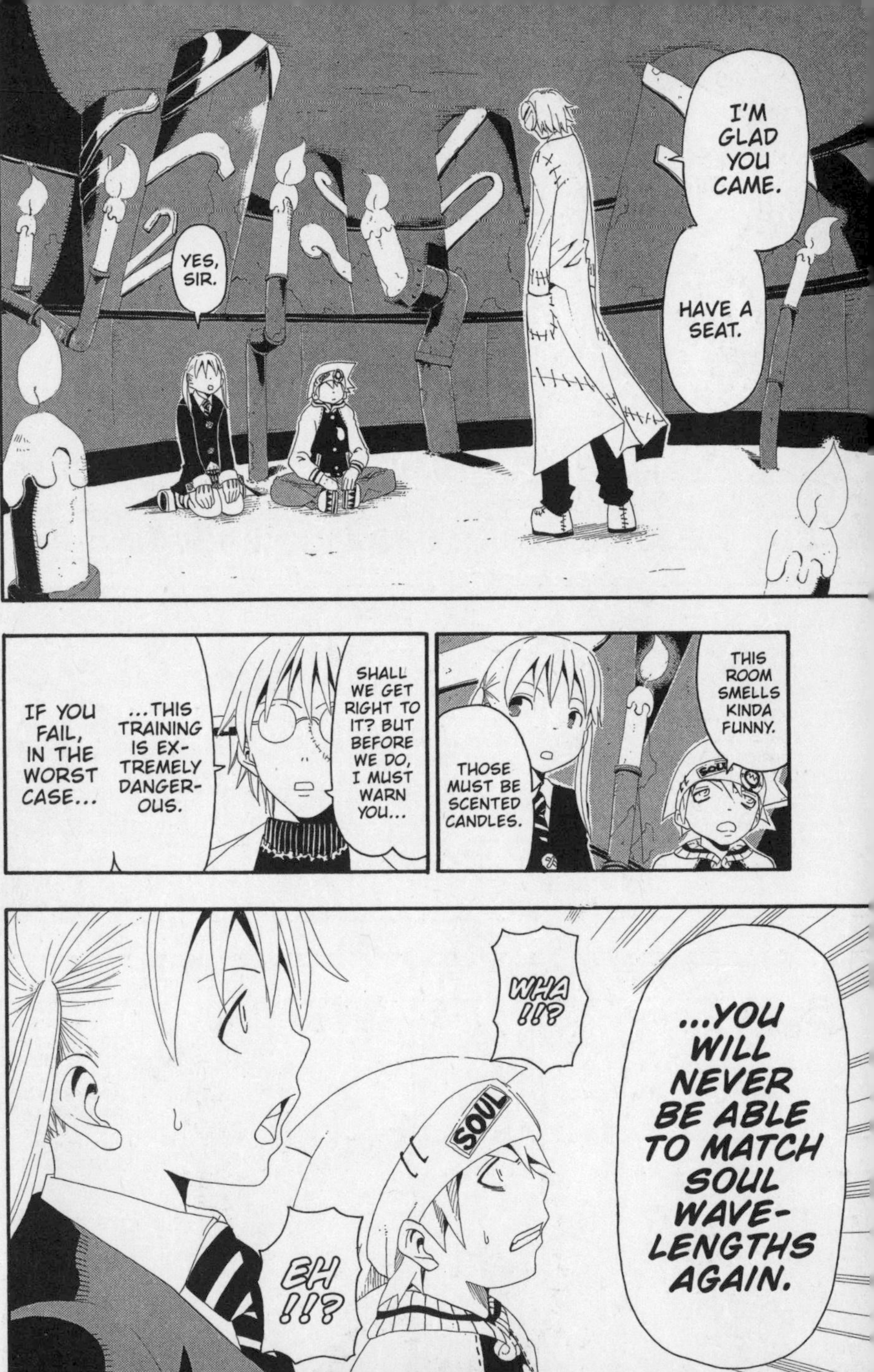
I'M GLAD YOU CAME.
HAVE A SEAT.
YES, SIR.
THIS ROOM SMELLS KINDA FUNNY.
THOSE MUST BE SCENTED CANDLES.
SHALL WE GET RIGHT TO IT? BUT BEFORE WE DO, I MUST WARN YOU...
...THIS TRAINING IS EXTREMELY DANGEROUS.
IF YOU FAIL, IN THE WORST CASE...
...YOU WILL NEVER BE ABLE TO MATCH SOUL WAVELENGTHS AGAIN.
WHA!!?
EH!!?

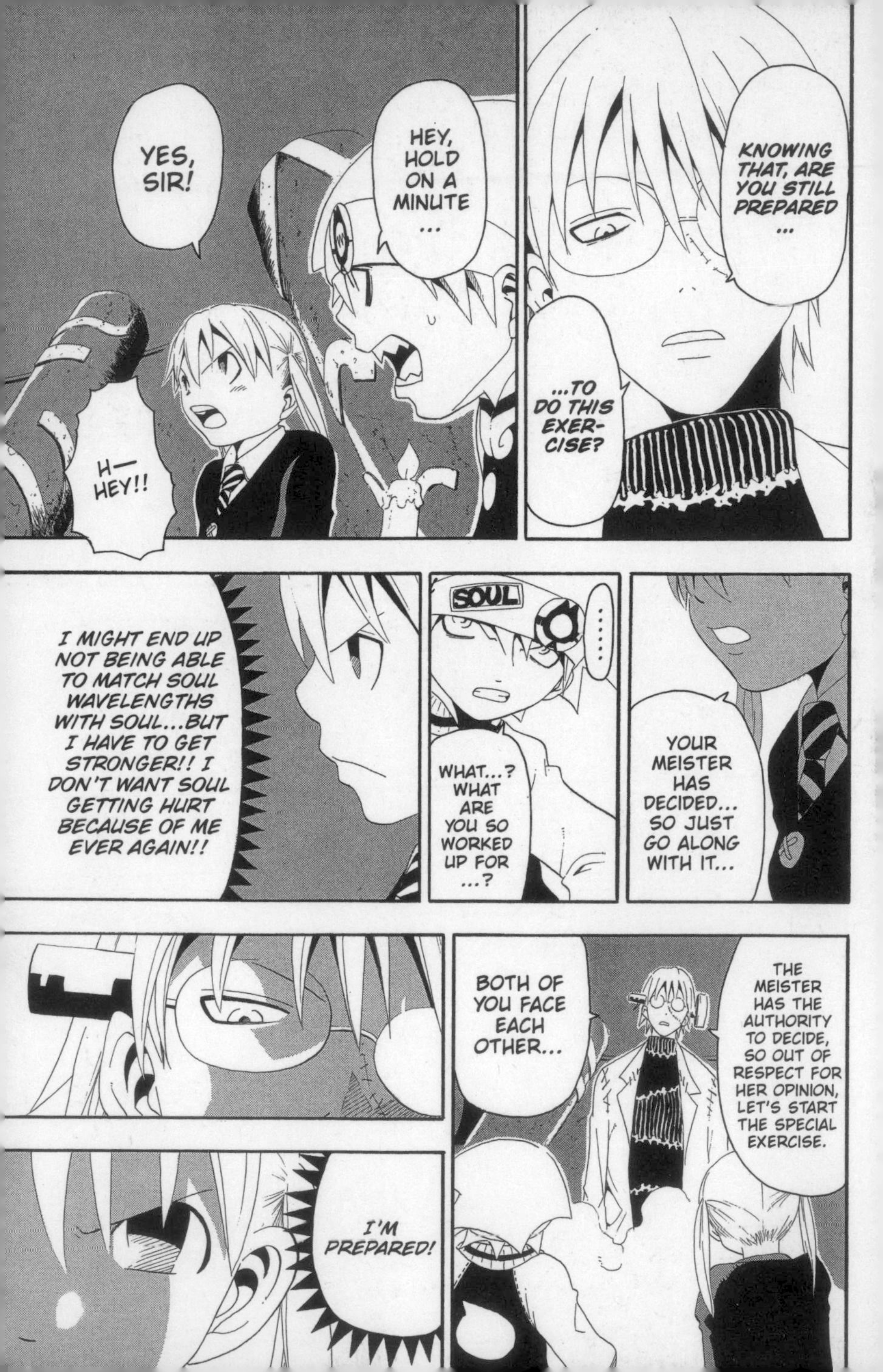
KNOWING THAT, ARE YOU STILL PREPARED ...
...TO DO THIS EXER-CISE?
HEY, HOLD ON A MINUTE ...
YES, SIR!
H— HEY!!
YOUR MEISTER HAS DECIDED... SO JUST GO ALONG WITH IT...
......
WHAT...? WHAT ARE YOU SO WORKED UP FOR ...?
I MIGHT END UP NOT BEING ABLE TO MATCH SOUL WAVELENGTHS WITH SOUL...BUT I HAVE TO GET STRONGER!! I DON'T WANT SOUL GETTING HURT BECAUSE OF ME EVER AGAIN!!
THE MEISTER HAS THE AUTHORITY TO DECIDE, SO OUT OF RESPECT FOR HER OPINION, LET'S START THE SPECIAL EXERCISE.
BOTH OF YOU FACE EACH OTHER...
I'M PREPARED!

HUH!?

NOW I WANT EACH OF YOU TO POINT OUT THE OTHER'S FAULTS.

YES.

TH-THAT'S OUR TRAINING?

THAT'S RIGHT.

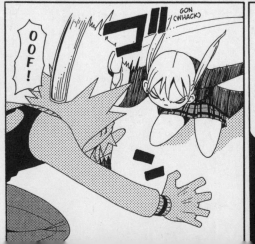

OOF!

GON (WHACK)

SHE'S STUBBORN, RECKLESS, HER HOBBIES ARE READING AND PUZZLES, SHE'S GLOOMY, HER ANKLES ARE *FAT*—

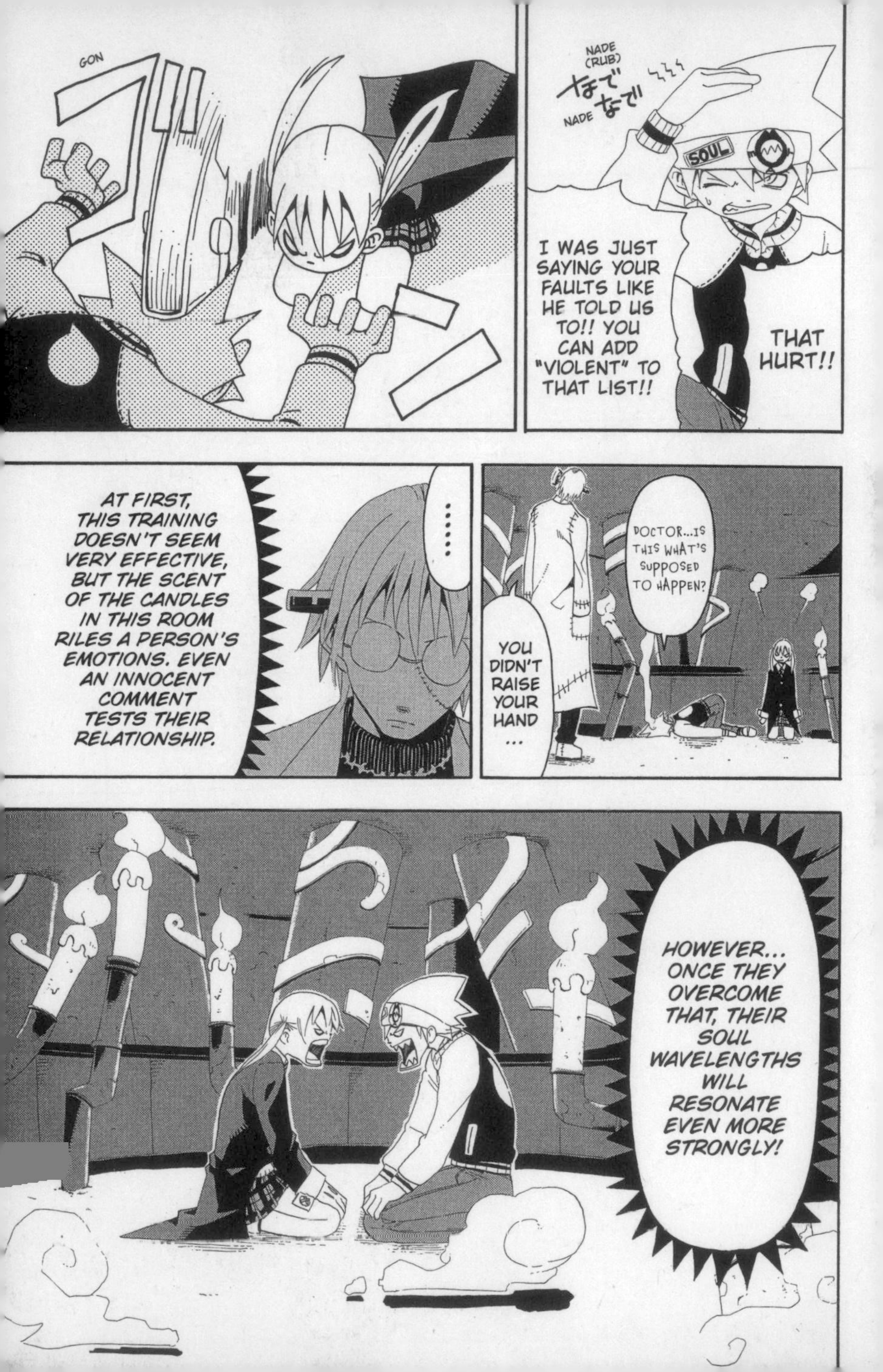
NADE (RUB)
なで
NADE
なで
THAT HURT!!
I WAS JUST SAYING YOUR FAULTS LIKE HE TOLD US TO!! YOU CAN ADD "VIOLENT" TO THAT LIST!!
GON
DOCTOR...IS THIS WHAT'S SUPPOSED TO HAPPEN?
YOU DIDN'T RAISE YOUR HAND ...
......
AT FIRST, THIS TRAINING DOESN'T SEEM VERY EFFECTIVE, BUT THE SCENT OF THE CANDLES IN THIS ROOM RILES A PERSON'S EMOTIONS. EVEN AN INNOCENT COMMENT TESTS THEIR RELATIONSHIP.
HOWEVER... ONCE THEY OVERCOME THAT, THEIR SOUL WAVELENGTHS WILL RESONATE EVEN MORE STRONGLY!

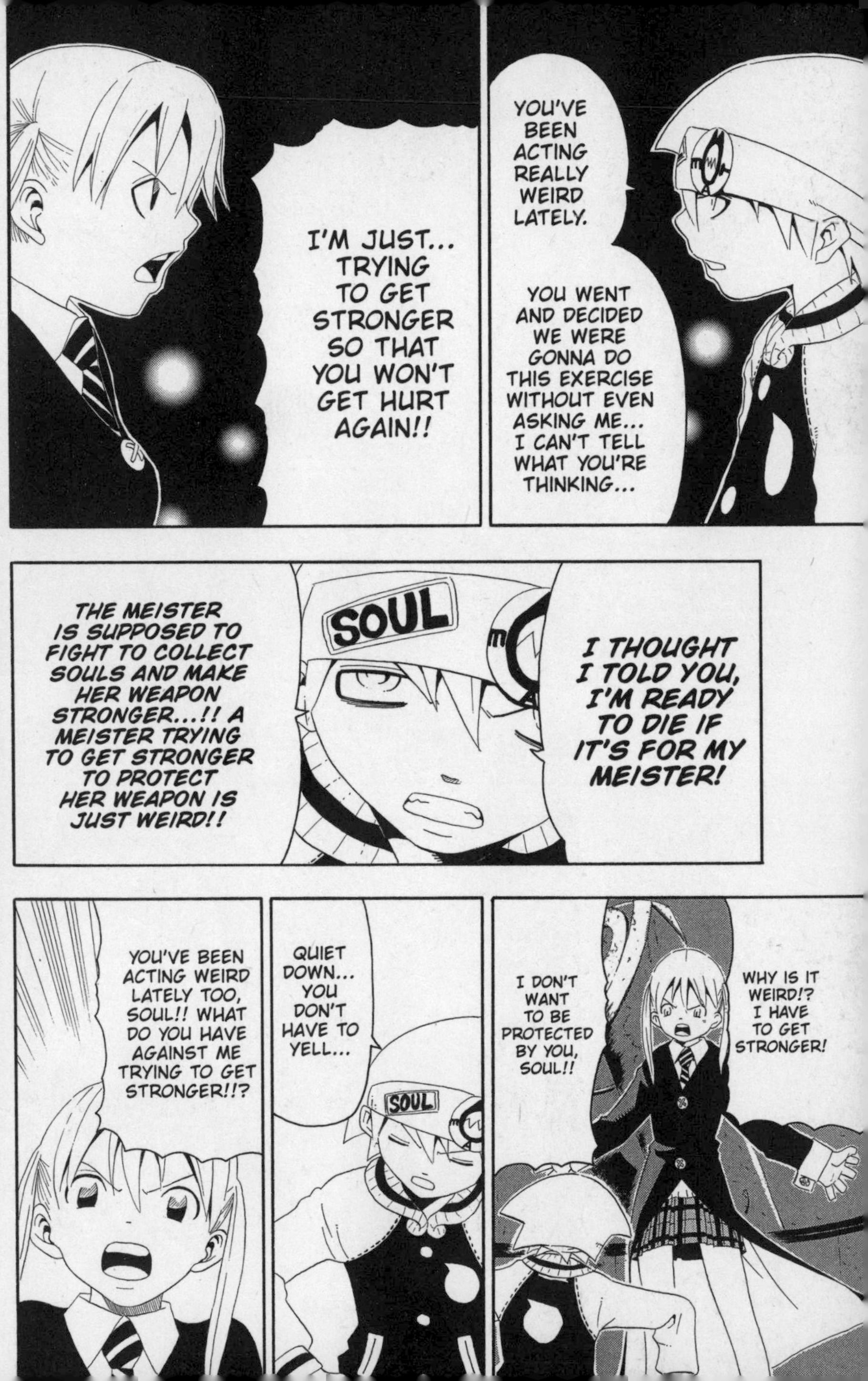
YOU'VE BEEN ACTING REALLY WEIRD LATELY.
YOU WENT AND DECIDED WE WERE GONNA DO THIS EXERCISE WITHOUT EVEN ASKING ME... I CAN'T TELL WHAT YOU'RE THINKING...
I'M JUST... TRYING TO GET STRONGER SO THAT YOU WON'T GET HURT AGAIN!!
I THOUGHT I TOLD YOU, I'M READY TO DIE IF IT'S FOR MY MEISTER!
THE MEISTER IS SUPPOSED TO FIGHT TO COLLECT SOULS AND MAKE HER WEAPON STRONGER...!! A MEISTER TRYING TO GET STRONGER TO PROTECT HER WEAPON IS JUST WEIRD!!
SOUL
WHY IS IT WEIRD!? I HAVE TO GET STRONGER!
I DON'T WANT TO BE PROTECTED BY YOU, SOUL!!
QUIET DOWN... YOU DON'T HAVE TO YELL...
SOUL
YOU'VE BEEN ACTING WEIRD LATELY TOO, SOUL!! WHAT DO YOU HAVE AGAINST ME TRYING TO GET STRONGER!!?

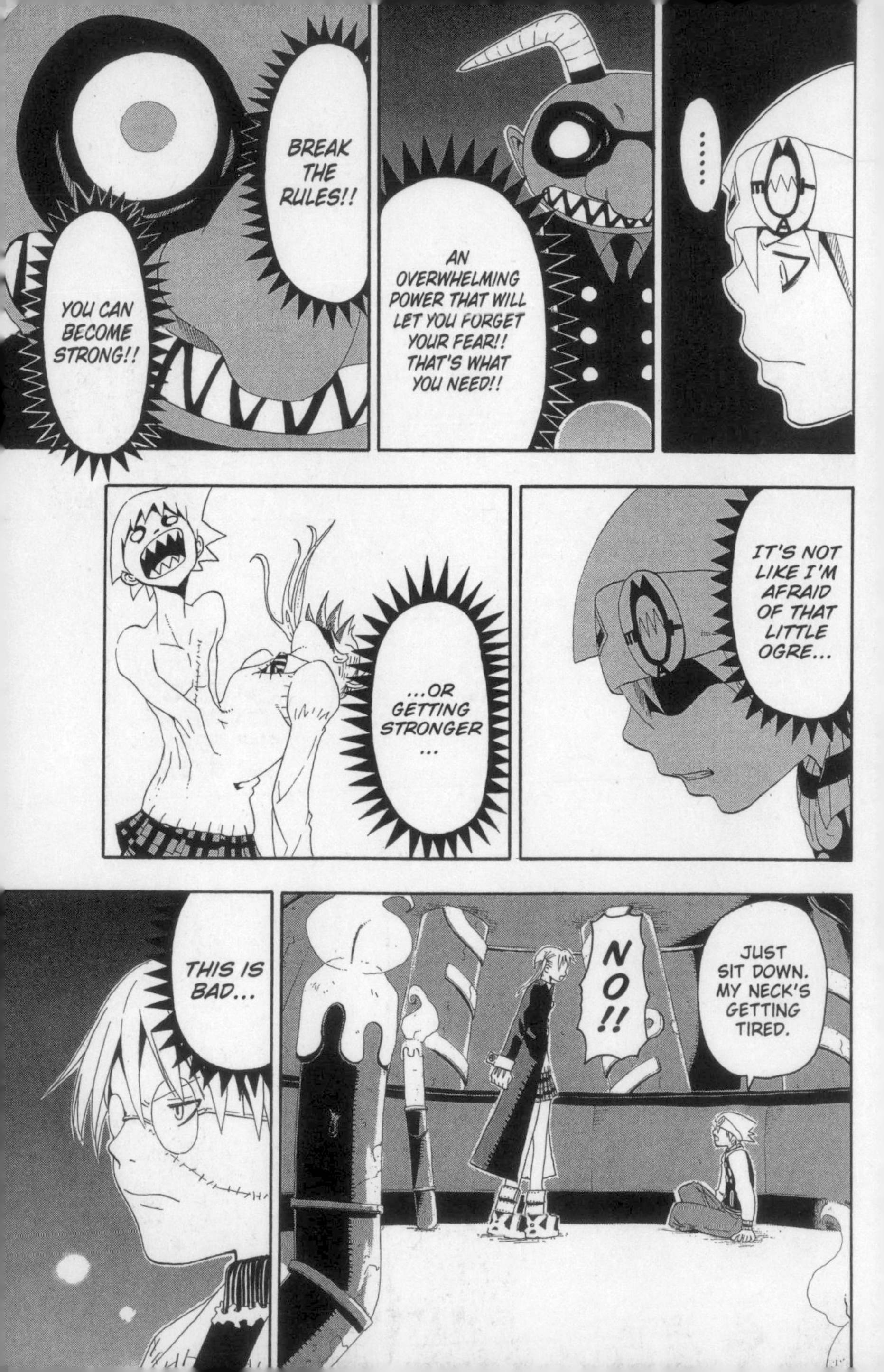
......
AN OVERWHELMING POWER THAT WILL LET YOU FORGET YOUR FEAR!! THAT'S WHAT YOU NEED!!
BREAK THE RULES!!
YOU CAN BECOME STRONG!!
IT'S NOT LIKE I'M AFRAID OF THAT LITTLE OGRE...
...OR GETTING STRONGER ...
JUST SIT DOWN. MY NECK'S GETTING TIRED.
NO!!
THIS IS BAD...

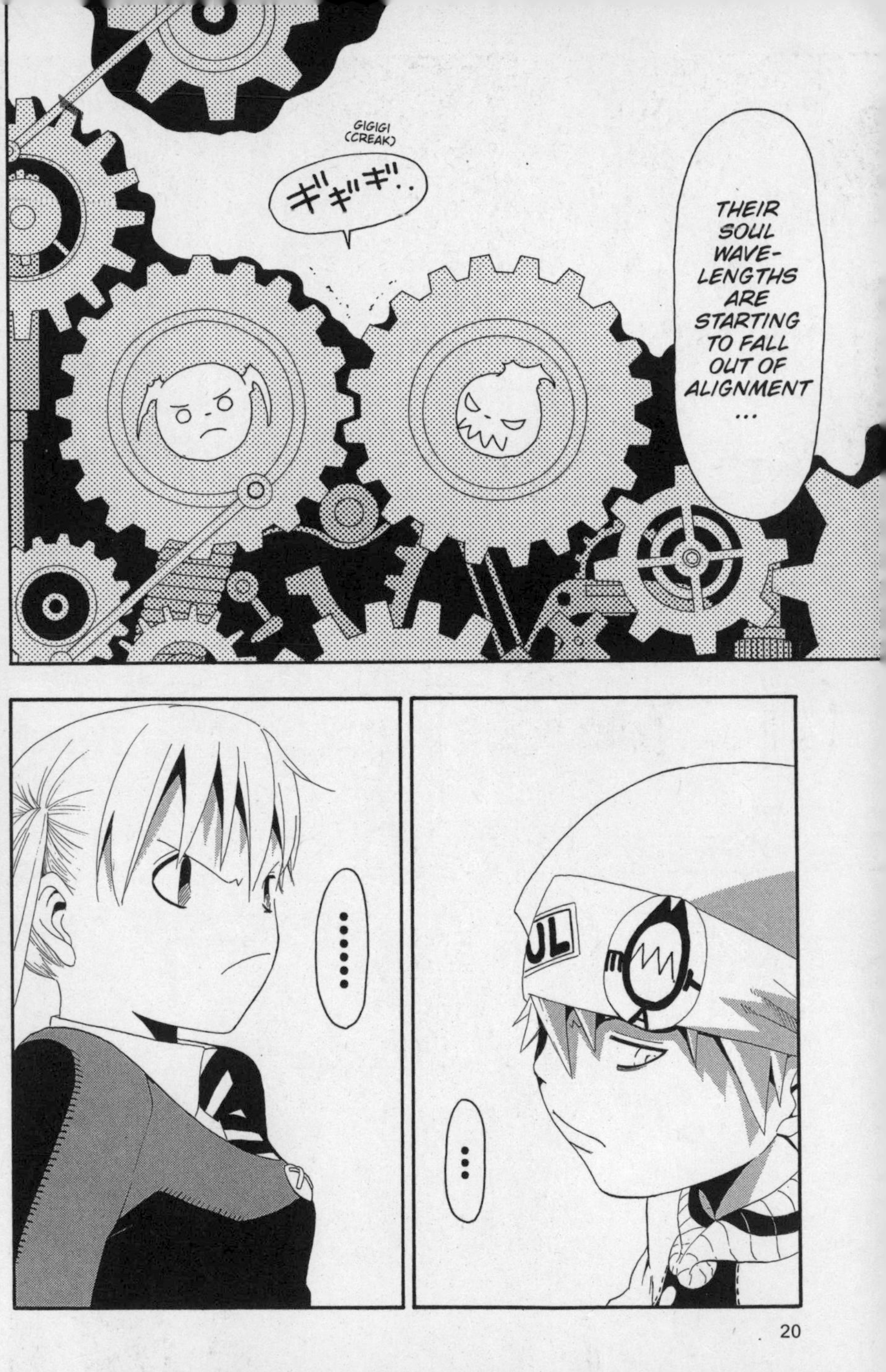
THEIR SOUL WAVE-LENGTHS ARE STARTING TO FALL OUT OF ALIGNMENT ...
GIGIGI (CREAK)
ギギギ..
...
......

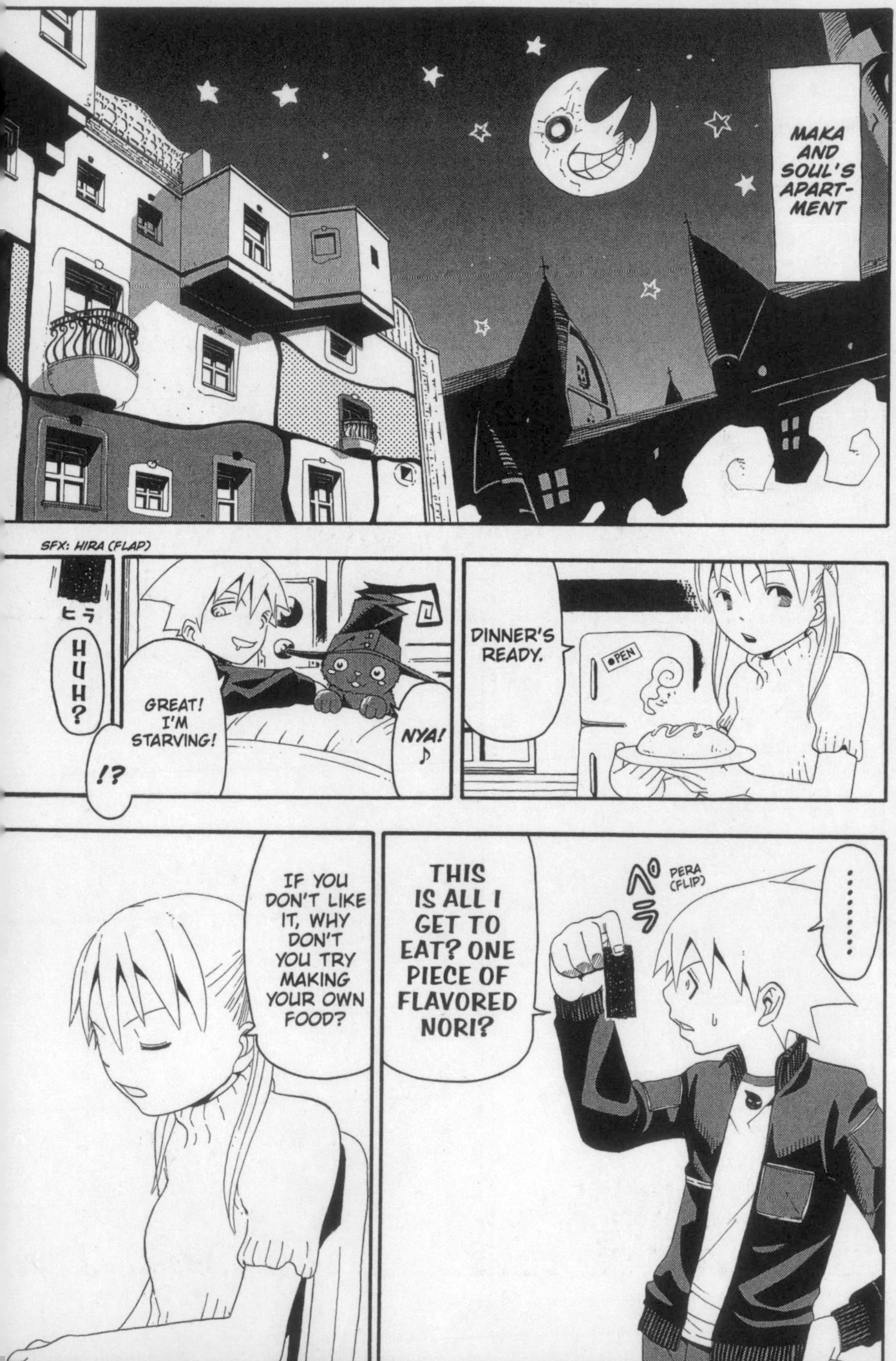
MAKA AND SOUL'S APARTMENT
DINNER'S READY.
GREAT! I'M STARVING!
NYA! ♪
SFX: HIRA (FLAP)
ヒラ
HUH?
!?
....
ペラ
PERA (FLIP)
THIS IS ALL I GET TO EAT? ONE PIECE OF FLAVORED NORI?
IF YOU DON'T LIKE IT, WHY DON'T YOU TRY MAKING YOUR OWN FOOD?

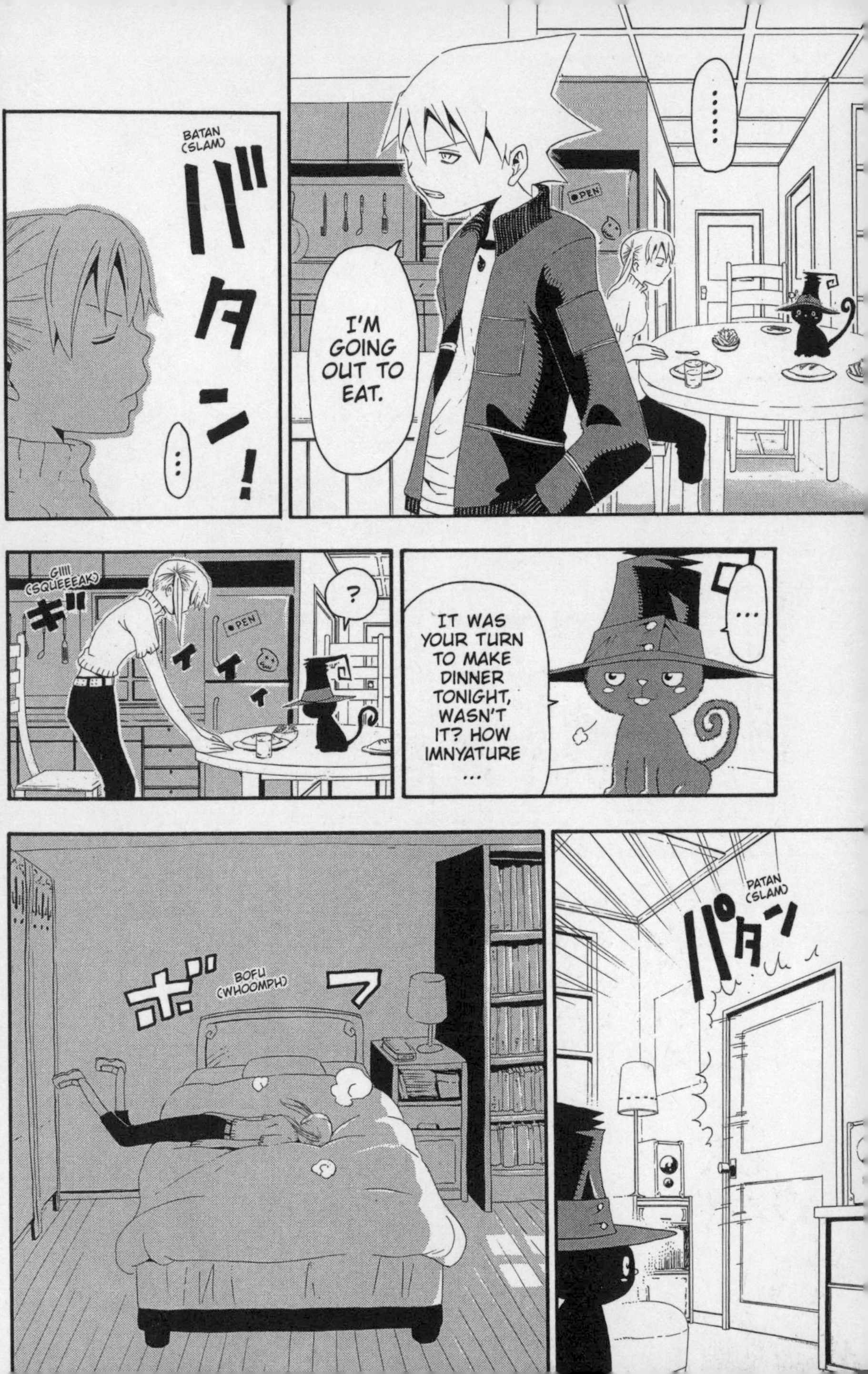
......
I'M GOING OUT TO EAT.
BATAN (SLAM)
バターン!
...
...
IT WAS YOUR TURN TO MAKE DINNER TONIGHT, WASN'T IT? HOW IMNYATURE ...
GIIII (SQUEEEAK)
ギィィ
?
PATAN (SLAM)
パタン
BOFU (WHOOMPH)
ボフ

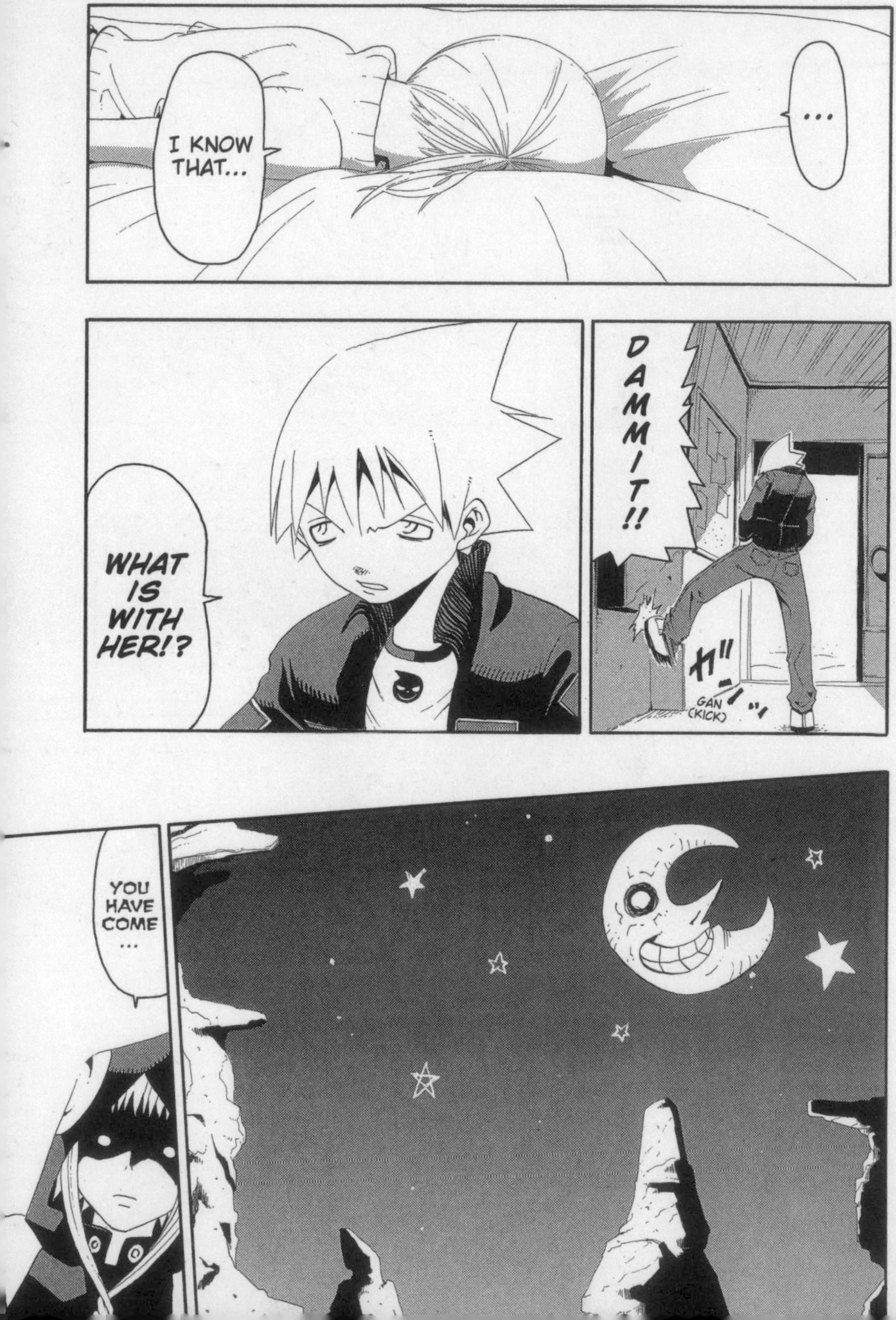
...
I KNOW THAT...
DAMMIT!!
GAN (KICK)
WHAT IS WITH HER!?
YOU HAVE COME ...

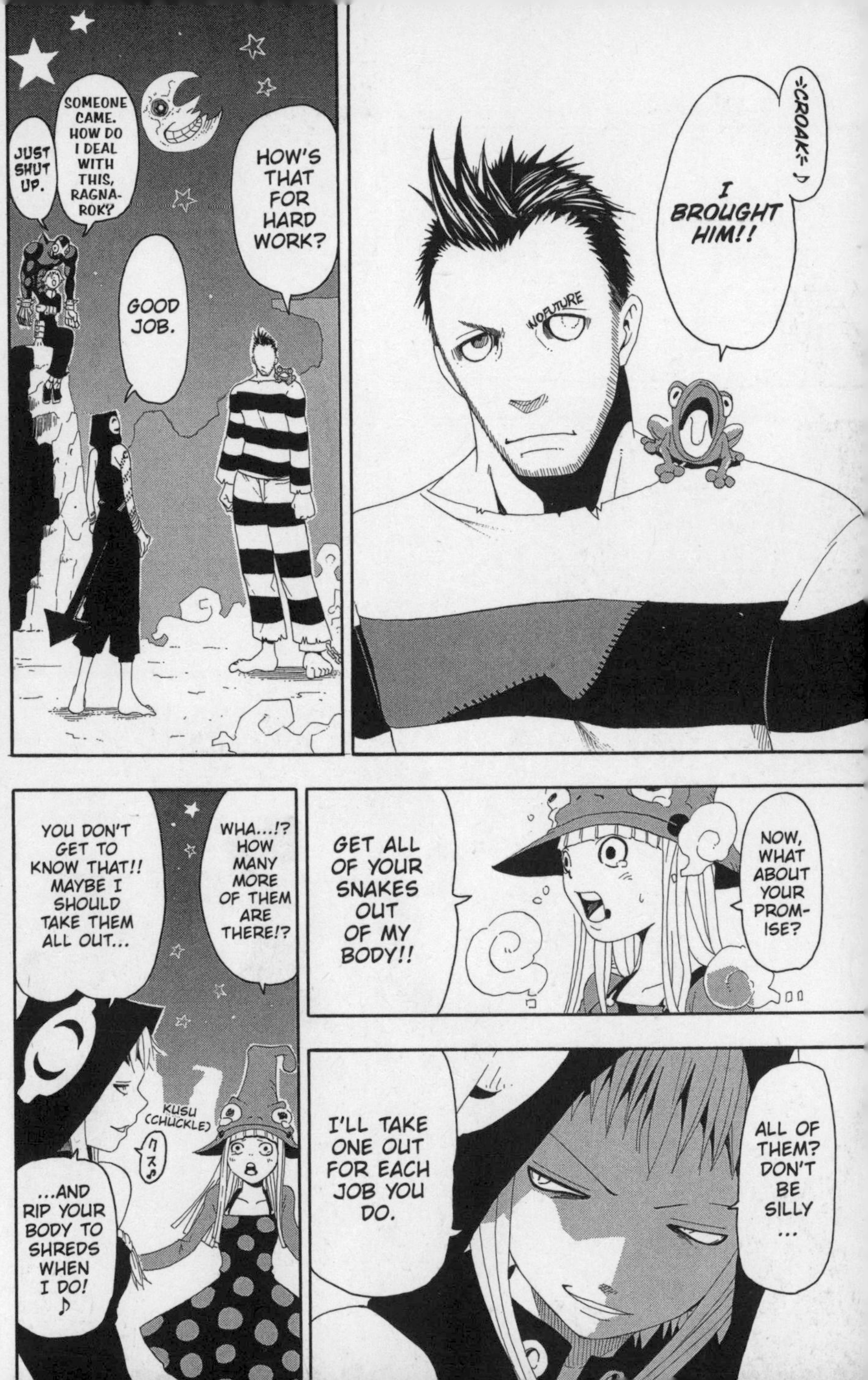
~CROAK~ ♪
I BROUGHT HIM!!
NOFUTURE
HOW'S THAT FOR HARD WORK?
SOMEONE CAME. HOW DO I DEAL WITH THIS, RAGNAROK?
JUST SHUT UP.
GOOD JOB.
NOW, WHAT ABOUT YOUR PROMISE?
GET ALL OF YOUR SNAKES OUT OF MY BODY!!
ALL OF THEM? DON'T BE SILLY ...
I'LL TAKE ONE OUT FOR EACH JOB YOU DO.
WHA...!? HOW MANY MORE OF THEM ARE THERE!?
YOU DON'T GET TO KNOW THAT!! MAYBE I SHOULD TAKE THEM ALL OUT...
KUSU (CHUCKLE)
...AND RIP YOUR BODY TO SHREDS WHEN I DO! ♪

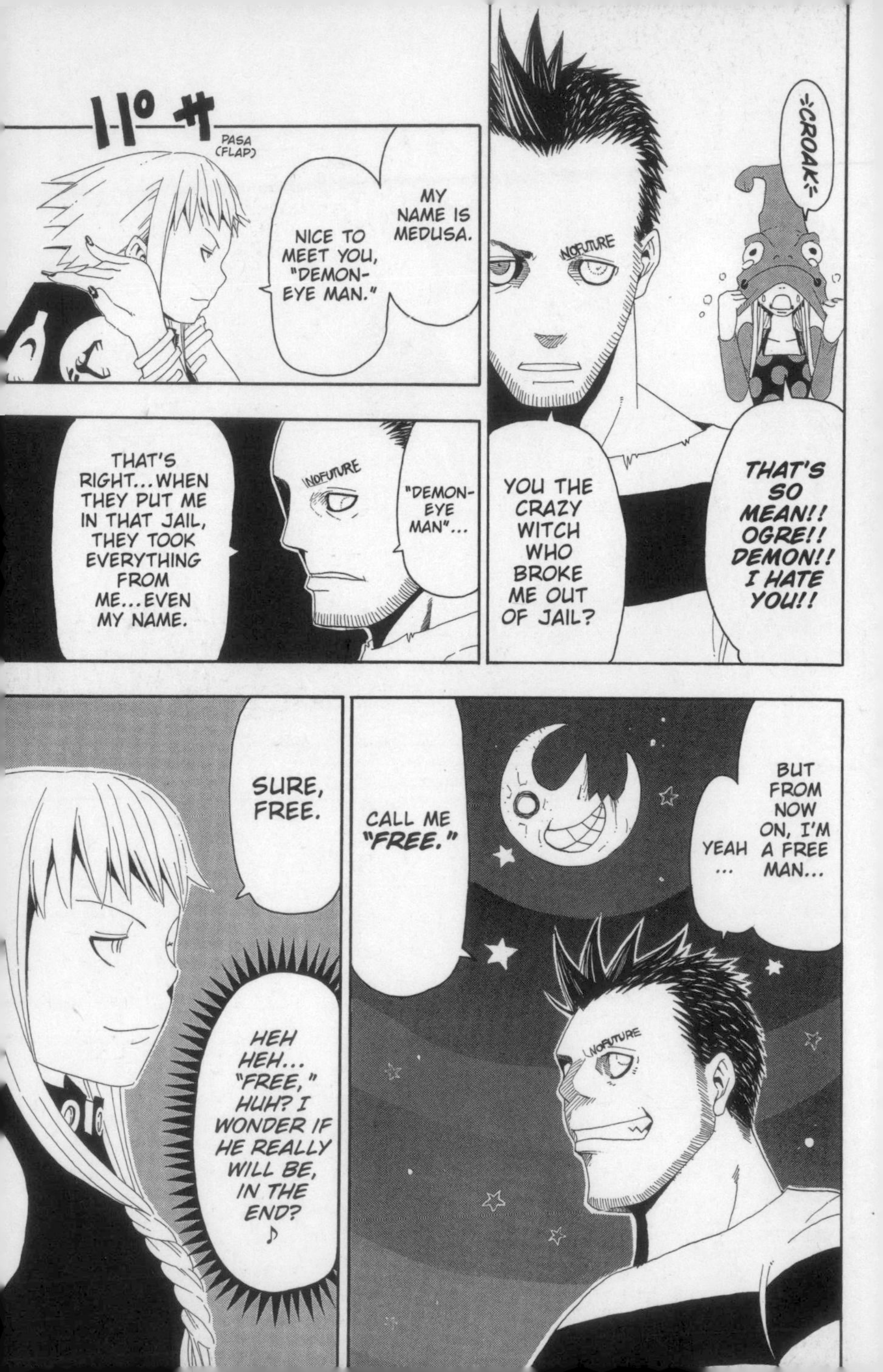
CROAK
NOFUTURE
THAT'S SO MEAN!! OGRE!! DEMON!! I HATE YOU!!
YOU THE CRAZY WITCH WHO BROKE ME OUT OF JAIL?
PASA (FLAP)
MY NAME IS MEDUSA.
NICE TO MEET YOU, "DEMON-EYE MAN."
"DEMON-EYE MAN"...
NOFUTURE
THAT'S RIGHT...WHEN THEY PUT ME IN THAT JAIL, THEY TOOK EVERYTHING FROM ME...EVEN MY NAME.
BUT FROM NOW ON, I'M A FREE MAN...
YEAH...
CALL ME "FREE."
NOFUTURE
SURE, FREE.
HEH HEH... "FREE," HUH? I WONDER IF HE REALLY WILL BE, IN THE END? ♪

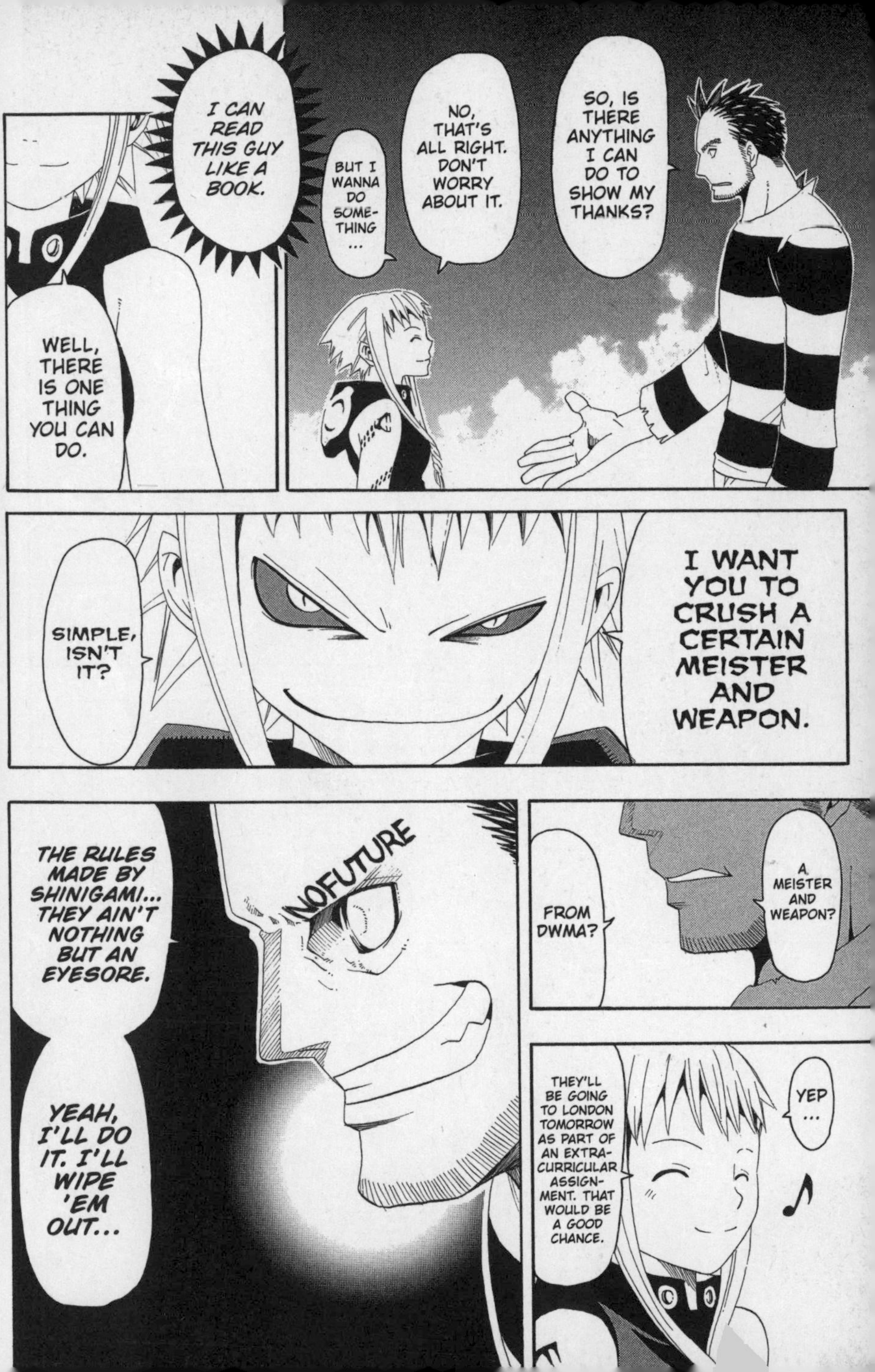
SO, IS THERE ANYTHING I CAN DO TO SHOW MY THANKS?
NO, THAT'S ALL RIGHT. DON'T WORRY ABOUT IT.
BUT I WANNA DO SOME-THING ...
I CAN READ THIS GUY LIKE A BOOK.
WELL, THERE IS ONE THING YOU CAN DO.
I WANT YOU TO CRUSH A CERTAIN MEISTER AND WEAPON.
SIMPLE, ISN'T IT?
A MEISTER AND WEAPON?
FROM DWMA?
YEP ...
THEY'LL BE GOING TO LONDON TOMORROW AS PART OF AN EXTRA-CURRICULAR ASSIGN-MENT. THAT WOULD BE A GOOD CHANCE.
THE RULES MADE BY SHINIGAMI... THEY AIN'T NOTHING BUT AN EYESORE.
NOFUTURE
YEAH, I'LL DO IT. I'LL WIPE 'EM OUT...

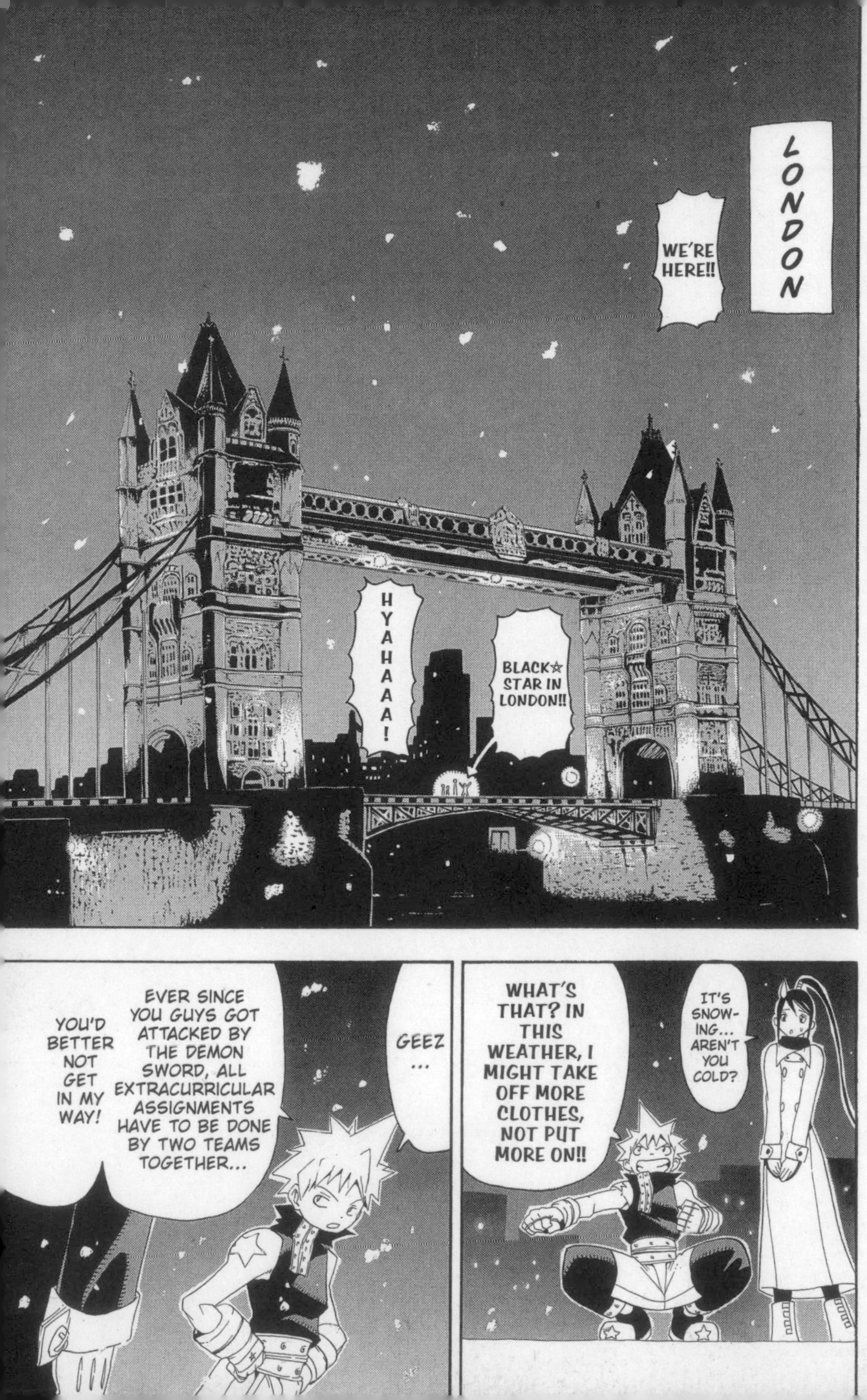
LONDON
WE'RE HERE!!
BLACK☆ STAR IN LONDON!!
HYAHAAAA!
IT'S SNOWING... AREN'T YOU COLD?
WHAT'S THAT? IN THIS WEATHER, I MIGHT TAKE OFF MORE CLOTHES, NOT PUT MORE ON!!
GEEZ...
EVER SINCE YOU GUYS GOT ATTACKED BY THE DEMON SWORD, ALL EXTRACURRICULAR ASSIGNMENTS HAVE TO BE DONE BY TWO TEAMS TOGETHER...
YOU'D BETTER NOT GET IN MY WAY!

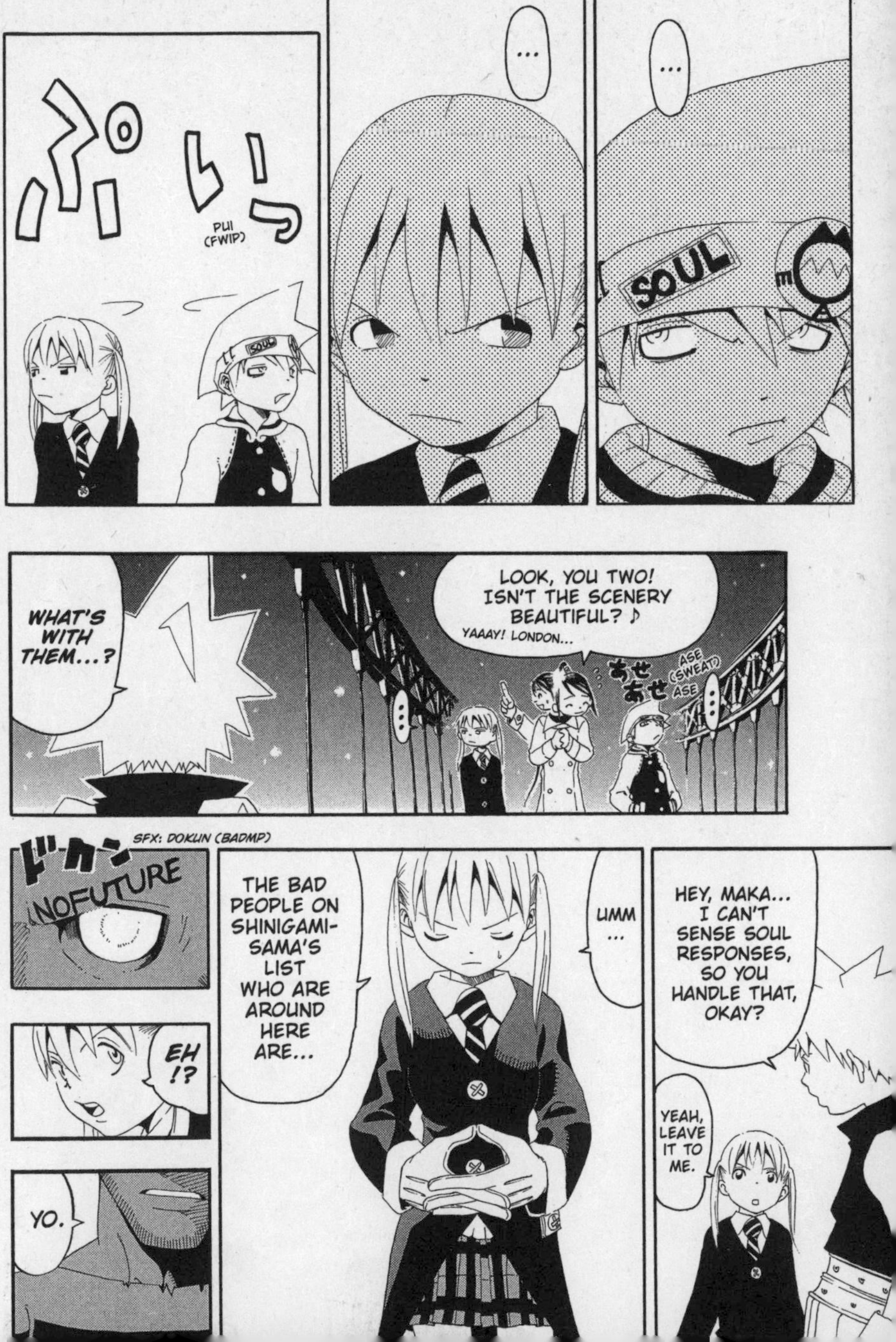
...
...
PUI (FWIP)
LOOK, YOU TWO! ISN'T THE SCENERY BEAUTIFUL? ♪
YAAAY! LONDON...
あせあせ ASE ASE (SWEAT)
...
...
WHAT'S WITH THEM...?
HEY, MAKA... I CAN'T SENSE SOUL RESPONSES, SO YOU HANDLE THAT, OKAY?
YEAH, LEAVE IT TO ME.
UMM...
THE BAD PEOPLE ON SHINIGAMI-SAMA'S LIST WHO ARE AROUND HERE ARE...
SFX: DOKUN (BADMP)
NOFUTURE
EH!?
YO.

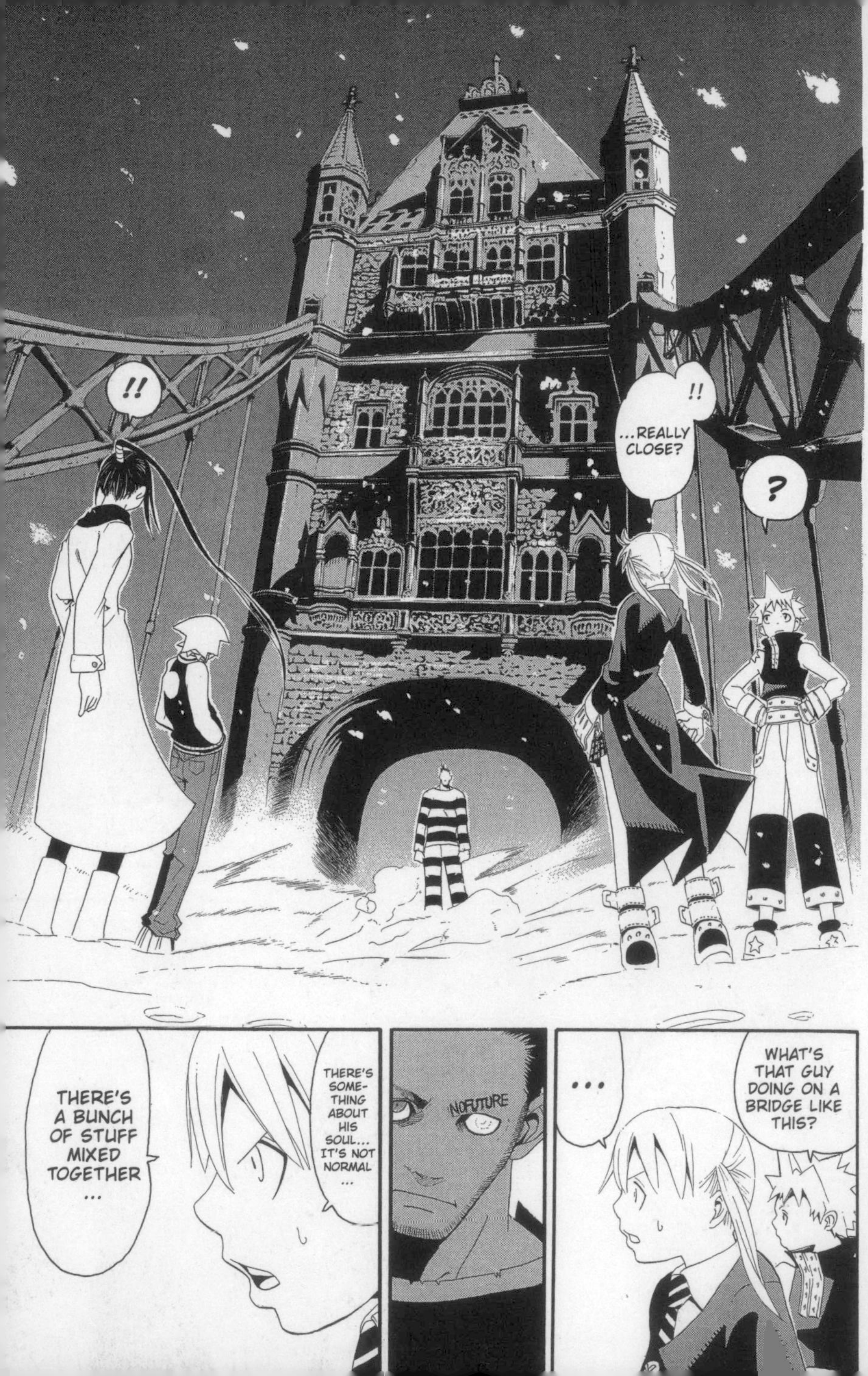
!!
...REALLY CLOSE?
?
!!
WHAT'S THAT GUY DOING ON A BRIDGE LIKE THIS?
...
NOFUTURE
THERE'S SOME-THING ABOUT HIS SOUL... IT'S NOT NORMAL ...
THERE'S A BUNCH OF STUFF MIXED TOGETHER ...

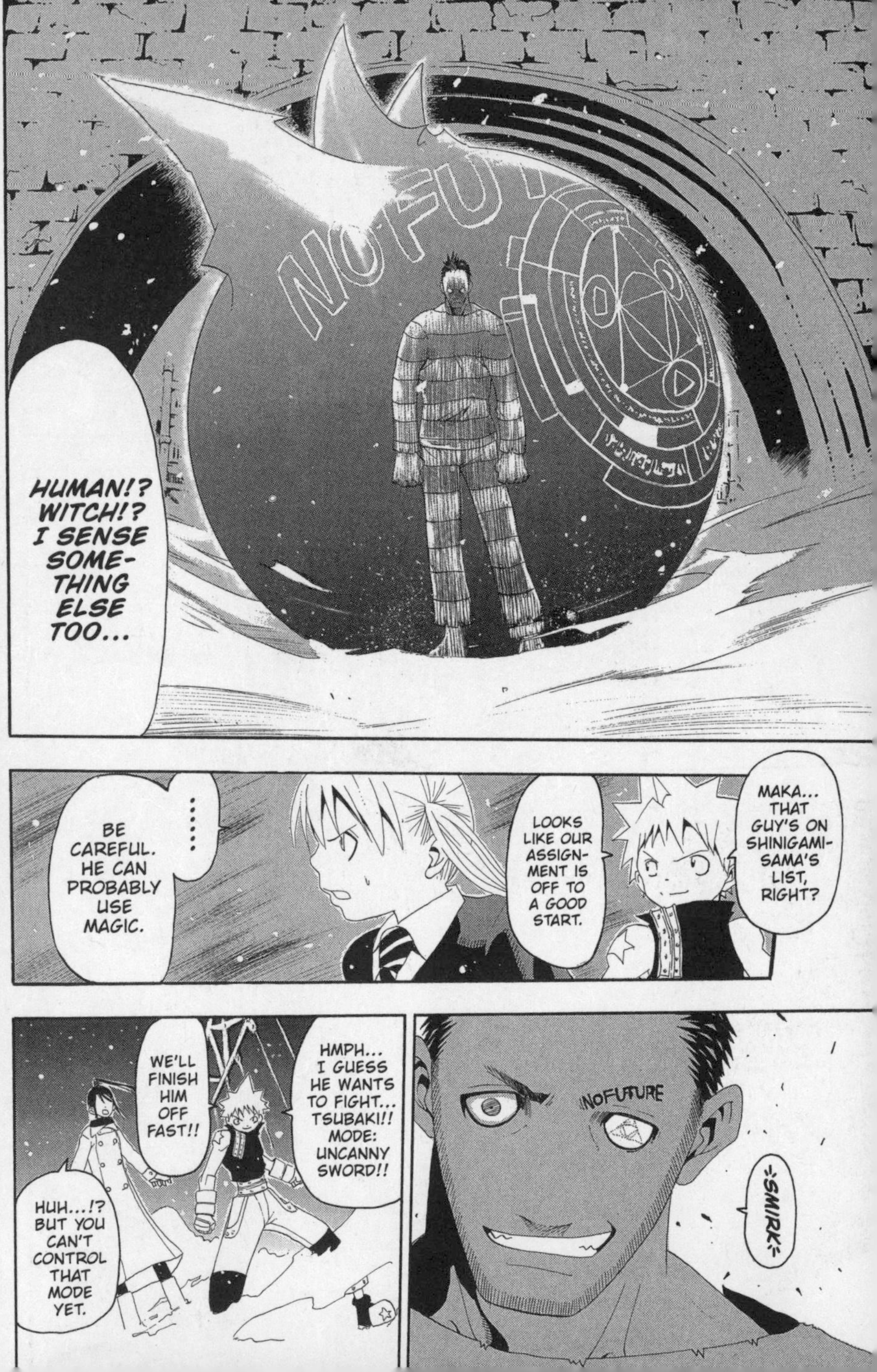
HUMAN!? WITCH!? I SENSE SOME-THING ELSE TOO...
MAKA... THAT GUY'S ON SHINIGAMI-SAMA'S LIST, RIGHT?
LOOKS LIKE OUR ASSIGN-MENT IS OFF TO A GOOD START.
......
BE CAREFUL. HE CAN PROBABLY USE MAGIC.
NOFUTURE
SMIRK
HMPH... I GUESS HE WANTS TO FIGHT... TSUBAKI!! MODE: UNCANNY SWORD!!
WE'LL FINISH HIM OFF FAST!!
HUH...!? BUT YOU CAN'T CONTROL THAT MODE YET.

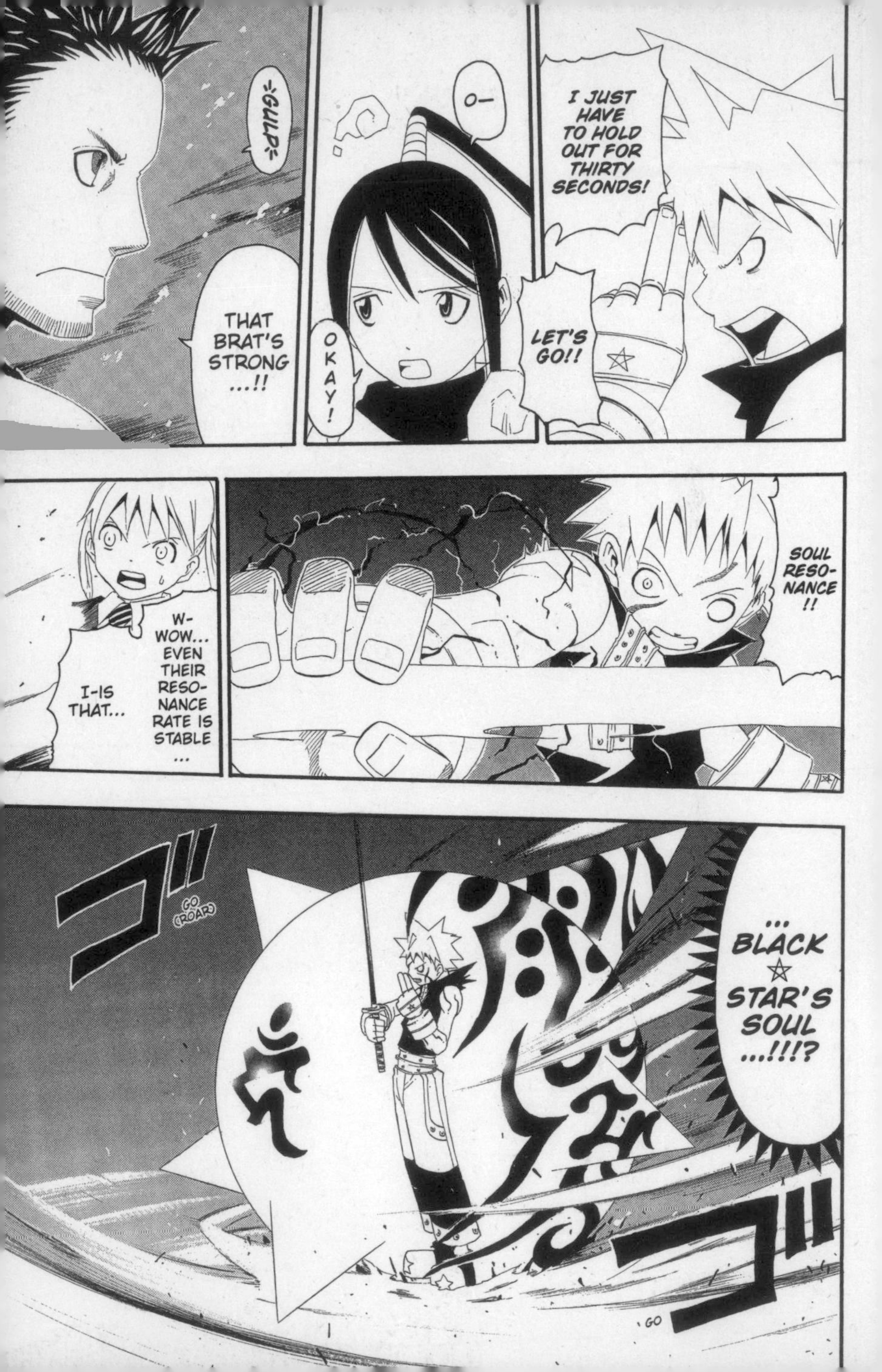
I JUST HAVE TO HOLD OUT FOR THIRTY SECONDS!
LET'S GO!!
O—
OKAY!
-GULP-
THAT BRAT'S STRONG ...!!
SOUL RESO-NANCE !!
W-WOW... EVEN THEIR RESO-NANCE RATE IS STABLE ...
I-IS THAT...
... BLACK☆STAR'S SOUL ...!!!?
ゴ
GO (ROAR)
ゴ
GO

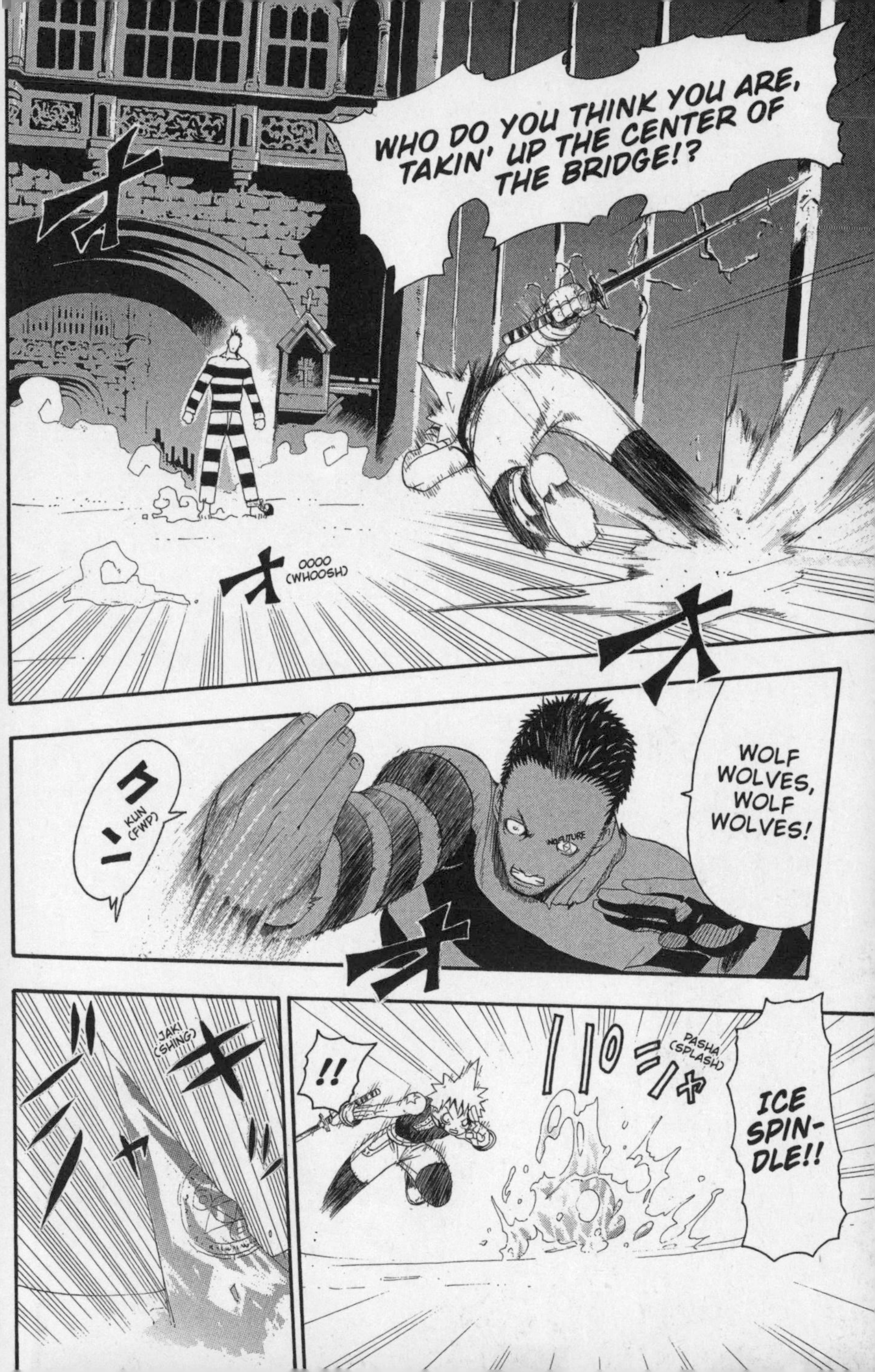
WHO DO YOU THINK YOU ARE, TAKIN' UP THE CENTER OF THE BRIDGE!?
OOOO (WHOOSH)
WOLF WOLVES, WOLF WOLVES!
NO FUTURE
KUN (FWP)
ICE SPIN-DLE!!
PASHA (SPLASH)
!!
JAKI (SHING)

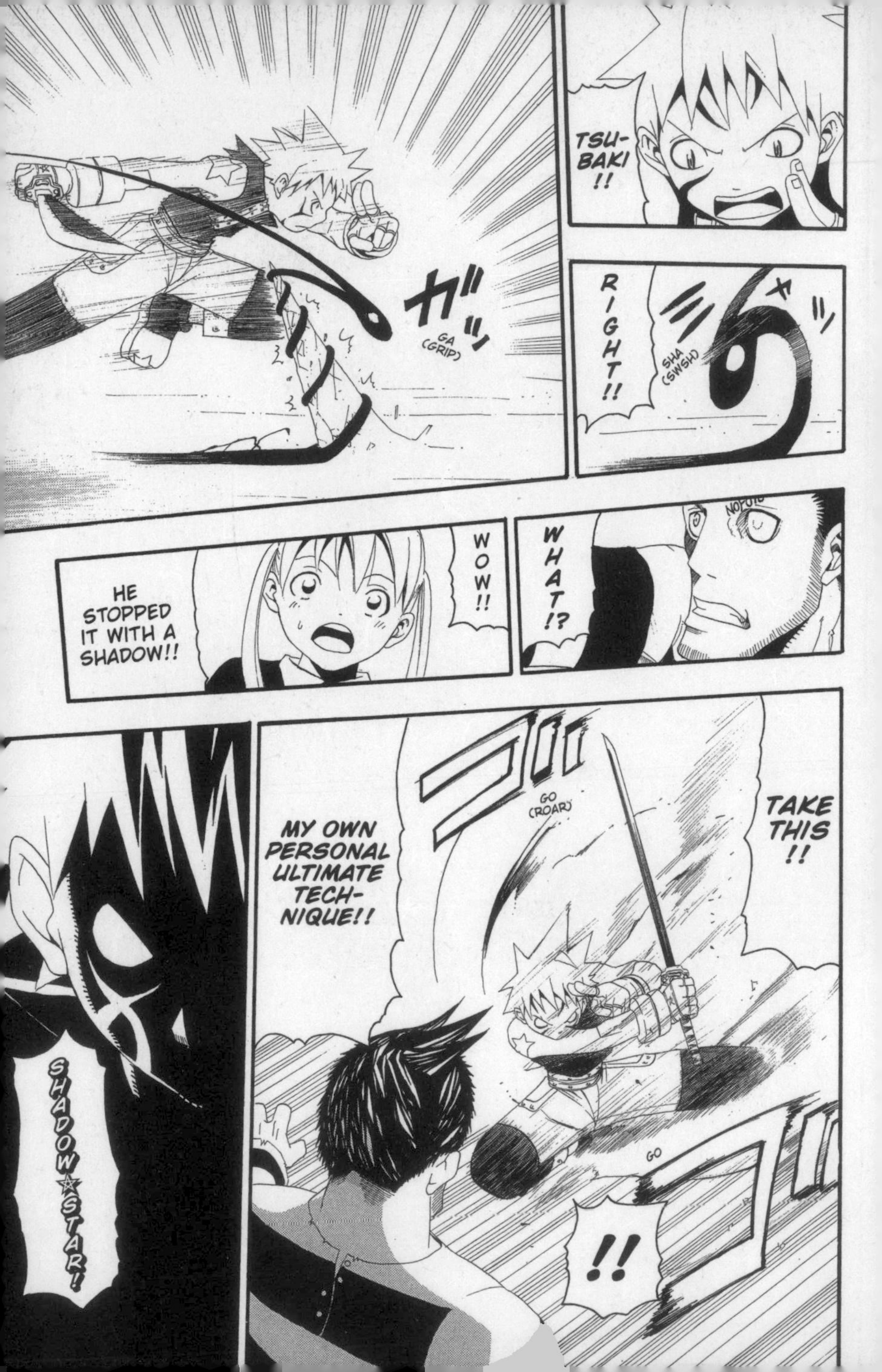

TSU-BAKI!!
RIGHT!!
SHA (SWSH)
GA (GRIP)
WHAT!?
WOW!!
HE STOPPED IT WITH A SHADOW!!
TAKE THIS!!
MY OWN PERSONAL ULTIMATE TECH-NIQUE!!
GO (ROAR)
GO
!!
SHADOW☆STAR!

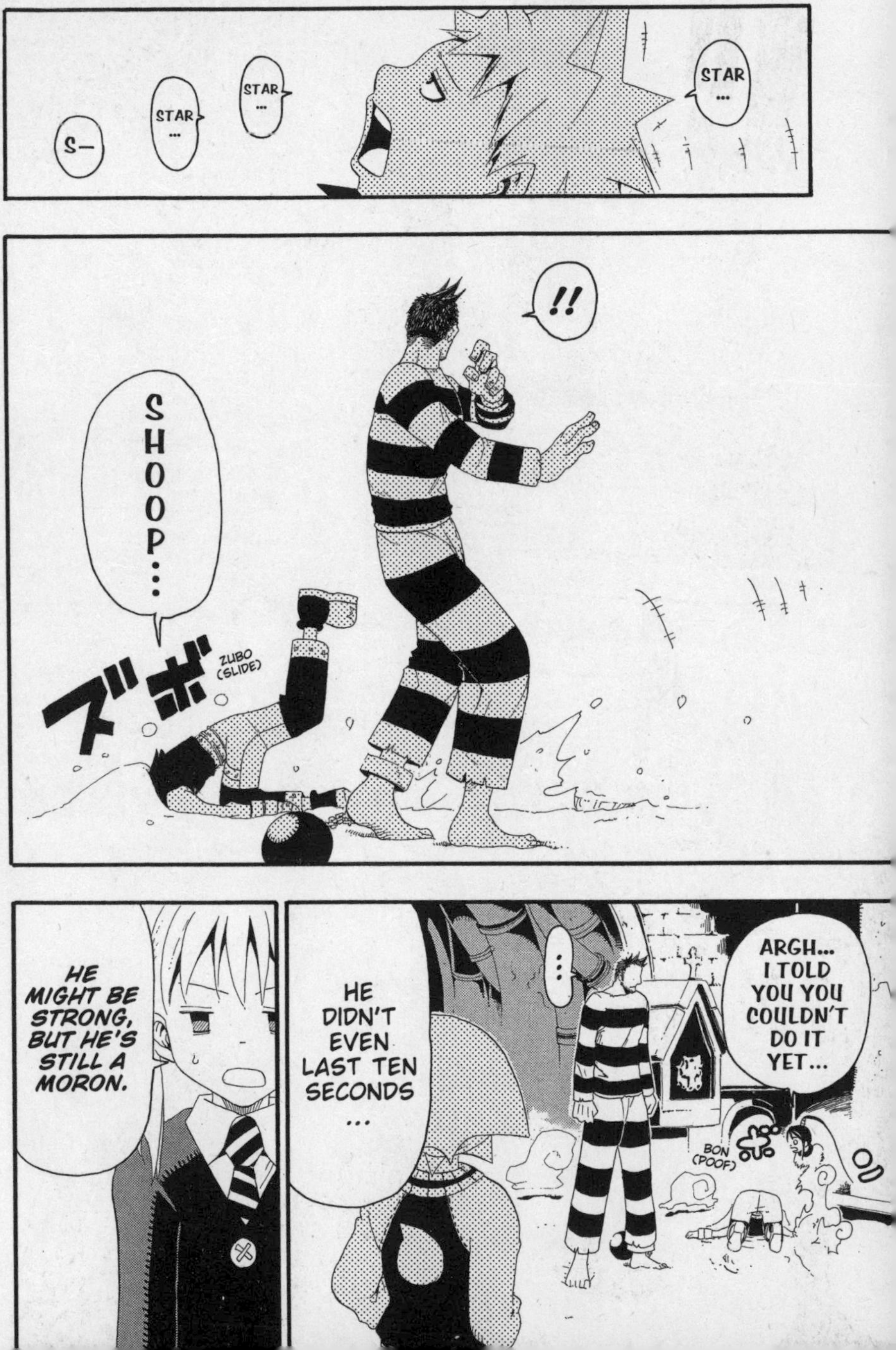

STAR ...
STAR ...
STAR ...
S—
!!
SHOOP...
ズボ
ZUBO (SLIDE)
ARGH... I TOLD YOU YOU COULDN'T DO IT YET...
BON (POOF)
...
HE DIDN'T EVEN LAST TEN SECONDS ...
HE MIGHT BE STRONG, BUT HE'S STILL A MORON.

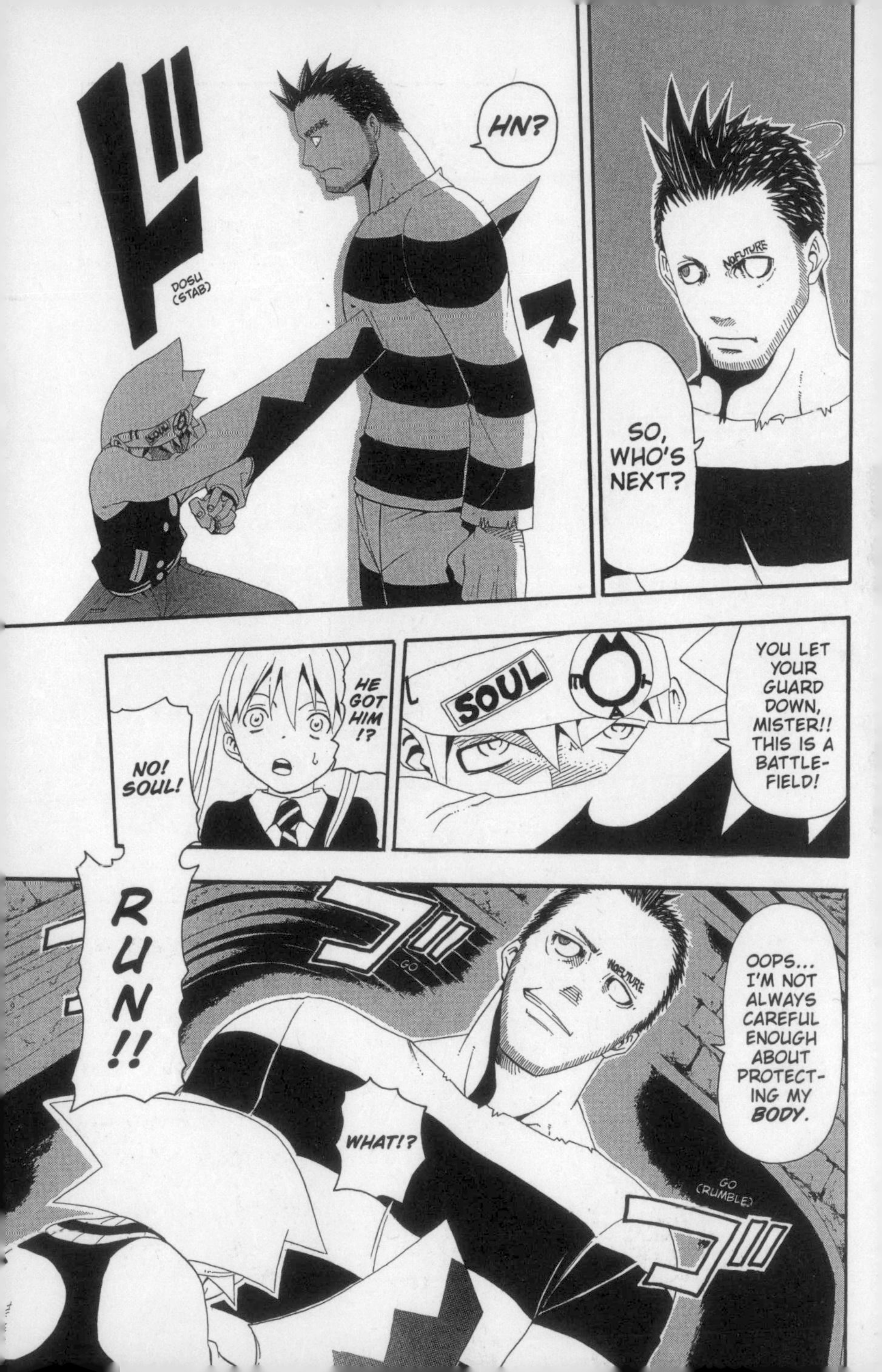
SO, WHO'S NEXT?
HN?
DOSU (STAB)
YOU LET YOUR GUARD DOWN, MISTER!! THIS IS A BATTLE-FIELD!
HE GOT HIM!?
NO! SOUL!
OOPS... I'M NOT ALWAYS CAREFUL ENOUGH ABOUT PROTECT-ING MY *BODY*.
GO
RUN!!
WHAT!?
GO (RUMBLE)

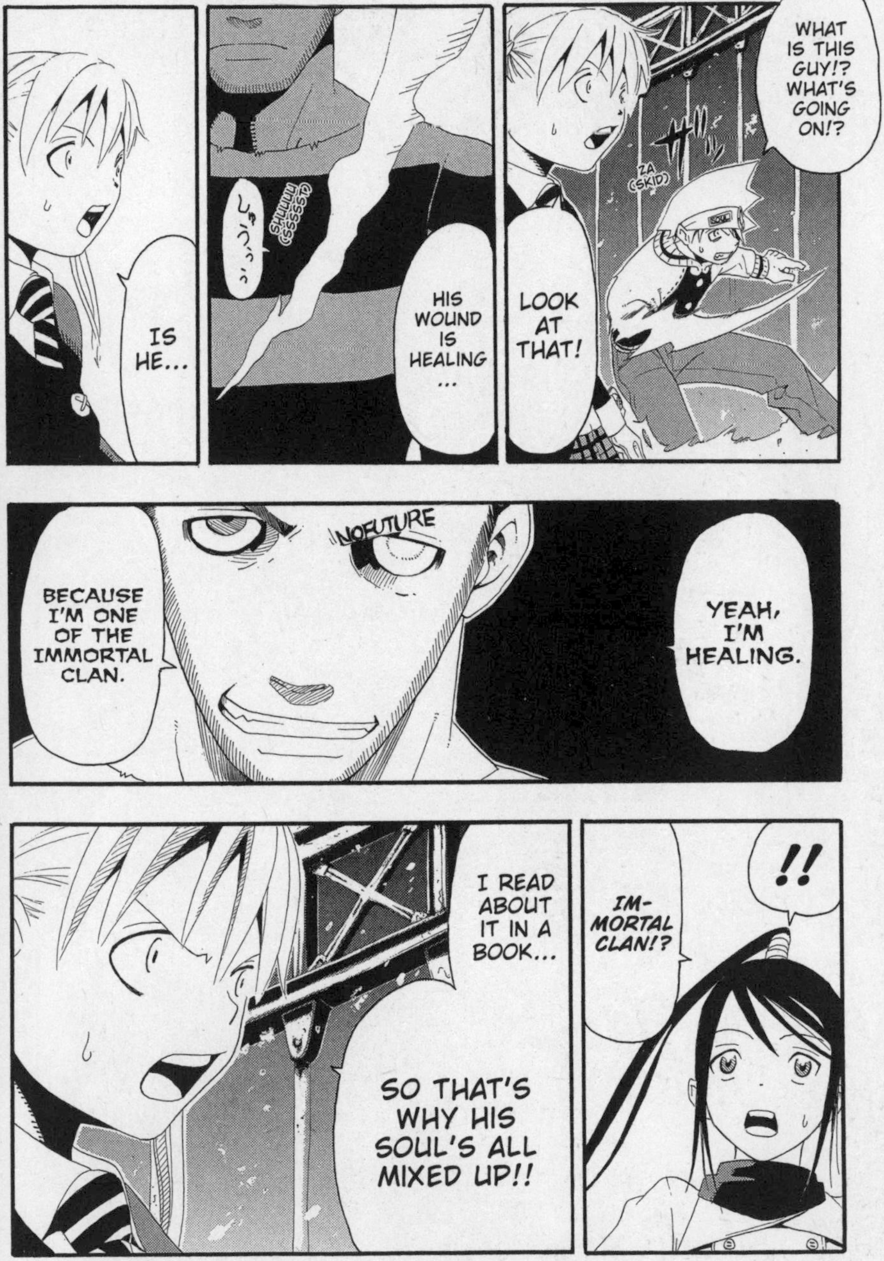
WHAT IS THIS GUY!? WHAT'S GOING ON!?
ZA (SKID)
LOOK AT THAT!
HIS WOUND IS HEALING...
しゅううう
SHUUUU (SSSSST)
IS HE...
YEAH, I'M HEALING.
NOFUTURE
BECAUSE I'M ONE OF THE IMMORTAL CLAN.
!!
IM-MORTAL CLAN!?
I READ ABOUT IT IN A BOOK...
SO THAT'S WHY HIS SOUL'S ALL MIXED UP!!

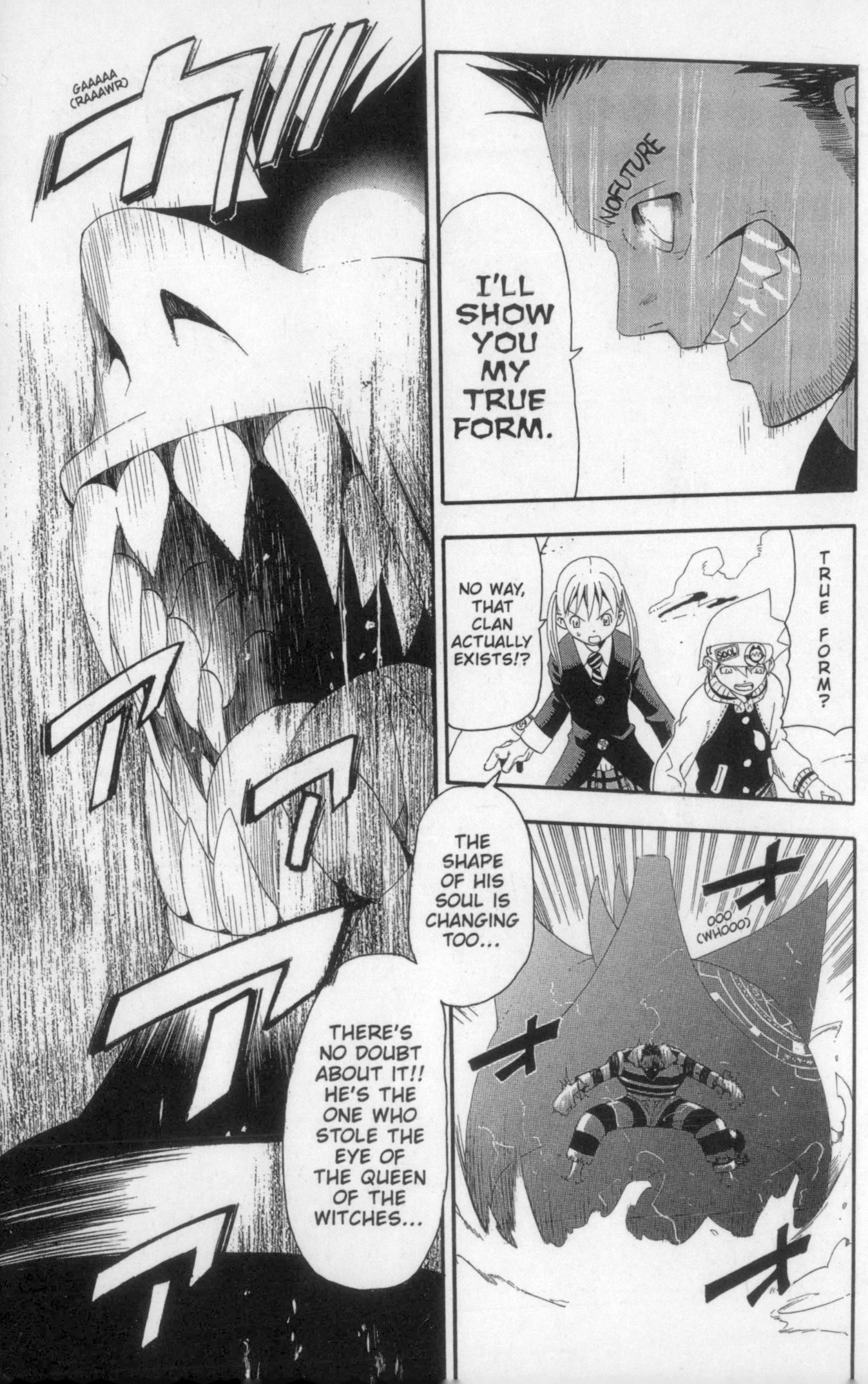
NOFUTURE
I'LL SHOW YOU MY TRUE FORM.
TRUE FORM?
NO WAY, THAT CLAN ACTUALLY EXISTS!?
OOO (WHOOO)
THE SHAPE OF HIS SOUL IS CHANGING TOO...
THERE'S NO DOUBT ABOUT IT!! HE'S THE ONE WHO STOLE THE EYE OF THE QUEEN OF THE WITCHES...
GAAAAA (RAAAWR)

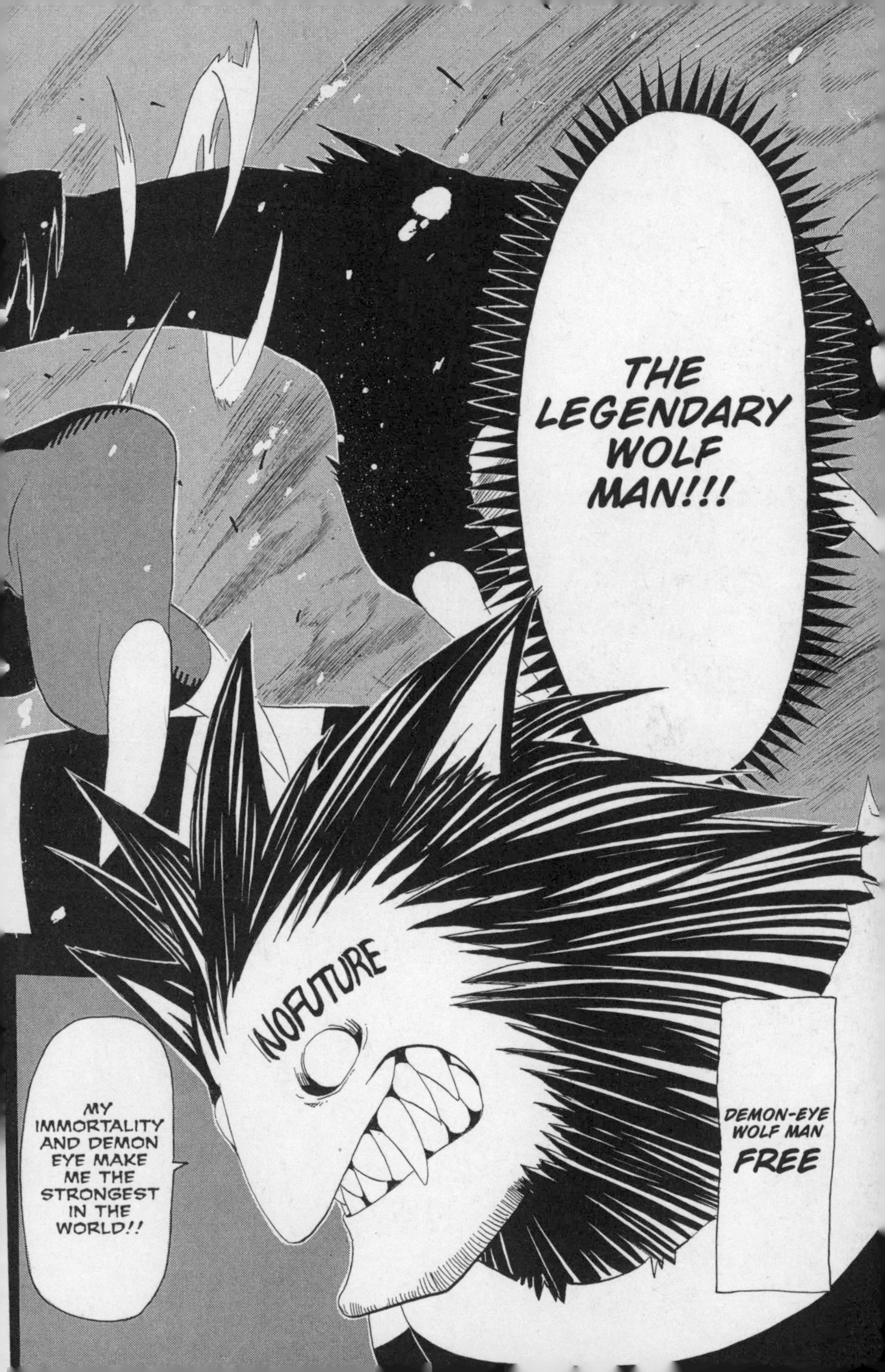

THE LEGENDARY WOLF MAN!!!
DEMON-EYE WOLF MAN FREE
NOFUTURE
MY IMMORTALITY AND DEMON EYE MAKE ME THE STRONGEST IN THE WORLD!!

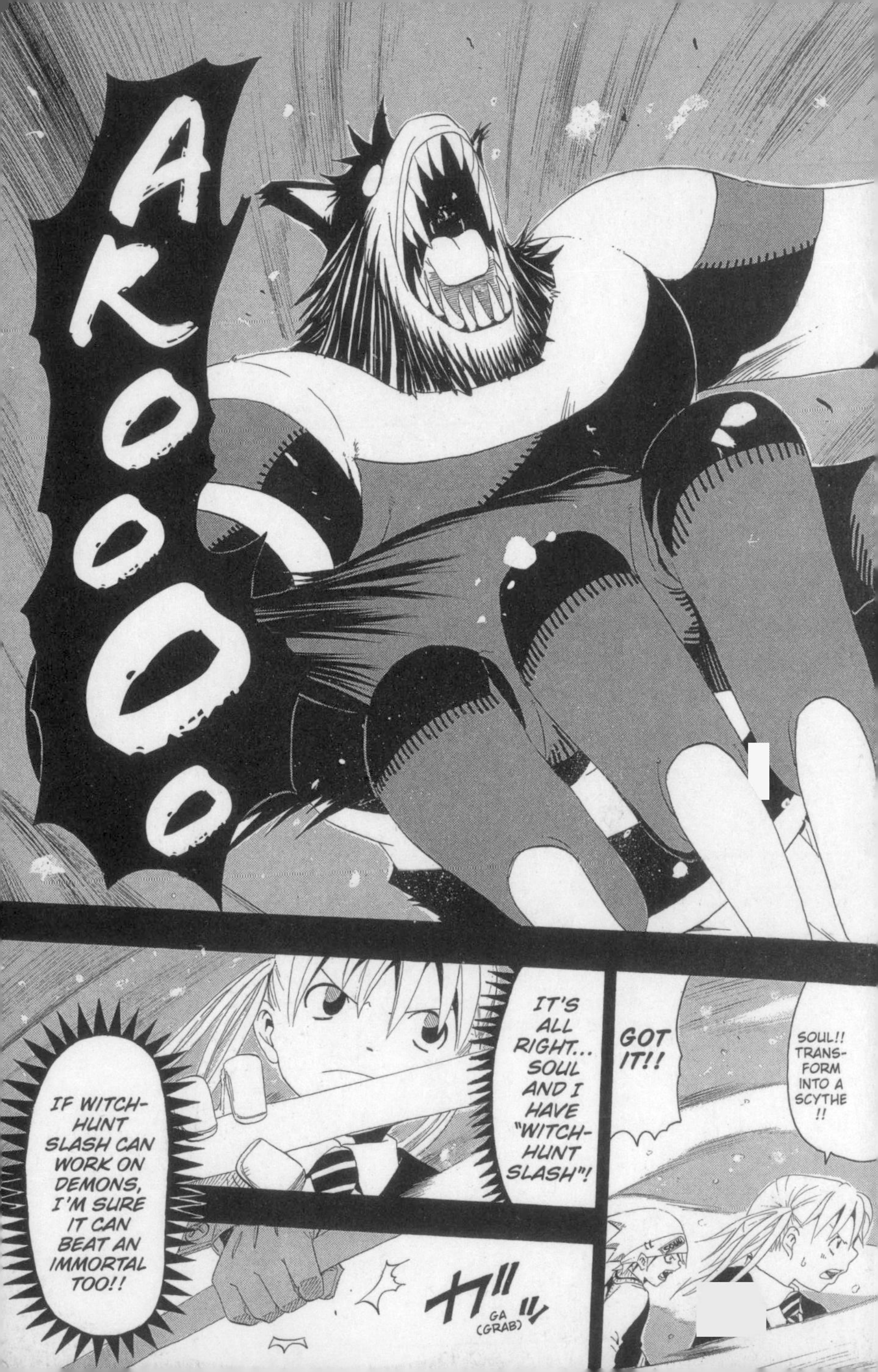
AROOOOO
SOUL!! TRANSFORM INTO A SCYTHE!!
GOT IT!!
IT'S ALL RIGHT... SOUL AND I HAVE "WITCH-HUNT SLASH"!
IF WITCH-HUNT SLASH CAN WORK ON DEMONS, I'M SURE IT CAN BEAT AN IMMORTAL TOO!!
GA (GRAB)

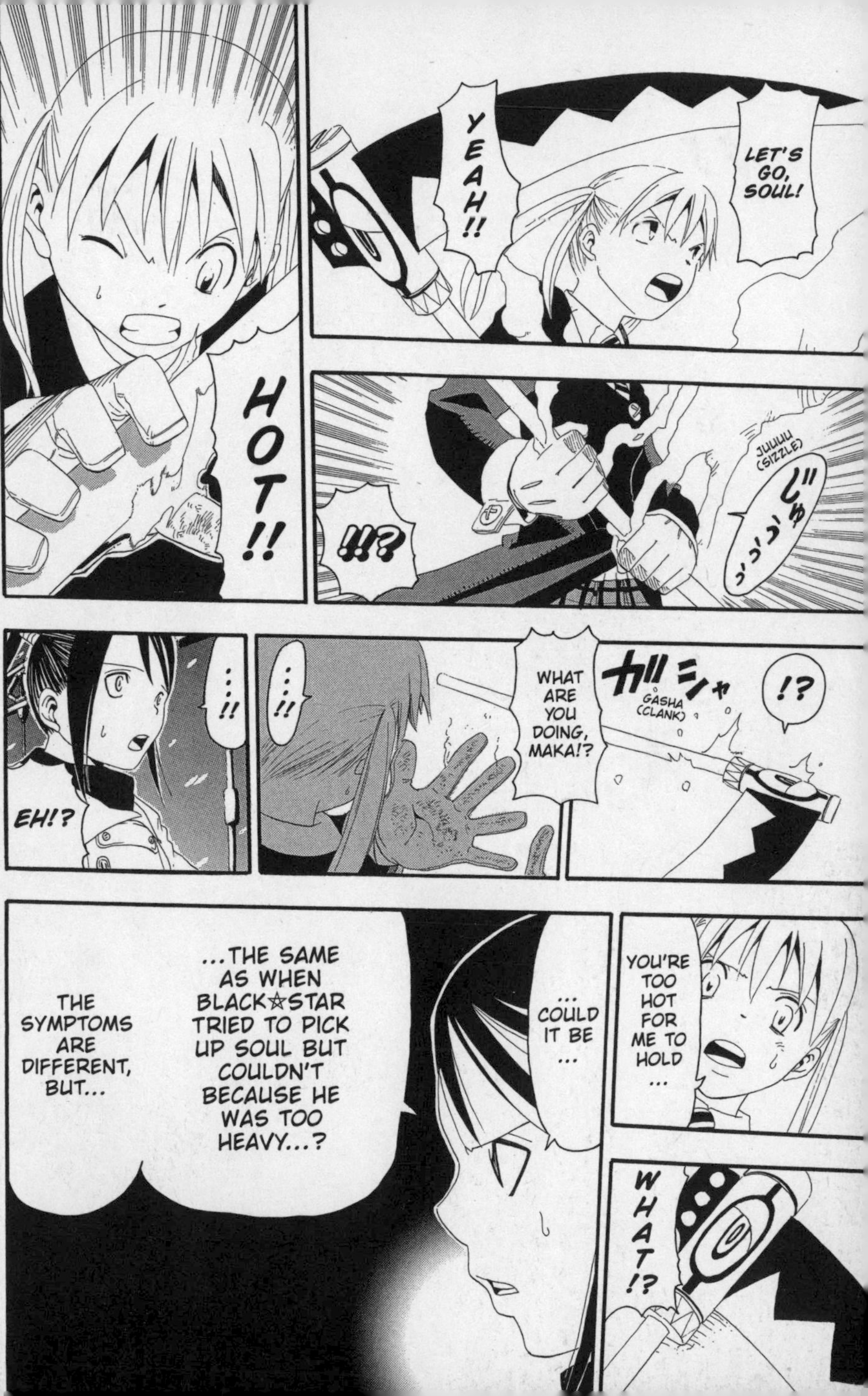
LET'S GO, SOUL!
YEAH!!
JUUUU (SIZZLE)
じゅううう
!!?
HOT!!
!?
ガシャ
GASHA (CLANK)
WHAT ARE YOU DOING, MAKA!?
...!!
...!!
EH!?
YOU'RE TOO HOT FOR ME TO HOLD...
WHAT!?
...COULD IT BE...
...THE SAME AS WHEN BLACK☆STAR TRIED TO PICK UP SOUL BUT COULDN'T BECAUSE HE WAS TOO HEAVY...?
THE SYMPTOMS ARE DIFFERENT, BUT...

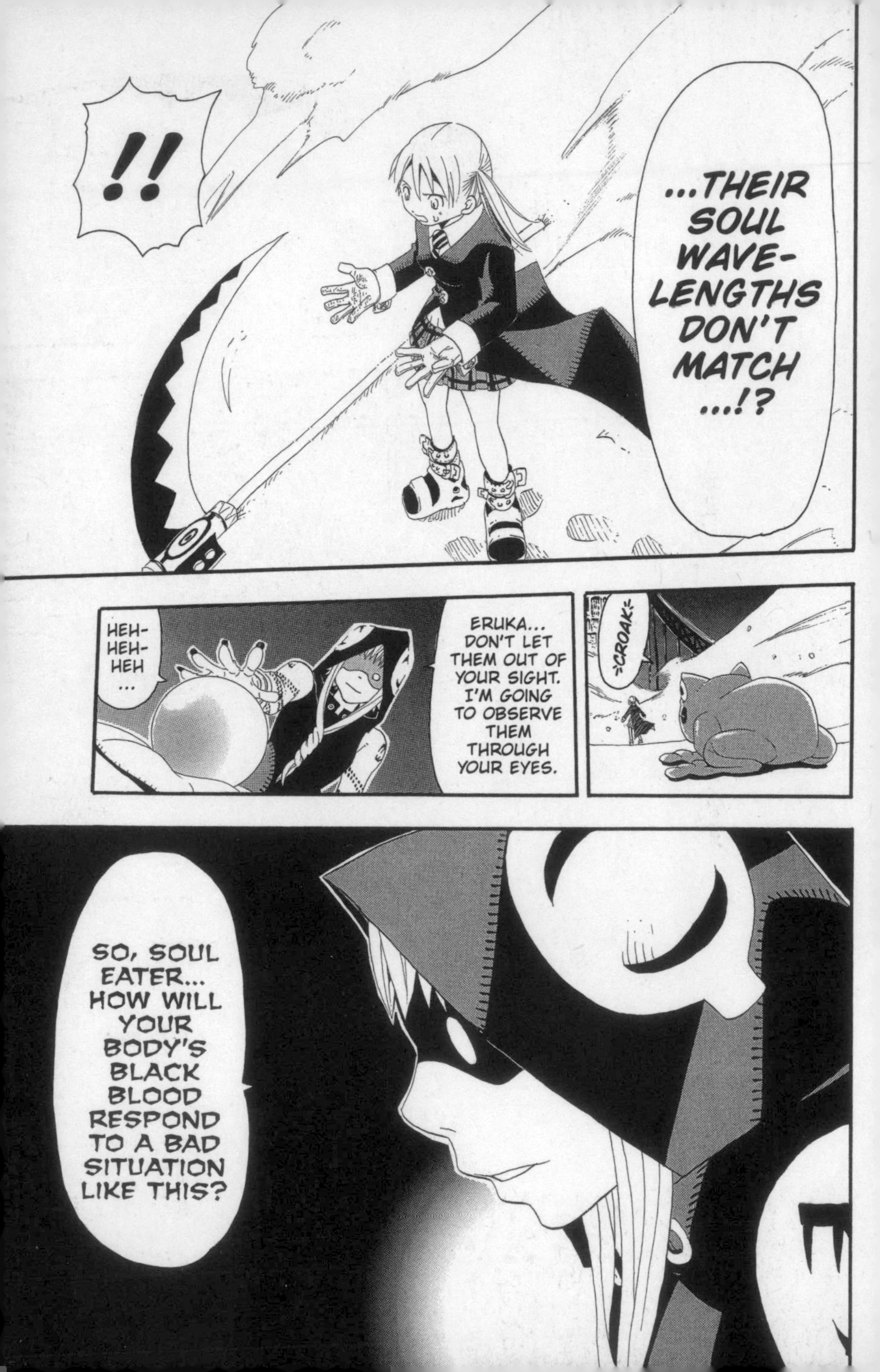
...THEIR SOUL WAVE-LENGTHS DON'T MATCH ...!?
!!
CROAK
ERUKA... DON'T LET THEM OUT OF YOUR SIGHT. I'M GOING TO OBSERVE THEM THROUGH YOUR EYES.
HEH-HEH-HEH ...
SO, SOUL EATER... HOW WILL YOUR BODY'S BLACK BLOOD RESPOND TO A BAD SITUATION LIKE THIS?

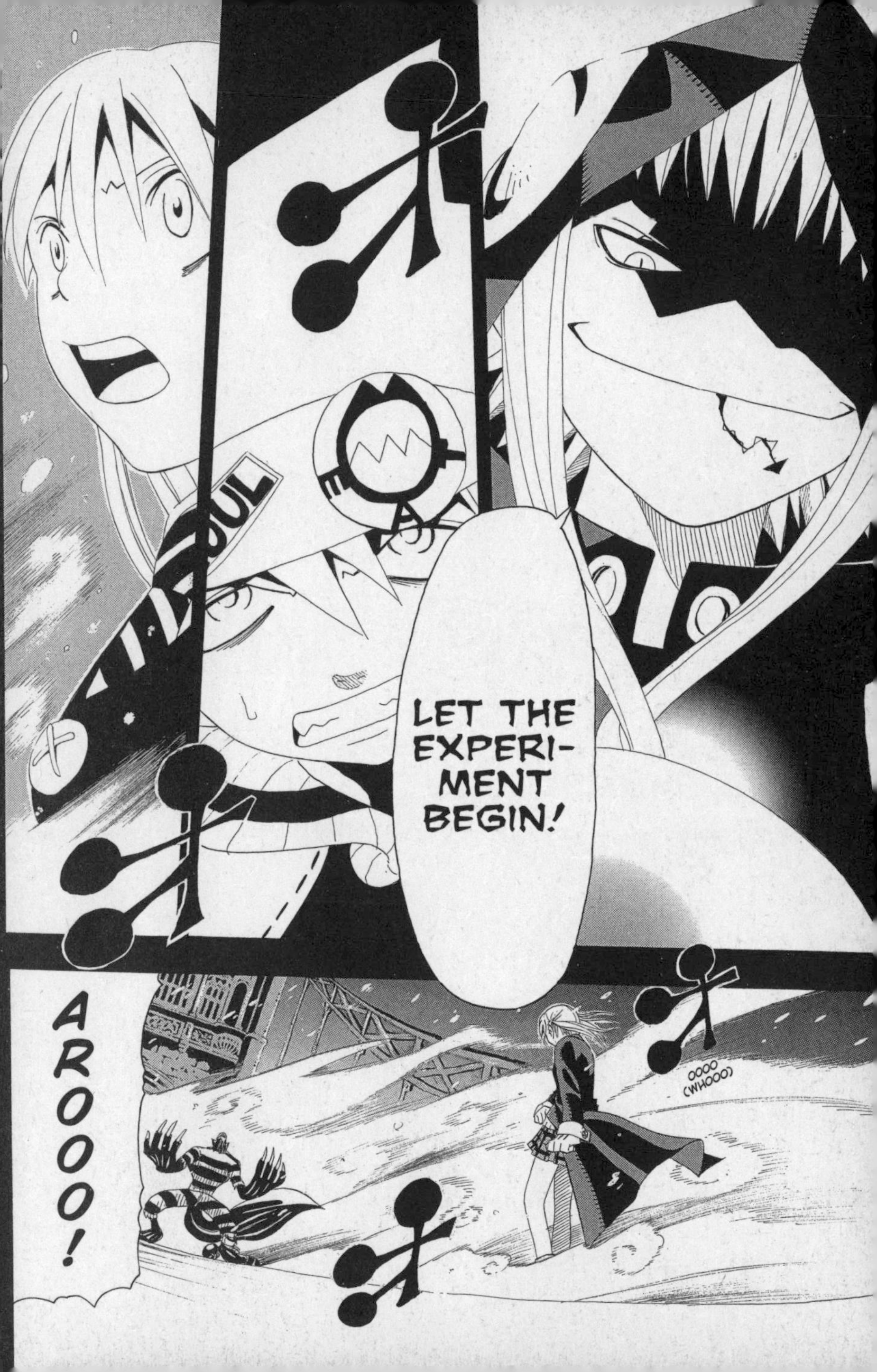
LET THE EXPERIMENT BEGIN!
OOOO (WHOOO)
AROOOO!

SOUL EATER

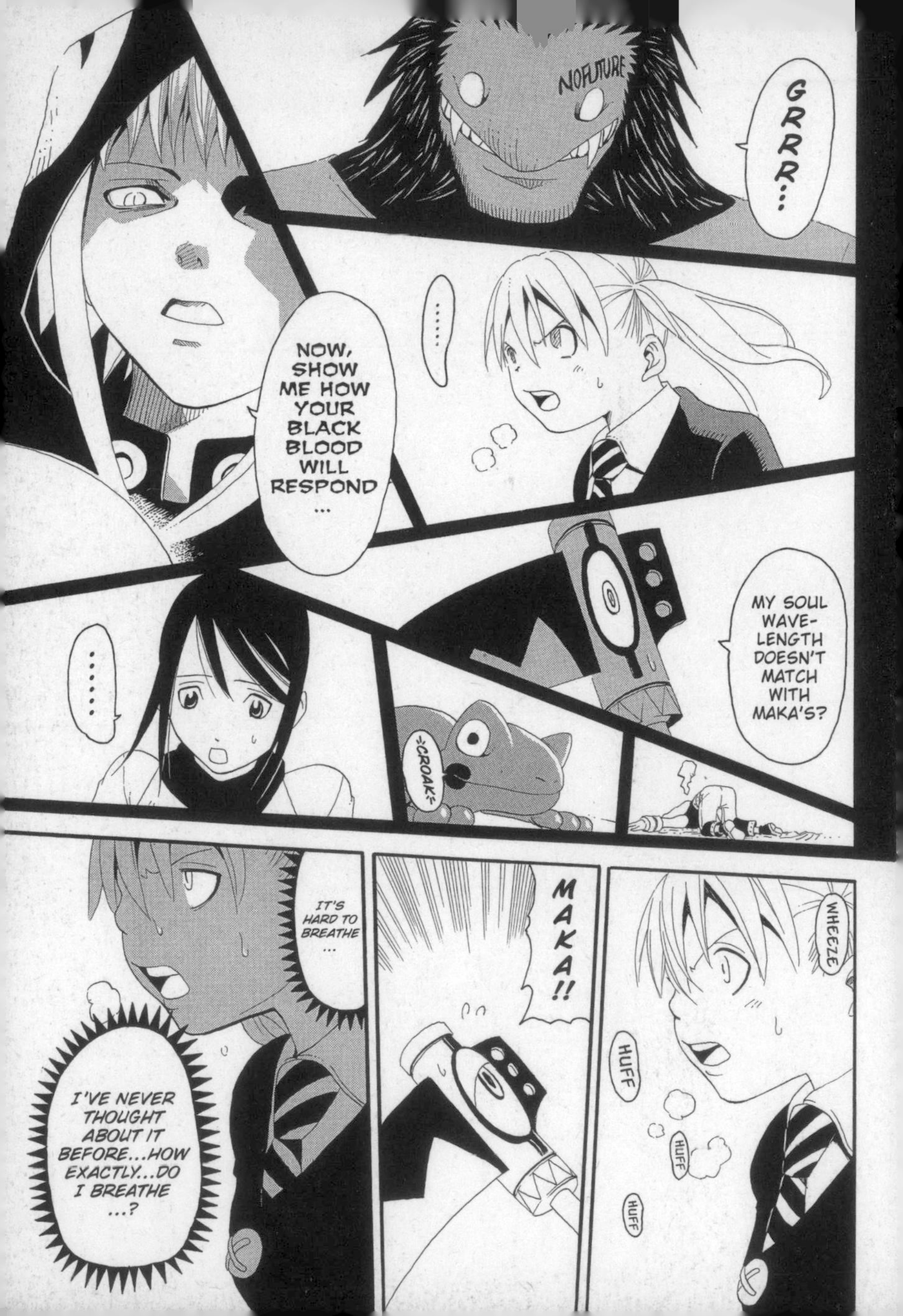
NOFUTURE
GRRR...
......
NOW, SHOW ME HOW YOUR BLACK BLOOD WILL RESPOND...
MY SOUL WAVE-LENGTH DOESN'T MATCH WITH MAKA'S?
CROAK
......
WHEEZE
HUFF
HUFF
HUFF
MAKA!!
IT'S HARD TO BREATHE...
I'VE NEVER THOUGHT ABOUT IT BEFORE...HOW EXACTLY...DO I BREATHE...?

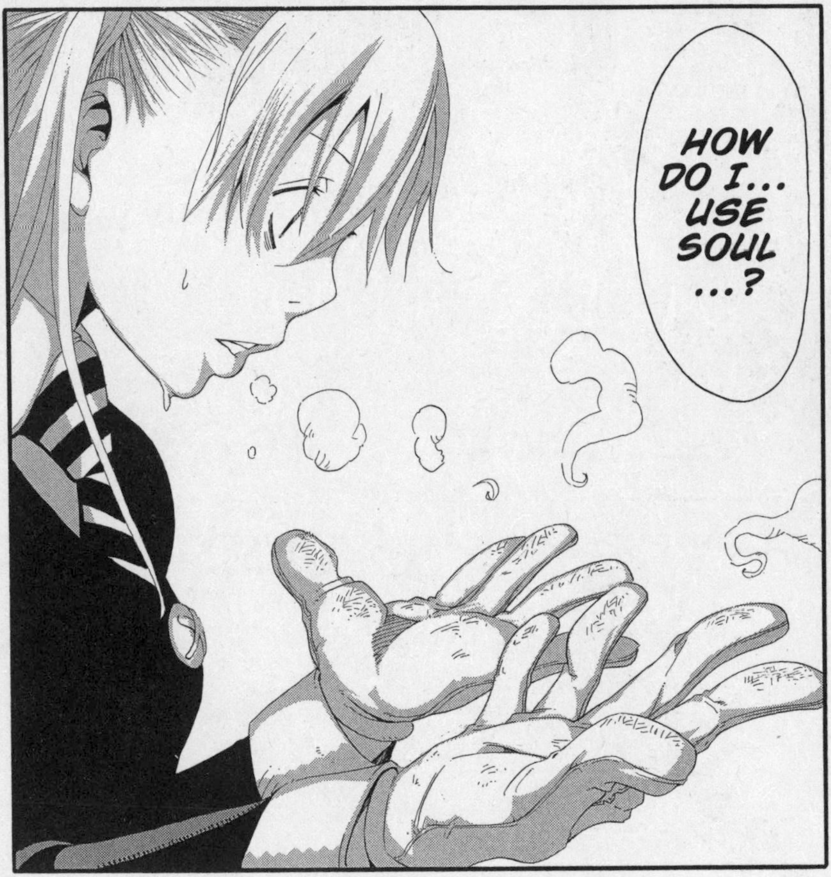
HOW DO I... USE SOUL ...?

CHAPTER 11: THE EXPERIMENT (PART 2)

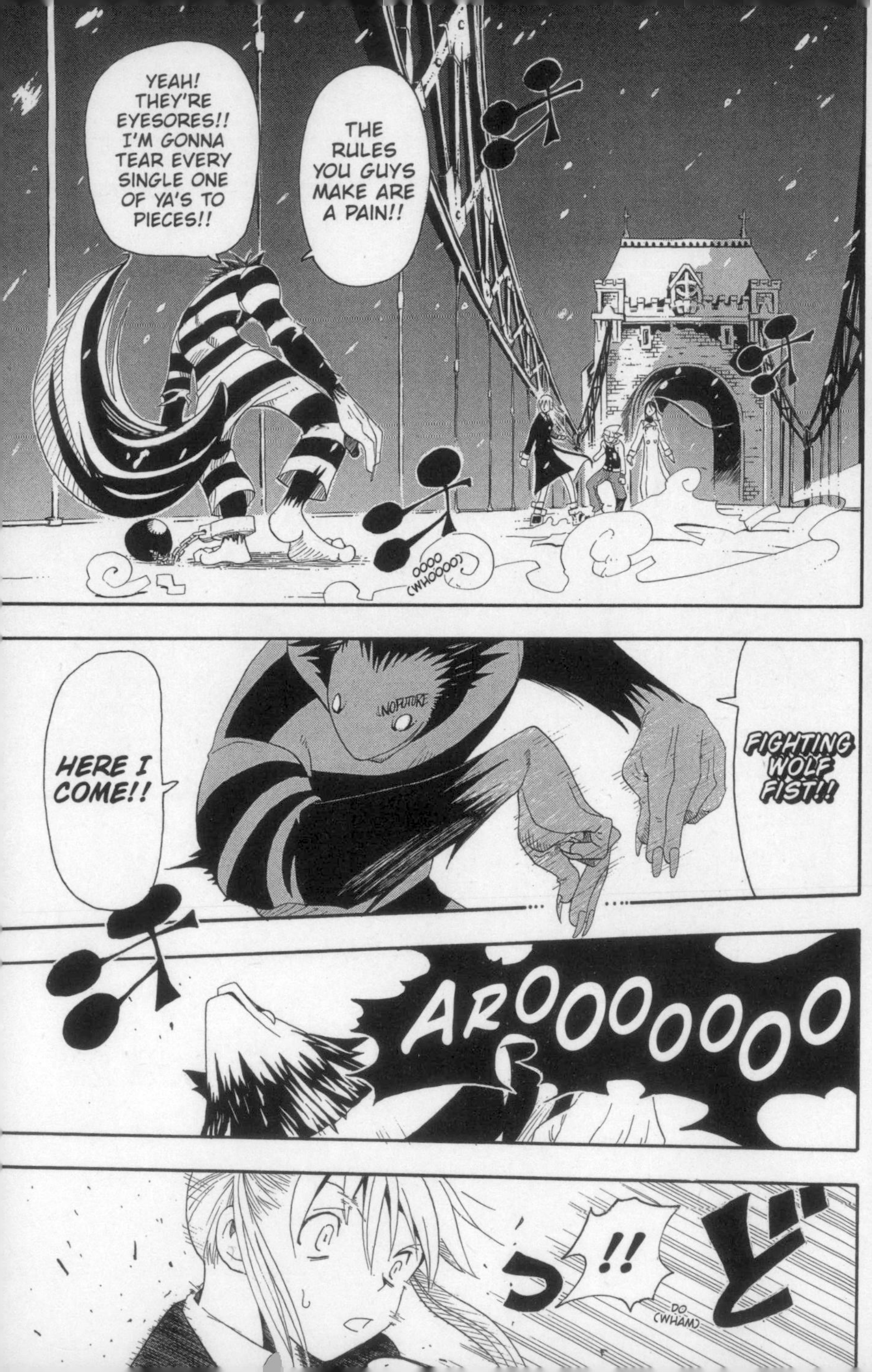
THE RULES YOU GUYS MAKE ARE A PAIN!!
YEAH! THEY'RE EYESORES!! I'M GONNA TEAR EVERY SINGLE ONE OF YA'S TO PIECES!!
OOOO (WHOOOO)
FIGHTING WOLF FIST!!
NO FUTURE
HERE I COME!!
AROOOOOOOO
!!
DO (WHAM)

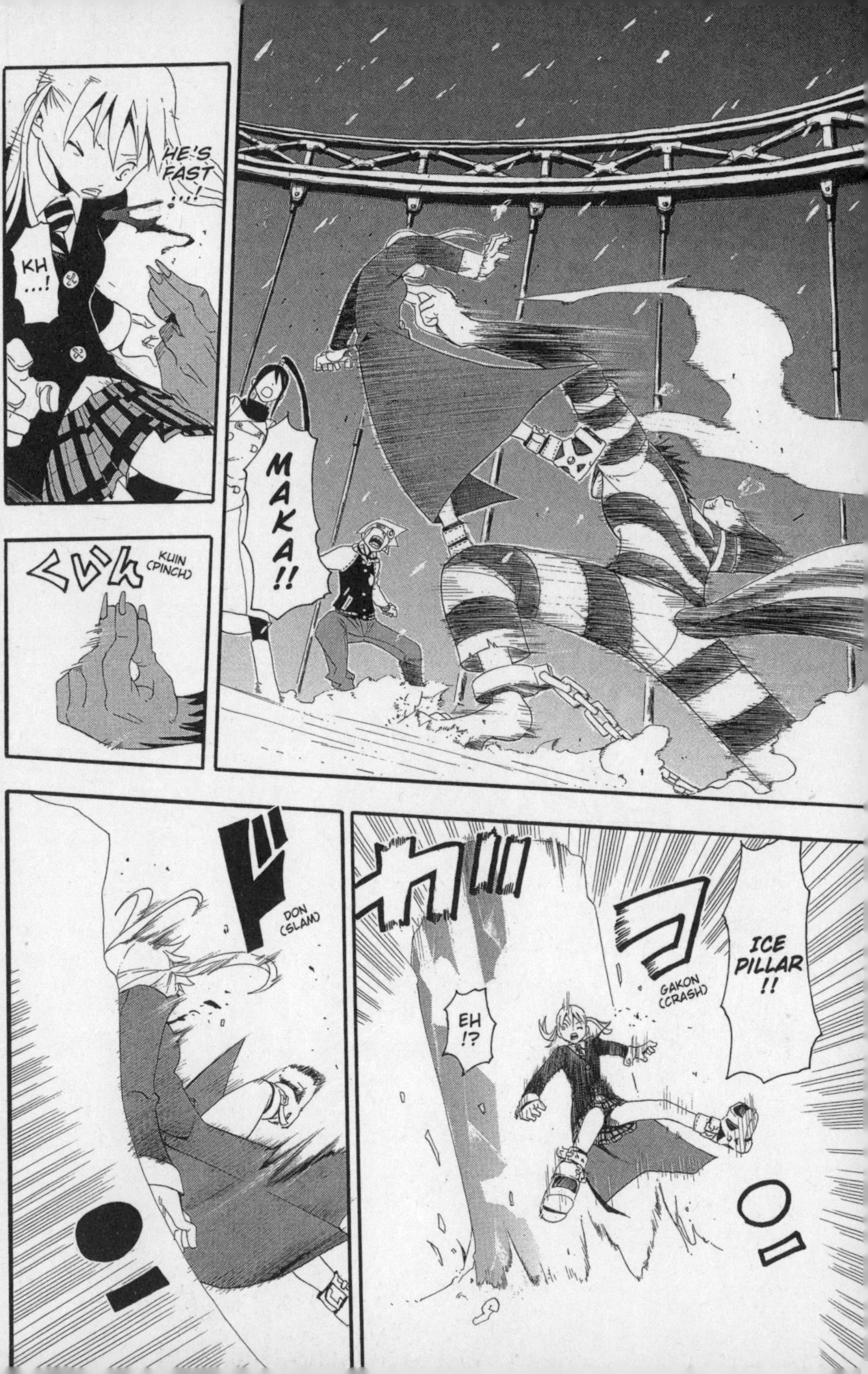
MAKA!!
HE'S FAST...!!
KH ...!
くいん
KUIN (PINCH)
ICE PILLAR !!
GAKON (CRASH)
EH !?
ド
DON (SLAM)

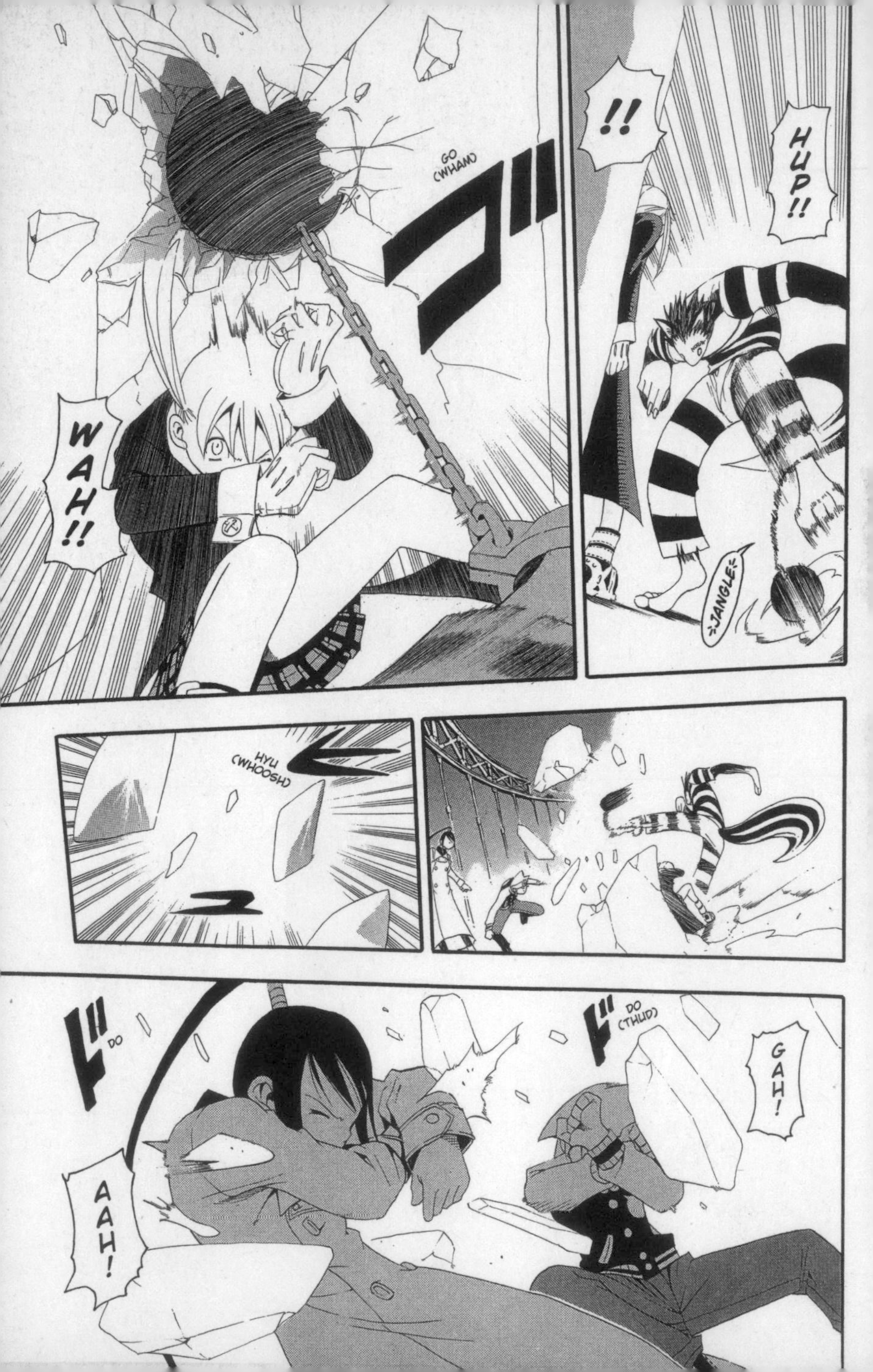
!!
HUP!!
JANGLE
GO (WHAM)
WAH!!
HYU (WHOOSH)
DO (THUD)
GAH!
DO
AAH!

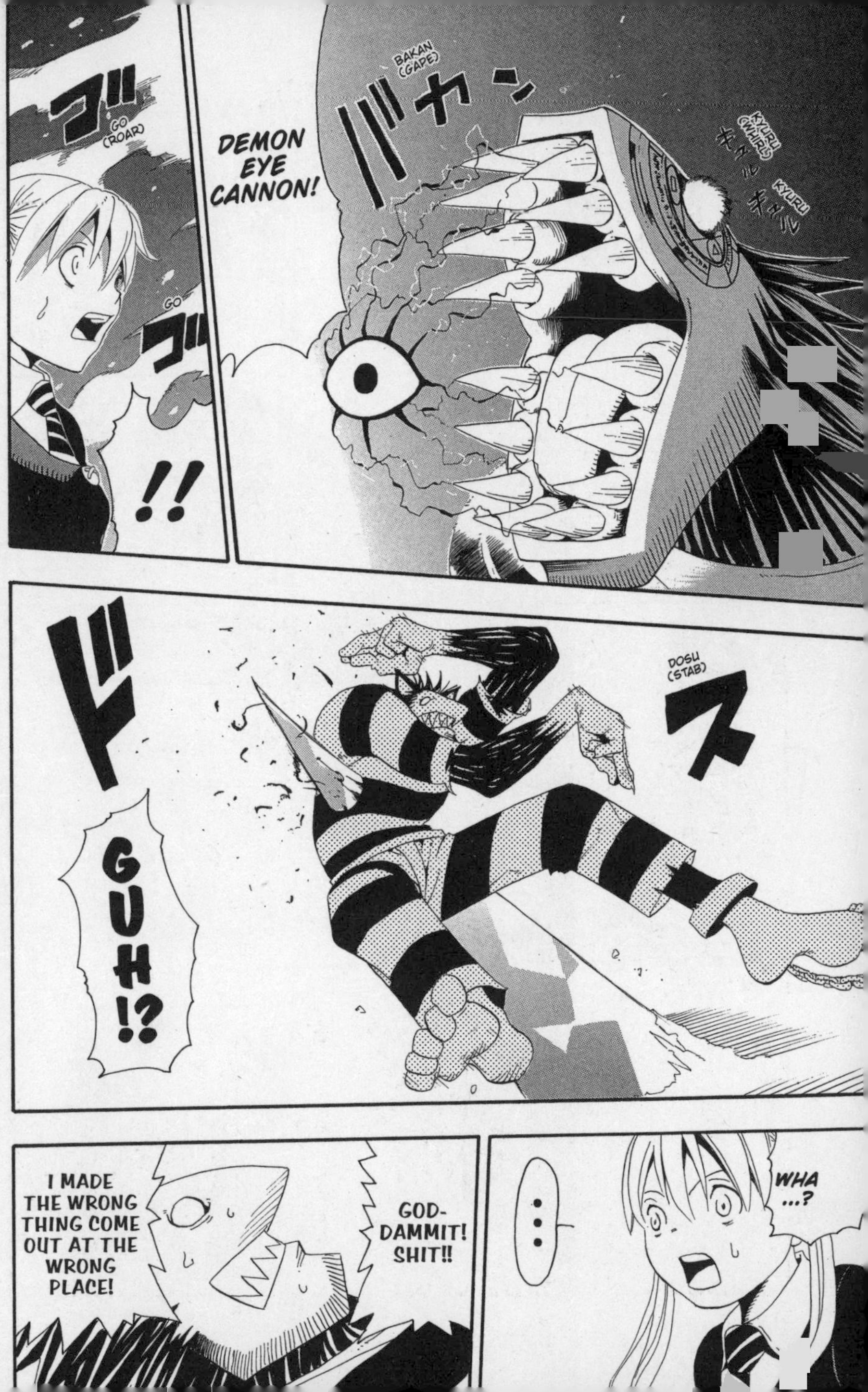
BAKAN (GAPE)
KYURU (WHIRL)
KYURU
DEMON EYE CANNON!
GO (ROAR)
GO
!!
DOSU (STAB)
GUH!?
WHA ...?
...
GOD-DAMMIT! SHIT!!
I MADE THE WRONG THING COME OUT AT THE WRONG PLACE!

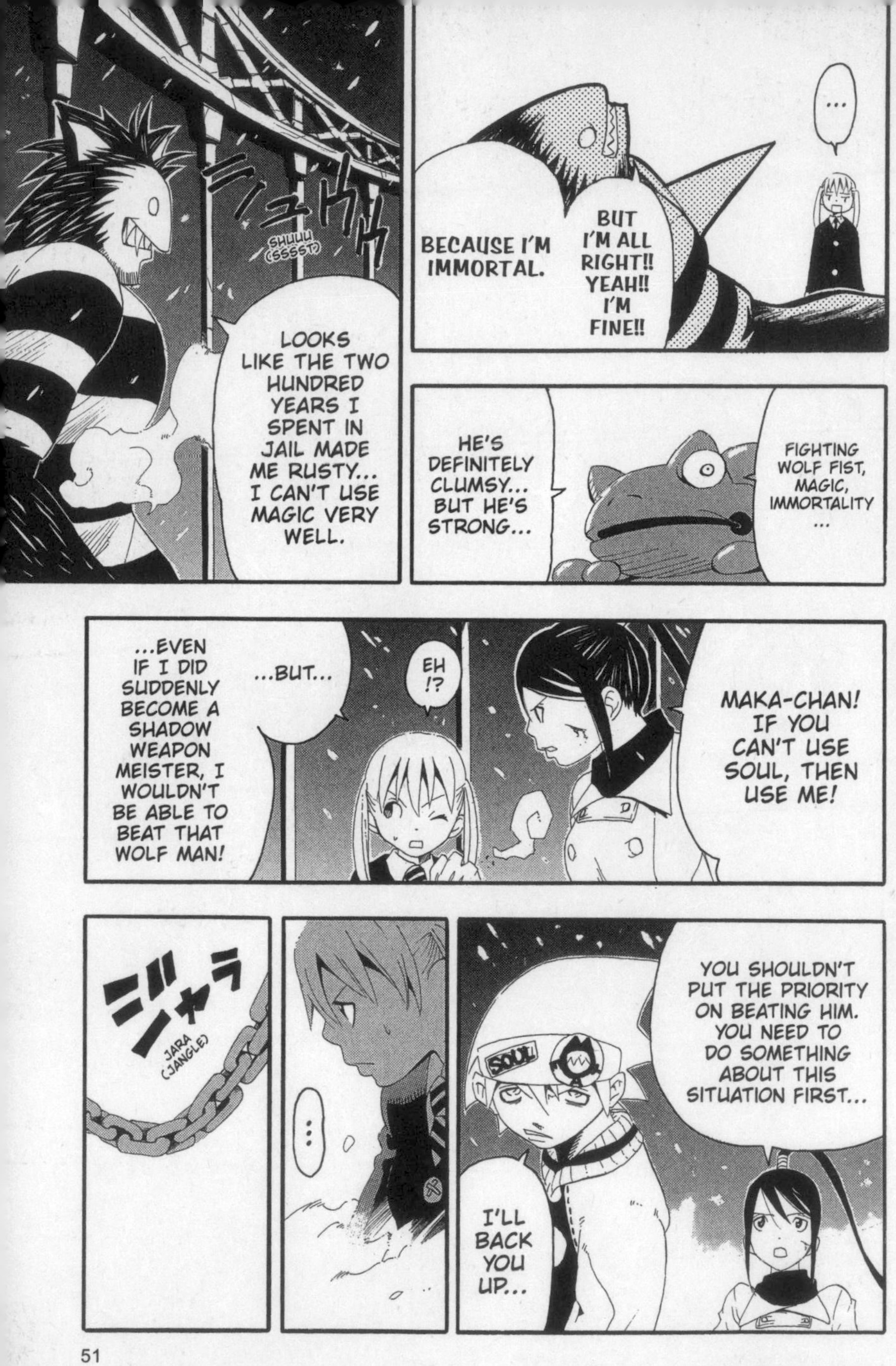
...
BUT I'M ALL RIGHT!! YEAH!! I'M FINE!!
BECAUSE I'M IMMORTAL.
FIGHTING WOLF FIST, MAGIC, IMMORTALITY ...
HE'S DEFINITELY CLUMSY... BUT HE'S STRONG...
SHUUU (SSSST)
LOOKS LIKE THE TWO HUNDRED YEARS I SPENT IN JAIL MADE ME RUSTY... I CAN'T USE MAGIC VERY WELL.
MAKA-CHAN! IF YOU CAN'T USE SOUL, THEN USE ME!
EH !?
...BUT...
...EVEN IF I DID SUDDENLY BECOME A SHADOW WEAPON MEISTER, I WOULDN'T BE ABLE TO BEAT THAT WOLF MAN!
YOU SHOULDN'T PUT THE PRIORITY ON BEATING HIM. YOU NEED TO DO SOMETHING ABOUT THIS SITUATION FIRST...
I'LL BACK YOU UP...
SOUL
...
JARA (JANGLE)

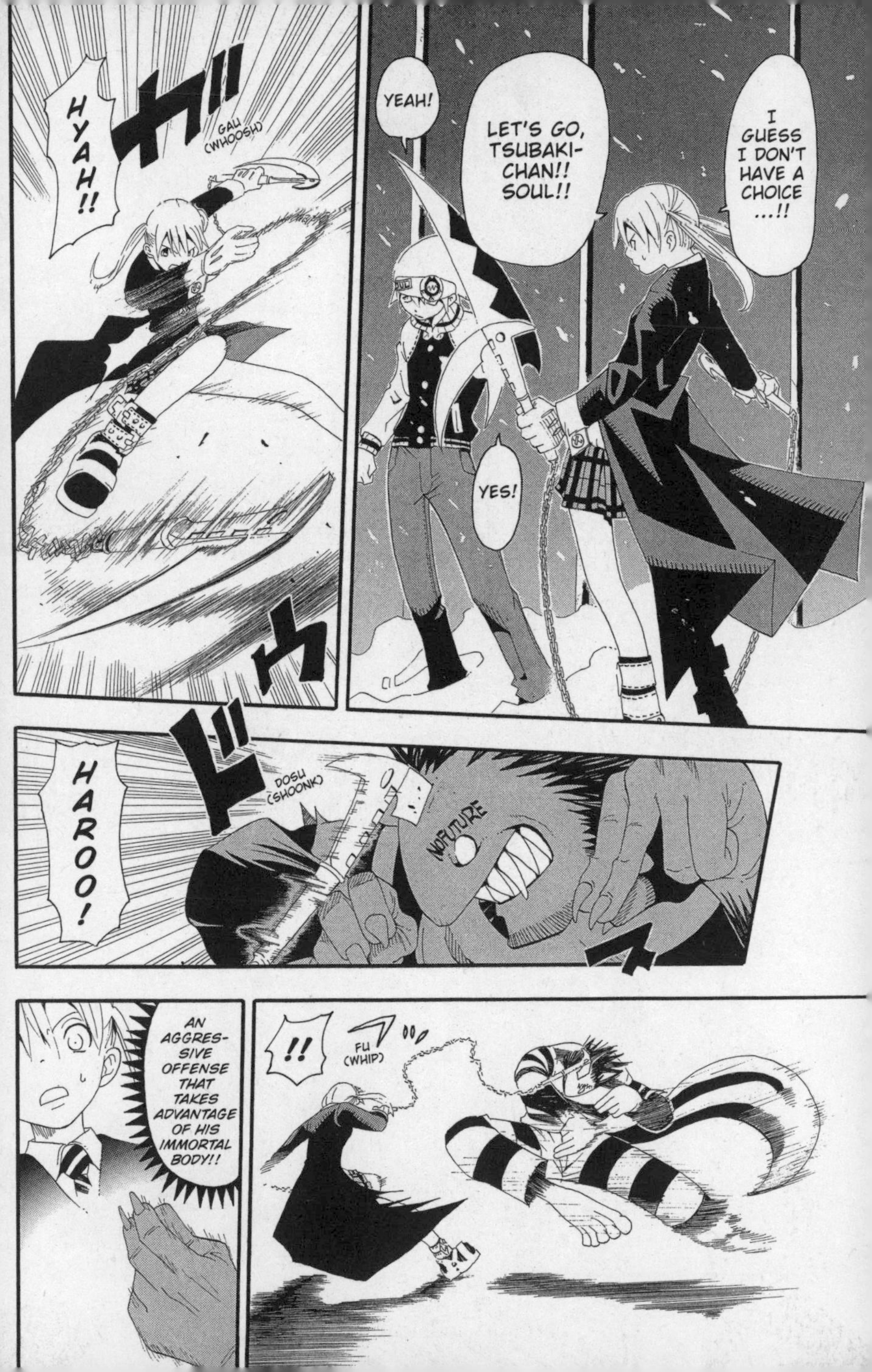
I GUESS I DON'T HAVE A CHOICE ...!!
LET'S GO, TSUBAKI-CHAN!! SOUL!!
YEAH!
YES!
GAU (WHOOSH)
HYAH!!
DOSU (SHOONK)
NOFUTURE
HAROOO!
FU (WHIP)
!!
AN AGGRES-SIVE OFFENSE THAT TAKES ADVANTAGE OF HIS IMMORTAL BODY!!

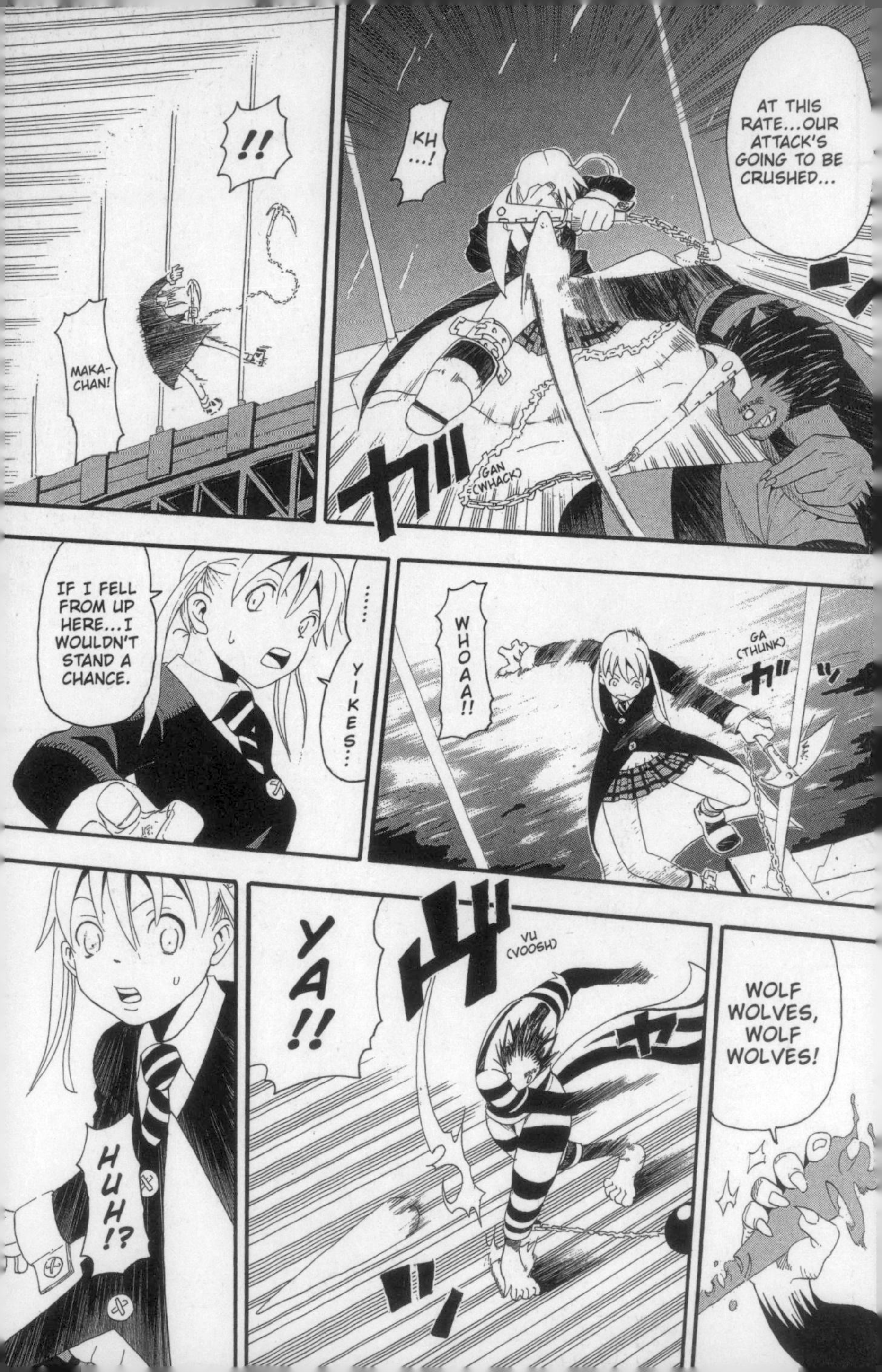
AT THIS RATE...OUR ATTACK'S GOING TO BE CRUSHED...
KH ...!
GAN (WHACK)
!!
MAKA-CHAN!
WHOAA!!
GA (THUNK)
......YIKES...
IF I FELL FROM UP HERE...I WOULDN'T STAND A CHANCE.
WOLF WOLVES, WOLF WOLVES!
YA!!
VU (VOOSH)
HUH!?

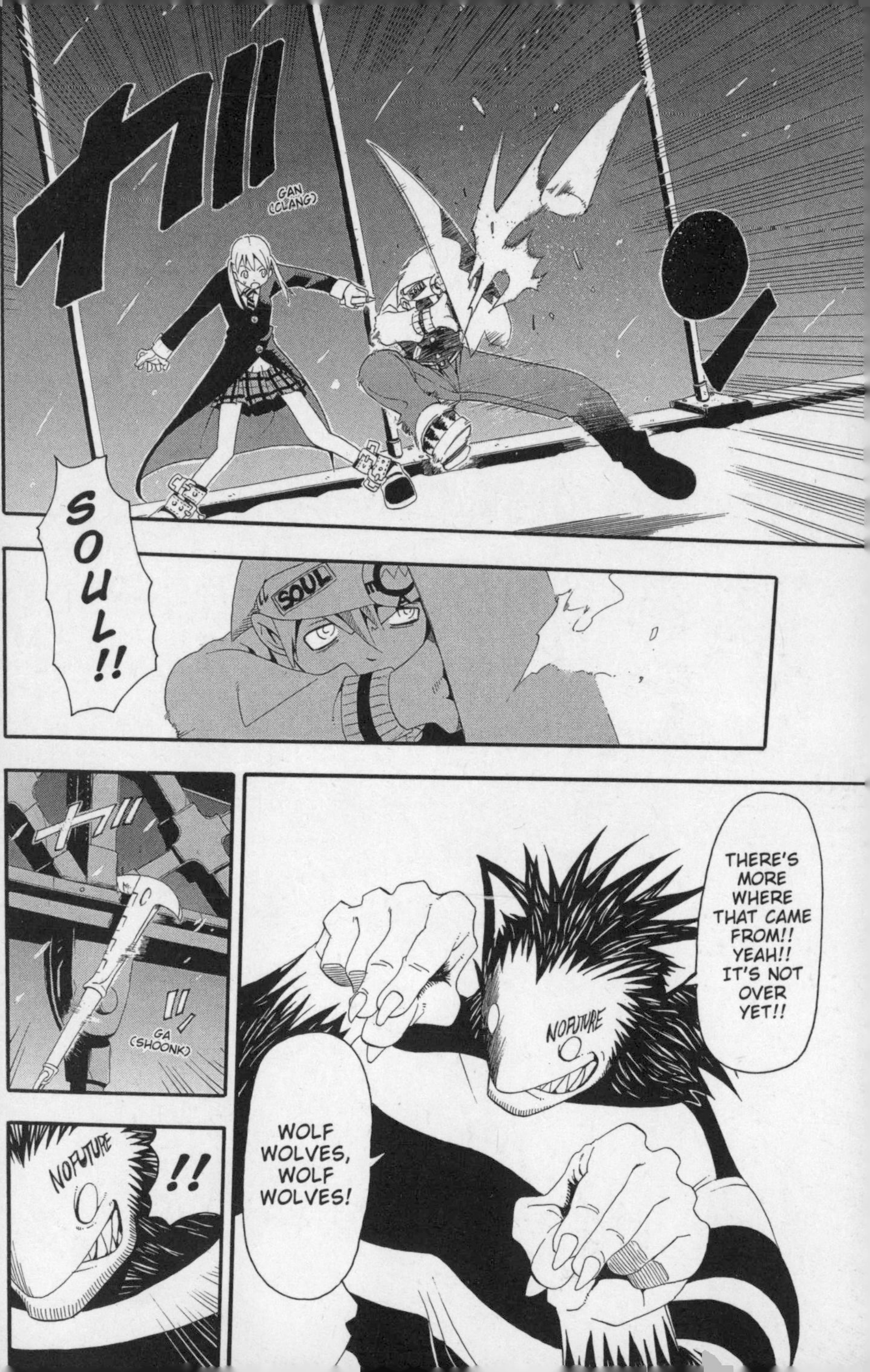
GAN (CLANG)
SOUL!!
THERE'S MORE WHERE THAT CAME FROM!! YEAH!! IT'S NOT OVER YET!!
NOFUTURE
WOLF WOLVES, WOLF WOLVES!
GA (SHOONK)
NOFUTURE
!!

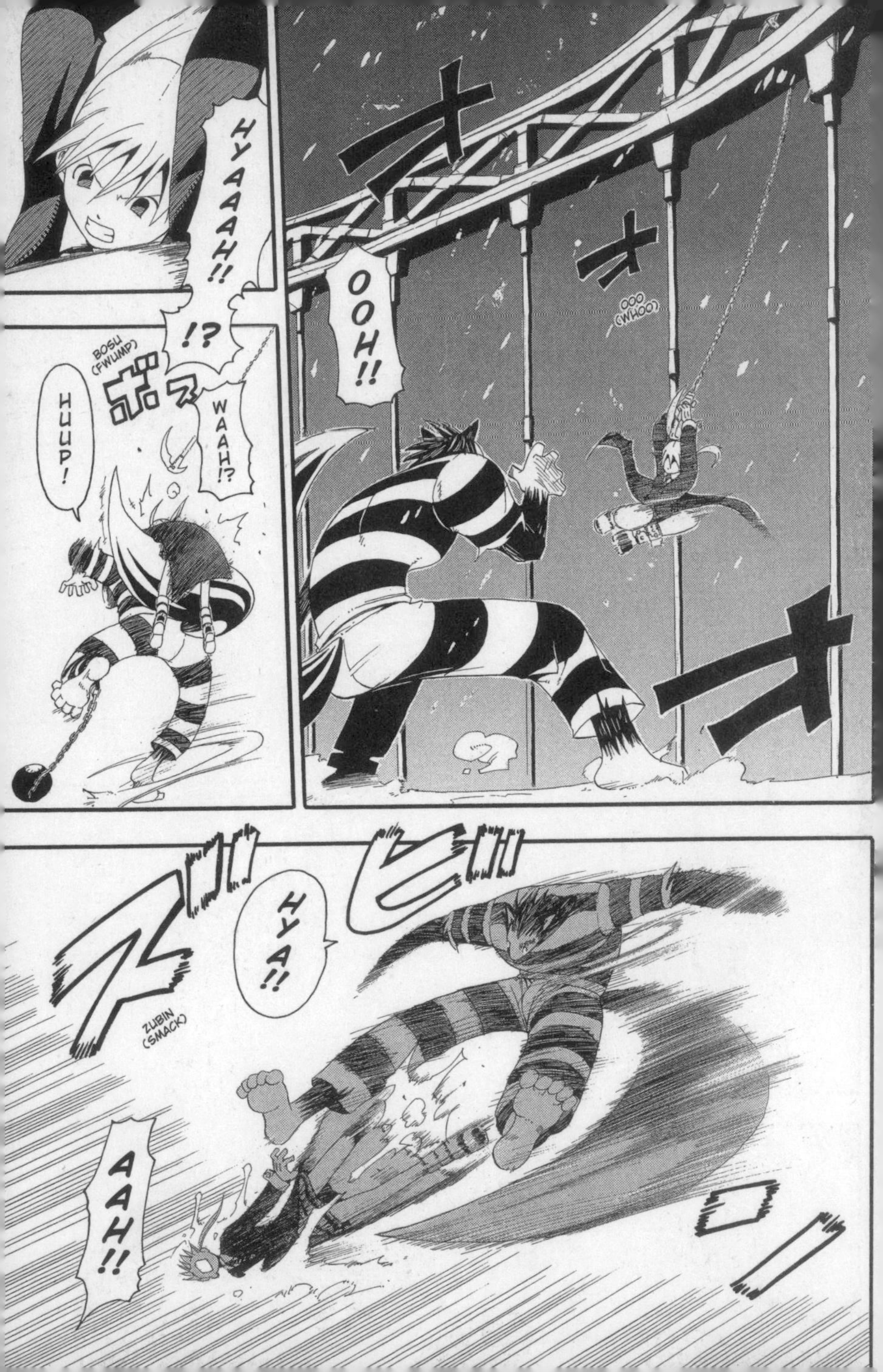

OOH!!
OOO (WHOO)
HYAAAAH!!
!?
WAAAH!?
BOSU (FWUMP)
HUUUP!
HYA!!
ZUBIN (SMACK)
AAAH!!

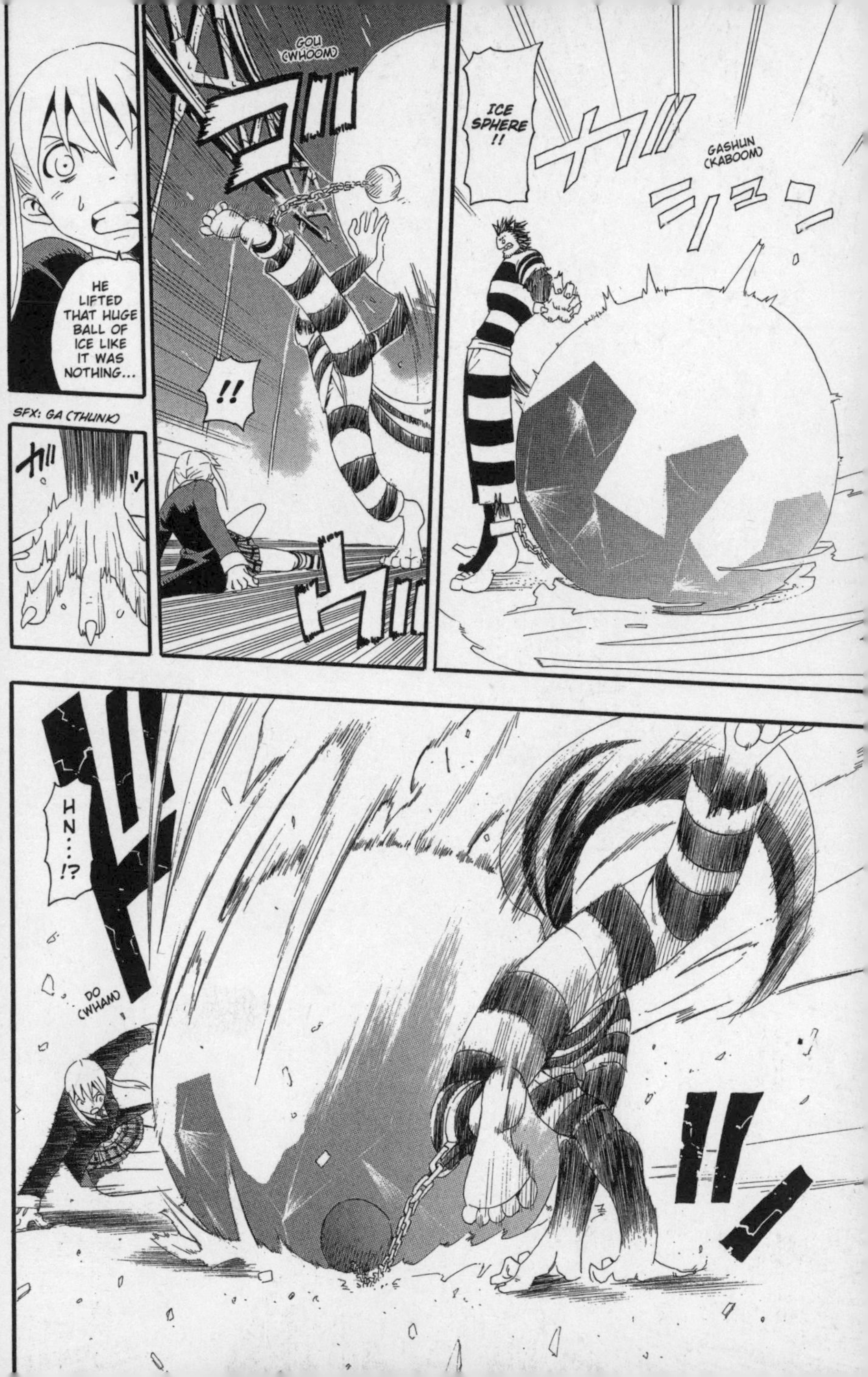
ICE SPHERE !!
GASHUN (KABOOM)
GOU (WHOOM)
!!
HE LIFTED THAT HUGE BALL OF ICE LIKE IT WAS NOTHING...
SFX: GA (THUNK)
HN...!?
DO (WHAM)

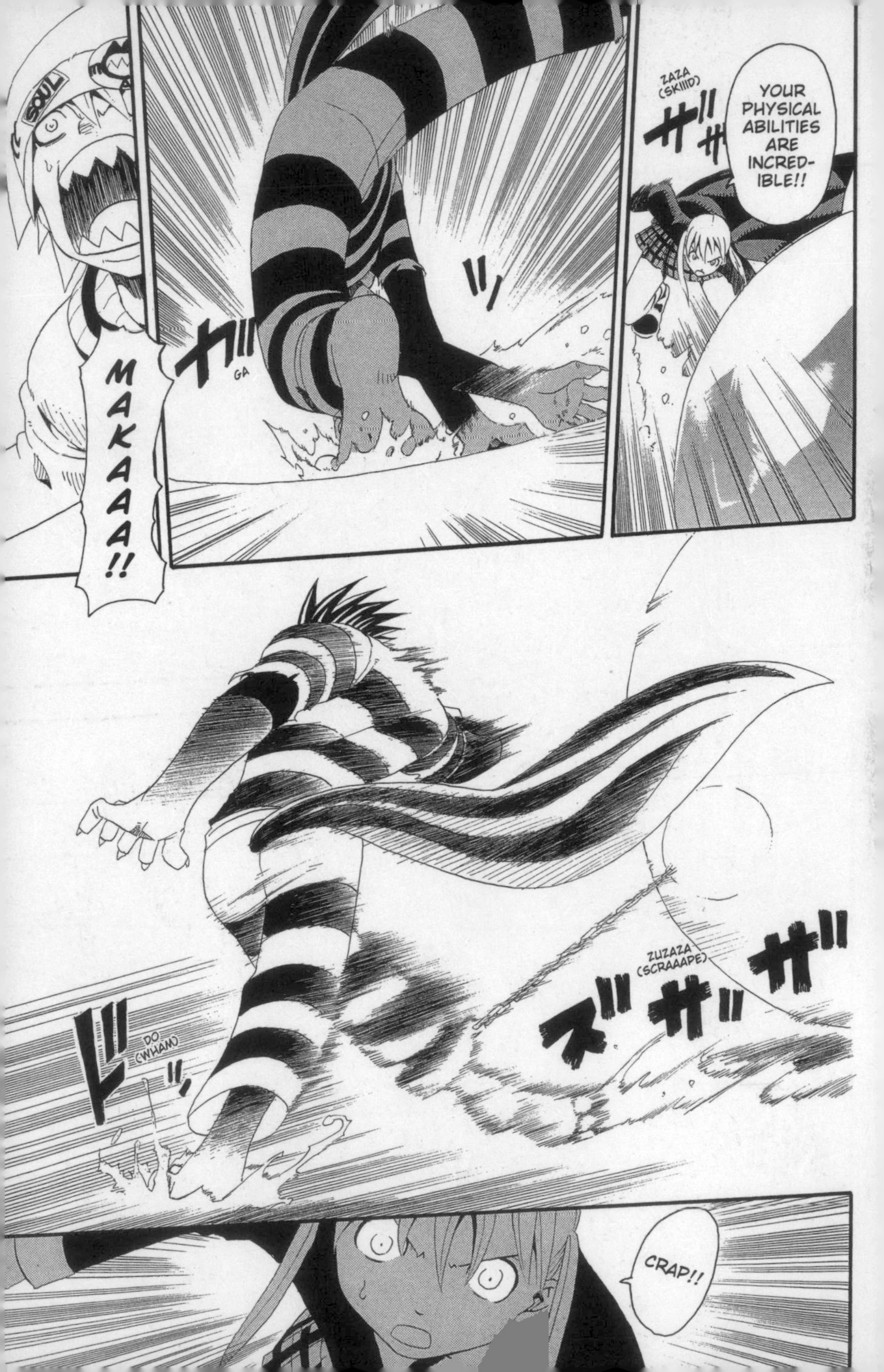
ZAZA (SKIIID)
YOUR PHYSICAL ABILITIES ARE INCRED-IBLE!!
GA
MAKAAAAA!!
ZUZAZA (SCRAAAPE)
DO (WHAM)
CRAP!!

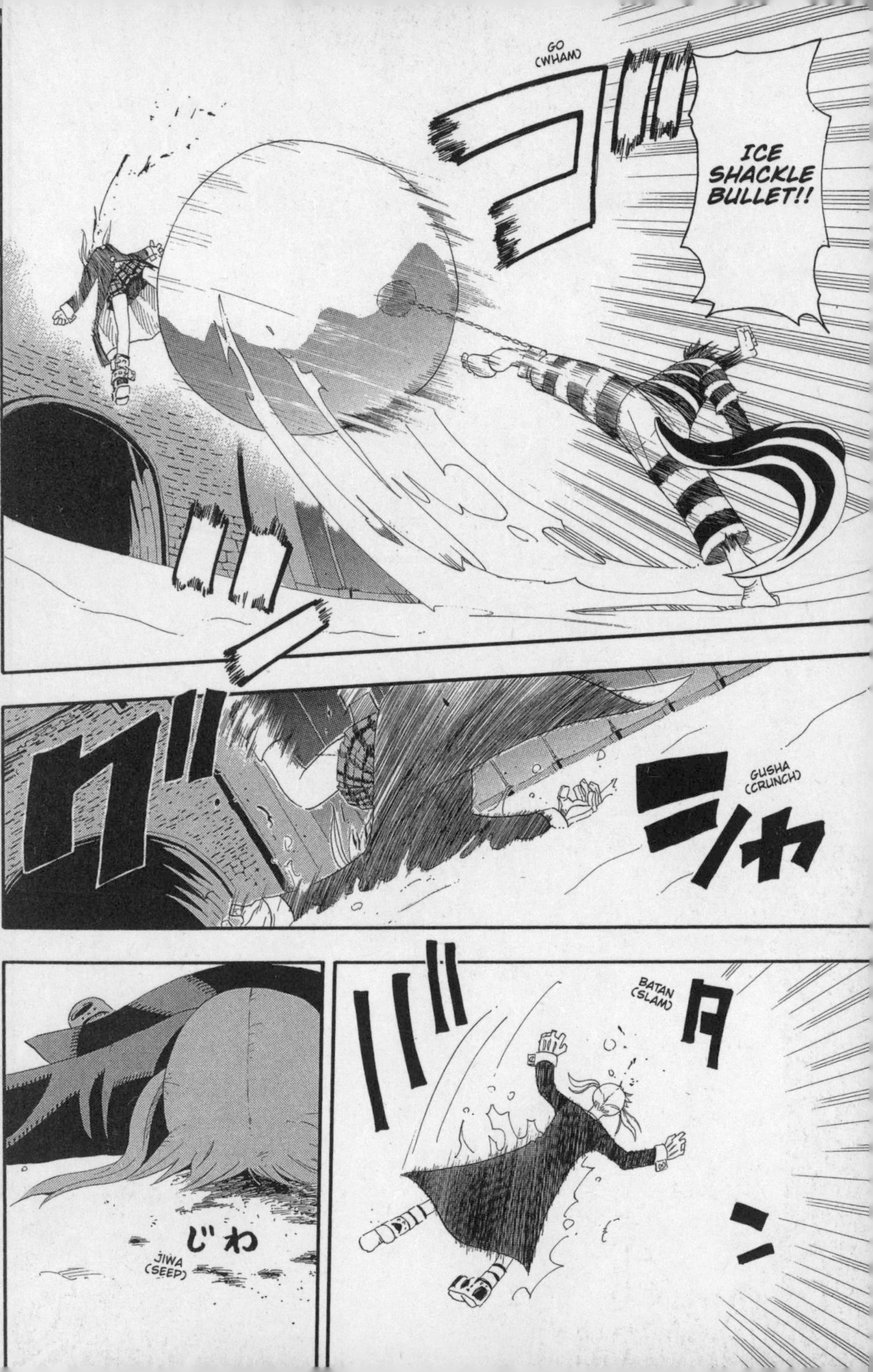
ICE SHACKLE BULLET!!
GO (WHAM)
GUSHA (CRUNCH)
BATAN (SLAM)
じわ
JIWA (SEEP)

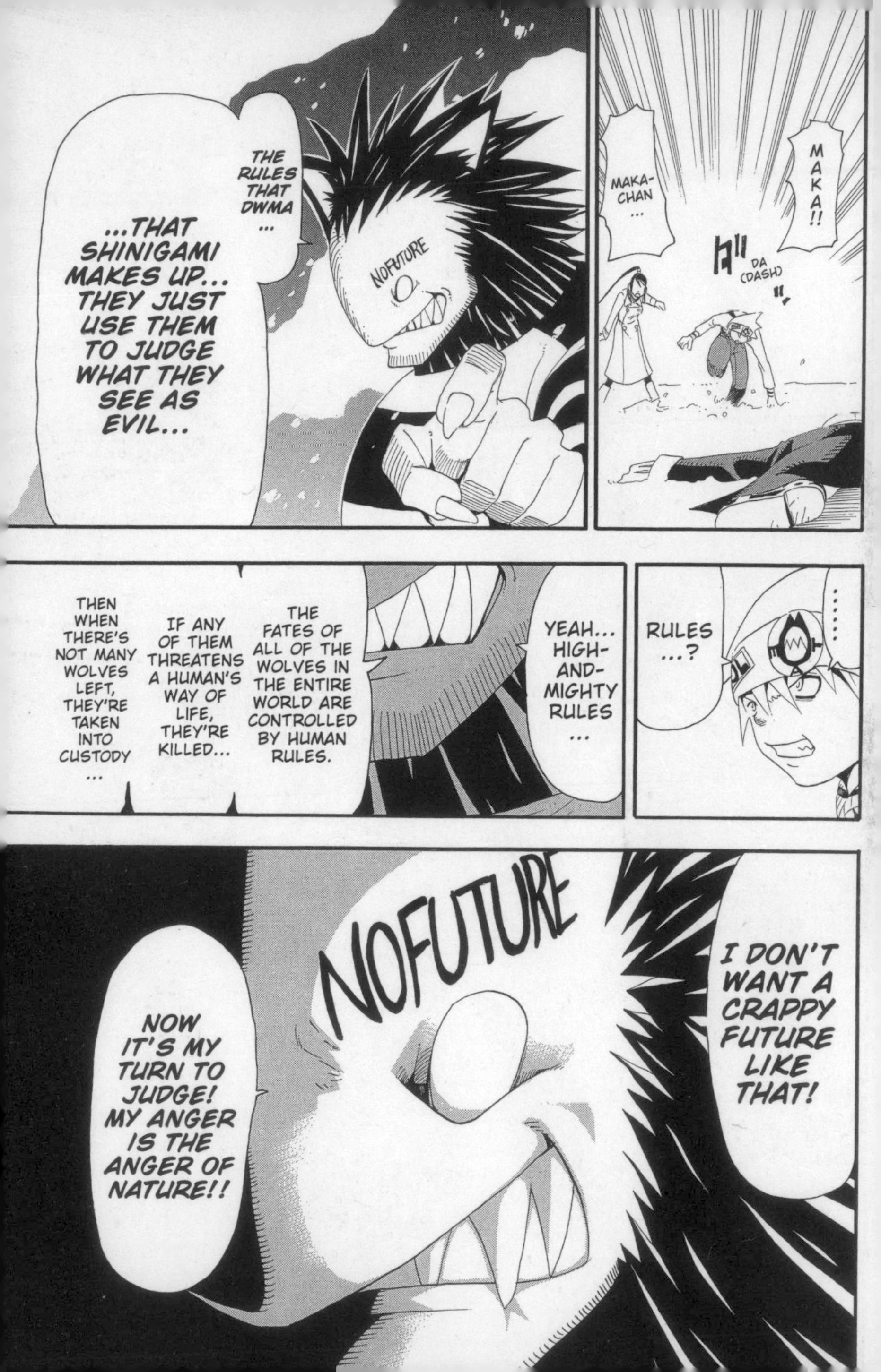

MAKA!!
MAKA-CHAN ...
DA (DASH)
THE RULES THAT DWMA ...
...THAT SHINIGAMI MAKES UP... THEY JUST USE THEM TO JUDGE WHAT THEY SEE AS EVIL...
NOFUTURE
......
RULES ...?
YEAH... HIGH-AND-MIGHTY RULES ...
THE FATES OF ALL OF THE WOLVES IN THE ENTIRE WORLD ARE CONTROLLED BY HUMAN RULES.
IF ANY OF THEM THREATENS A HUMAN'S WAY OF LIFE, THEY'RE KILLED...
THEN WHEN THERE'S NOT MANY WOLVES LEFT, THEY'RE TAKEN INTO CUSTODY ...
I DON'T WANT A CRAPPY FUTURE LIKE THAT!
NOFUTURE
NOW IT'S MY TURN TO JUDGE! MY ANGER IS THE ANGER OF NATURE!!

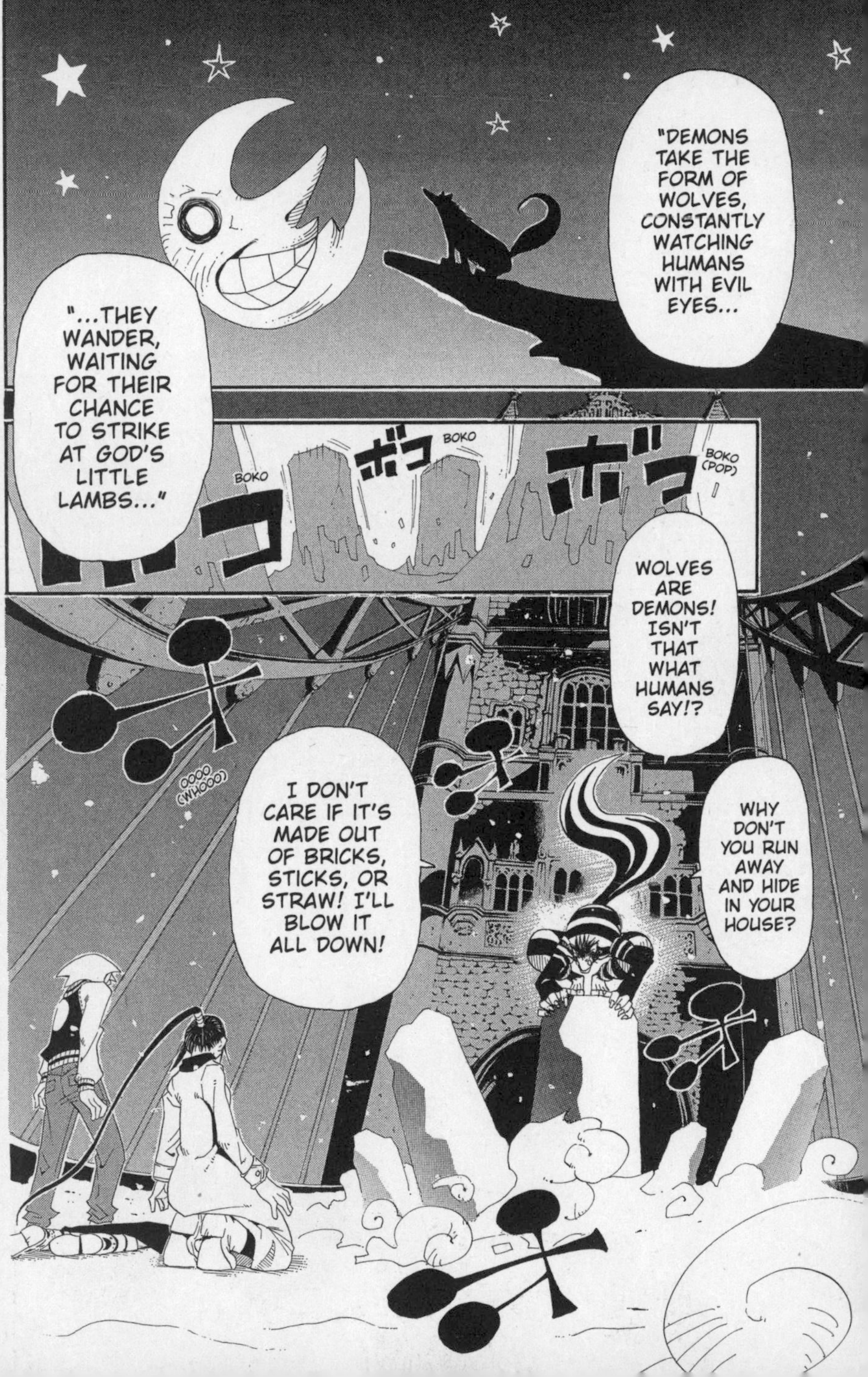
"DEMONS TAKE THE FORM OF WOLVES, CONSTANTLY WATCHING HUMANS WITH EVIL EYES...
"...THEY WANDER, WAITING FOR THEIR CHANCE TO STRIKE AT GOD'S LITTLE LAMBS..."
BOKO (POP)
BOKO
BOKO
WOLVES ARE DEMONS! ISN'T THAT WHAT HUMANS SAY!?
WHY DON'T YOU RUN AWAY AND HIDE IN YOUR HOUSE?
I DON'T CARE IF IT'S MADE OUT OF BRICKS, STICKS, OR STRAW! I'LL BLOW IT ALL DOWN!

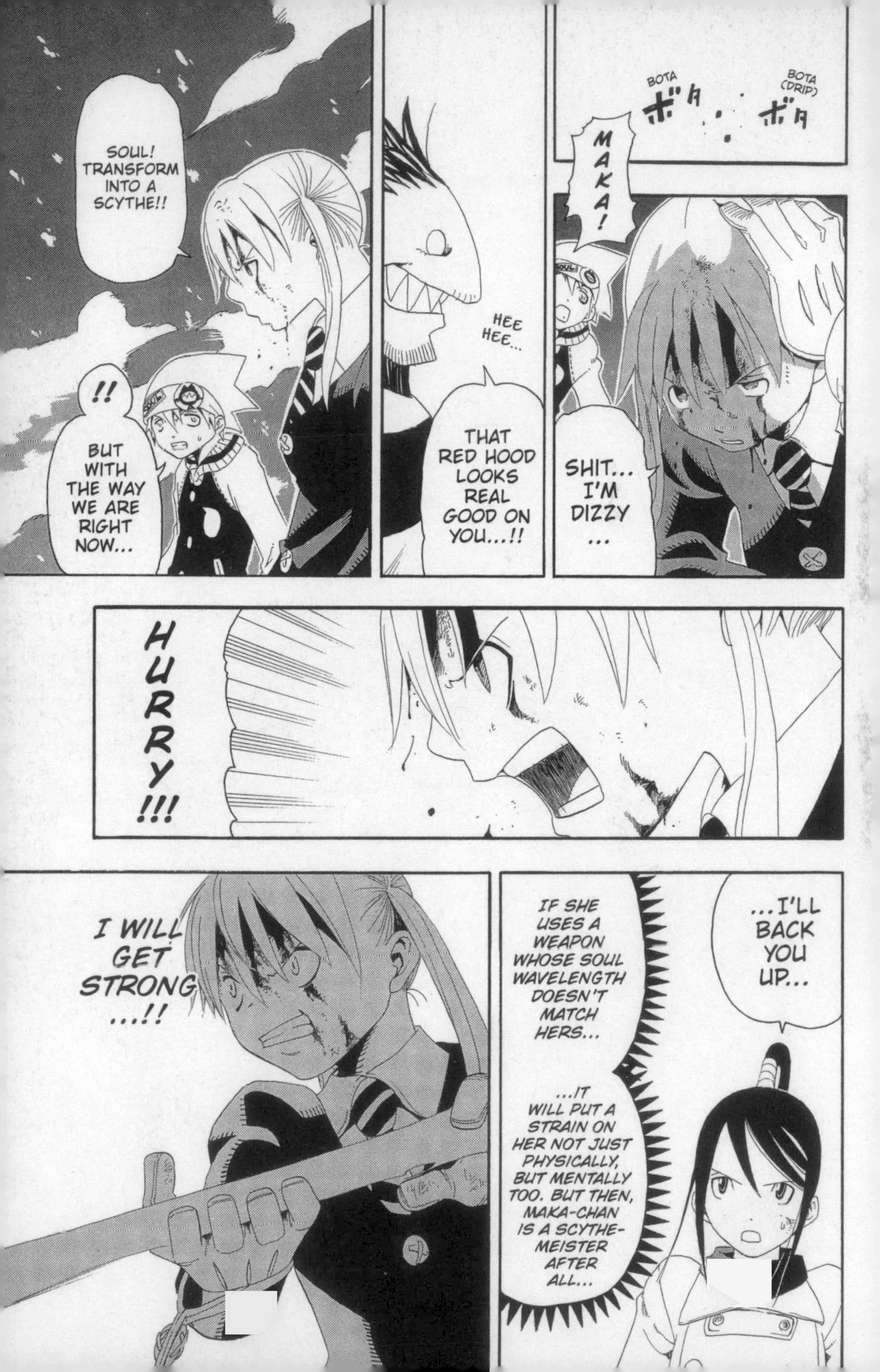
BOTA
BOTA (DRIP)
ボタ ボタ
MAKA!
SHIT... I'M DIZZY...
HEE HEE...
THAT RED HOOD LOOKS REAL GOOD ON YOU...!!
SOUL! TRANSFORM INTO A SCYTHE!!
!!
BUT WITH THE WAY WE ARE RIGHT NOW...
HURRY!!!
...I'LL BACK YOU UP...
IF SHE USES A WEAPON WHOSE SOUL WAVELENGTH DOESN'T MATCH HERS...
...IT WILL PUT A STRAIN ON HER NOT JUST PHYSICALLY, BUT MENTALLY TOO. BUT THEN, MAKA-CHAN IS A SCYTHE-MEISTER AFTER ALL...
I WILL GET STRONG...!!

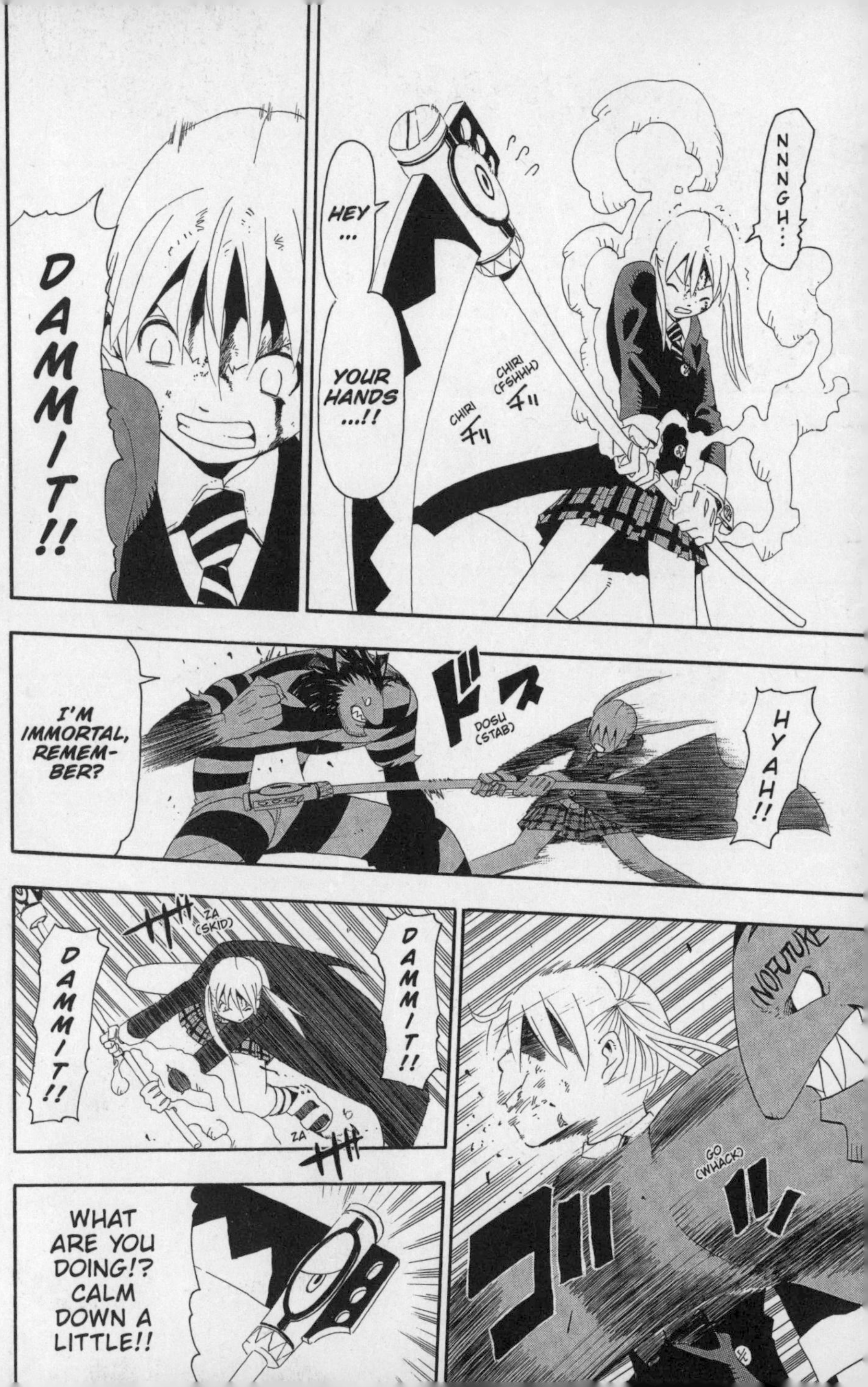
NNNGH...
CHIRI (FSHHH) チリ
CHIRI チリ
HEY ...
YOUR HANDS ...!!
DAMMIT!!
HYAH!!
ドス
DOSU (STAB)
I'M IMMORTAL, REMEMBER?
NOFUTURE
ゴッ
GO (WHACK)
DAMMIT!!
ZA (SKID)
DAMMIT!!
ZA
WHAT ARE YOU DOING!? CALM DOWN A LITTLE!!

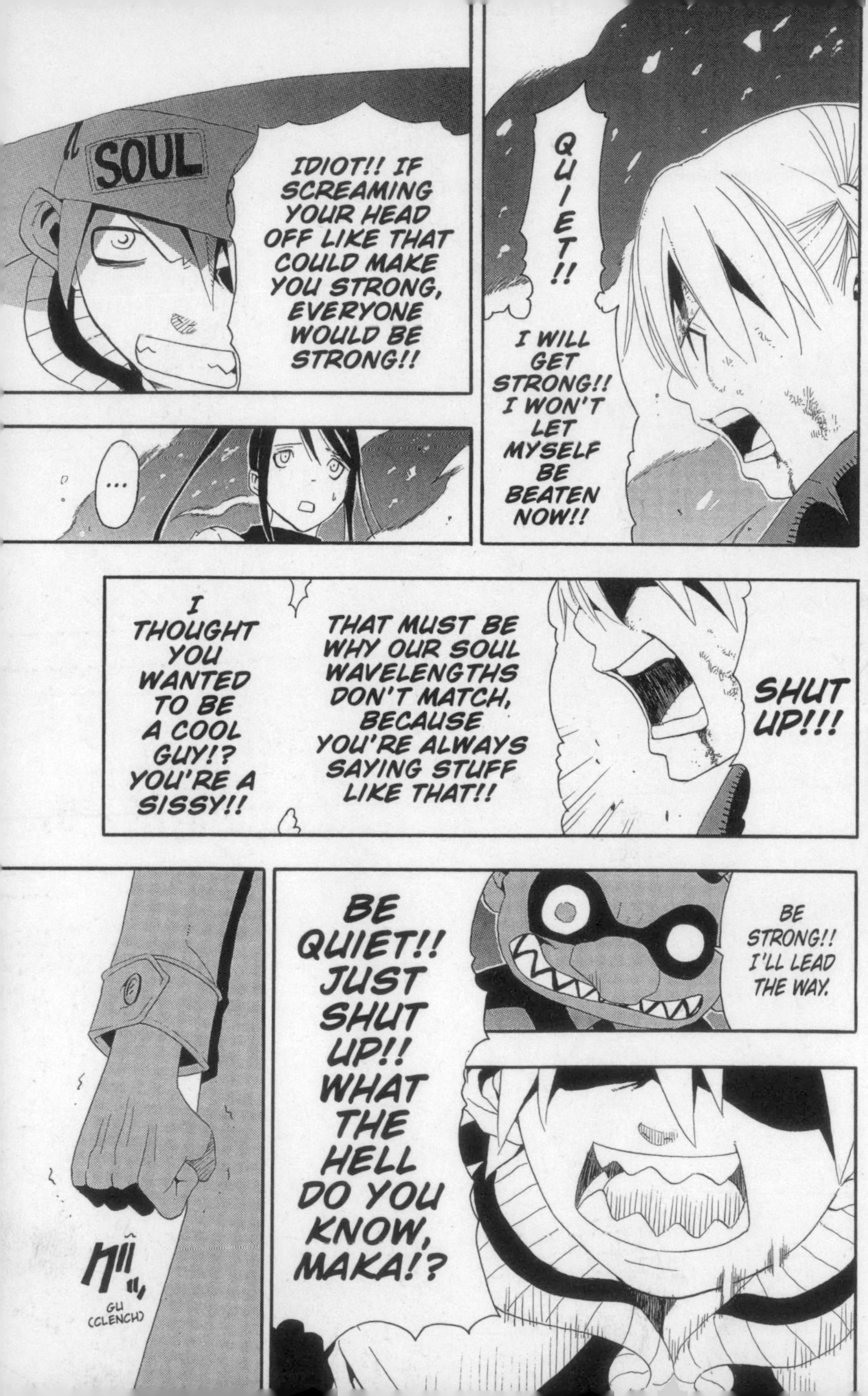
QUIET!!
I WILL GET STRONG!! I WON'T LET MYSELF BE BEATEN NOW!!
IDIOT!! IF SCREAMING YOUR HEAD OFF LIKE THAT COULD MAKE YOU STRONG, EVERYONE WOULD BE STRONG!!
...
SHUT UP!!!
THAT MUST BE WHY OUR SOUL WAVELENGTHS DON'T MATCH, BECAUSE YOU'RE ALWAYS SAYING STUFF LIKE THAT!!
I THOUGHT YOU WANTED TO BE A COOL GUY!? YOU'RE A SISSY!!
BE STRONG!! I'LL LEAD THE WAY.
BE QUIET!! JUST SHUT UP!! WHAT THE HELL DO YOU KNOW, MAKA!?
GU (CLENCH)

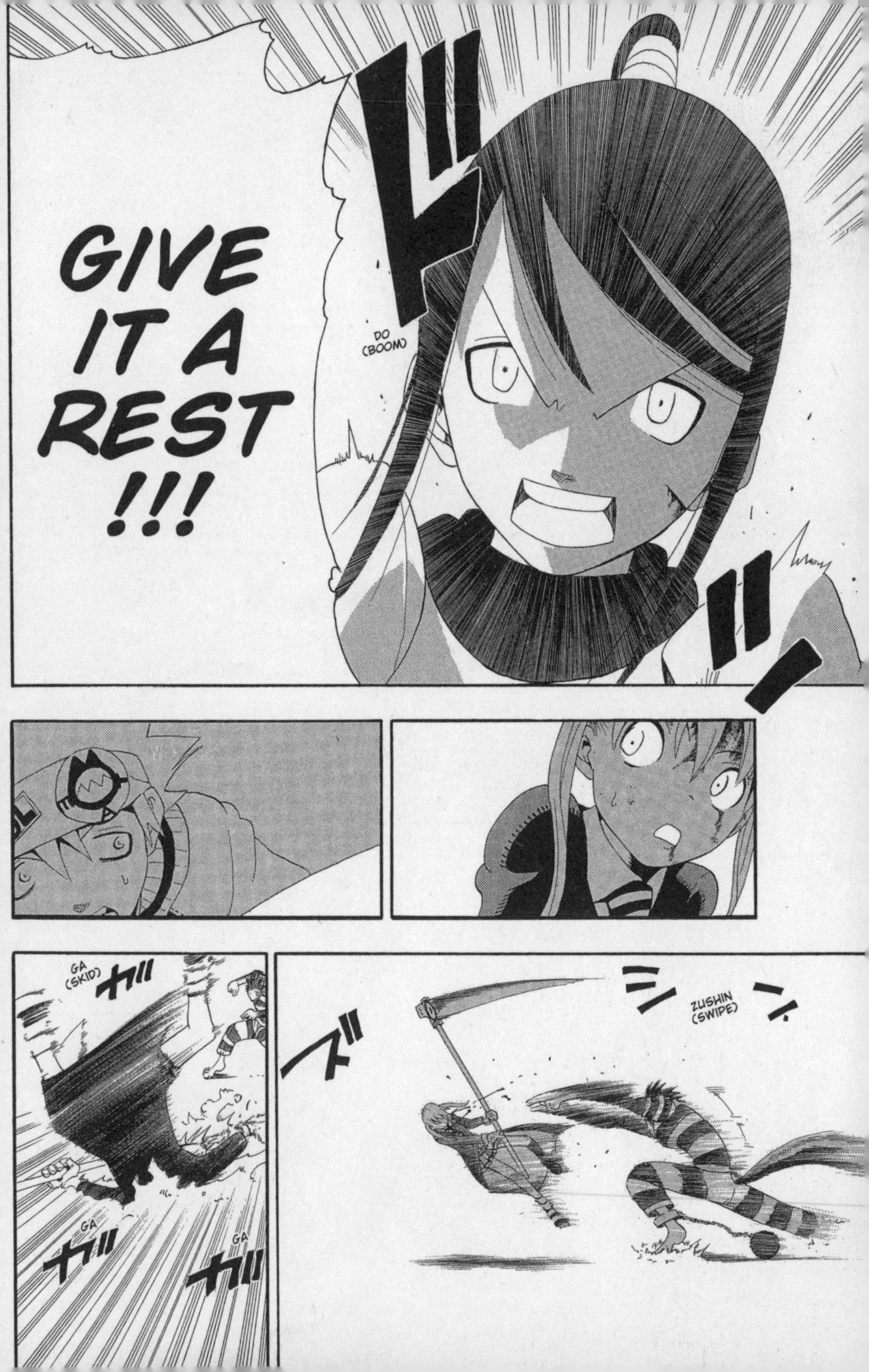
DO (BOOM)
GIVE IT A REST!!!
GA (SKID)
GA
GA
ZUSHIN (SWIPE)

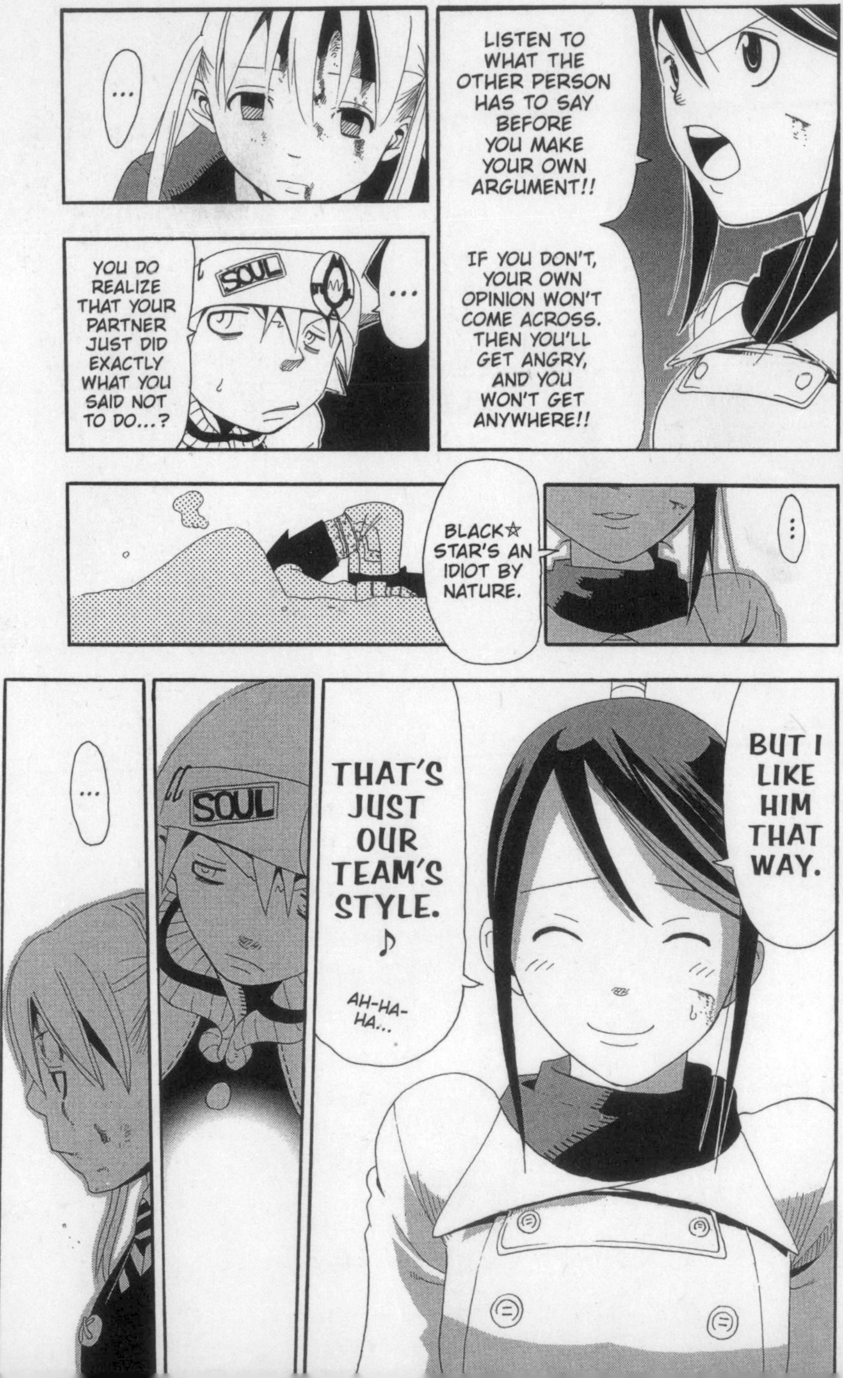
LISTEN TO WHAT THE OTHER PERSON HAS TO SAY BEFORE YOU MAKE YOUR OWN ARGUMENT!!
IF YOU DON'T, YOUR OWN OPINION WON'T COME ACROSS. THEN YOU'LL GET ANGRY, AND YOU WON'T GET ANYWHERE!!
...
...
SOUL
YOU DO REALIZE THAT YOUR PARTNER JUST DID EXACTLY WHAT YOU SAID NOT TO DO...?
...
BLACK☆STAR'S AN IDIOT BY NATURE.
BUT I LIKE HIM THAT WAY.
THAT'S JUST OUR TEAM'S STYLE. ♪
AH-HA-HA...
SOUL
...

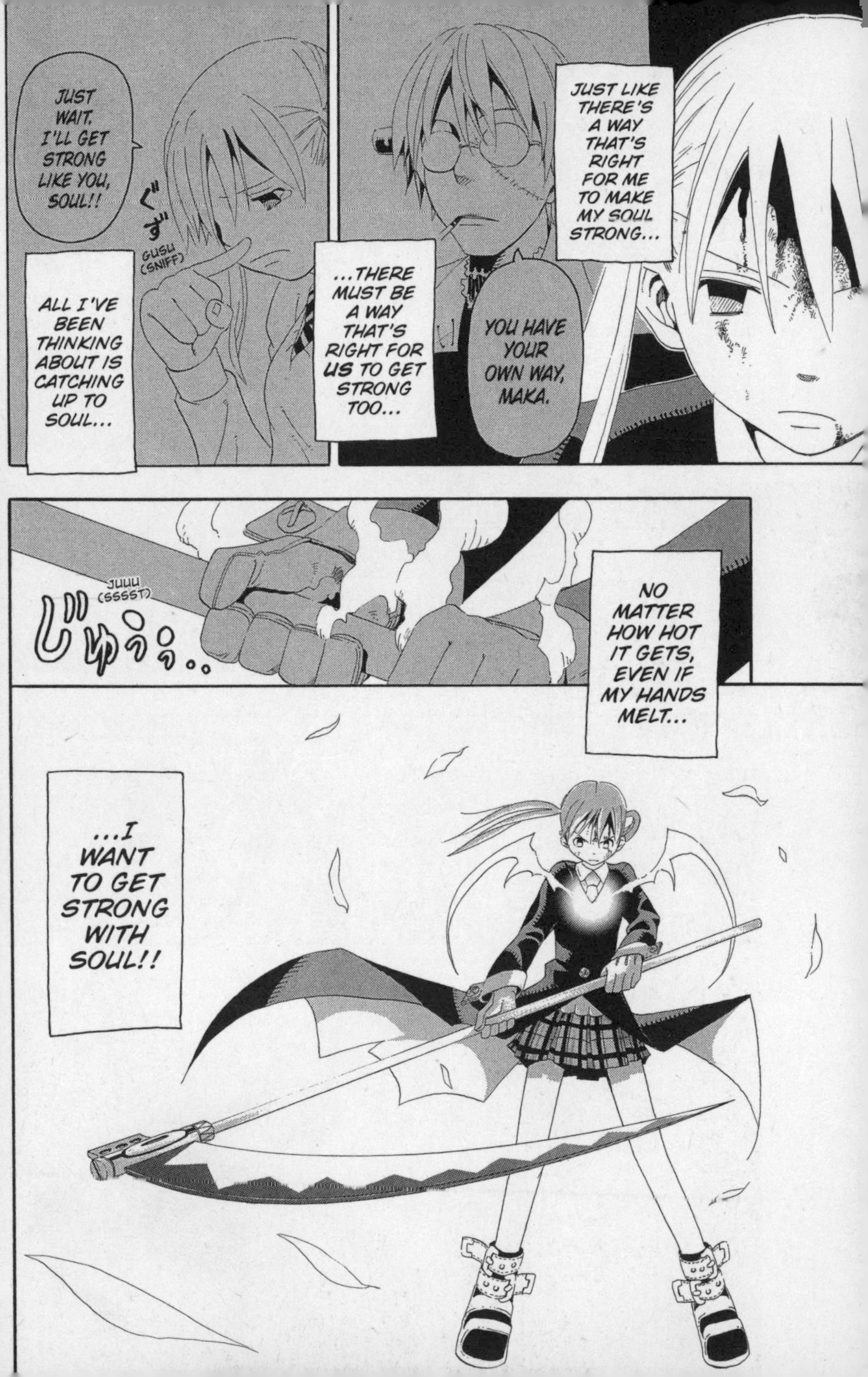
JUST LIKE THERE'S A WAY THAT'S RIGHT FOR ME TO MAKE MY SOUL STRONG...
YOU HAVE YOUR OWN WAY, MAKA.
...THERE MUST BE A WAY THAT'S RIGHT FOR US TO GET STRONG TOO...
JUST WAIT. I'LL GET STRONG LIKE YOU, SOUL!!
ぐず
GUSU (SNIFF)
ALL I'VE BEEN THINKING ABOUT IS CATCHING UP TO SOUL...
NO MATTER HOW HOT IT GETS, EVEN IF MY HANDS MELT...
じゅぅぅ...
JUUU (SSSST)
...I WANT TO GET STRONG WITH SOUL!!

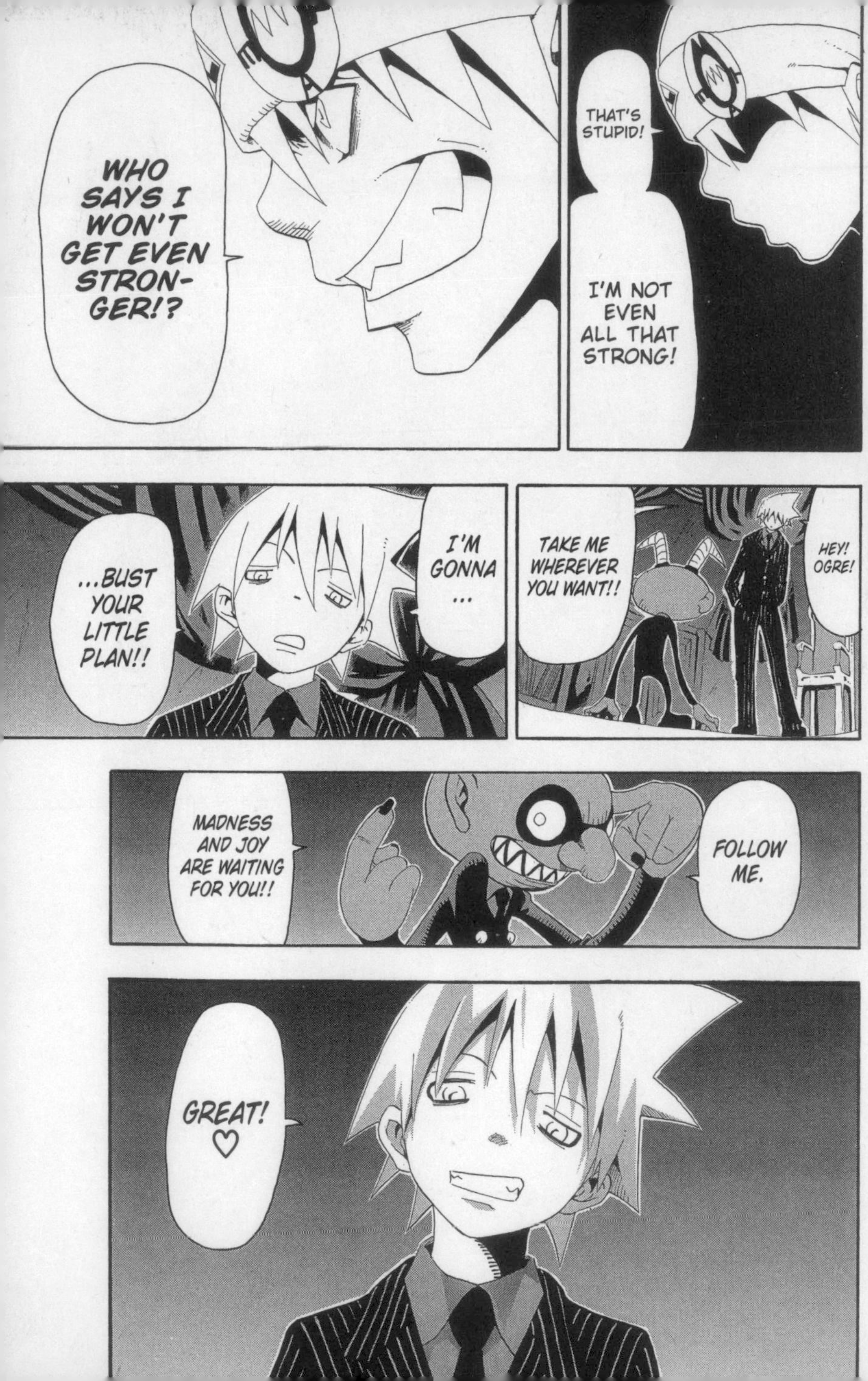
THAT'S STUPID!
I'M NOT EVEN ALL THAT STRONG!
WHO SAYS I WON'T GET EVEN STRONGER!?
HEY! OGRE!
TAKE ME WHEREVER YOU WANT!!
I'M GONNA ...
...BUST YOUR LITTLE PLAN!!
FOLLOW ME.
MADNESS AND JOY ARE WAITING FOR YOU!!
GREAT! ♡

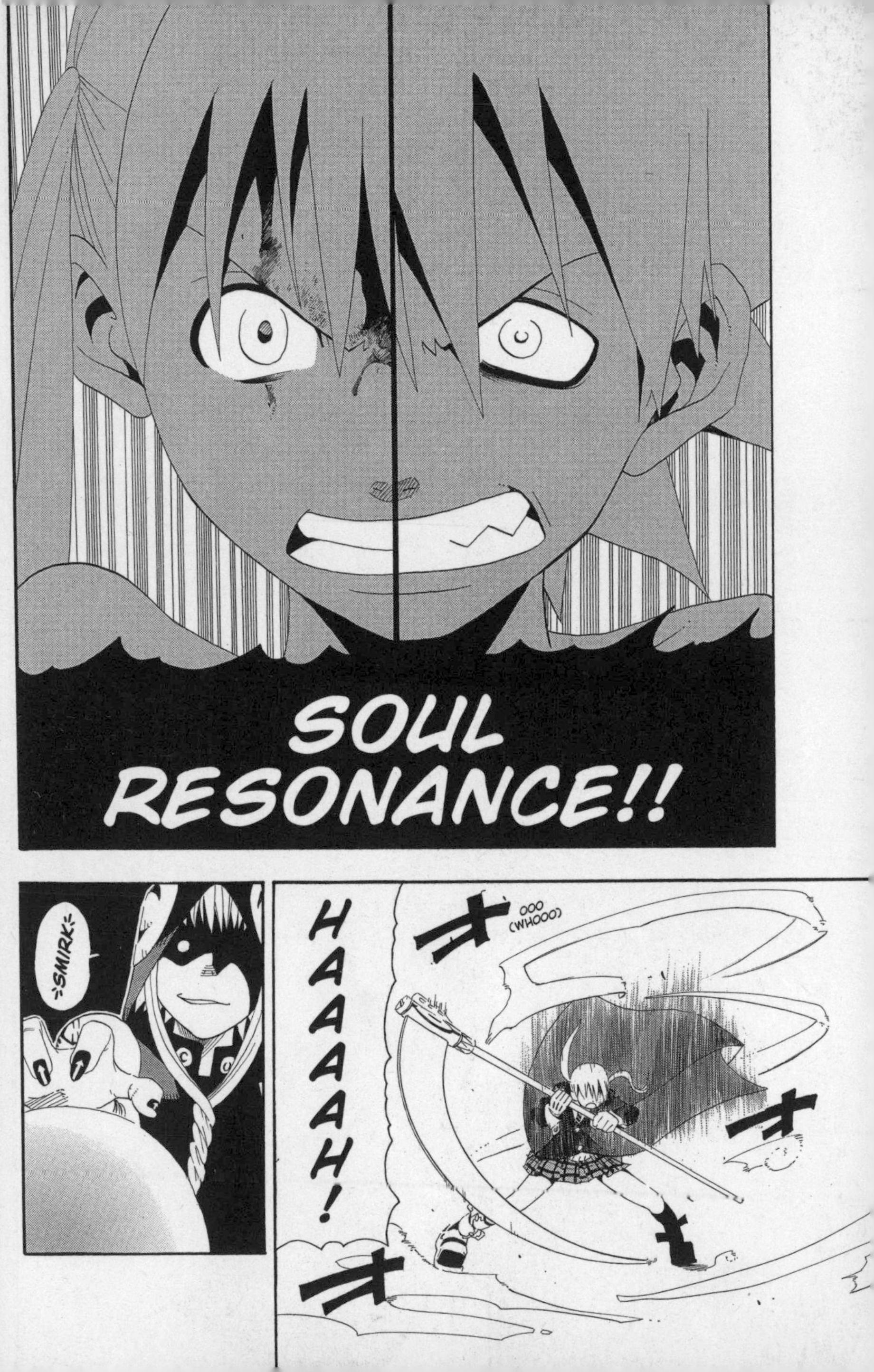
SOUL RESONANCE!!
HAAAAAH!
OOO (WHOOO)
SMIRK

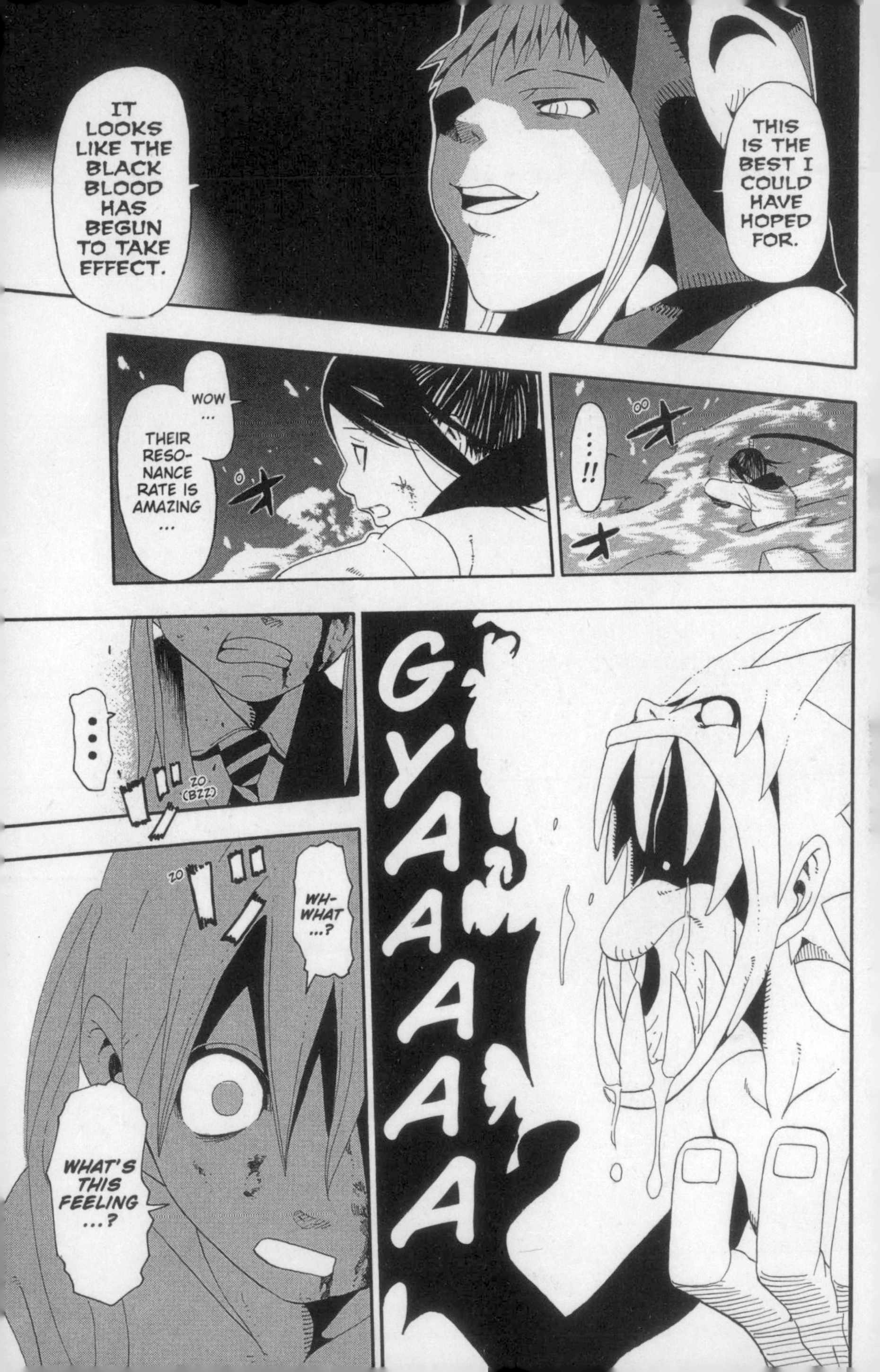
THIS IS THE BEST I COULD HAVE HOPED FOR.
IT LOOKS LIKE THE BLACK BLOOD HAS BEGUN TO TAKE EFFECT.
...!!
WOW ... THEIR RESONANCE RATE IS AMAZING ...
GYAAAAA
...
ZO (BZZ)
ZO
WH-WHAT ...?
WHAT'S THIS FEELING ...?

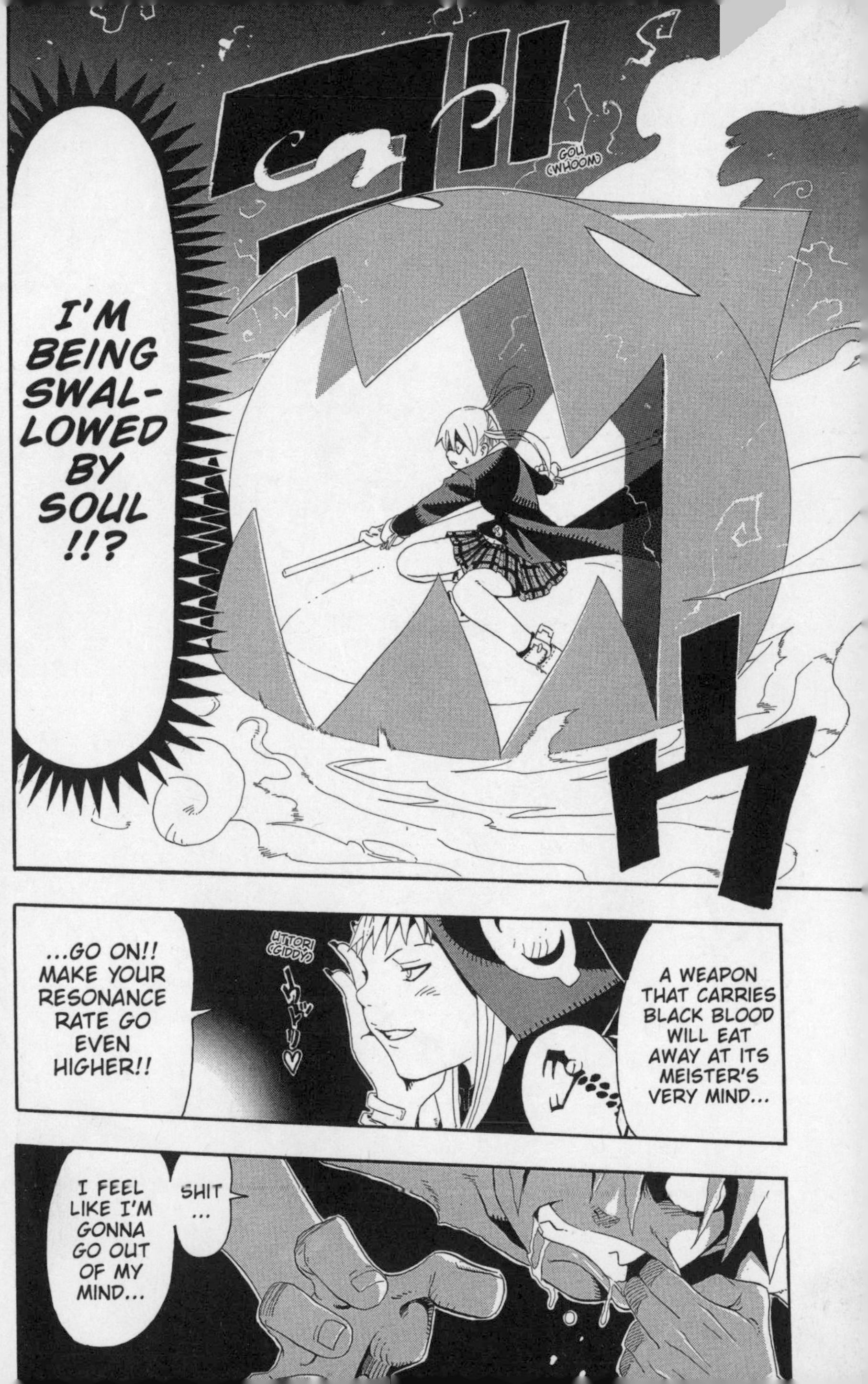
GOU (WHOOM)
I'M BEING SWAL-LOWED BY SOUL!!?
A WEAPON THAT CARRIES BLACK BLOOD WILL EAT AWAY AT ITS MEISTER'S VERY MIND...
UTTORI (GIDDY)
...GO ON!! MAKE YOUR RESONANCE RATE GO EVEN HIGHER!!
SHIT...
I FEEL LIKE I'M GONNA GO OUT OF MY MIND...

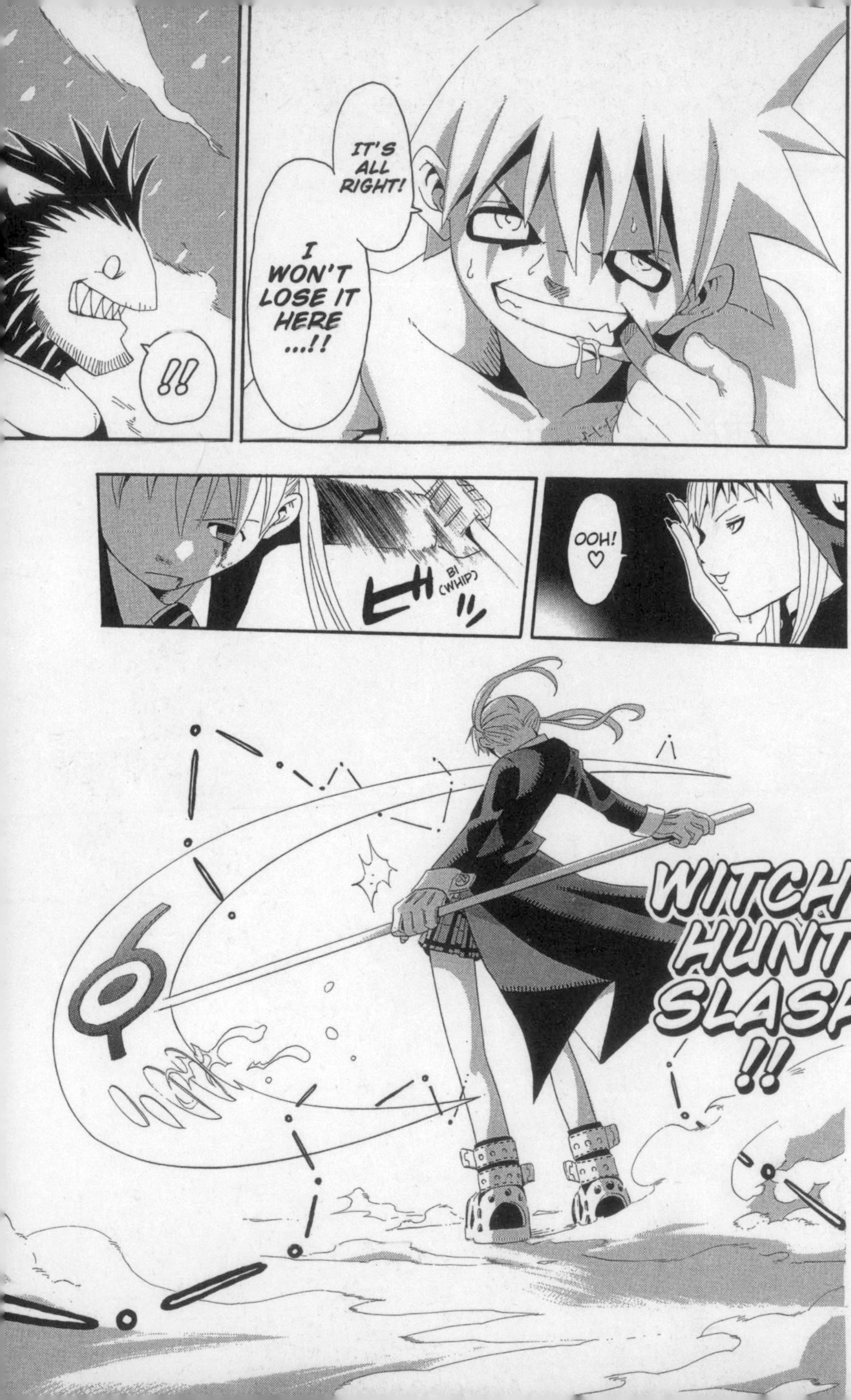
IT'S ALL RIGHT!
I WON'T LOSE IT HERE ...!!
!!
OOH! ♡
BI (WHIP)
WITCH-HUNT SLASH !!

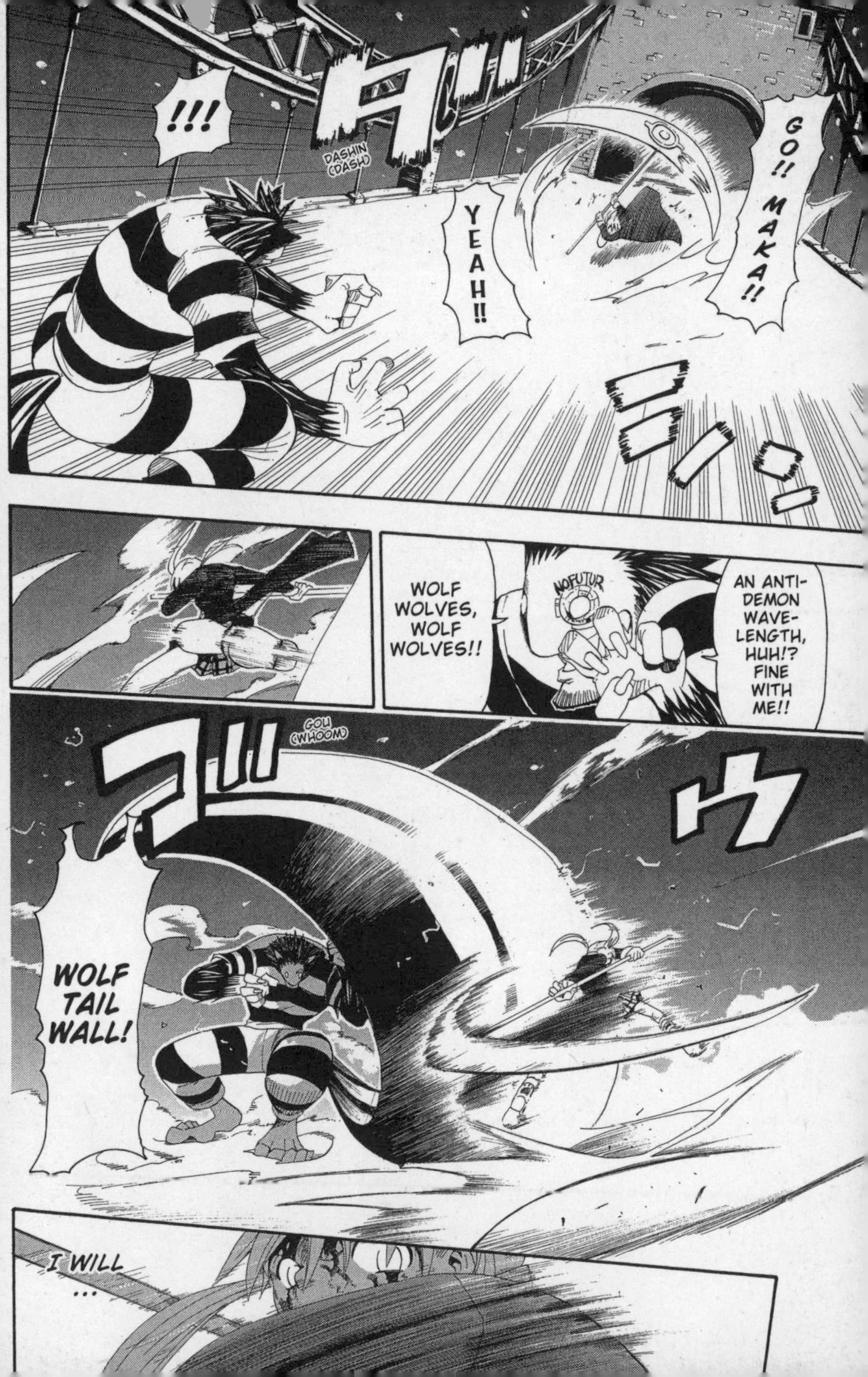
GO!! MAKA!!
YEAH!!
!!!
DASHIN (DASH)
AN ANTI-DEMON WAVE-LENGTH, HUH!? FINE WITH ME!!
NOFUTUR
WOLF WOLVES, WOLF WOLVES!!
GOU (WHOOM)
WOLF TAIL WALL!
I WILL ...

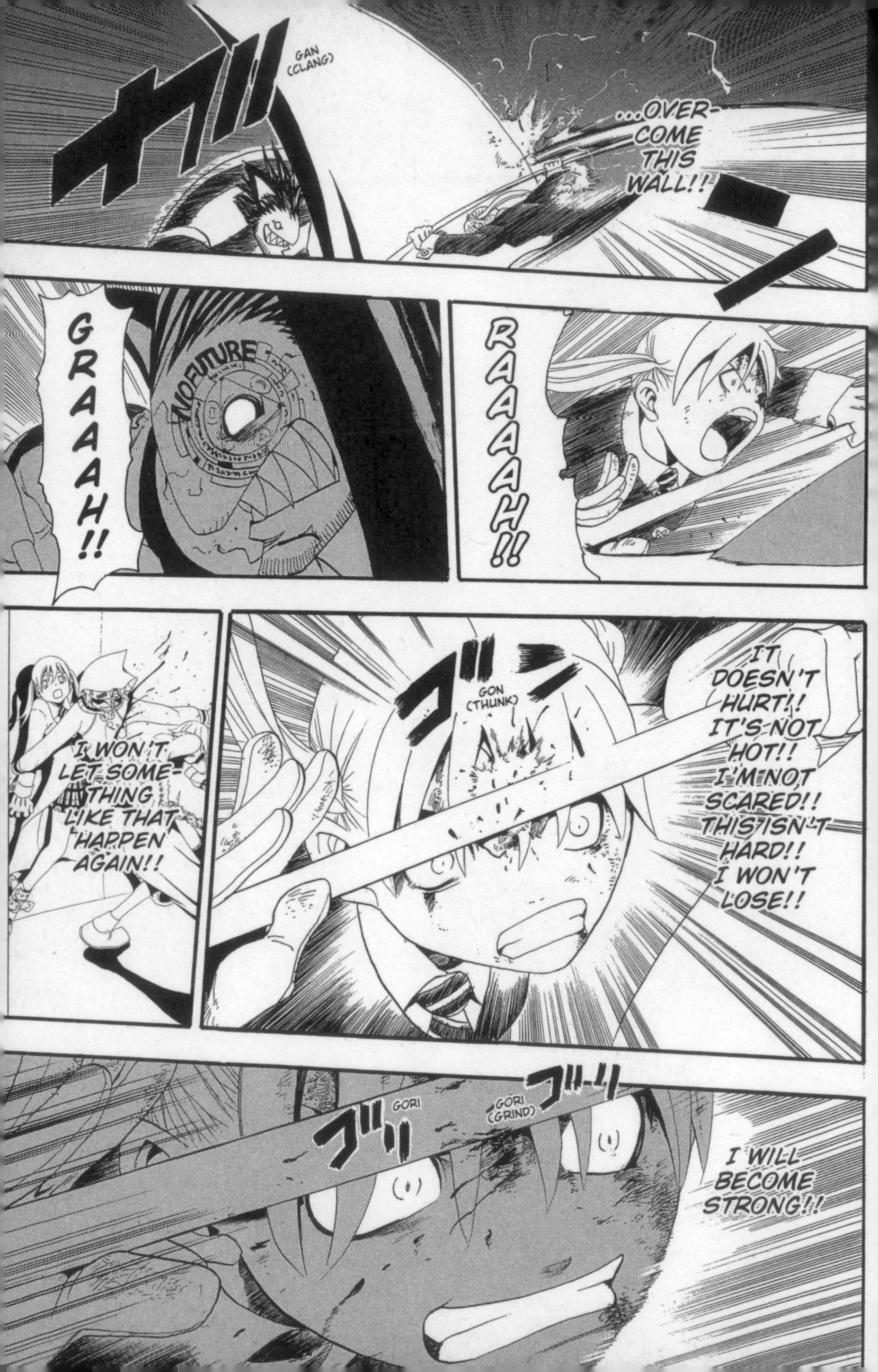
GAN (CLANG)
...OVER-COME THIS WALL!!
RAAAAAH!!
GRAAAAH!!
NO FUTURE
IT DOESN'T HURT!! IT'S NOT HOT!! I'M NOT SCARED!! THIS ISN'T HARD!! I WON'T LOSE!!
GON (THUNK)
I WON'T LET SOME-THING LIKE THAT HAPPEN AGAIN!!
I WILL BECOME STRONG!!
GORI (GRIND)
GORI

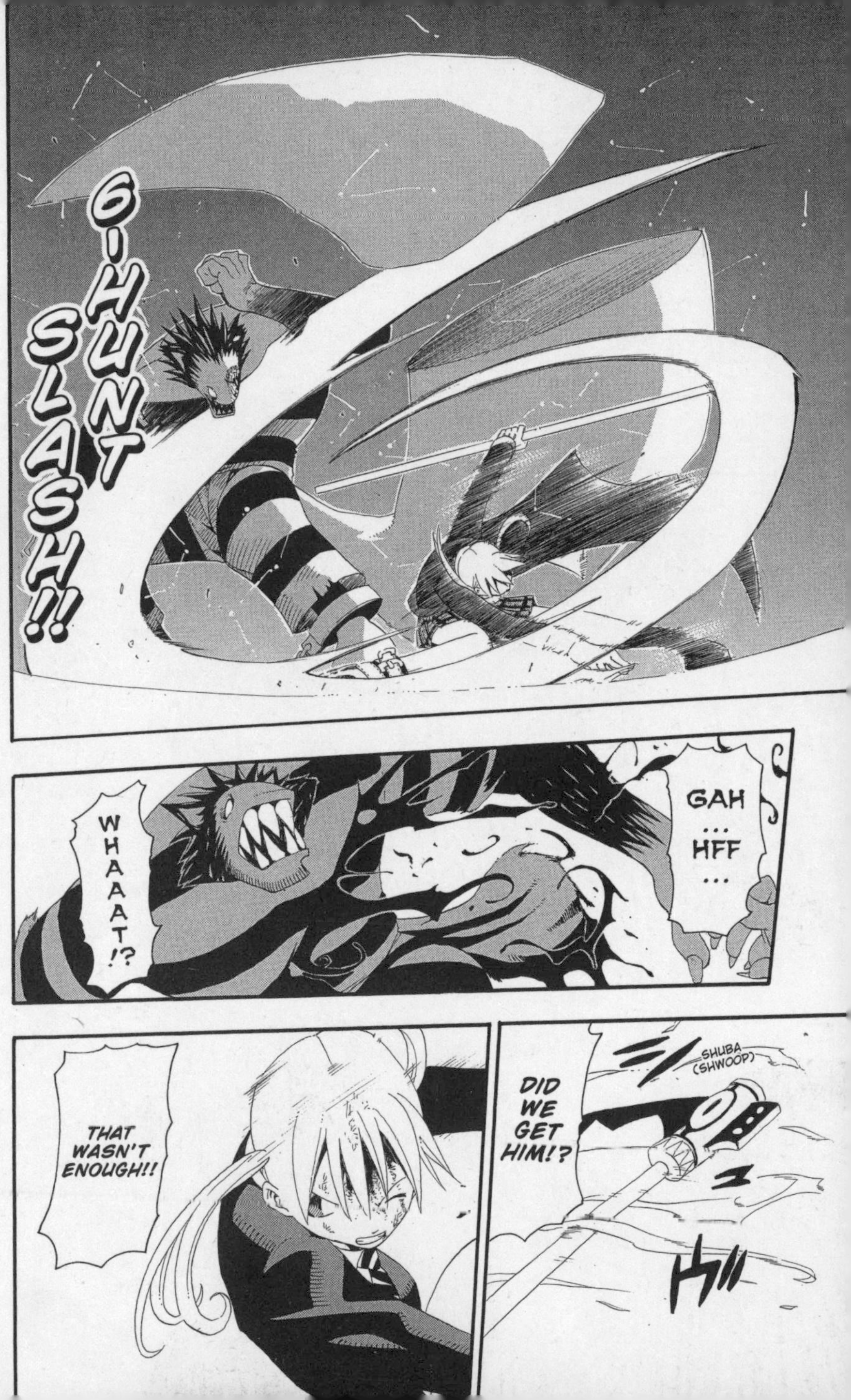
HUNT SLASH!!
GAH ... HFF ...
WHAAAT!?
SHUBA (SHWOOP)
DID WE GET HIM!?
THAT WASN'T ENOUGH!!

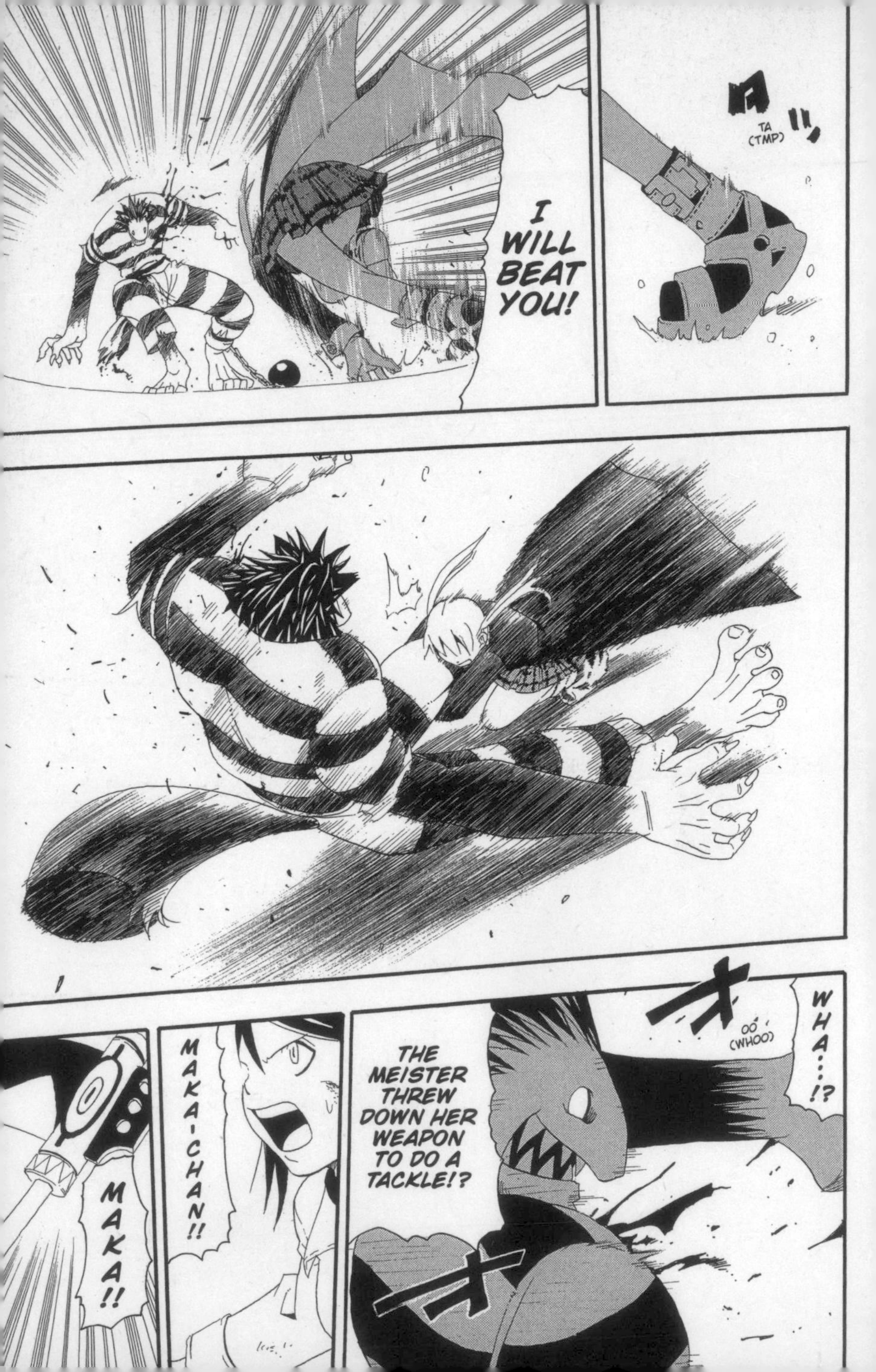

TA (TMP)
I WILL BEAT YOU!
WHA...!?
OO (WHOO)
THE MEISTER THREW DOWN HER WEAPON TO DO A TACKLE!?
MAKA-CHAN!!
MAKA!!

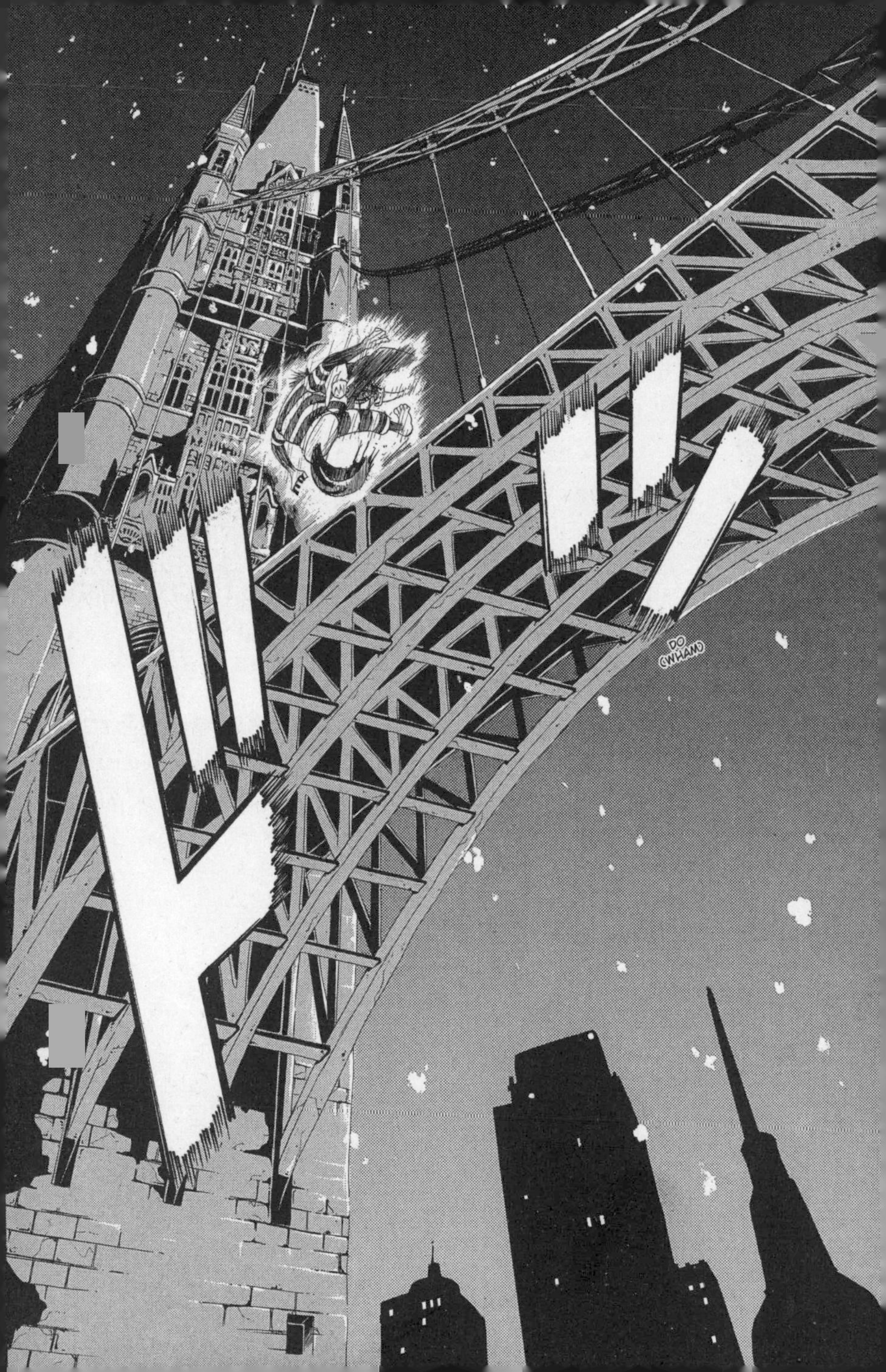
DO
(WHAM)

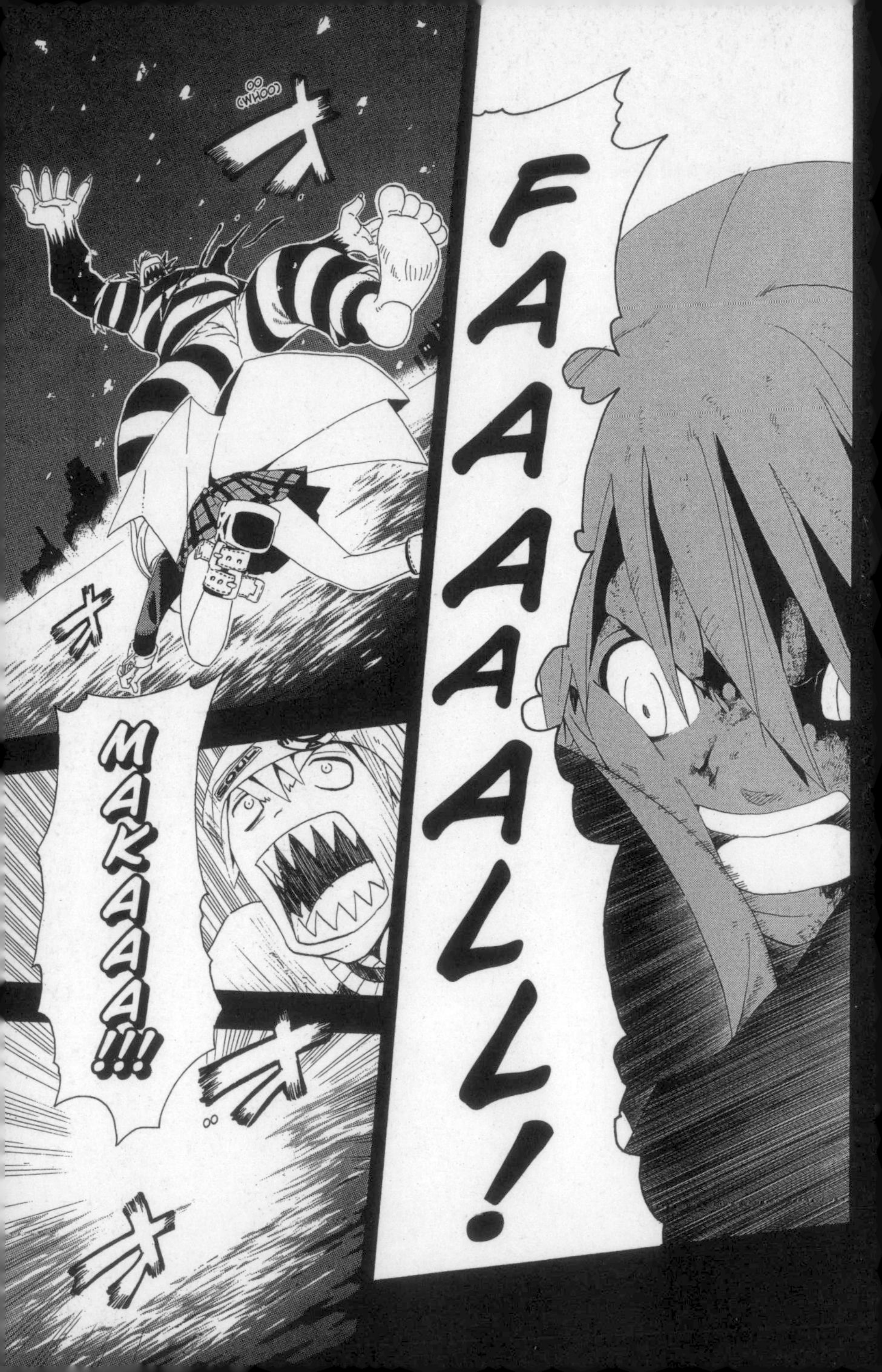
FAAAAALL!
(WHOO)
MAKAAA!!!

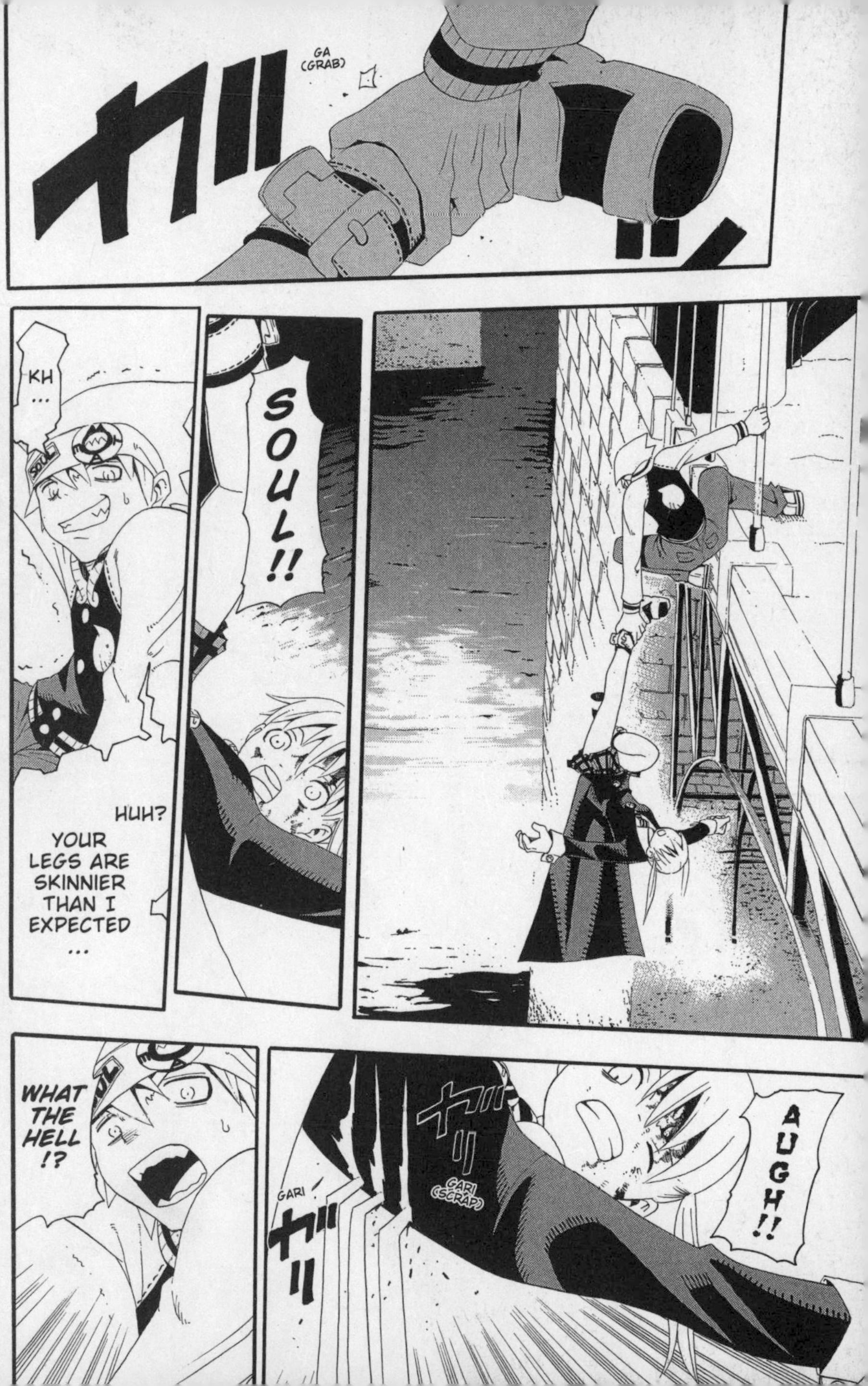
GA (GRAB)
SOUL!!
KH ...
HUH?
YOUR LEGS ARE SKINNIER THAN I EXPECTED ...
AUGH!!
GARI (SCRAP)
GARI
WHAT THE HELL !?

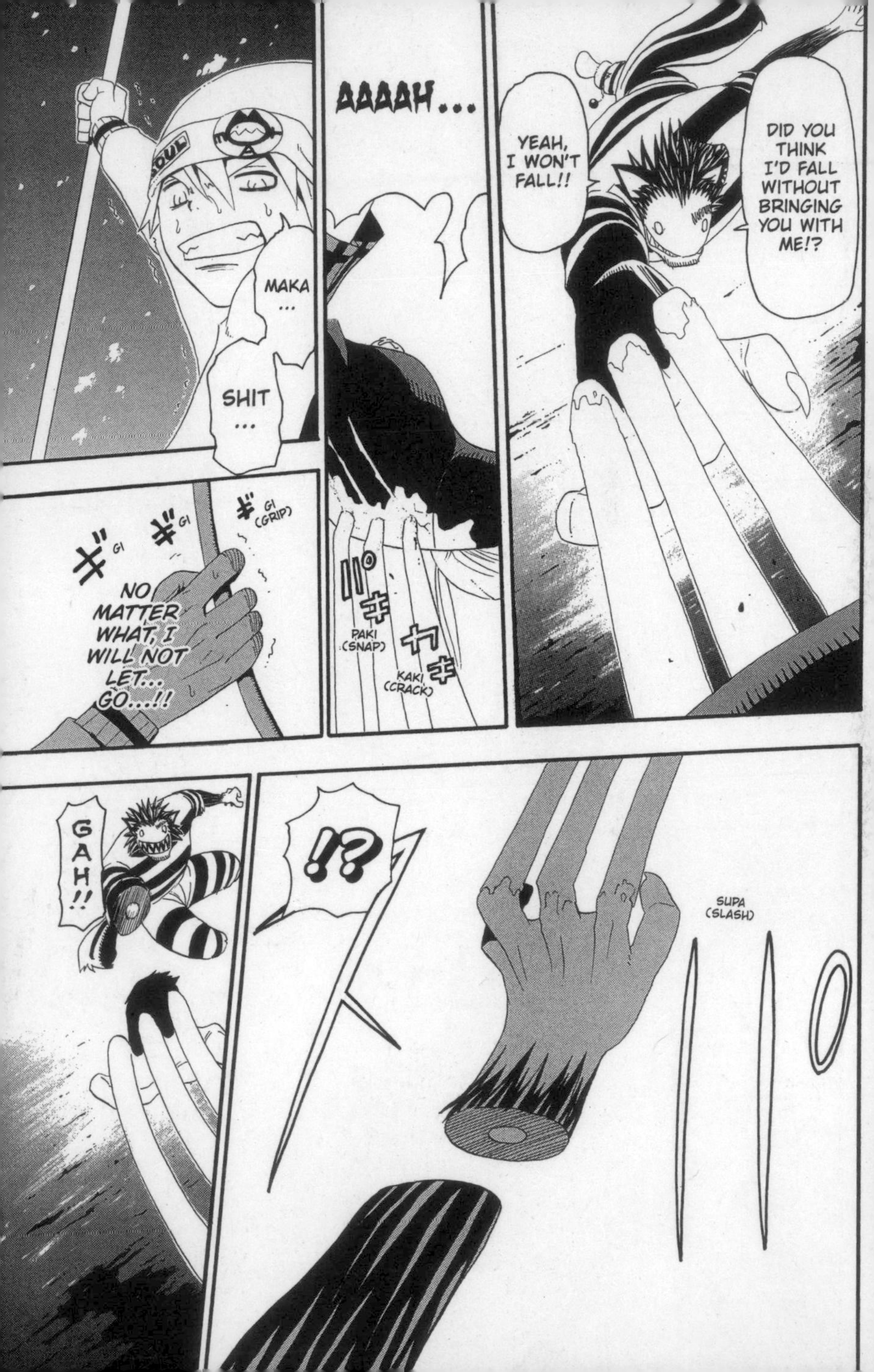
DID YOU THINK I'D FALL WITHOUT BRINGING YOU WITH ME!?
YEAH, I WON'T FALL!!
AAAAH...
PAKI (SNAP)
KAKI (CRACK)
MAKA...
SHIT...
GI (GRIP)
GI
GI
NO MATTER WHAT, I WILL NOT LET... GO...!!
SUPA (SLASH)
!?
GAH!!

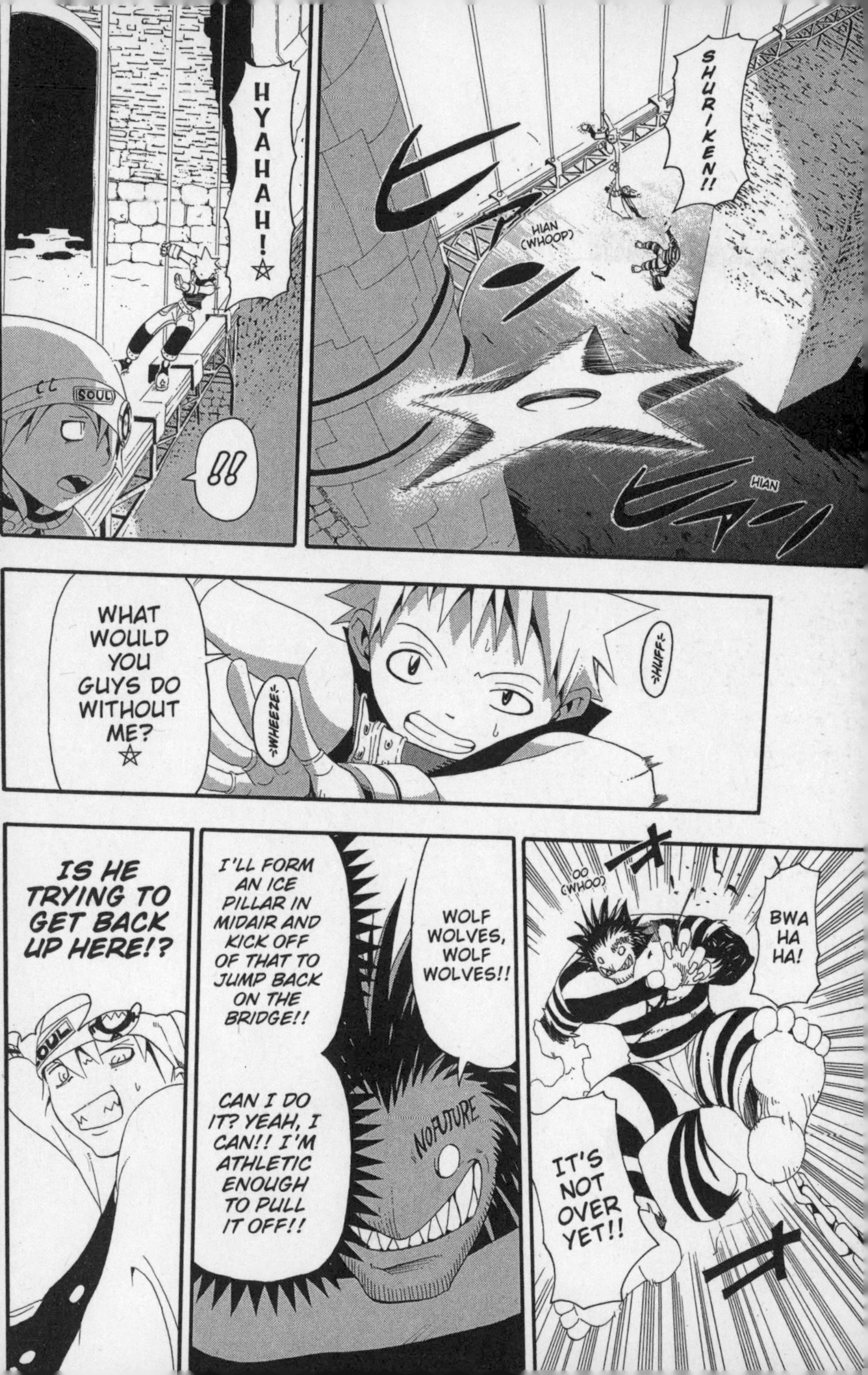
SHURIKEN!!
HIAN (WHOOP)
HIAN
HYAHAH!☆
!!
WHAT WOULD YOU GUYS DO WITHOUT ME?☆
HUFF
WHEEZE
OO (WHOO)
BWA HA HA!
IT'S NOT OVER YET!!
I'LL FORM AN ICE PILLAR IN MIDAIR AND KICK OFF OF THAT TO JUMP BACK ON THE BRIDGE!!
WOLF WOLVES, WOLF WOLVES!!
CAN I DO IT? YEAH, I CAN!! I'M ATHLETIC ENOUGH TO PULL IT OFF!!
NO FUTURE
IS HE TRYING TO GET BACK UP HERE!?

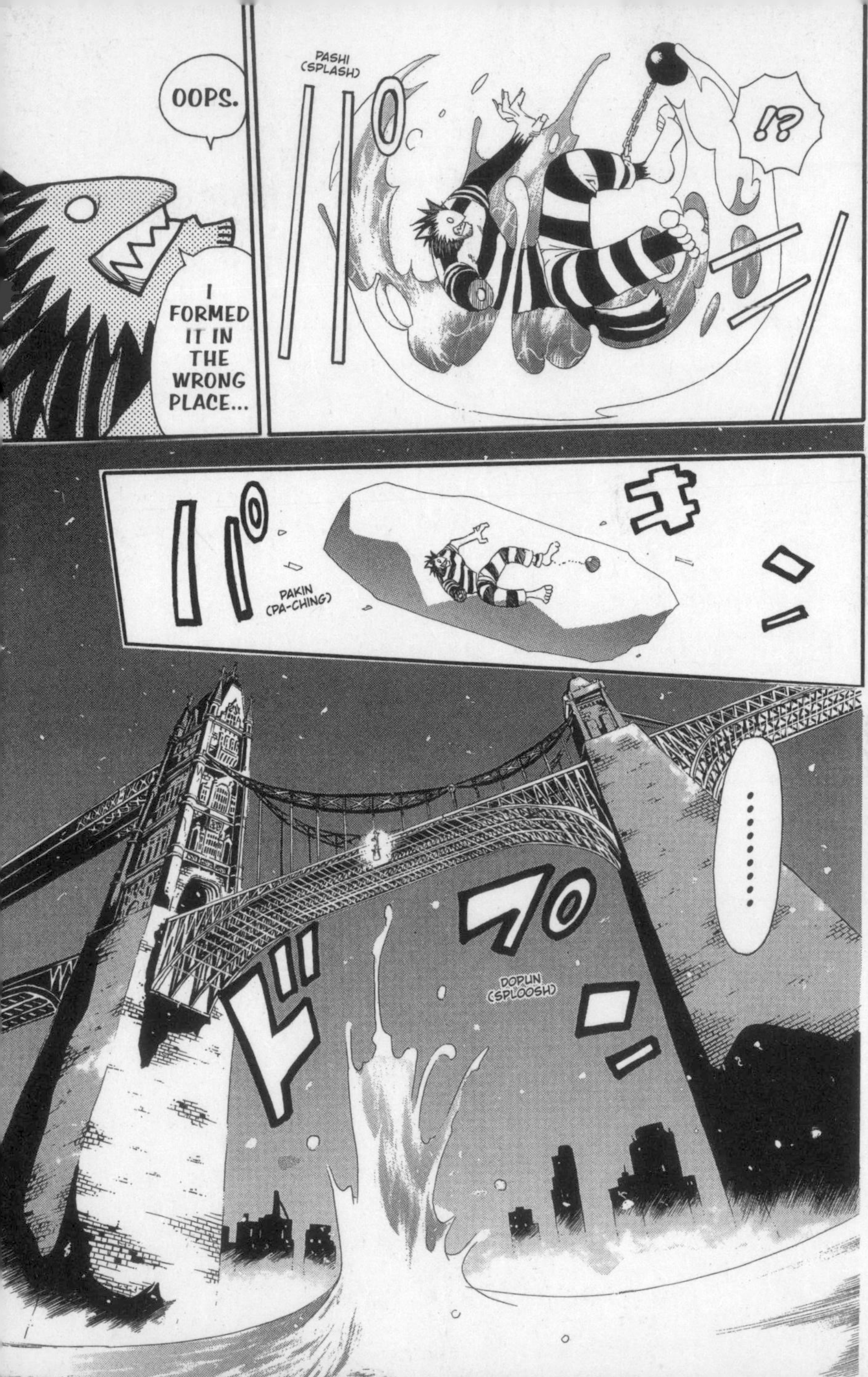
PASHI (SPLASH)
!?
OOPS.
I FORMED IT IN THE WRONG PLACE...
PAKIN (PA-CHING)
......
DOPUN (SPLOOSH)

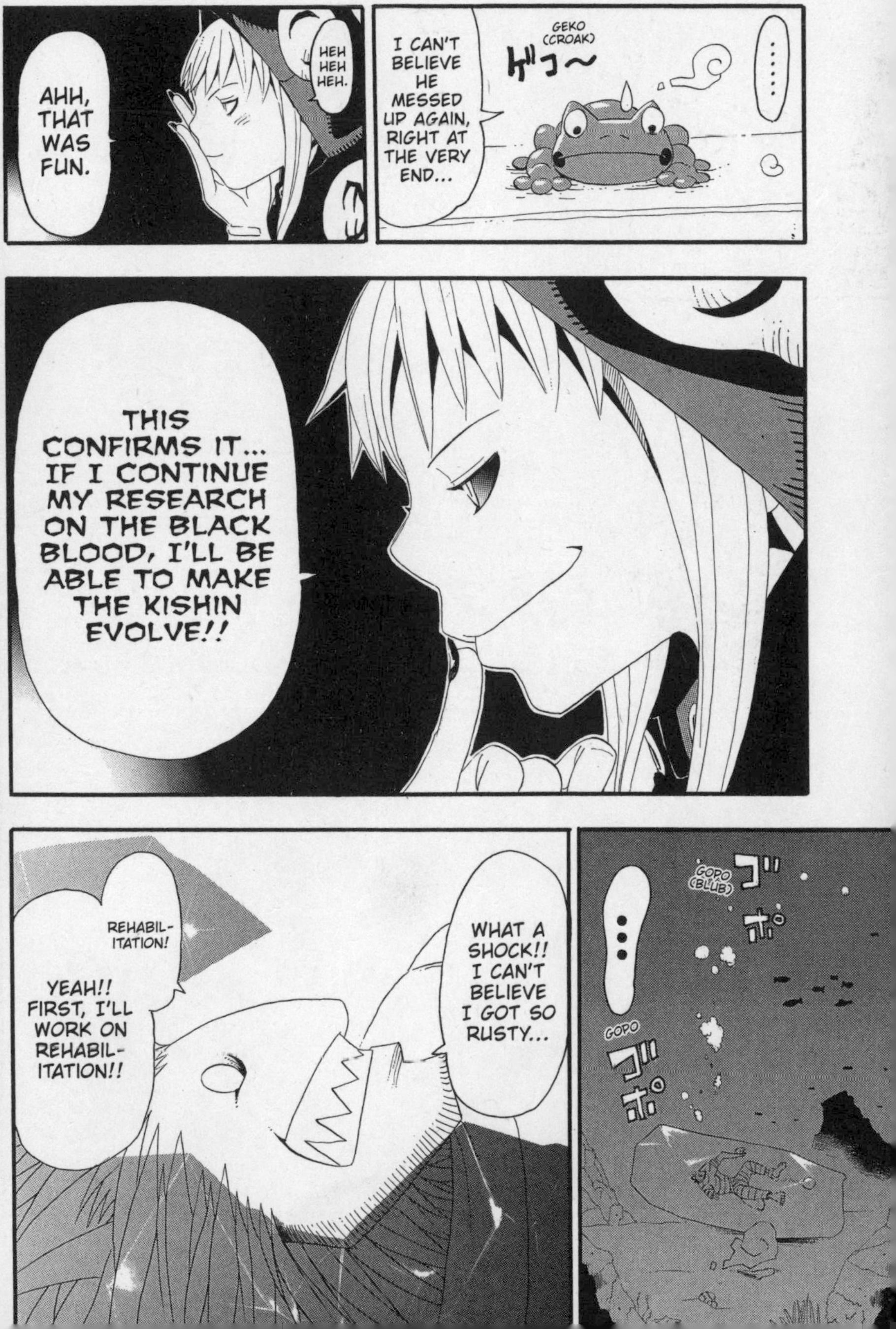
......
GEKO (CROAK)
ゲコ～
I CAN'T BELIEVE HE MESSED UP AGAIN, RIGHT AT THE VERY END...
HEH HEH HEH.
AHH, THAT WAS FUN.
THIS CONFIRMS IT... IF I CONTINUE MY RESEARCH ON THE BLACK BLOOD, I'LL BE ABLE TO MAKE THE KISHIN EVOLVE!!
...
GOPO (BLUB)
ゴポ
GOPO
ゴポ
WHAT A SHOCK!! I CAN'T BELIEVE I GOT SO RUSTY...
REHABIL-ITATION!
YEAH!! FIRST, I'LL WORK ON REHABIL-ITATION!!

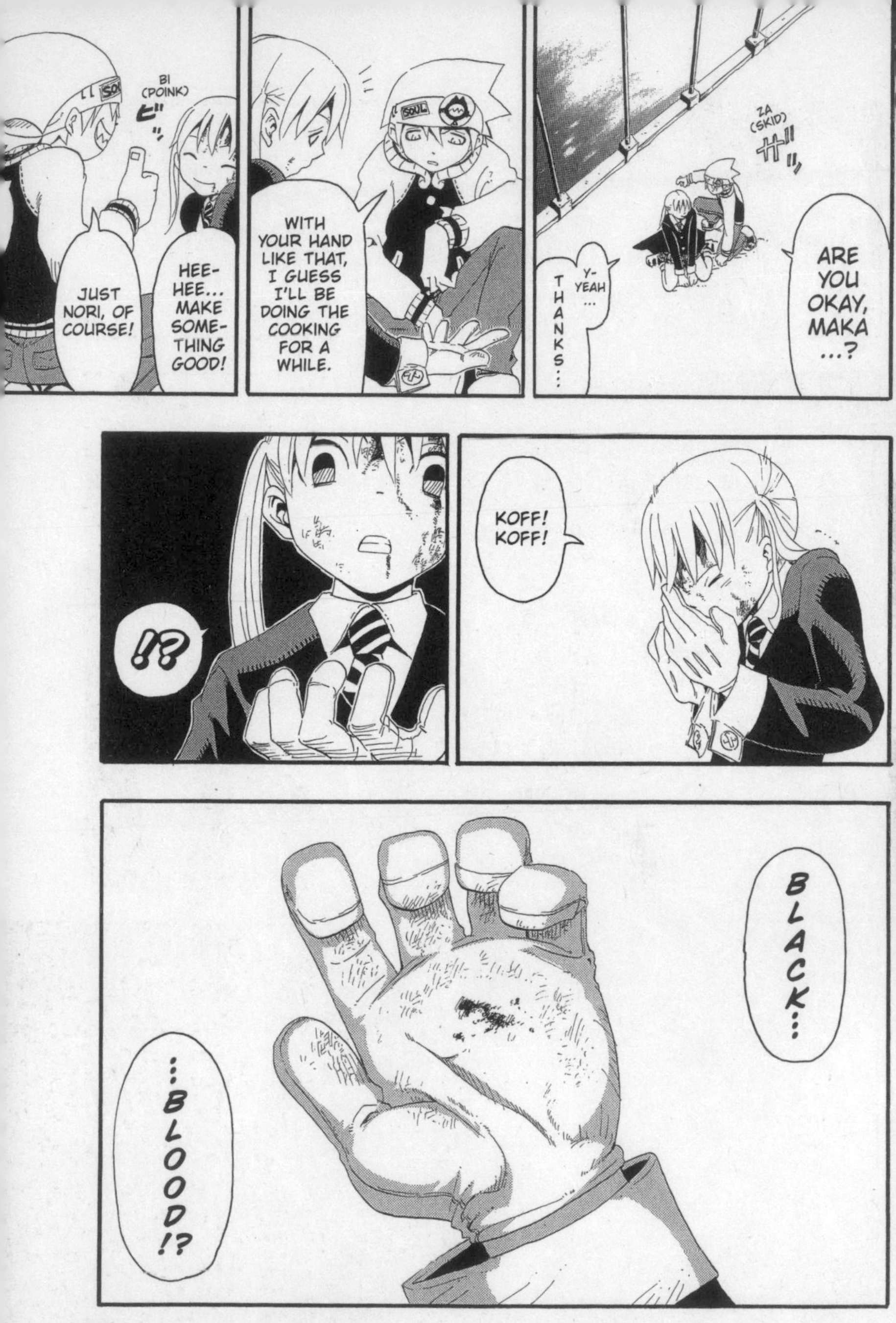
ZA (SKID)
ARE YOU OKAY, MAKA...?
Y-YEAH...
THANKS...
WITH YOUR HAND LIKE THAT, I GUESS I'LL BE DOING THE COOKING FOR A WHILE.
BI (POINK)
HEE-HEE... MAKE SOME-THING GOOD!
JUST NORI, OF COURSE!
KOFF! KOFF!
!?
BLACK...
...BLOOD!?

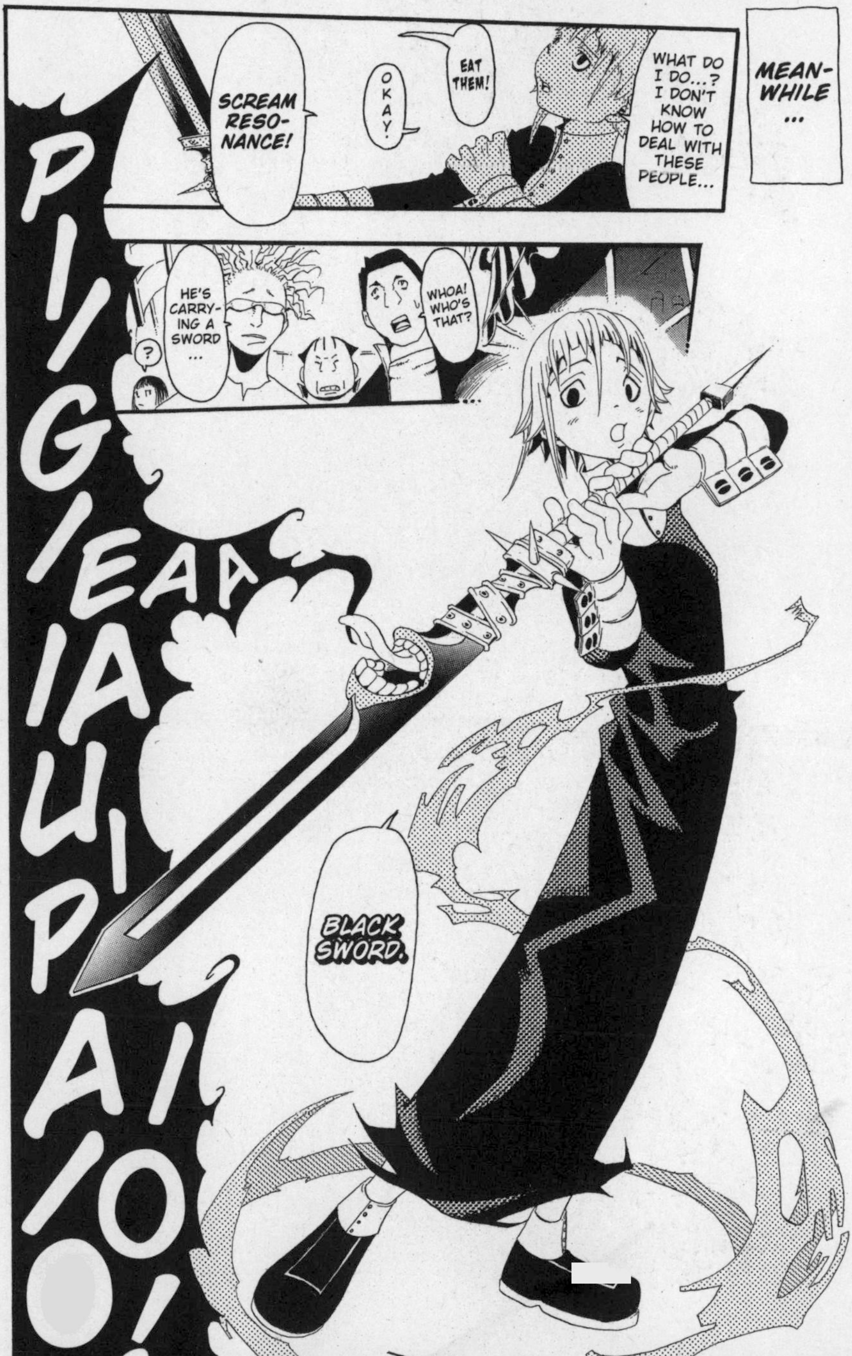
MEAN-WHILE ...
WHAT DO I DO...? I DON'T KNOW HOW TO DEAL WITH THESE PEOPLE...
EAT THEM!
OKAY.
SCREAM RESO-NANCE!
WHOA! WHO'S THAT?
HE'S CARRY-ING A SWORD ...
?
...
BLACK SWORD.
PI/G/EAA/IA/U/P/A/I/O/O!

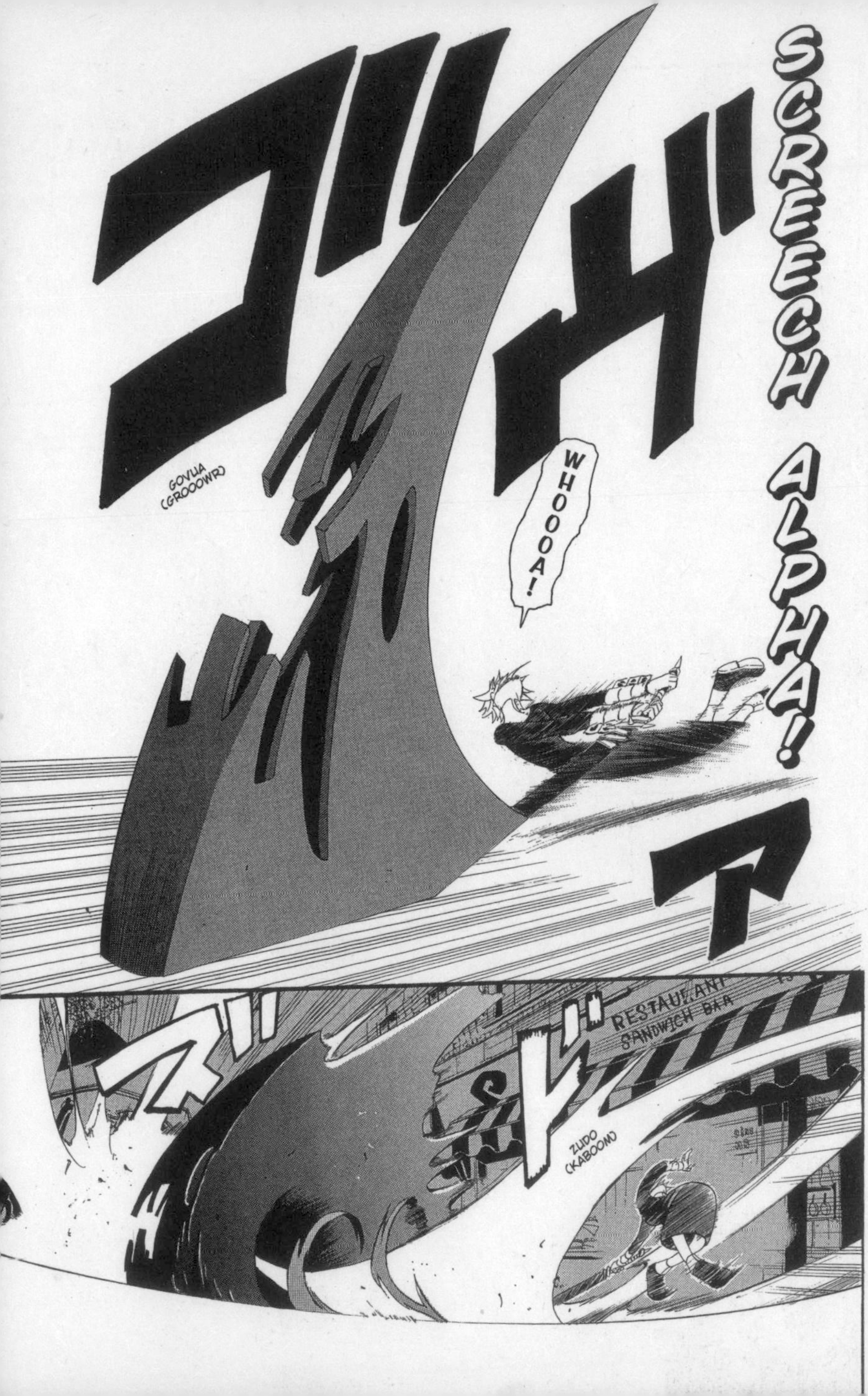
SCREECH ALPHA!
WHOOOOA!
GOVUA (GROOOWR)
RESTAURANT
SANDWICH BAR
ZUDO (KABOOM)

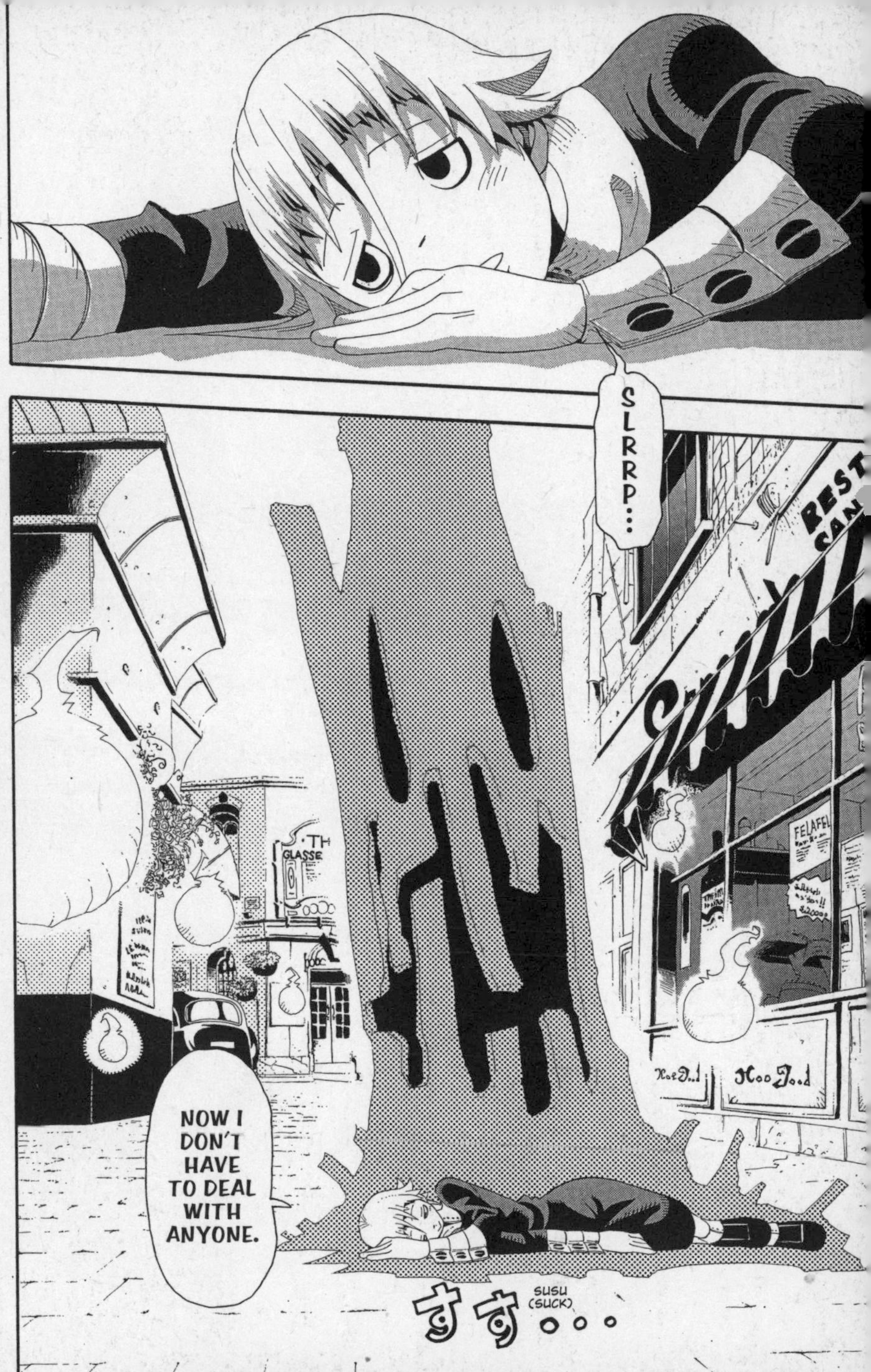
SLRRP...
NOW I DON'T HAVE TO DEAL WITH ANYONE.
すす。。。
SUSU (SUCK)

SOUL EATER

CHAPTER 12: ULTIMATE WRITTEN EXAM

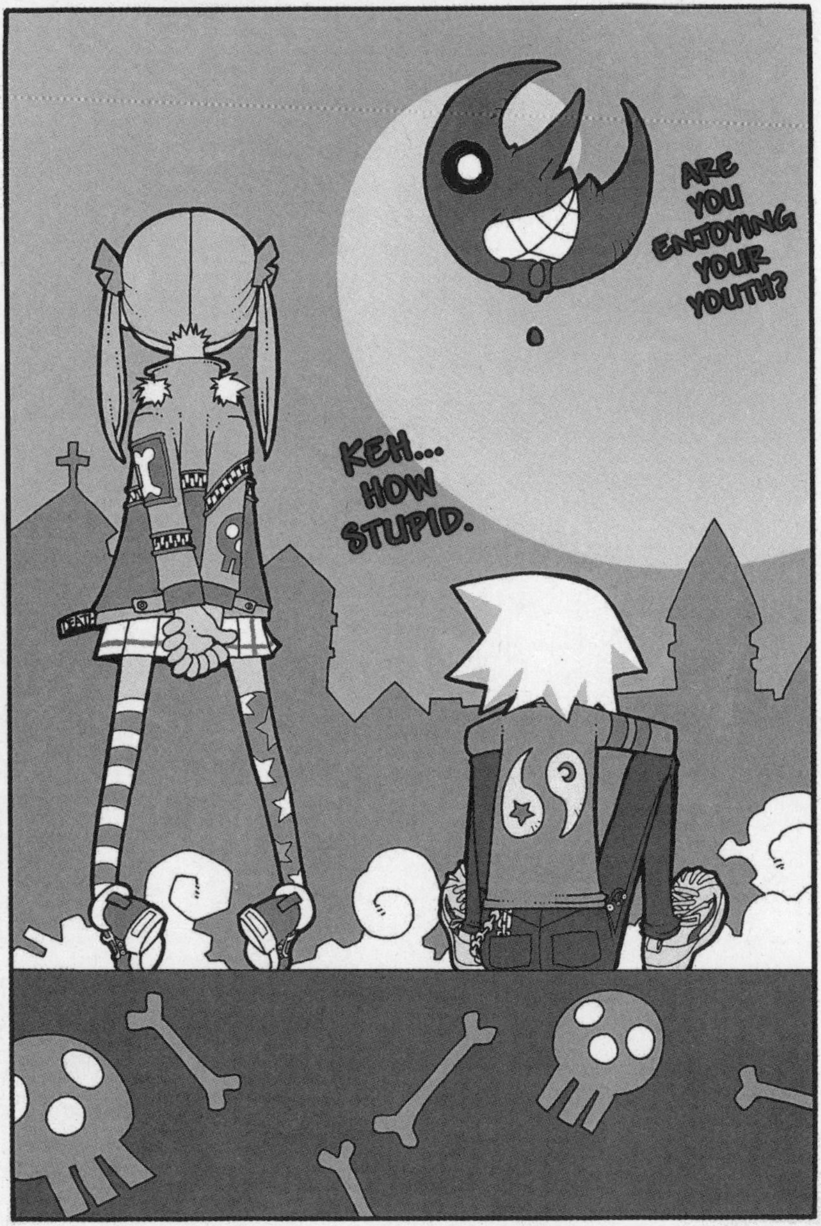
ARE YOU ENJOYING YOUR YOUTH?
KEH... HOW STUPID.

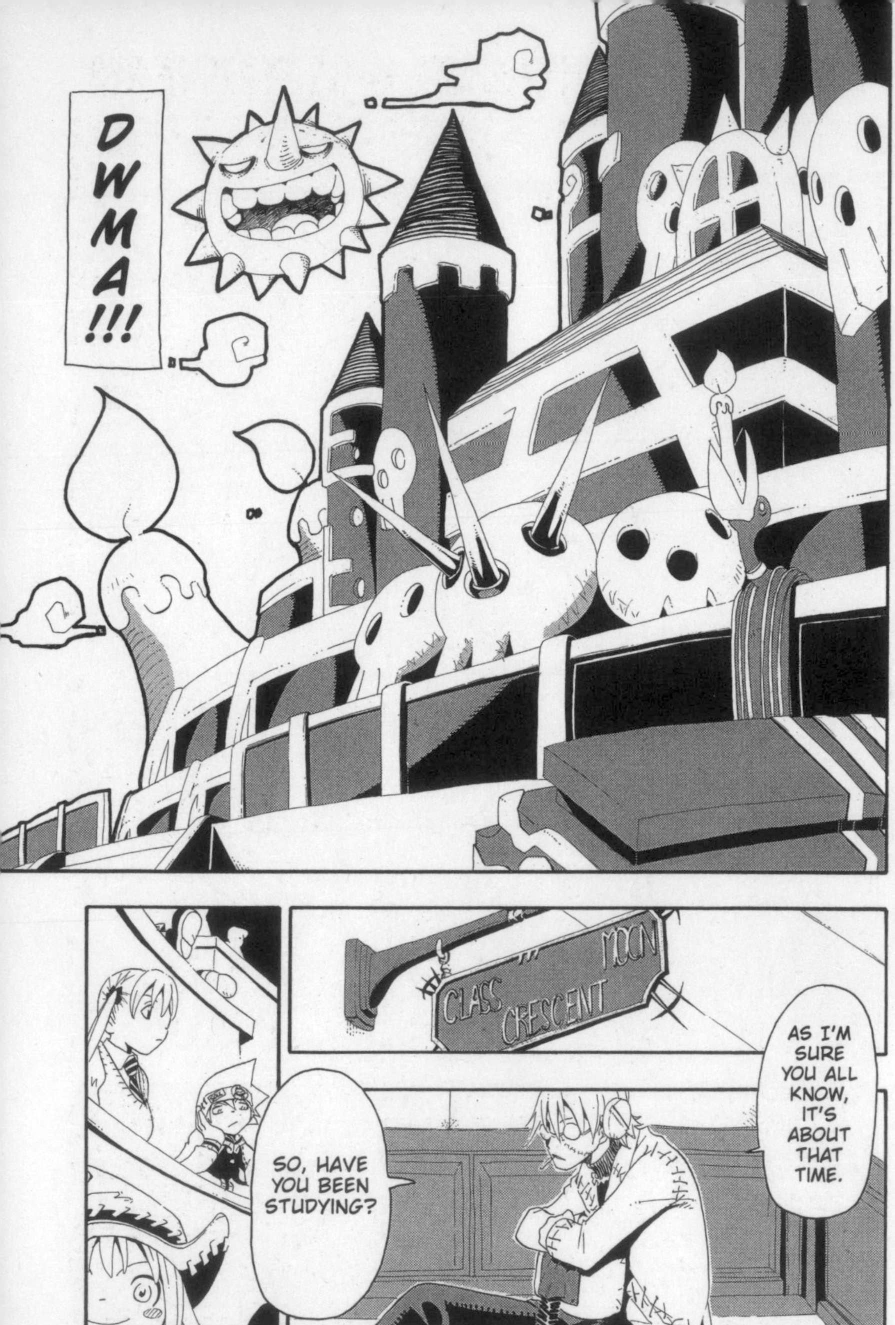
DWMA!!!
CLASS CRESCENT MOON
AS I'M SURE YOU ALL KNOW, IT'S ABOUT THAT TIME.
SO, HAVE YOU BEEN STUDYING?

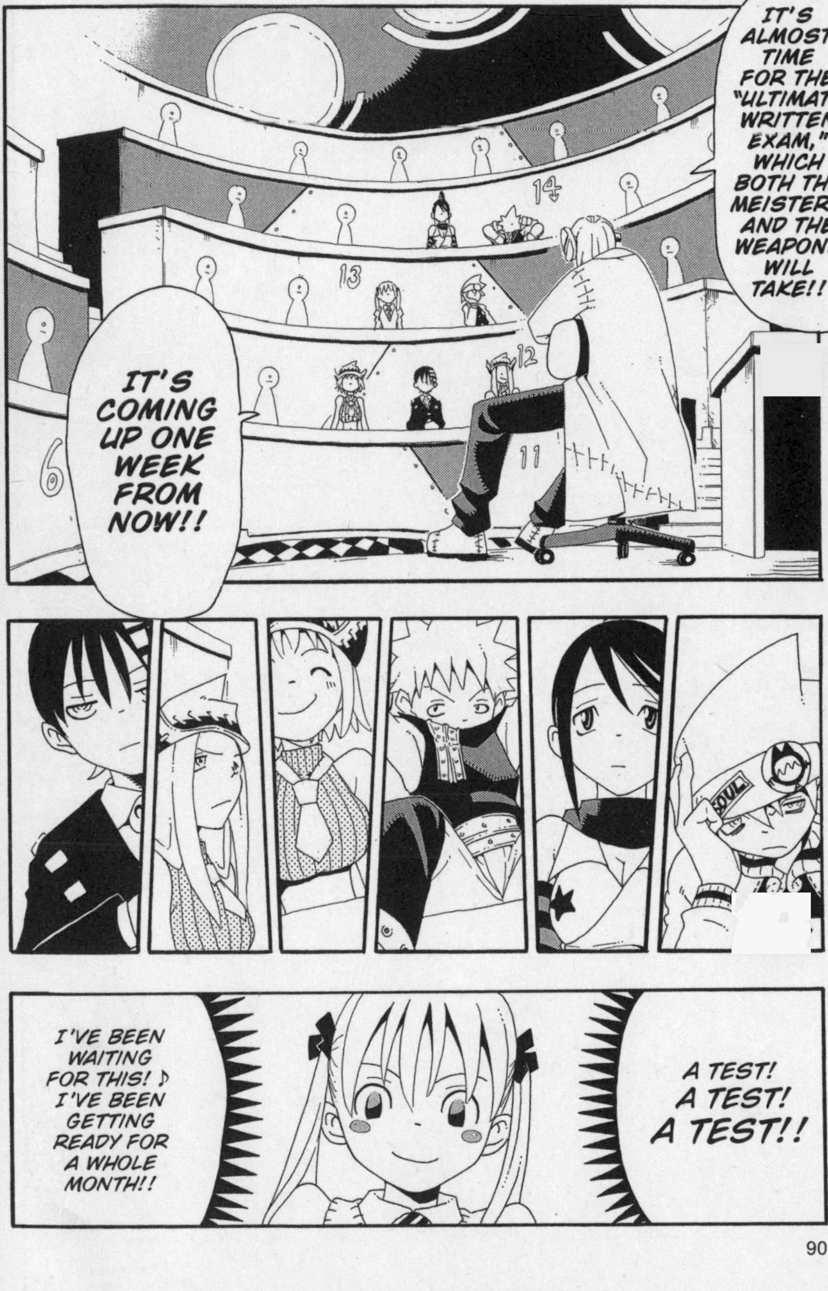
IT'S ALMOST TIME FOR THE "ULTIMATE WRITTEN EXAM," WHICH BOTH THE MEISTERS AND THE WEAPONS WILL TAKE!!
IT'S COMING UP ONE WEEK FROM NOW!!
A TEST! A TEST! A TEST!!
I'VE BEEN WAITING FOR THIS! ♪ I'VE BEEN GETTING READY FOR A WHOLE MONTH!!

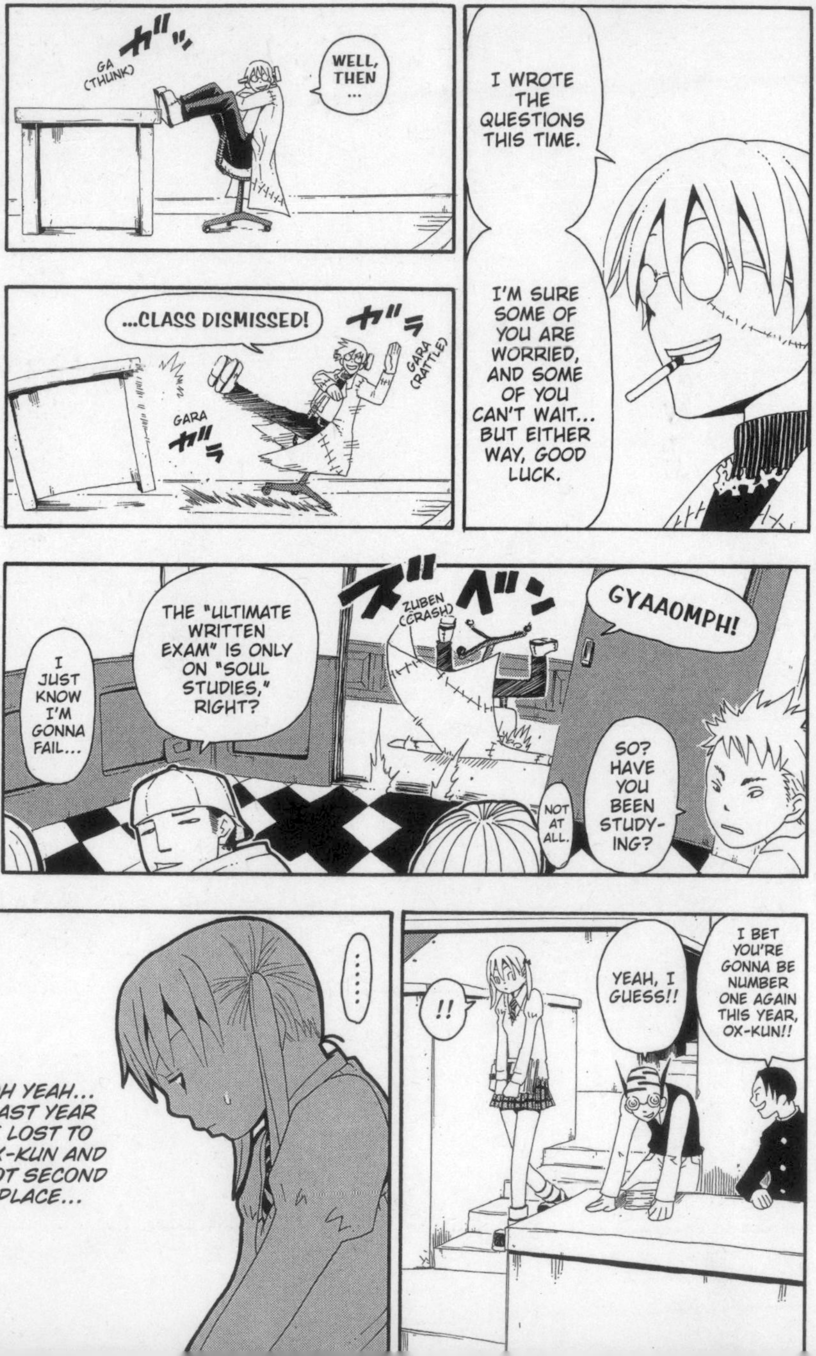
I WROTE THE QUESTIONS THIS TIME.
I'M SURE SOME OF YOU ARE WORRIED, AND SOME OF YOU CAN'T WAIT... BUT EITHER WAY, GOOD LUCK.
GA (THUNK)
WELL, THEN ...
...CLASS DISMISSED!
GARA (RATTLE)
GARA
GYAAOMPH!
ZUBEN (CRASH)
SO? HAVE YOU BEEN STUDY-ING?
NOT AT ALL.
THE "ULTIMATE WRITTEN EXAM" IS ONLY ON "SOUL STUDIES," RIGHT?
I JUST KNOW I'M GONNA FAIL...
I BET YOU'RE GONNA BE NUMBER ONE AGAIN THIS YEAR, OX-KUN!!
YEAH, I GUESS!!
!!
......
OH YEAH... LAST YEAR I LOST TO OX-KUN AND GOT SECOND PLACE...

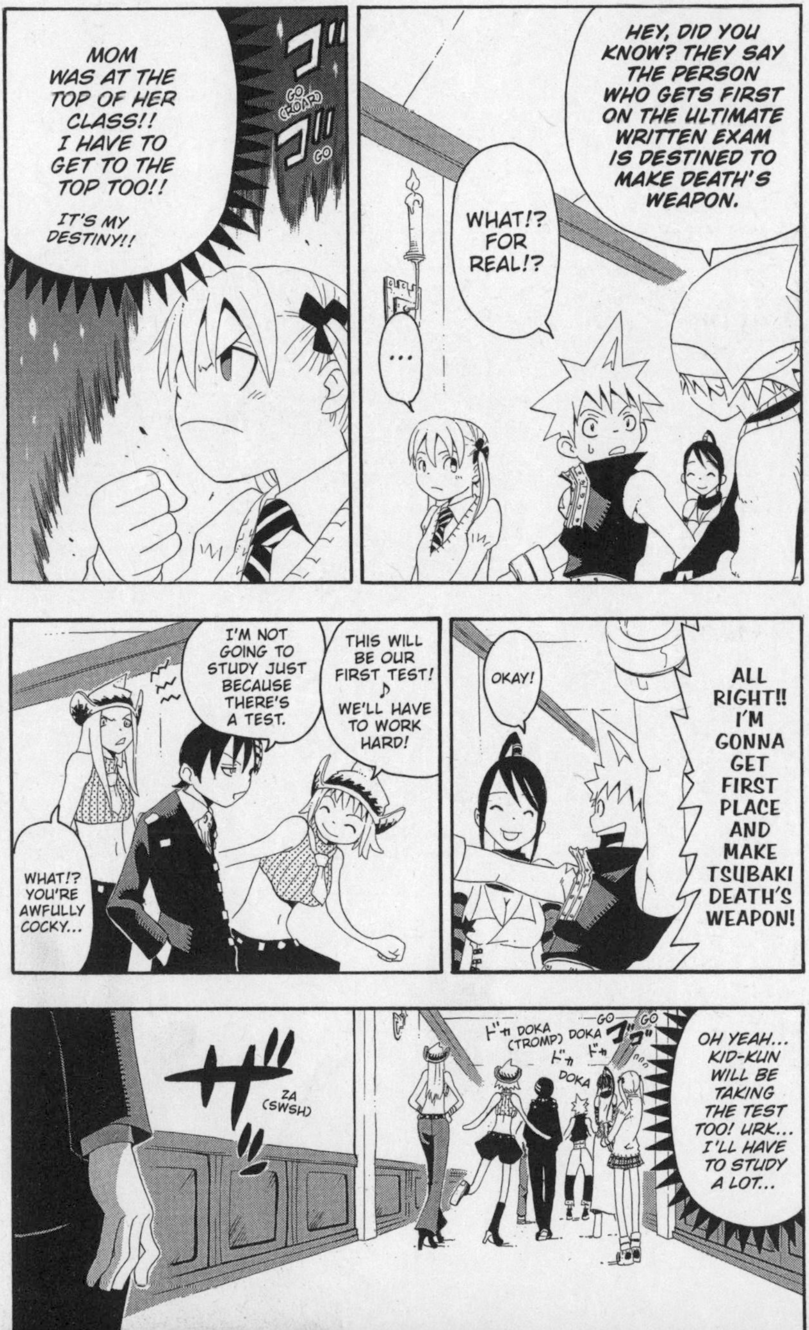
HEY, DID YOU KNOW? THEY SAY THE PERSON WHO GETS FIRST ON THE ULTIMATE WRITTEN EXAM IS DESTINED TO MAKE DEATH'S WEAPON.
WHAT!? FOR REAL!?
...
GO (ROAR) GO
MOM WAS AT THE TOP OF HER CLASS!! I HAVE TO GET TO THE TOP TOO!!
IT'S MY DESTINY!!
ALL RIGHT!! I'M GONNA GET FIRST PLACE AND MAKE TSUBAKI DEATH'S WEAPON!
OKAY!
THIS WILL BE OUR FIRST TEST! ♪ WE'LL HAVE TO WORK HARD!
I'M NOT GOING TO STUDY JUST BECAUSE THERE'S A TEST.
WHAT!? YOU'RE AWFULLY COCKY...
OH YEAH... KID-KUN WILL BE TAKING THE TEST TOO! URK... I'LL HAVE TO STUDY A LOT...
GO GO
DOKA (TROMP) DOKA DOKA
ZA (SWSH)

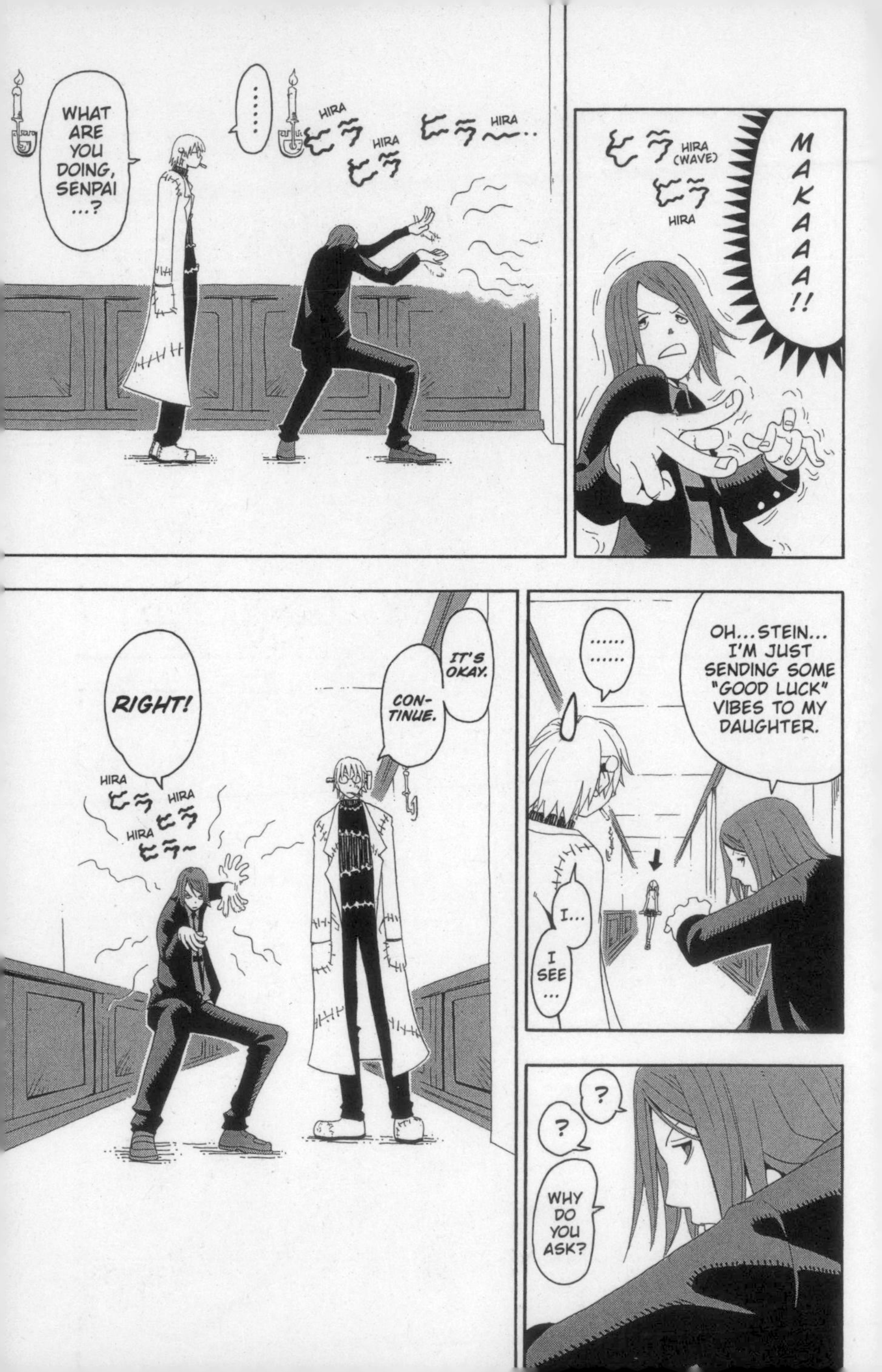
MAKAAAA!!
HIRA (WAVE)
HIRA
HIRA...
HIRA
HIRA
......
WHAT ARE YOU DOING, SENPAI...?
OH...STEIN... I'M JUST SENDING SOME "GOOD LUCK" VIBES TO MY DAUGHTER.
......
......
I...
I SEE...
?
?
WHY DO YOU ASK?
IT'S OKAY.
CONTINUE.
RIGHT!
HIRA
HIRA
HIRA

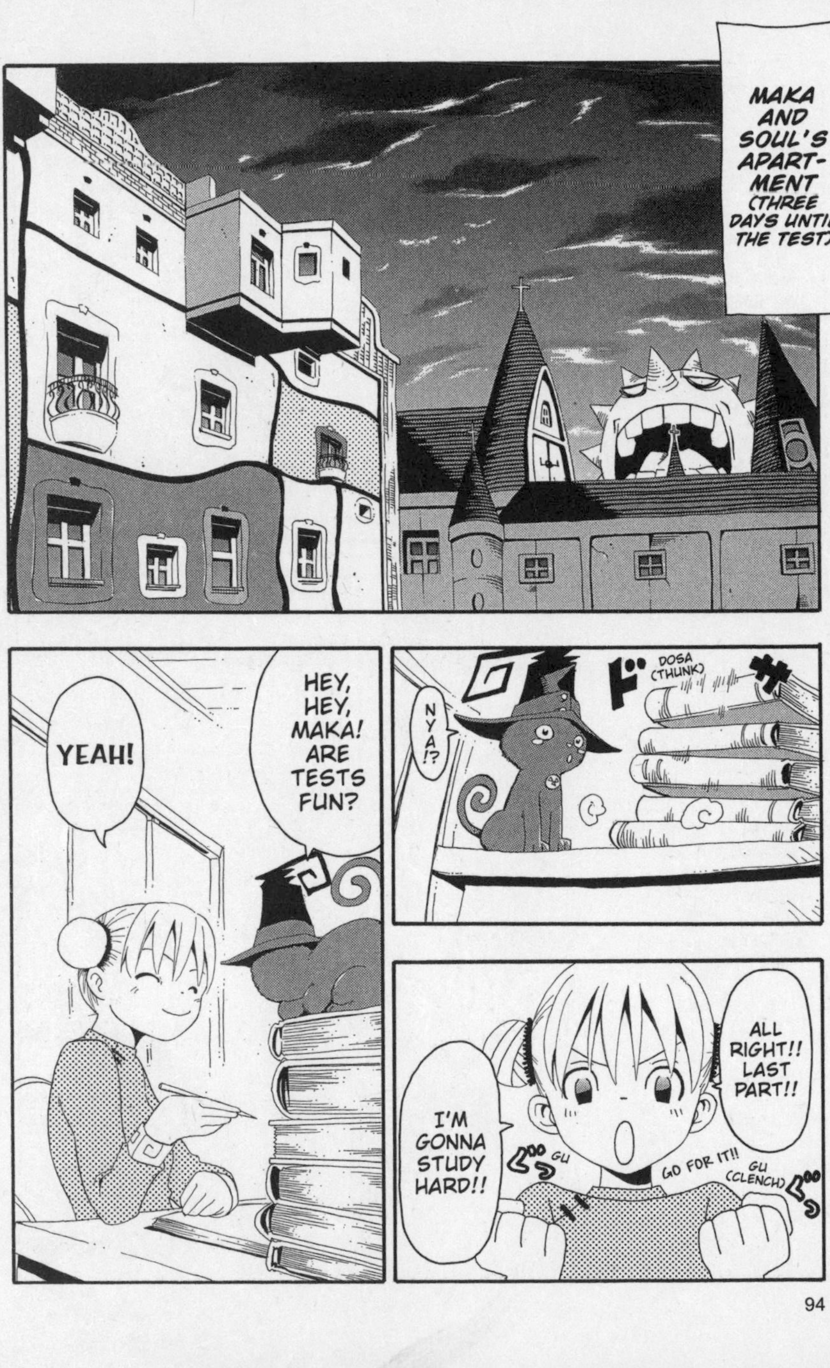
MAKA AND SOUL'S APARTMENT (THREE DAYS UNTIL THE TEST)
DOSA (THUNK)
NYA!?
ALL RIGHT!! LAST PART!!
GU (CLENCH)
GO FOR IT!!
GU
I'M GONNA STUDY HARD!!
HEY, HEY, MAKA! ARE TESTS FUN?
YEAH!

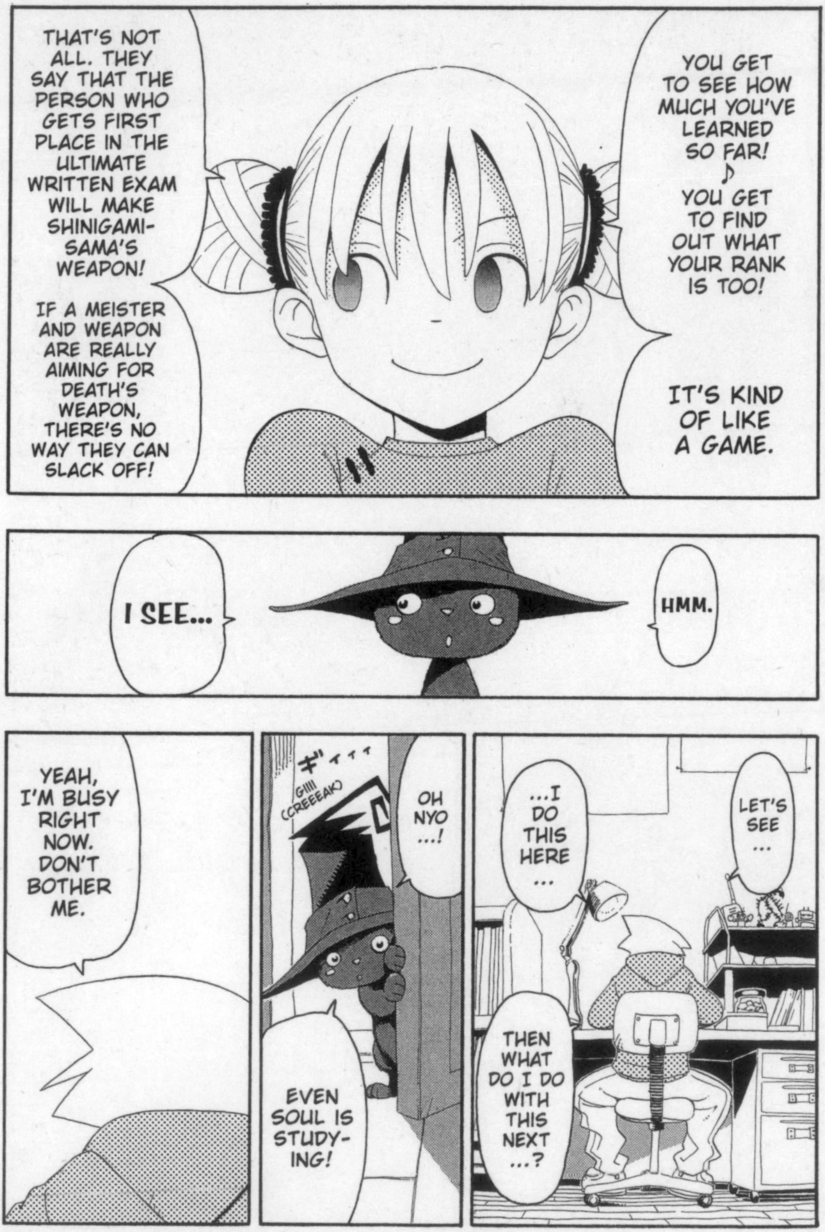
YOU GET TO SEE HOW MUCH YOU'VE LEARNED SO FAR! ♪
YOU GET TO FIND OUT WHAT YOUR RANK IS TOO!
IT'S KIND OF LIKE A GAME.
THAT'S NOT ALL. THEY SAY THAT THE PERSON WHO GETS FIRST PLACE IN THE ULTIMATE WRITTEN EXAM WILL MAKE SHINIGAMI-SAMA'S WEAPON!
IF A MEISTER AND WEAPON ARE REALLY AIMING FOR DEATH'S WEAPON, THERE'S NO WAY THEY CAN SLACK OFF!
HMM.
I SEE...
LET'S SEE ...
...I DO THIS HERE ...
THEN WHAT DO I DO WITH THIS NEXT ...?
ギィィィ
GIIII (CREEEAK)
OH NYO ...!
EVEN SOUL IS STUDY-ING!
YEAH, I'M BUSY RIGHT NOW. DON'T BOTHER ME.

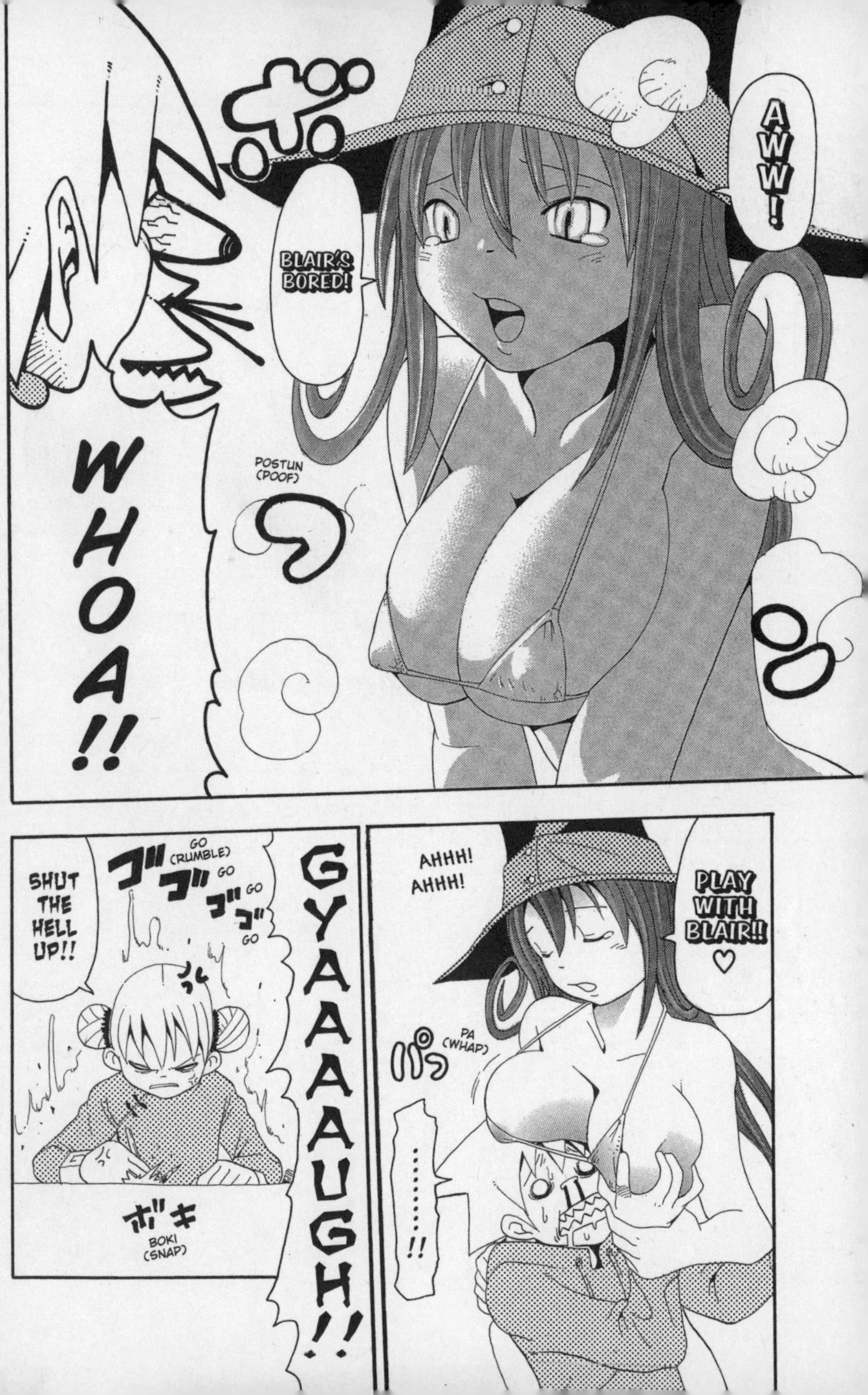
AWW!
BLAIR'S BORED!
POSTUN (POOF)
WHOA!!
PLAY WITH BLAIR!! ♡
AHHH! AHHH!
PA (WHAP)
......!!
GYAAAAAUGH!!
GO (RUMBLE) GO GO GO
SHUT THE HELL UP!!
BOKI (SNAP)

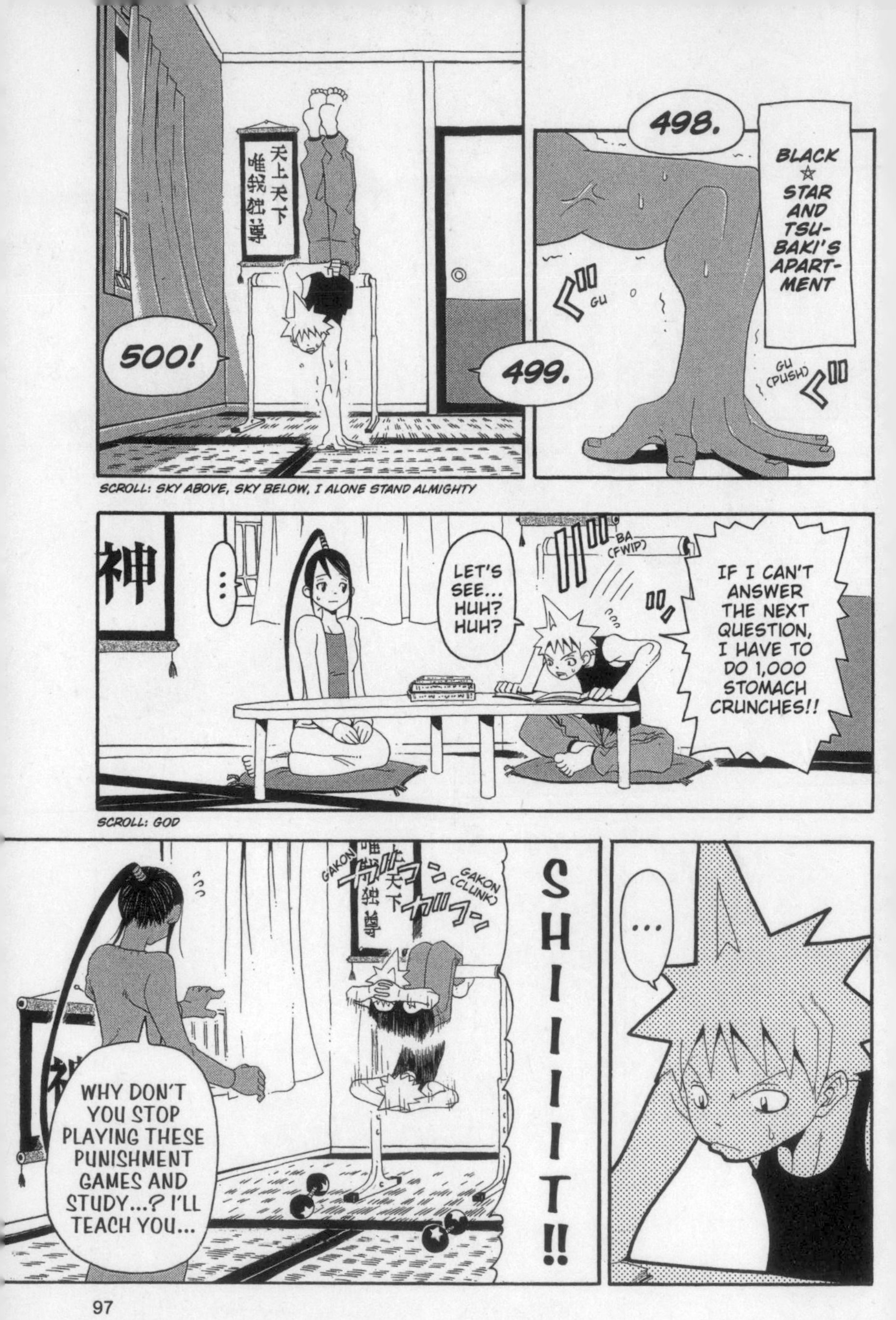
498.
BLACK ☆ STAR AND TSUBAKI'S APARTMENT
GU
499.
GU (PUSH)
500!
SCROLL: SKY ABOVE, SKY BELOW, I ALONE STAND ALMIGHTY
IF I CAN'T ANSWER THE NEXT QUESTION, I HAVE TO DO 1,000 STOMACH CRUNCHES!!
BA (FWIP)
LET'S SEE... HUH? HUH?
...
SCROLL: GOD
...
SHIIIIT!!
GAKON (CLUNK)
GAKON
WHY DON'T YOU STOP PLAYING THESE PUNISHMENT GAMES AND STUDY...? I'LL TEACH YOU...

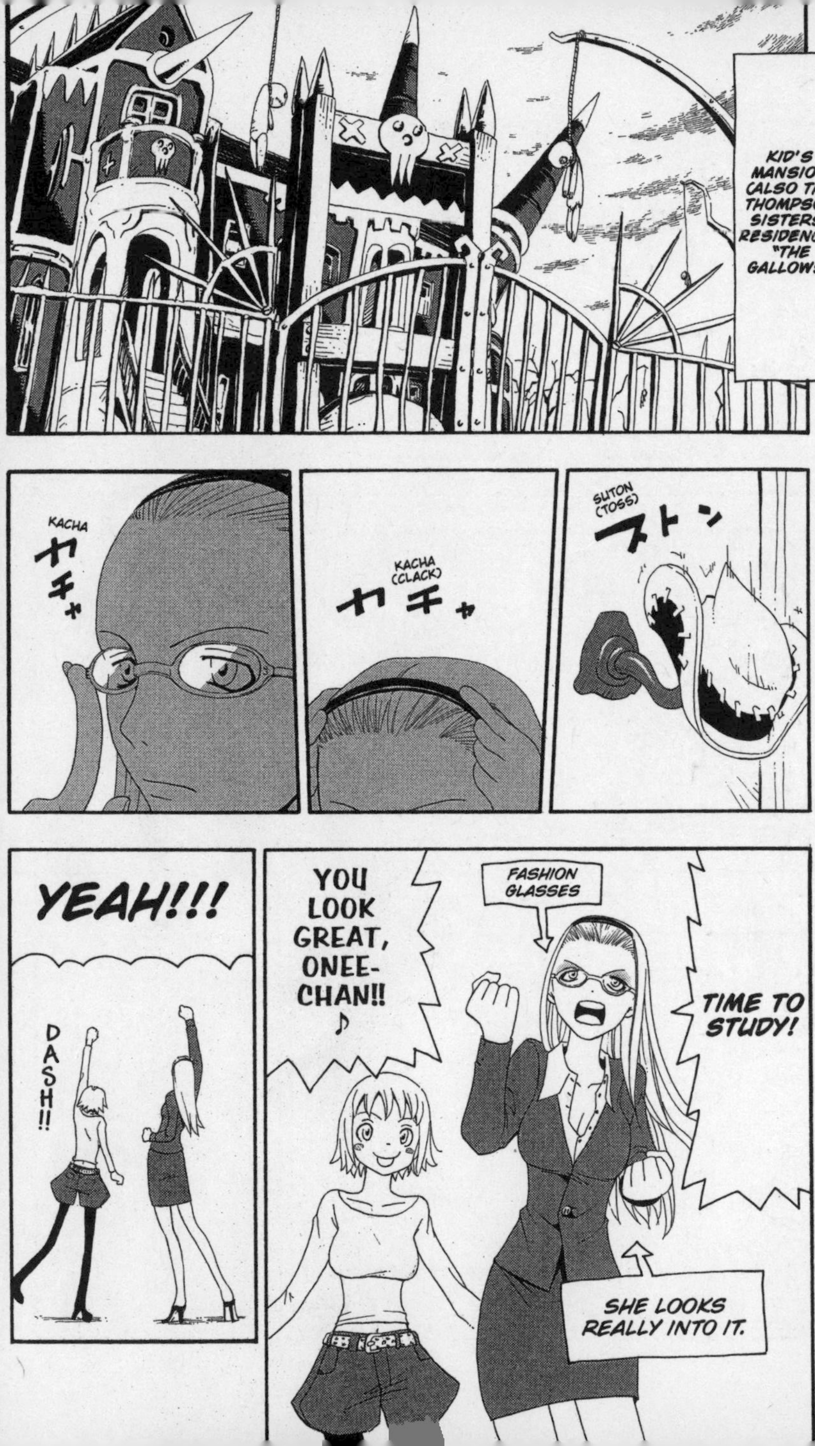
KID'S MANSION (ALSO THE THOMPSON SISTERS' RESIDENCE), "THE GALLOWS"
SUTON (TOSS)
ストン
KACHA (CLACK)
カチャ
KACHA
カチャ
TIME TO STUDY!
FASHION GLASSES
YOU LOOK GREAT, ONEE-CHAN!! ♪
SHE LOOKS REALLY INTO IT.
YEAH!!!
DASH!!

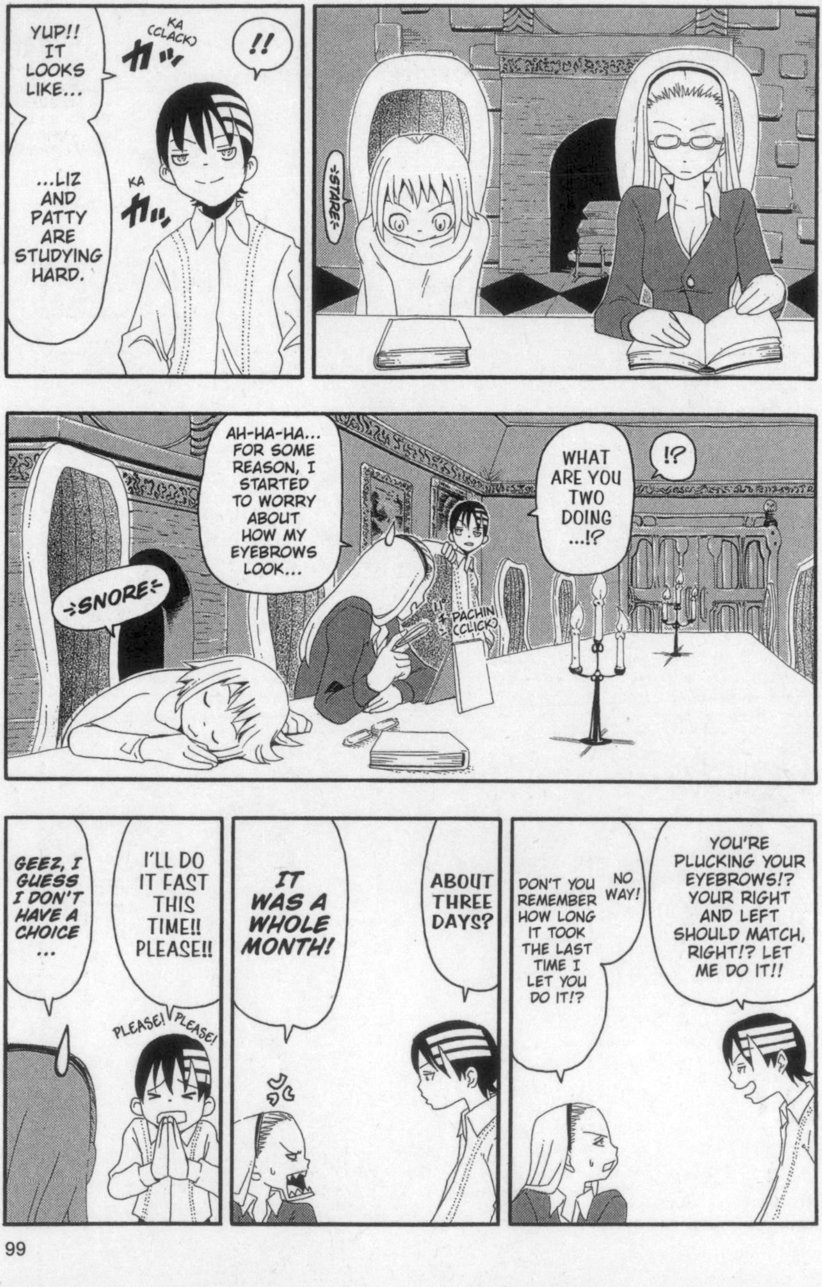
STARE
!!
KA (CLACK)
YUP!! IT LOOKS LIKE...
KA
...LIZ AND PATTY ARE STUDYING HARD.
!?
WHAT ARE YOU TWO DOING ...!?
AH-HA-HA... FOR SOME REASON, I STARTED TO WORRY ABOUT HOW MY EYEBROWS LOOK...
PACHIN (CLICK)
SNORE
YOU'RE PLUCKING YOUR EYEBROWS!? YOUR RIGHT AND LEFT SHOULD MATCH, RIGHT!? LET ME DO IT!!
NO WAY!
DON'T YOU REMEMBER HOW LONG IT TOOK THE LAST TIME I LET YOU DO IT!?
ABOUT THREE DAYS?
IT WAS A WHOLE MONTH!
I'LL DO IT FAST THIS TIME!! PLEASE!!
PLEASE! PLEASE!
GEEZ, I GUESS I DON'T HAVE A CHOICE ...

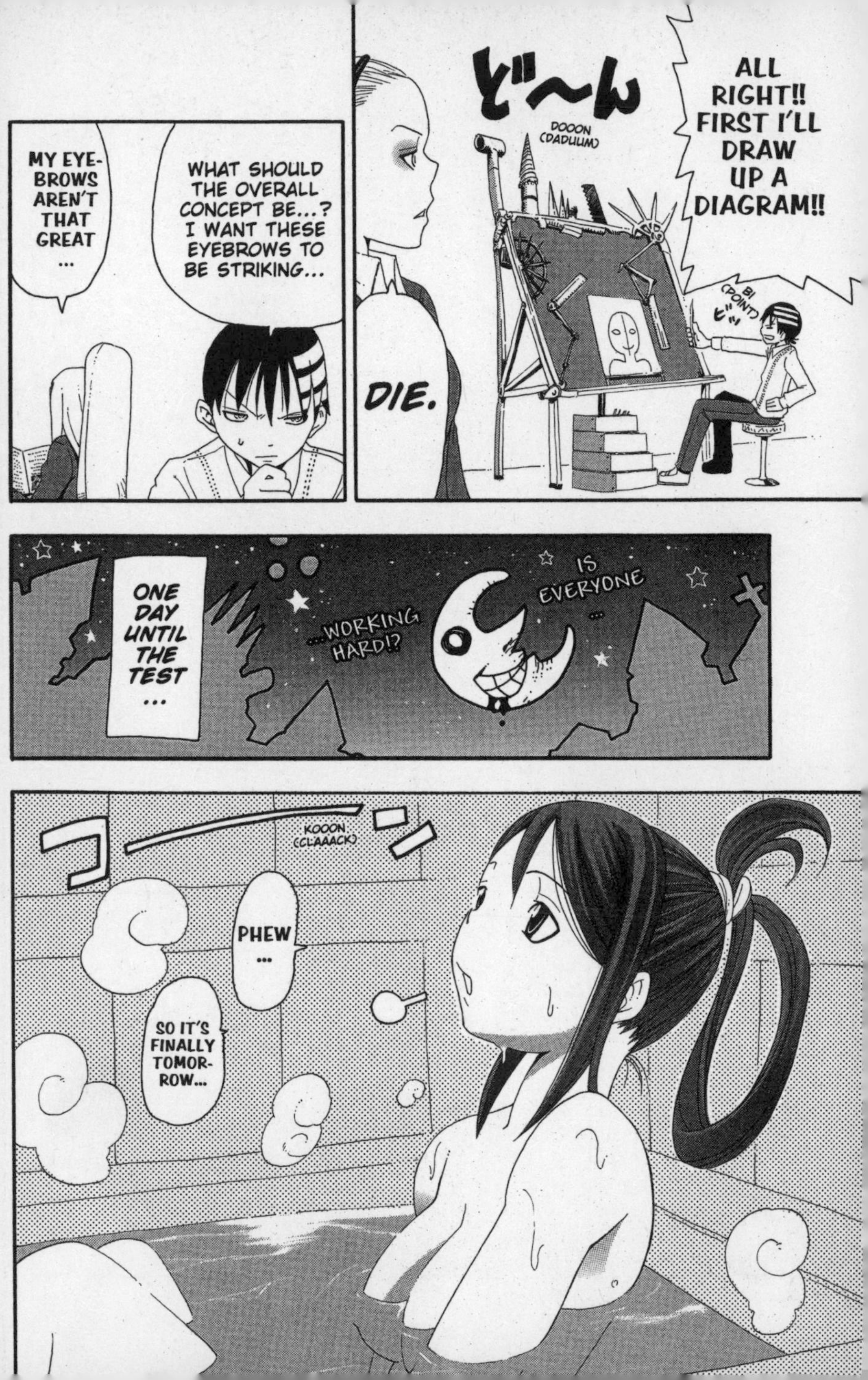
ALL RIGHT!! FIRST I'LL DRAW UP A DIAGRAM!!
BI (POINT)
ビッ
どへん
DOOON (DADUUM)
DIE.
WHAT SHOULD THE OVERALL CONCEPT BE...? I WANT THESE EYEBROWS TO BE STRIKING...
MY EYE-BROWS AREN'T THAT GREAT ...
IS EVERYONE ...
...WORKING HARD!?
ONE DAY UNTIL THE TEST ...
KOOON (CLAAACK)
PHEW ...
SO IT'S FINALLY TOMOR-ROW...

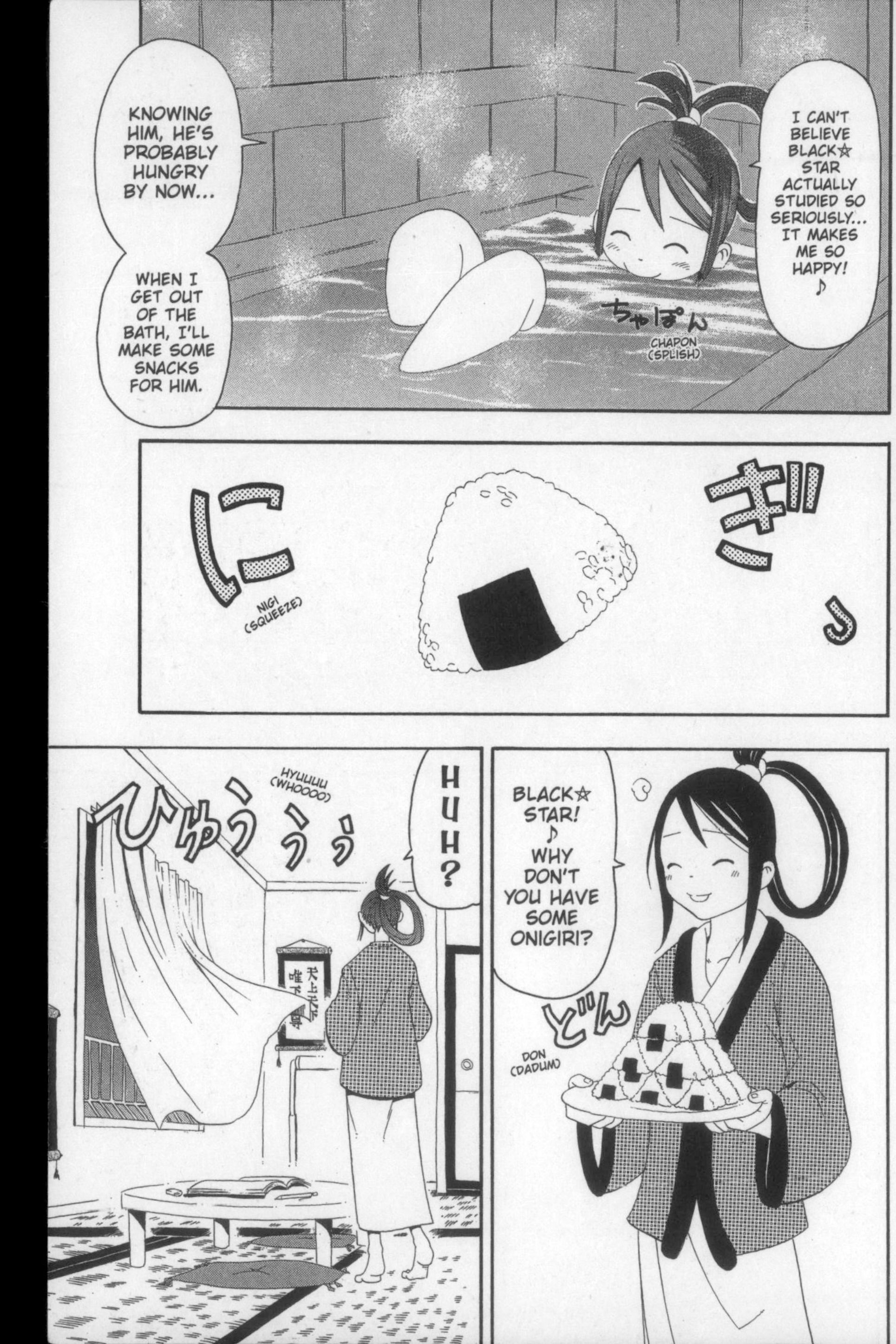
I CAN'T BELIEVE BLACK☆STAR ACTUALLY STUDIED SO SERIOUSLY... IT MAKES ME SO HAPPY! ♪
ちゃぽん
CHAPON (SPLISH)
KNOWING HIM, HE'S PROBABLY HUNGRY BY NOW...
WHEN I GET OUT OF THE BATH, I'LL MAKE SOME SNACKS FOR HIM.
にぎ♪
NIGI (SQUEEZE)
BLACK☆STAR! ♪ WHY DON'T YOU HAVE SOME ONIGIRI?
どん
DON (DADUM)
HUH?
ひゅううう
HYUUUU (WHOOOO)

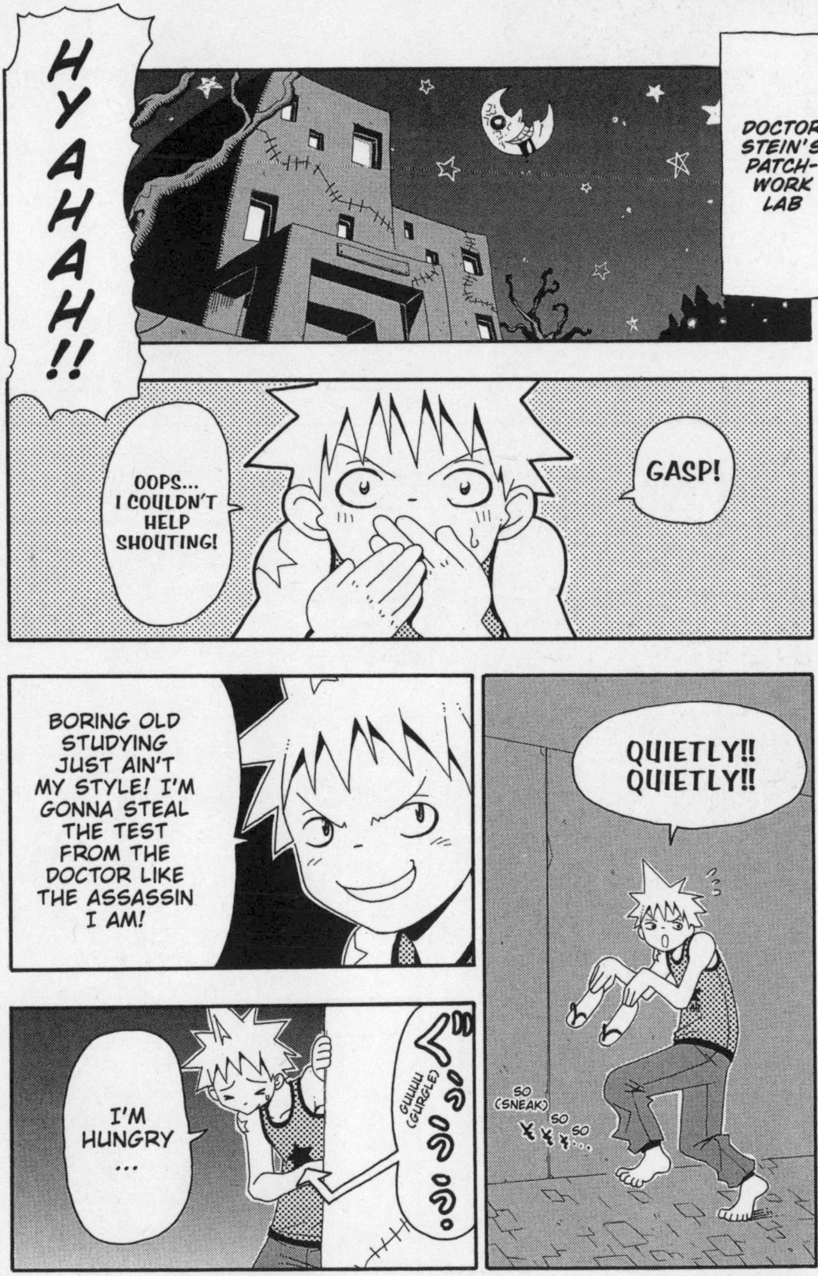
DOCTOR STEIN'S PATCHWORK LAB
HYAHAHAH!!
GASP!
OOPS... I COULDN'T HELP SHOUTING!
QUIETLY!! QUIETLY!!
SO (SNEAK) SO SO...
BORING OLD STUDYING JUST AIN'T MY STYLE! I'M GONNA STEAL THE TEST FROM THE DOCTOR LIKE THE ASSASSIN I AM!
GUUUU (GURGLE)
I'M HUNGRY ...

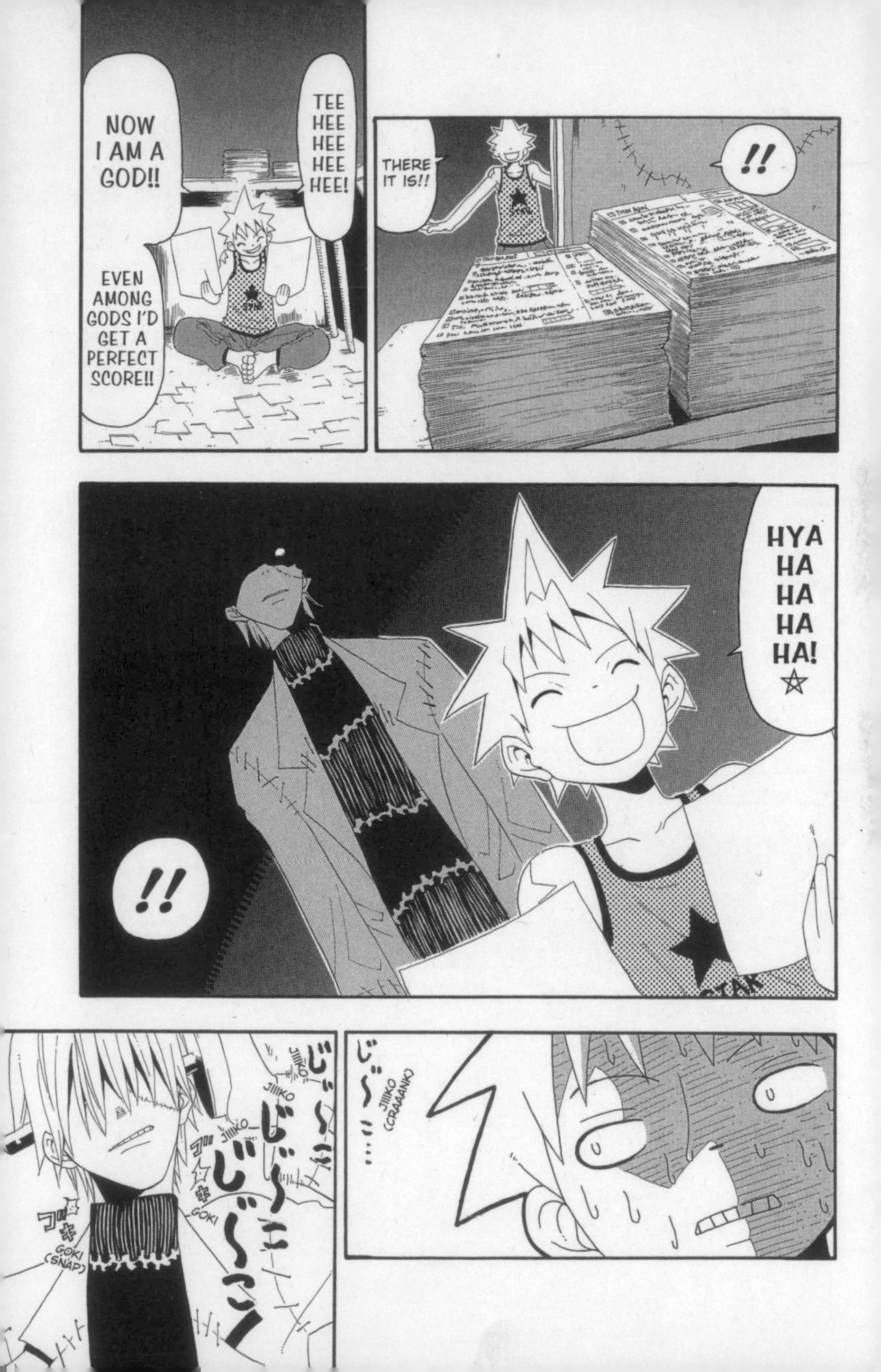
!!
THERE IT IS!!
TEE HEE HEE HEE HEE!
NOW I AM A GOD!!
EVEN AMONG GODS I'D GET A PERFECT SCORE!!
HYA HA HA HA HA! ☆
!!
JIIIKO (CRAAANK)
JIIIKO
JIIIKO
JIIIKO
GOKI
GOKI (SNAP)

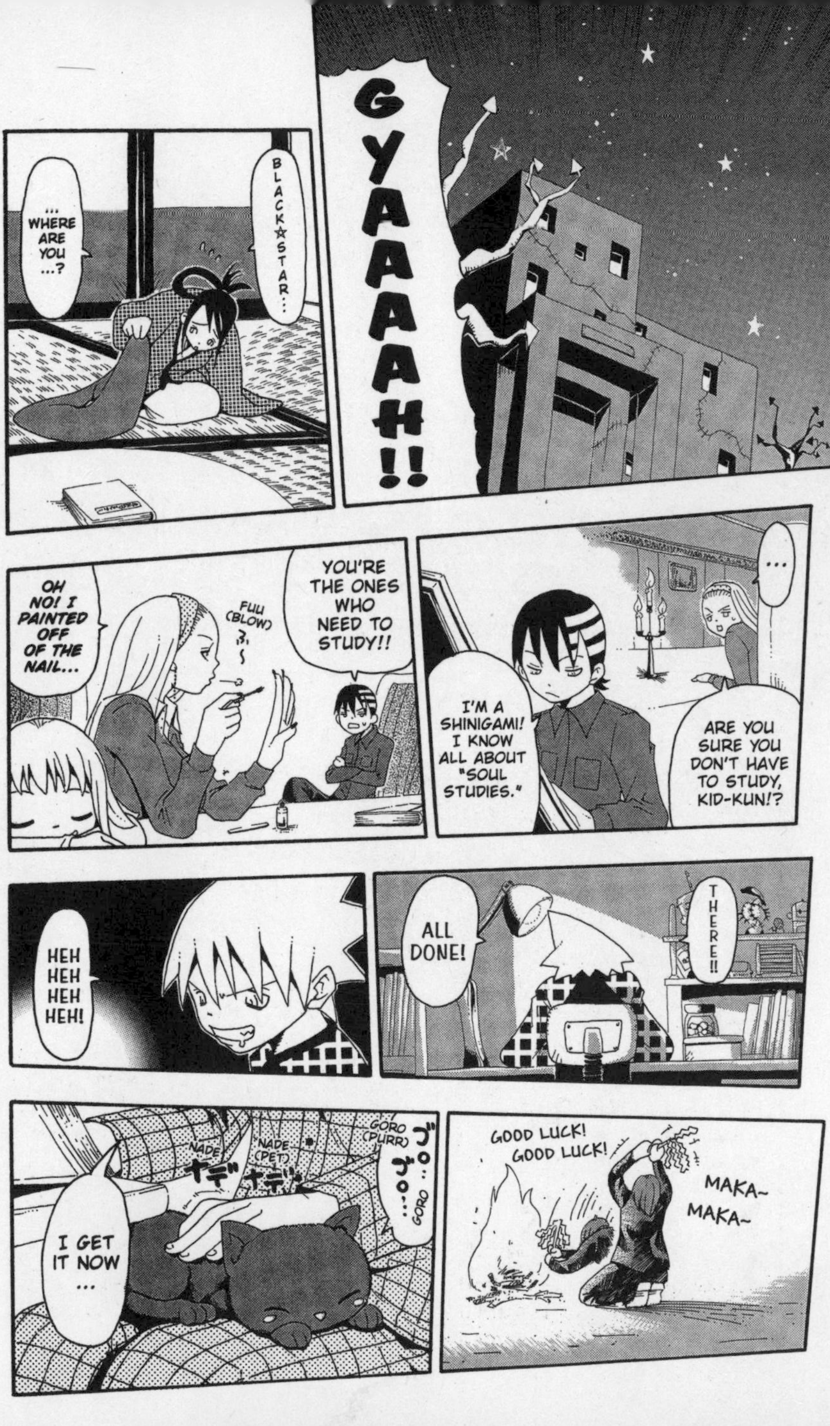
GYAAAH!!
BLACK☆STAR...
...WHERE ARE YOU...?
...
ARE YOU SURE YOU DON'T HAVE TO STUDY, KID-KUN!?
I'M A SHINIGAMI! I KNOW ALL ABOUT "SOUL STUDIES."
YOU'RE THE ONES WHO NEED TO STUDY!!
FUU (BLOW)
OH NO! I PAINTED OFF OF THE NAIL...
THERE!!
ALL DONE!
HEH HEH HEH HEH!
GOOD LUCK! GOOD LUCK!
MAKA~ MAKA~
GORO (PURR)
GORO
NADE (PET)
NADE
I GET IT NOW ...

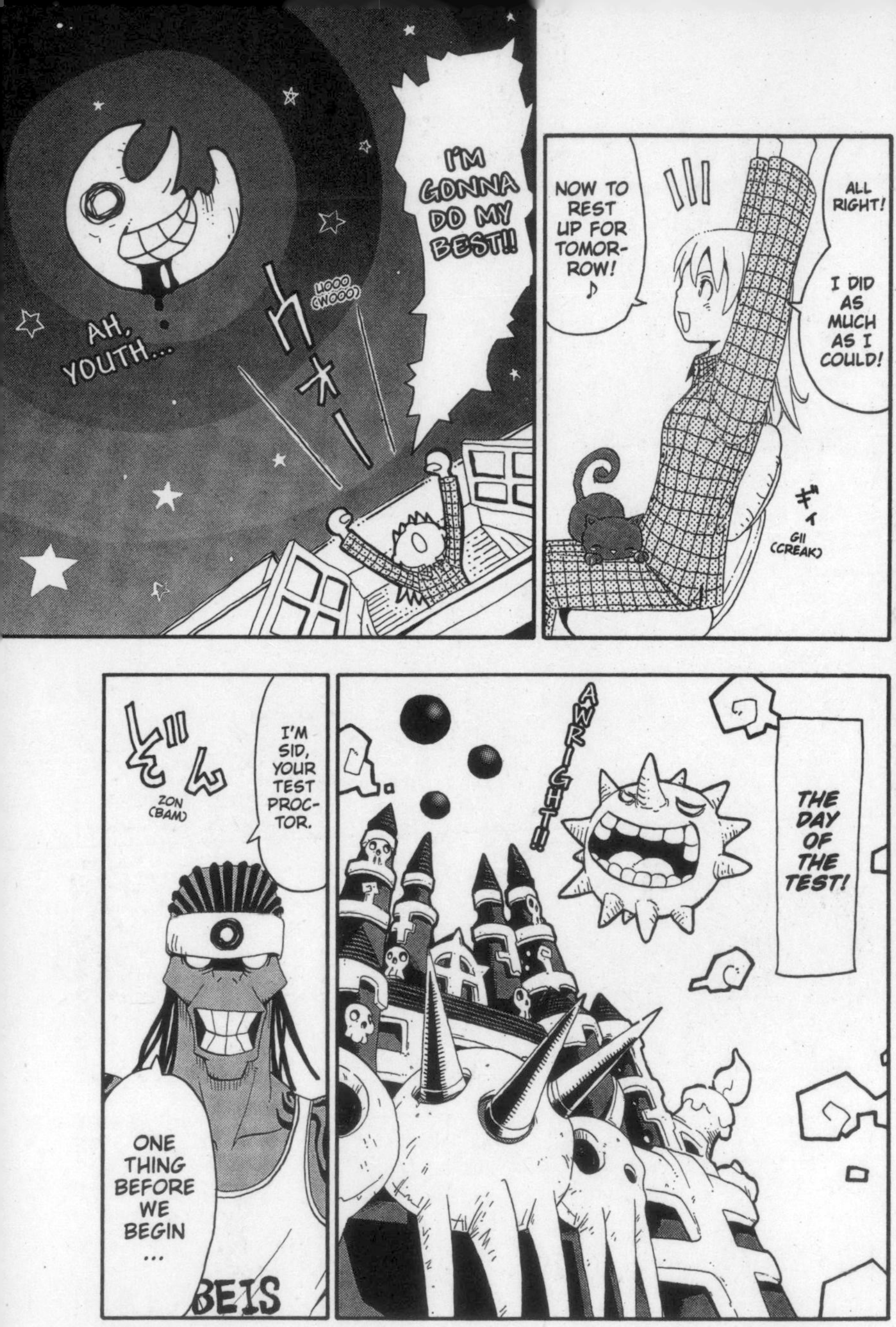
ALL RIGHT!
I DID AS MUCH AS I COULD!
NOW TO REST UP FOR TOMORROW! ♪
ギィ
GII (CREAK)
I'M GONNA DO MY BEST!!
WOOO (WOOO)
AH, YOUTH...
THE DAY OF THE TEST!
AWRIGHT!!
ぞん
ZON (BAM)
I'M SID, YOUR TEST PROCTOR.
ONE THING BEFORE WE BEGIN ...
BEIS

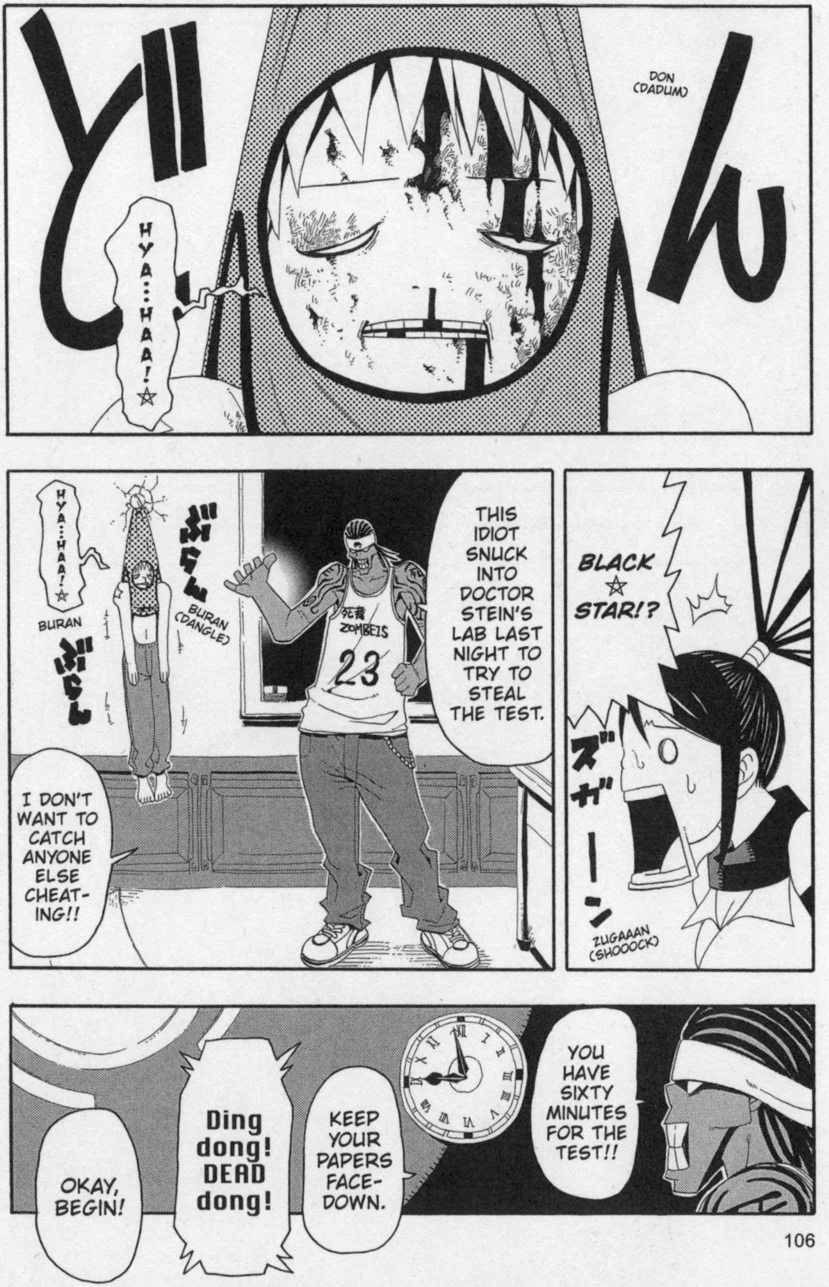
DON (DADUM)
HYA...HAA!☆
BLACK☆STAR!?
ZUGAAAN (SHOOOCK)
THIS IDIOT SNUCK INTO DOCTOR STEIN'S LAB LAST NIGHT TO TRY TO STEAL THE TEST.
ZOMBEIS
23
BURAN (DANGLE)
HYA...HAA!☆
BURAN
I DON'T WANT TO CATCH ANYONE ELSE CHEATING!!
YOU HAVE SIXTY MINUTES FOR THE TEST!!
KEEP YOUR PAPERS FACE-DOWN.
Ding dong! DEAD dong!
OKAY, BEGIN!

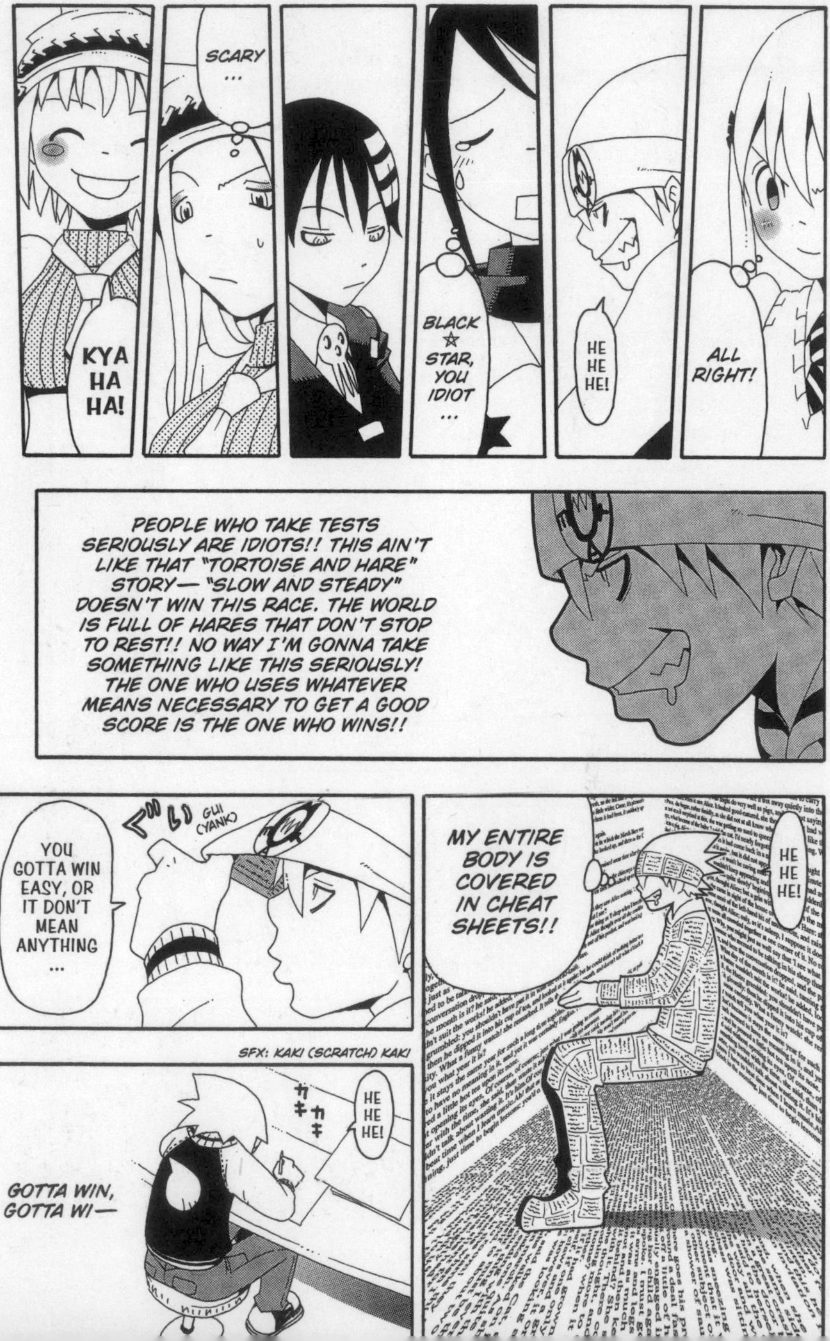
ALL RIGHT!
HE HE HE!
BLACK ☆ STAR, YOU IDIOT ...
SCARY ...
KYA HA HA!
PEOPLE WHO TAKE TESTS SERIOUSLY ARE IDIOTS!! THIS AIN'T LIKE THAT "TORTOISE AND HARE" STORY— "SLOW AND STEADY" DOESN'T WIN THIS RACE. THE WORLD IS FULL OF HARES THAT DON'T STOP TO REST!! NO WAY I'M GONNA TAKE SOMETHING LIKE THIS SERIOUSLY! THE ONE WHO USES WHATEVER MEANS NECESSARY TO GET A GOOD SCORE IS THE ONE WHO WINS!!
HE HE HE!
MY ENTIRE BODY IS COVERED IN CHEAT SHEETS!!
GUI (YANK)
YOU GOTTA WIN EASY, OR IT DON'T MEAN ANYTHING ...
SFX: KAKI (SCRATCH) KAKI
HE HE HE!
カキ カキ
GOTTA WIN, GOTTA WI—

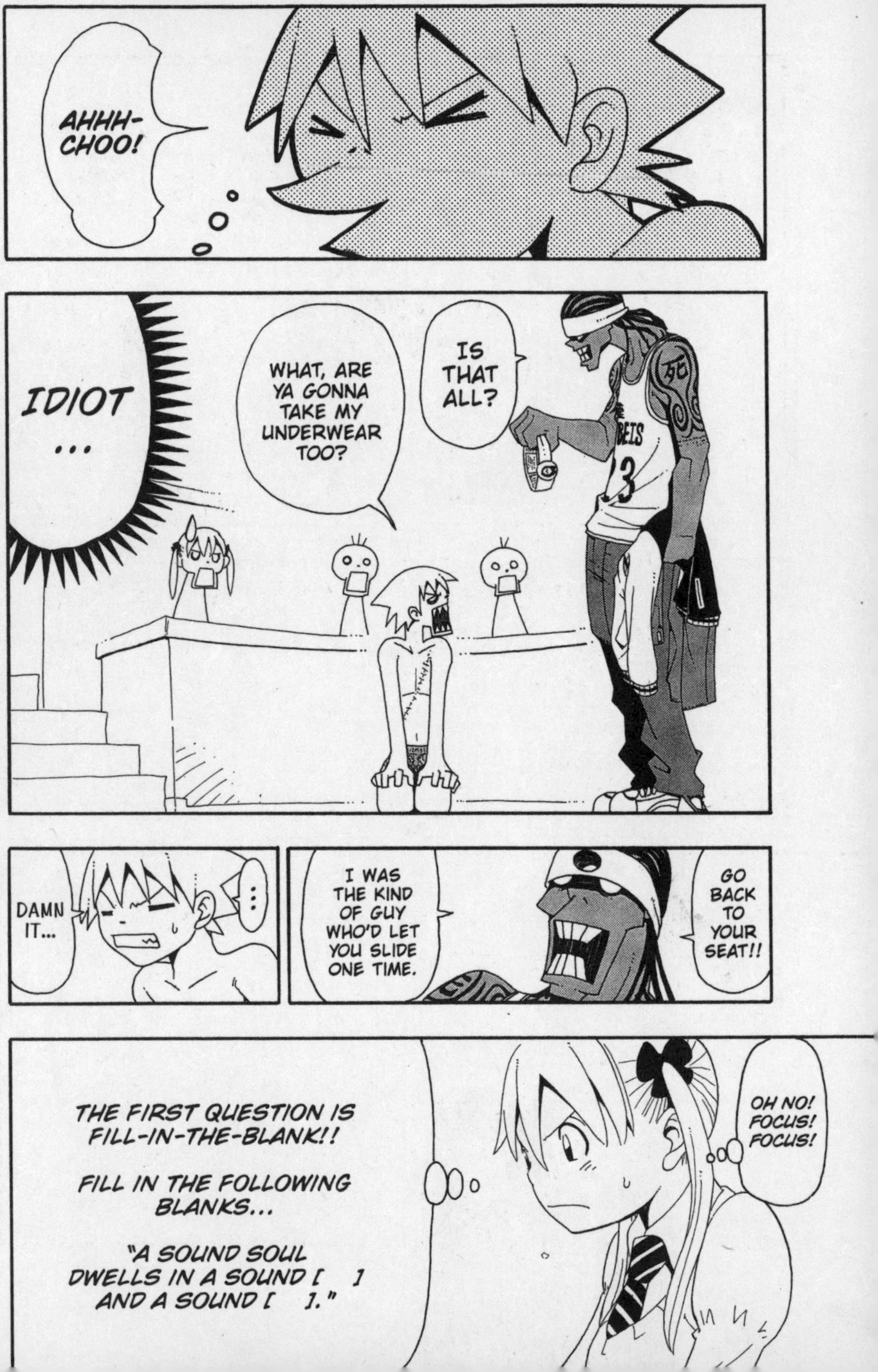
AHHH-CHOO!
IS THAT ALL?
WHAT, ARE YA GONNA TAKE MY UNDERWEAR TOO?
IDIOT ...
GO BACK TO YOUR SEAT!!
I WAS THE KIND OF GUY WHO'D LET YOU SLIDE ONE TIME.
...
DAMN IT...
OH NO! FOCUS! FOCUS!
THE FIRST QUESTION IS FILL-IN-THE-BLANK!!
FILL IN THE FOLLOWING BLANKS...
"A SOUND SOUL DWELLS IN A SOUND [ ] AND A SOUND [ ]."

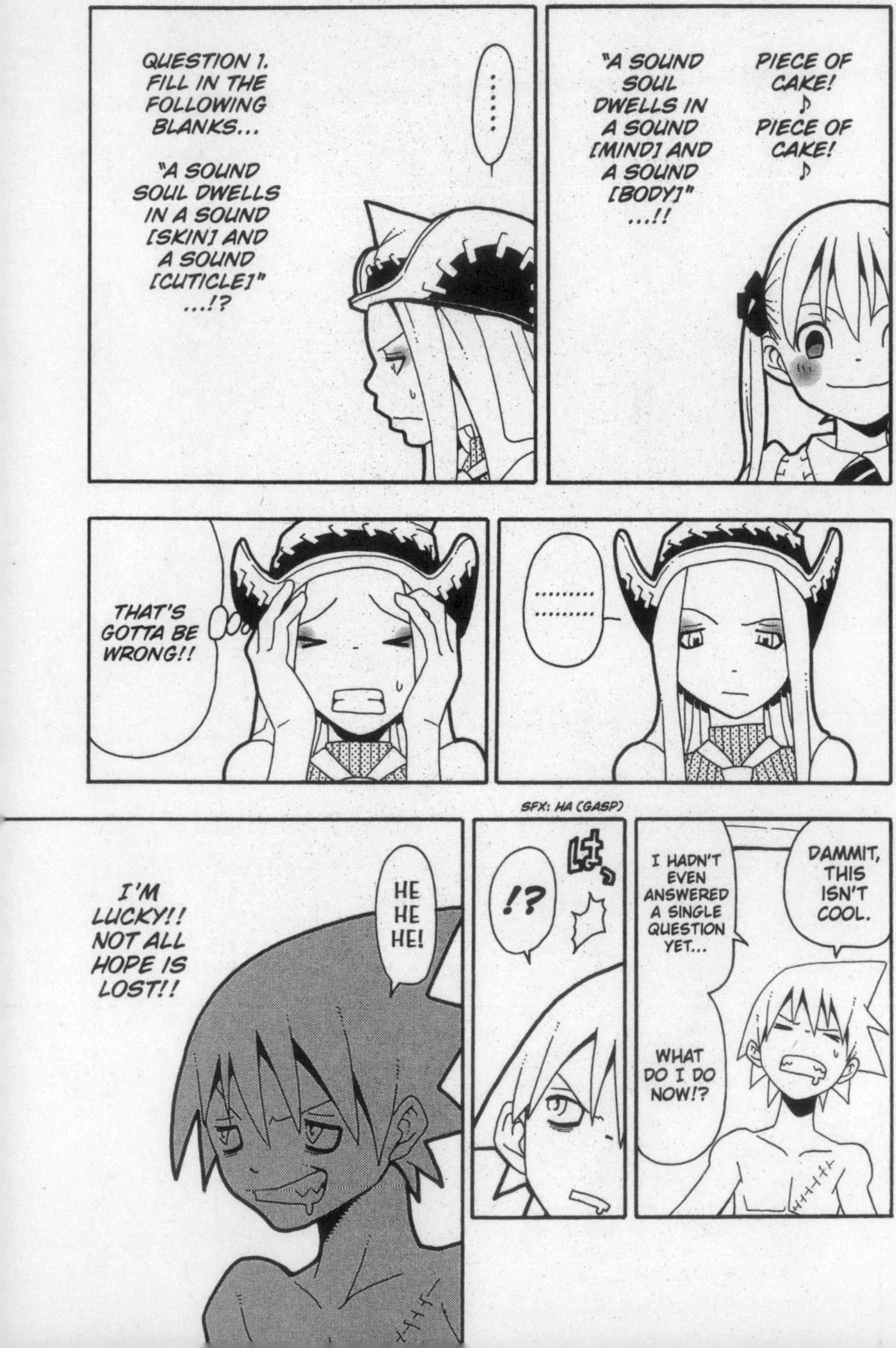
PIECE OF CAKE! ♪ PIECE OF CAKE! ♪
"A SOUND SOUL DWELLS IN A SOUND [MIND] AND A SOUND [BODY]" ...!!
......
QUESTION 1. FILL IN THE FOLLOWING BLANKS...
"A SOUND SOUL DWELLS IN A SOUND [SKIN] AND A SOUND [CUTICLE]" ...!?
....
THAT'S GOTTA BE WRONG!!
DAMMIT, THIS ISN'T COOL.
I HADN'T EVEN ANSWERED A SINGLE QUESTION YET...
WHAT DO I DO NOW!?
SFX: HA (GASP)
はっ
!?
HE HE HE!
I'M LUCKY!! NOT ALL HOPE IS LOST!!

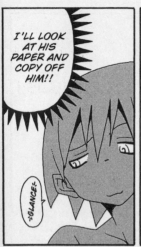

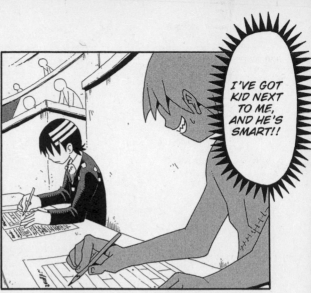

I'VE GOT KID NEXT TO ME, AND HE'S SMART!!
I'LL LOOK AT HIS PAPER AND COPY OFF HIM!!
GLANCE
カキ
KAKI (SCRATCH)
KAKI
カキ
name: Death the
DAMN IT...
I'M SO SAD...
I CAN'T WRITE IT JUST RIGHT...
....
KESHI (ERASE)
KESHI
HE'S STILL WRITING HIS NAME...

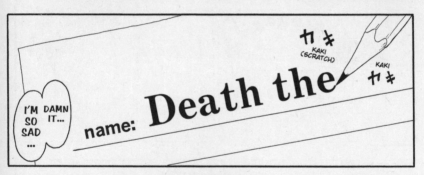

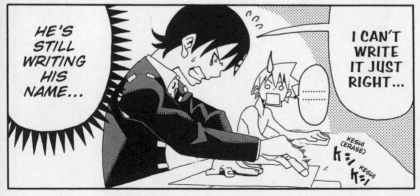

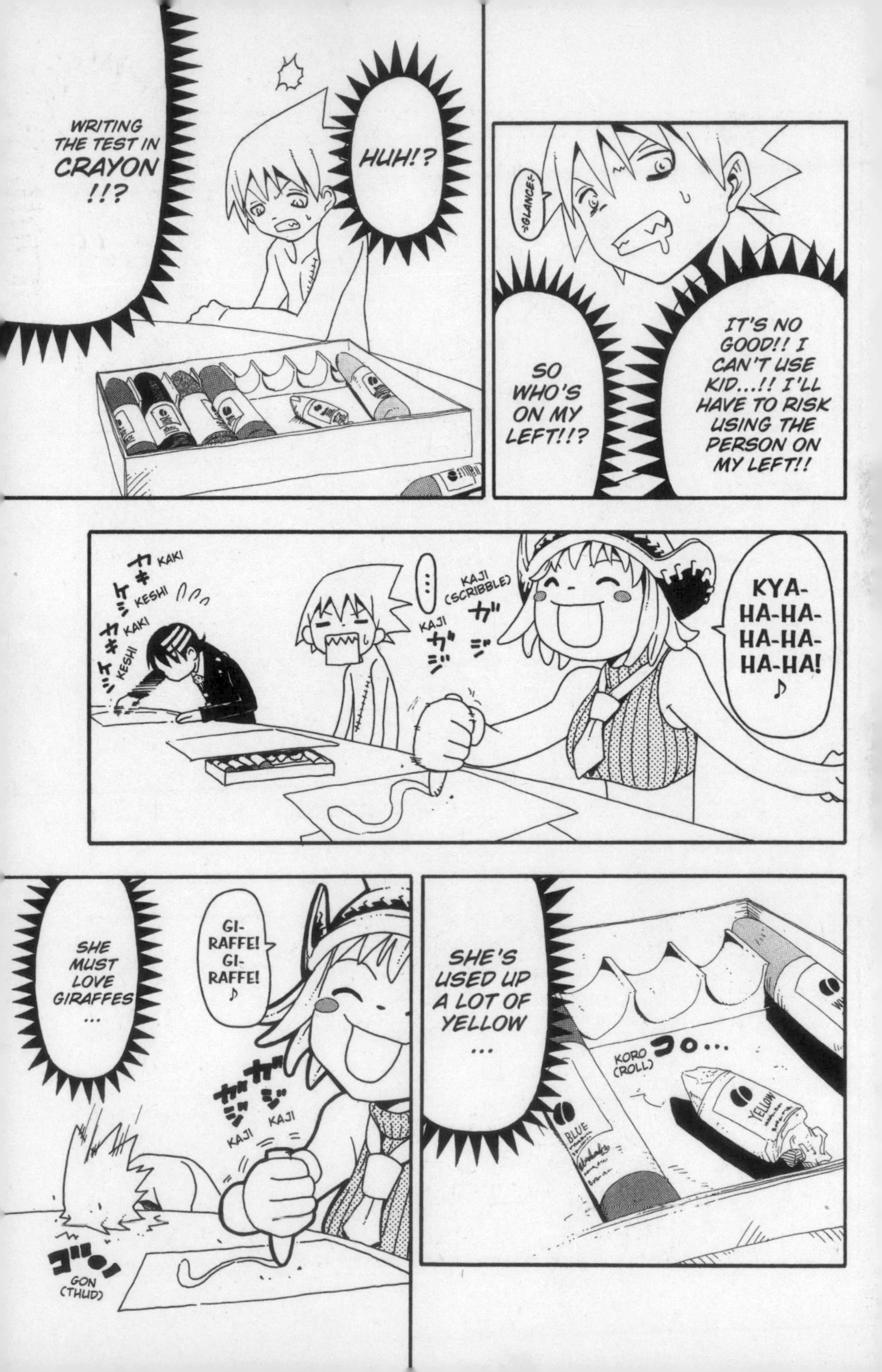

GLANCE
IT'S NO GOOD!! I CAN'T USE KID...!! I'LL HAVE TO RISK USING THE PERSON ON MY LEFT!!
SO WHO'S ON MY LEFT!!?
HUH!?
WRITING THE TEST IN CRAYON!!?
KYA-HA-HA-HA-HA-HA-HA! ♪
KAJI (SCRIBBLE)
KAJI
...
KAKI
KESHI
KAKI
KESHI
SHE'S USED UP A LOT OF YELLOW...
KORO (ROLL)
YELLOW
BLUE
SHE MUST LOVE GIRAFFES...
GI-RAFFE! GI-RAFFE! ♪
KAJI
KAJI
GON (THUD)

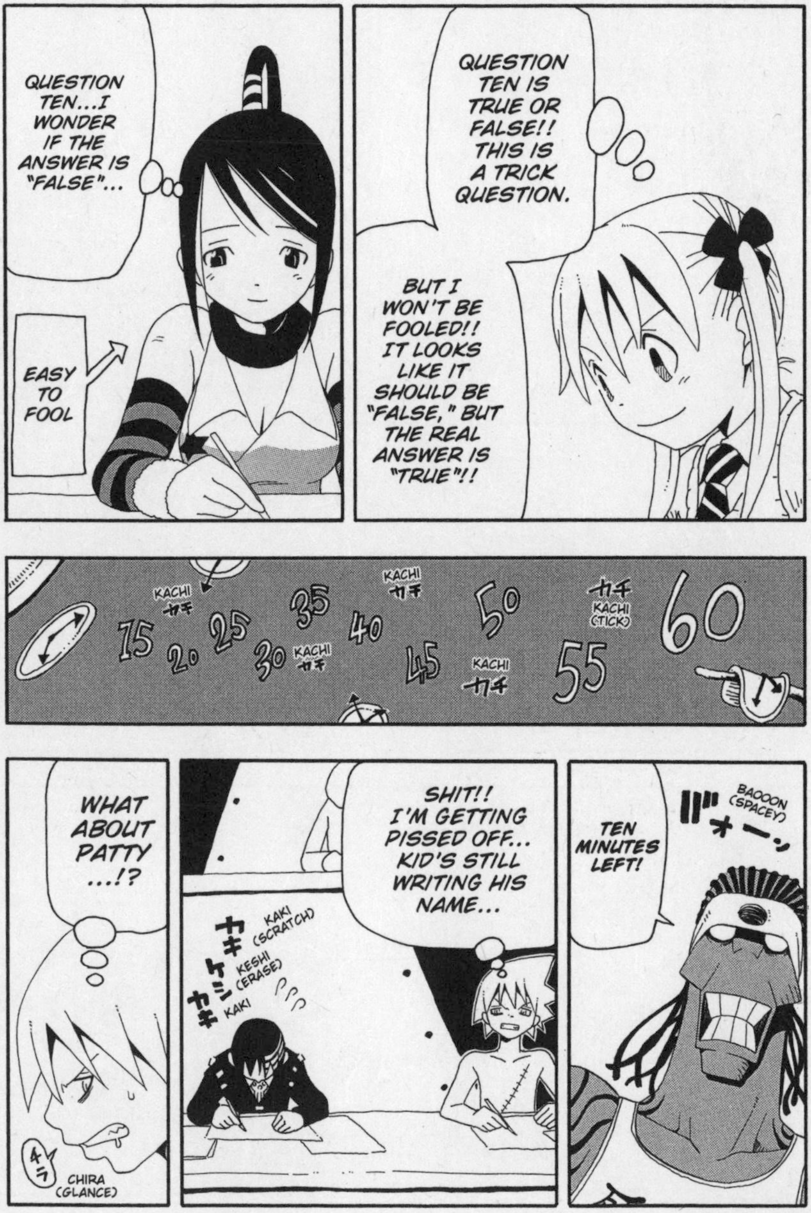
QUESTION TEN IS TRUE OR FALSE!! THIS IS A TRICK QUESTION.
BUT I WON'T BE FOOLED!! IT LOOKS LIKE IT SHOULD BE "FALSE," BUT THE REAL ANSWER IS "TRUE"!!
QUESTION TEN...I WONDER IF THE ANSWER IS "FALSE"...
EASY TO FOOL
60
カチ KACHI (TICK)
55
50
KACHI カチ
45
40
KACHI カチ
35
30
KACHI カチ
25
20
15
KACHI カチ
BAOOON (SPACEY)
TEN MINUTES LEFT!
SHIT!! I'M GETTING PISSED OFF... KID'S STILL WRITING HIS NAME...
カキ KAKI (SCRATCH)
ケシ KESHI (ERASE)
カキ KAKI
WHAT ABOUT PATTY ...!?
CHIRA (GLANCE)

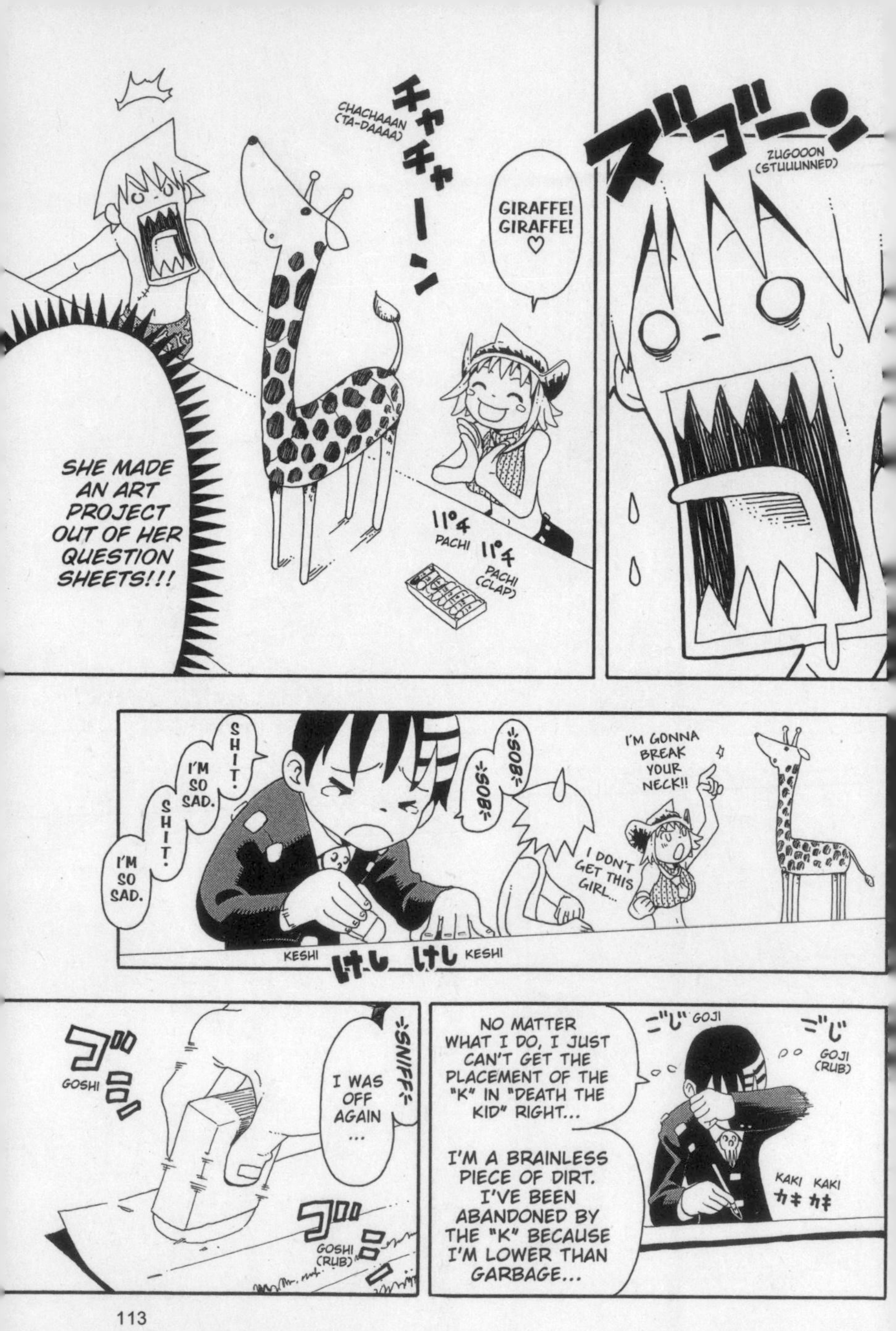

ズゴーン
ZUGOOON (STUUUNNED)
チャチャーン
CHACHAAAN (TA-DAAAA)
GIRAFFE! GIRAFFE! ♡
パチ PACHI
パチ PACHI (CLAP)
SHE MADE AN ART PROJECT OUT OF HER QUESTION SHEETS!!!
I'M GONNA BREAK YOUR NECK!!
I DON'T GET THIS GIRL...
-SOB- -SOB-
SHIT. I'M SO SAD.
SHIT! I'M SO SAD.
けし KESHI けし KESHI
ごじ GOJI ごじ GOJI (RUB)
NO MATTER WHAT I DO, I JUST CAN'T GET THE PLACEMENT OF THE "K" IN "DEATH THE KID" RIGHT...
I'M A BRAINLESS PIECE OF DIRT. I'VE BEEN ABANDONED BY THE "K" BECAUSE I'M LOWER THAN GARBAGE...
カキ KAKI カキ KAKI
-SNIFF-
I WAS OFF AGAIN...
ゴシ GOSHI ゴシ GOSHI (RUB)

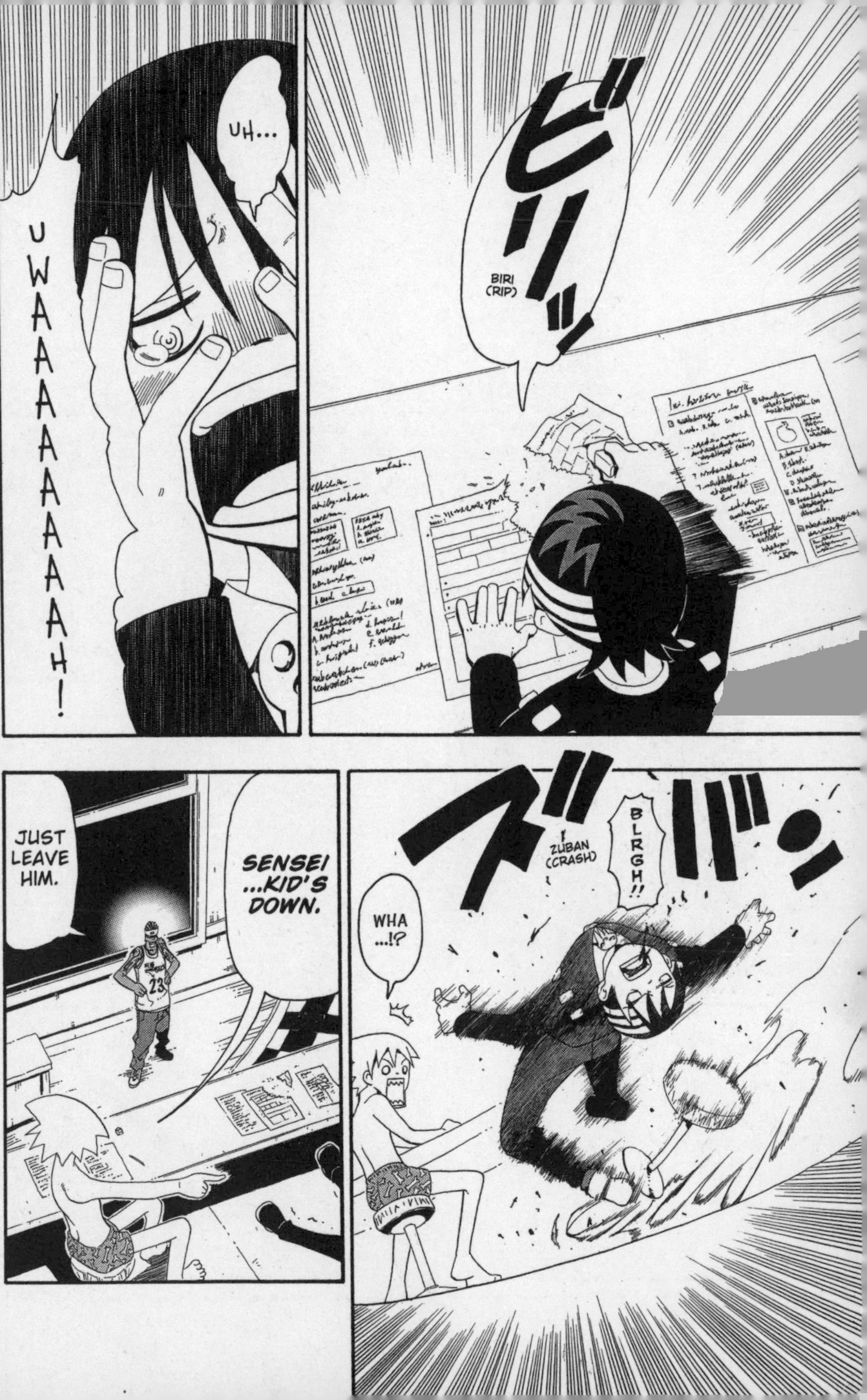
BIRI (RIP)
UH...
UWAAAAAAAAH!
BLRGH!!
ZUBAN (CRASH)
WHA ...!?
SENSEI ...KID'S DOWN.
JUST LEAVE HIM.

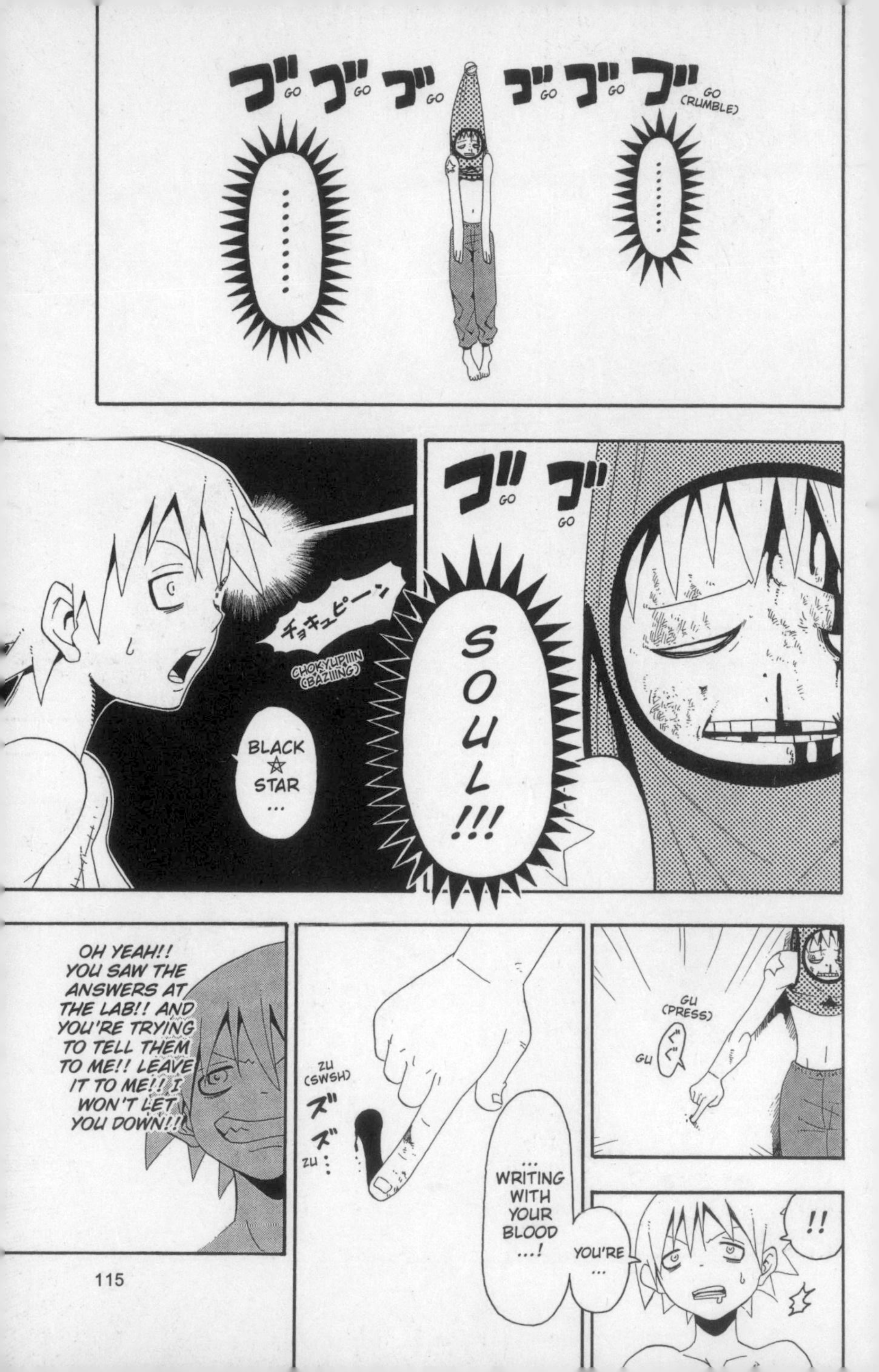
ゴ GO ゴ GO ゴ GO ゴ GO ゴ GO ゴ GO (RUMBLE)
......
......
ゴ GO ゴ GO
SOUL!!!
チョキュピーン
CHOKYUPIIIN (BAZIIING)
BLACK☆STAR ...
GU (PRESS)
ぐぐ
GU
!!
YOU'RE ...
... WRITING WITH YOUR BLOOD ...!
ZU (SWSH)
ズズ
ZU
OH YEAH!! YOU SAW THE ANSWERS AT THE LAB!! AND YOU'RE TRYING TO TELL THEM TO ME!! LEAVE IT TO ME!! I WON'T LET YOU DOWN!!

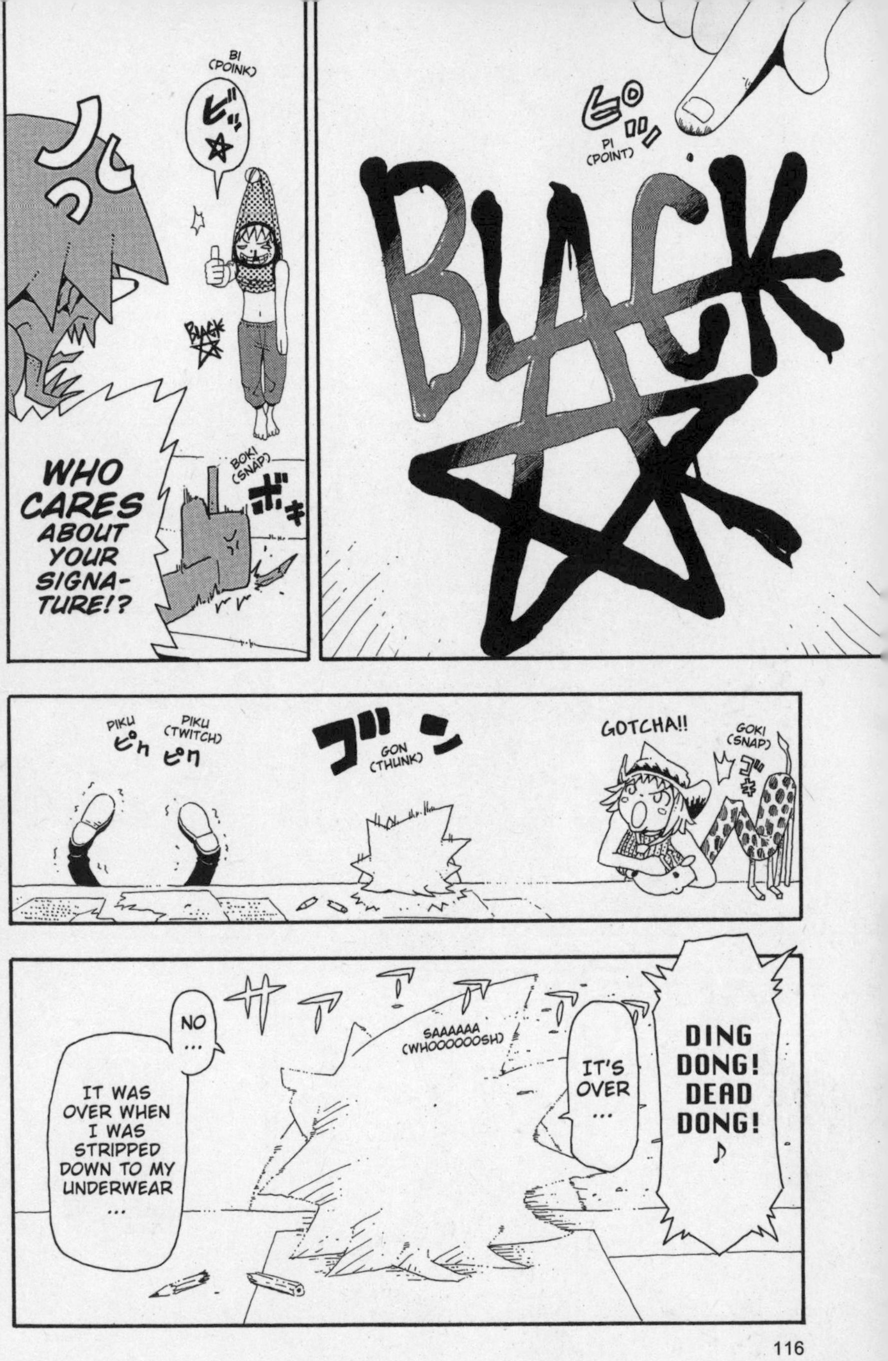
PI (POINT)
BLACK
BI (POINK)
BOKI (SNAP)
WHO CARES ABOUT YOUR SIGNA-TURE!?
GOKI (SNAP)
GOTCHA!!
GON (THUNK)
PIKU PIKU (TWITCH)
DING DONG! DEAD DONG! ♪
IT'S OVER ...
SAAAAAA (WHOOOOOOSH)
NO ...
IT WAS OVER WHEN I WAS STRIPPED DOWN TO MY UNDERWEAR ...

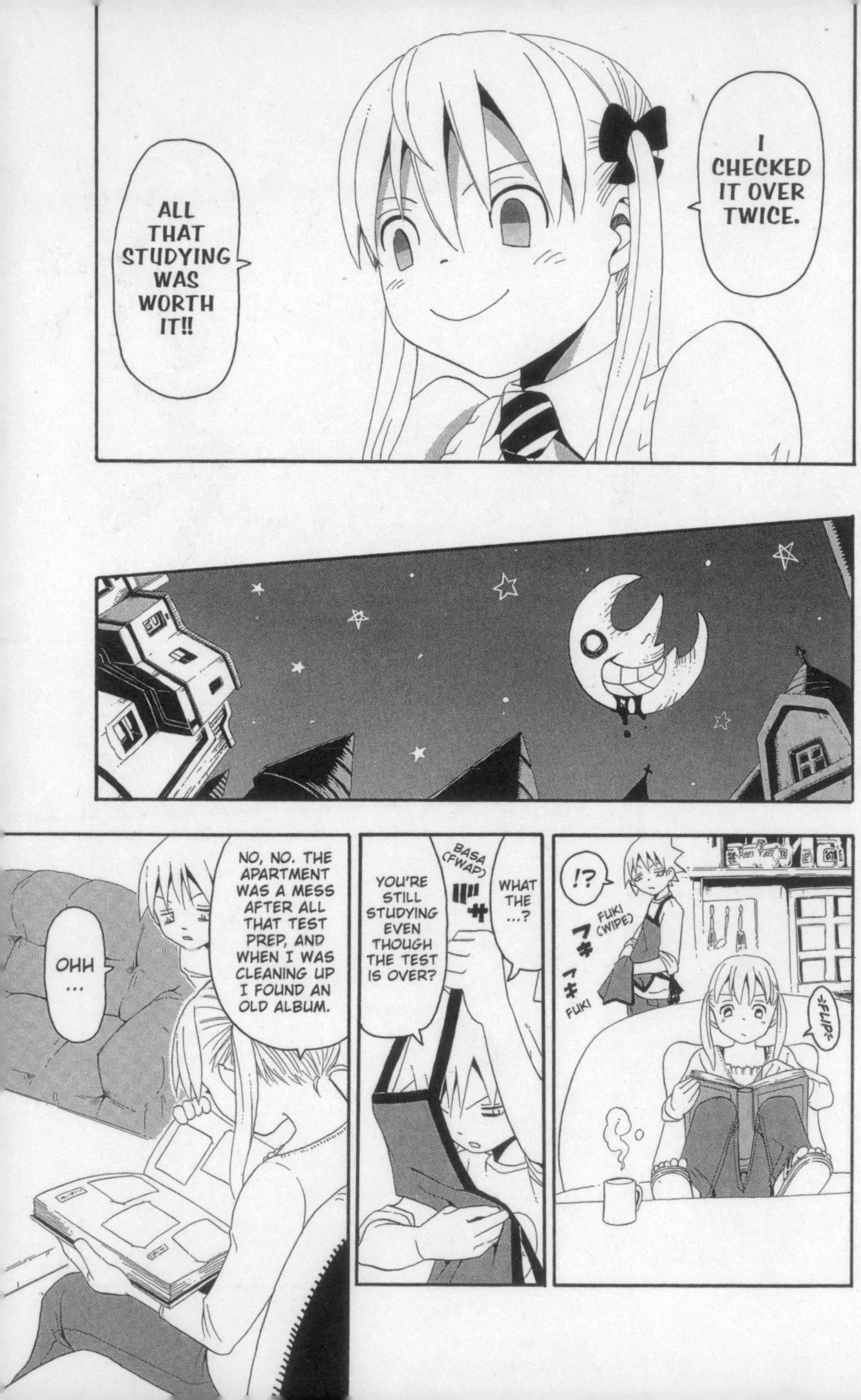
I CHECKED IT OVER TWICE.
ALL THAT STUDYING WAS WORTH IT!!
!?
FUKI (WIPE)
FUKI
FLIP
BASA (FWAP)
WHAT THE ...?
YOU'RE STILL STUDYING EVEN THOUGH THE TEST IS OVER?
NO, NO. THE APARTMENT WAS A MESS AFTER ALL THAT TEST PREP, AND WHEN I WAS CLEANING UP I FOUND AN OLD ALBUM.
OHH ...

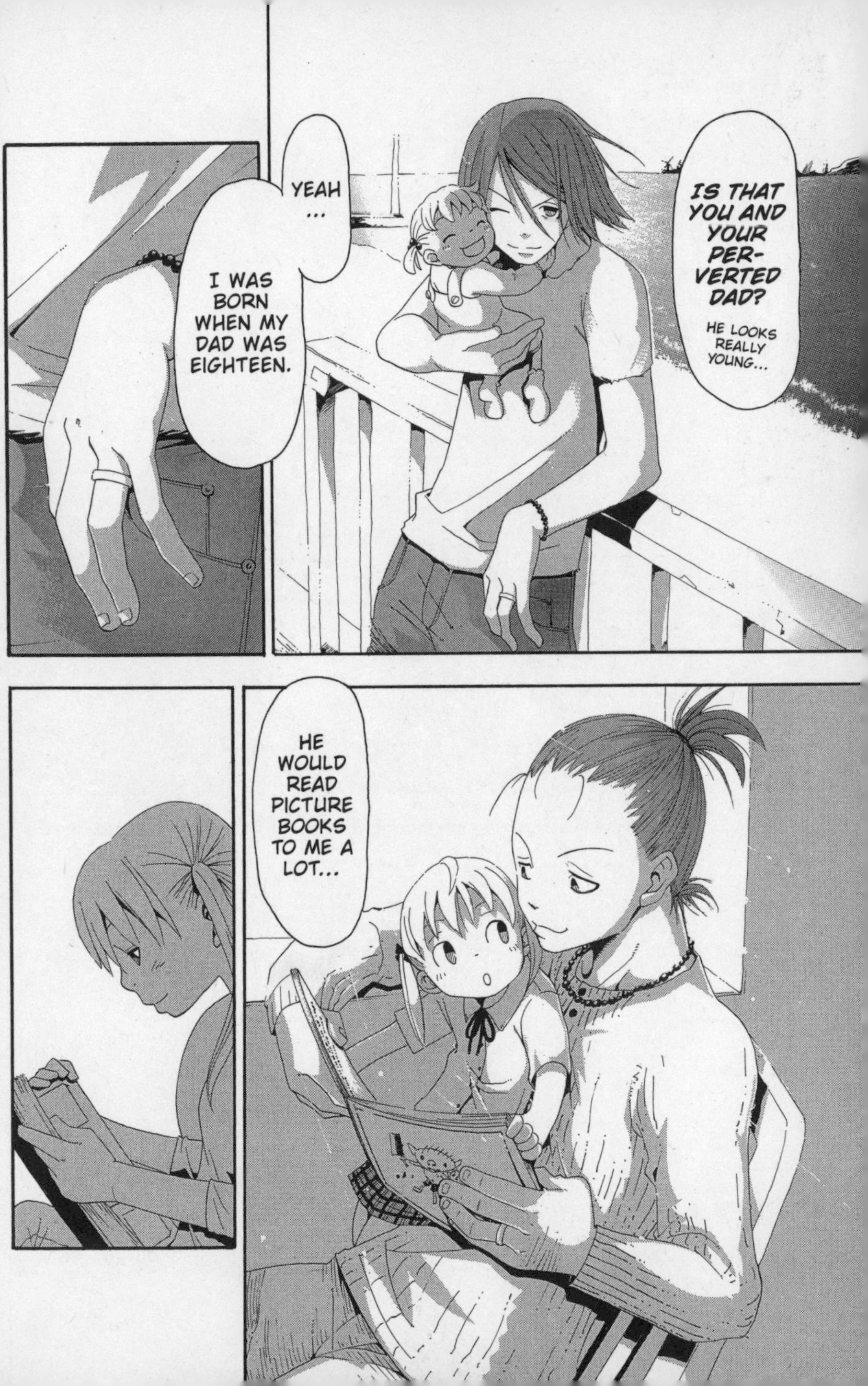
IS THAT YOU AND YOUR PER-VERTED DAD?
HE LOOKS REALLY YOUNG...
YEAH ...
I WAS BORN WHEN MY DAD WAS EIGHTEEN.
HE WOULD READ PICTURE BOOKS TO ME A LOT...

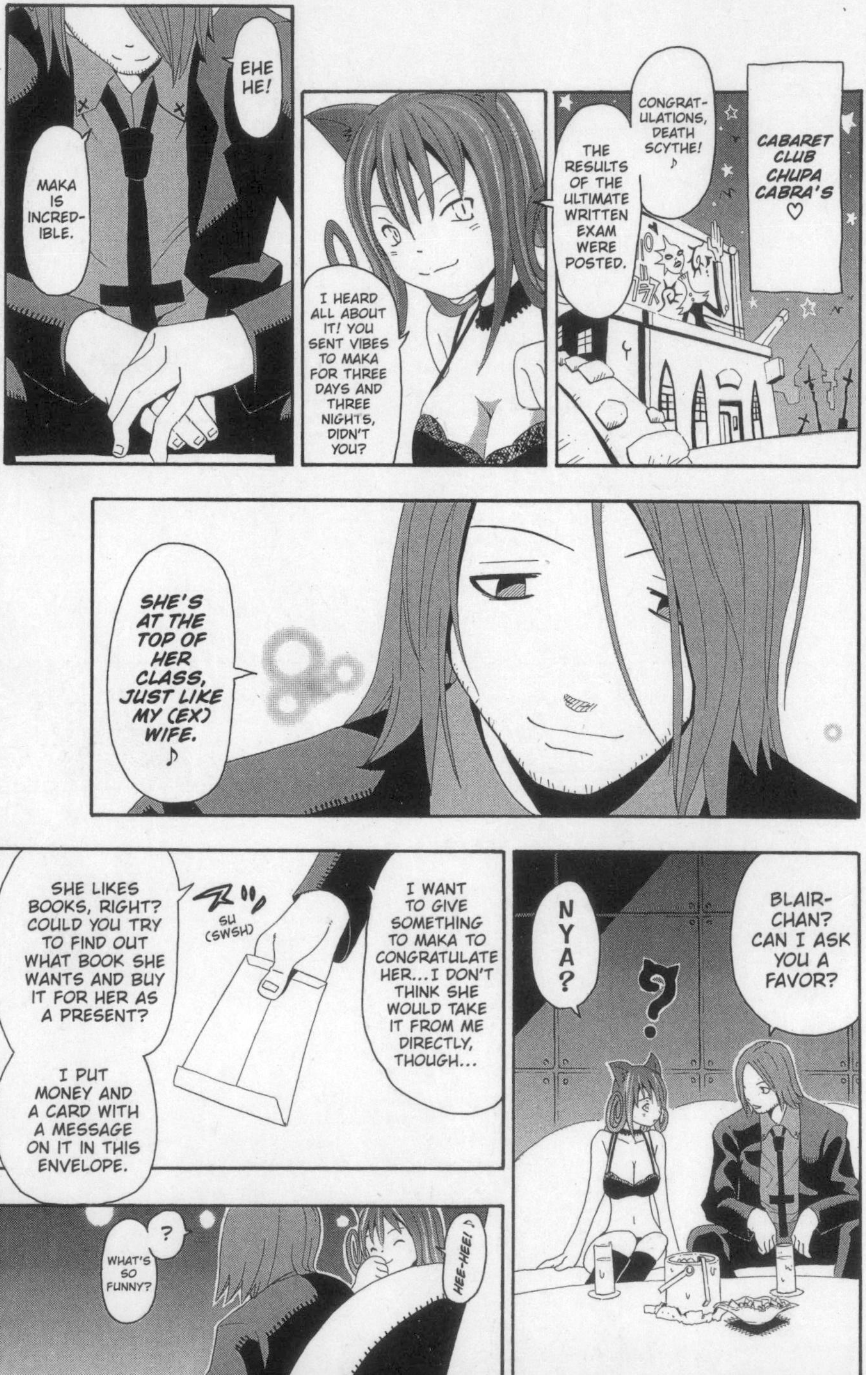
CABARET CLUB CHUPA CABRA'S ♡
CONGRATULATIONS, DEATH SCYTHE! ♪
THE RESULTS OF THE ULTIMATE WRITTEN EXAM WERE POSTED.
I HEARD ALL ABOUT IT! YOU SENT VIBES TO MAKA FOR THREE DAYS AND THREE NIGHTS, DIDN'T YOU?
EHE HE!
MAKA IS INCREDIBLE.
SHE'S AT THE TOP OF HER CLASS, JUST LIKE MY (EX) WIFE. ♪
BLAIR-CHAN? CAN I ASK YOU A FAVOR?
NYA?
I WANT TO GIVE SOMETHING TO MAKA TO CONGRATULATE HER... I DON'T THINK SHE WOULD TAKE IT FROM ME DIRECTLY, THOUGH...
SU (SWSH)
SHE LIKES BOOKS, RIGHT? COULD YOU TRY TO FIND OUT WHAT BOOK SHE WANTS AND BUY IT FOR HER AS A PRESENT?
I PUT MONEY AND A CARD WITH A MESSAGE ON IT IN THIS ENVELOPE.
HEE-HEE! ♪
?
WHAT'S SO FUNNY?

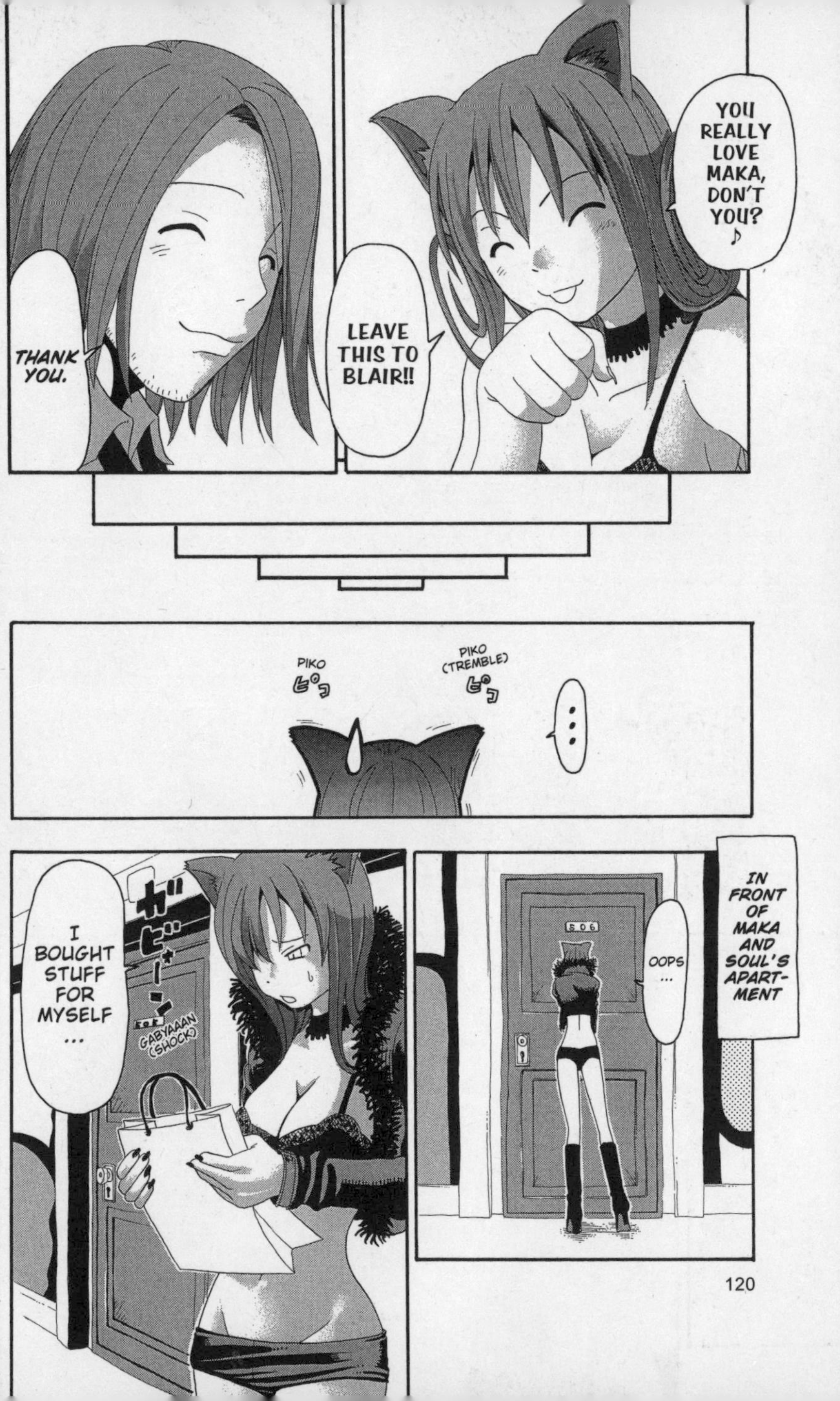
YOU REALLY LOVE MAKA, DON'T YOU? ♪
LEAVE THIS TO BLAIR!!
THANK YOU.
PIKO (TREMBLE)
...
PIKO
IN FRONT OF MAKA AND SOUL'S APARTMENT
OOPS ...
GABYAAAN (SHOCK)
I BOUGHT STUFF FOR MYSELF ...

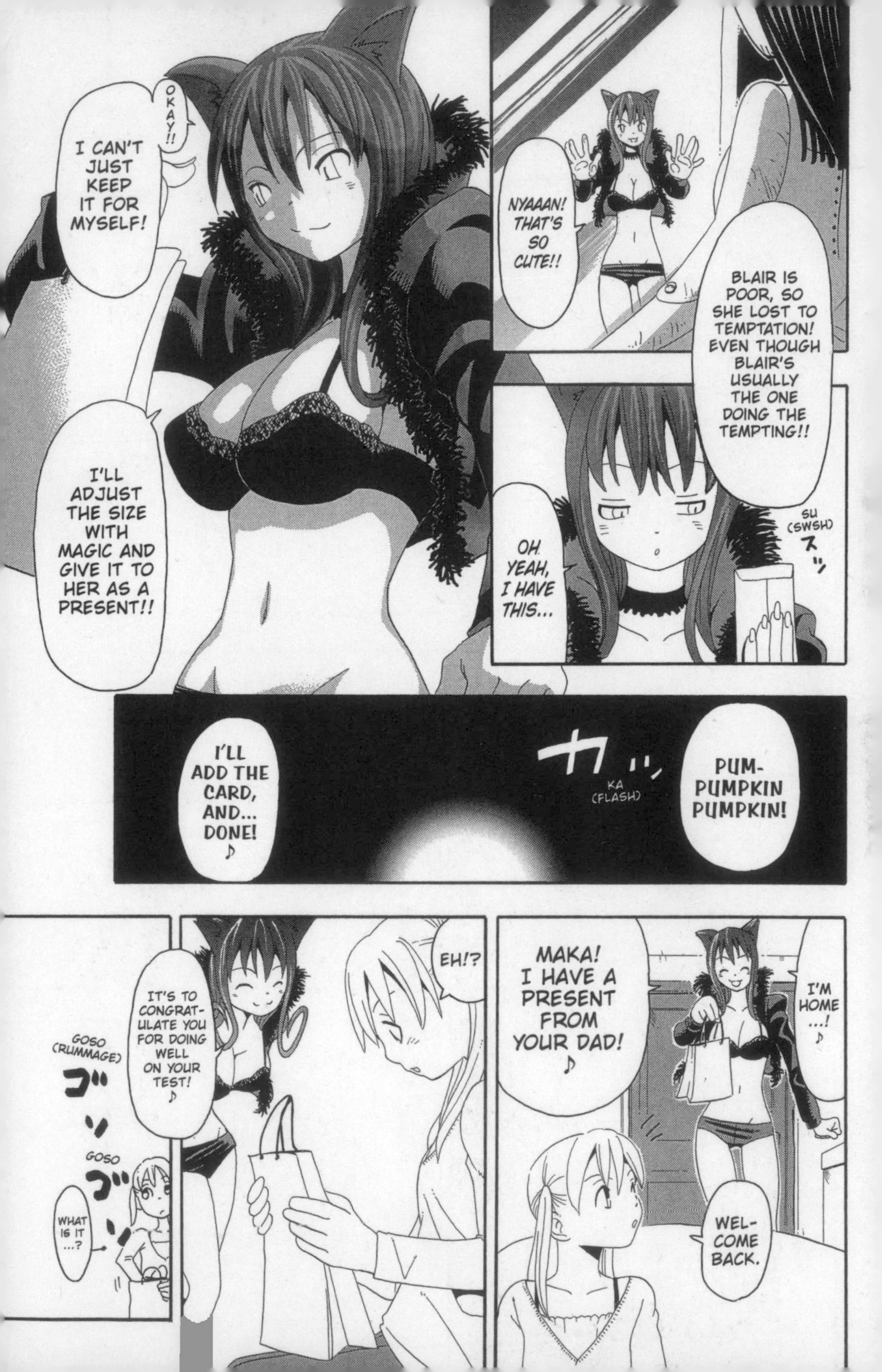
NYAAAN! THAT'S SO CUTE!!
BLAIR IS POOR, SO SHE LOST TO TEMPTATION! EVEN THOUGH BLAIR'S USUALLY THE ONE DOING THE TEMPTING!!
SU (SWSH)
OH. YEAH, I HAVE THIS...
OKAY!!
I CAN'T JUST KEEP IT FOR MYSELF!
I'LL ADJUST THE SIZE WITH MAGIC AND GIVE IT TO HER AS A PRESENT!!
PUM-PUMPKIN PUMPKIN!
KA (FLASH)
I'LL ADD THE CARD, AND... DONE! ♪
I'M HOME ...! ♪
MAKA! I HAVE A PRESENT FROM YOUR DAD! ♪
WEL-COME BACK.
EH!?
IT'S TO CONGRAT-ULATE YOU FOR DOING WELL ON YOUR TEST! ♪
GOSO (RUMMAGE)
GOSO
WHAT IS IT ...?

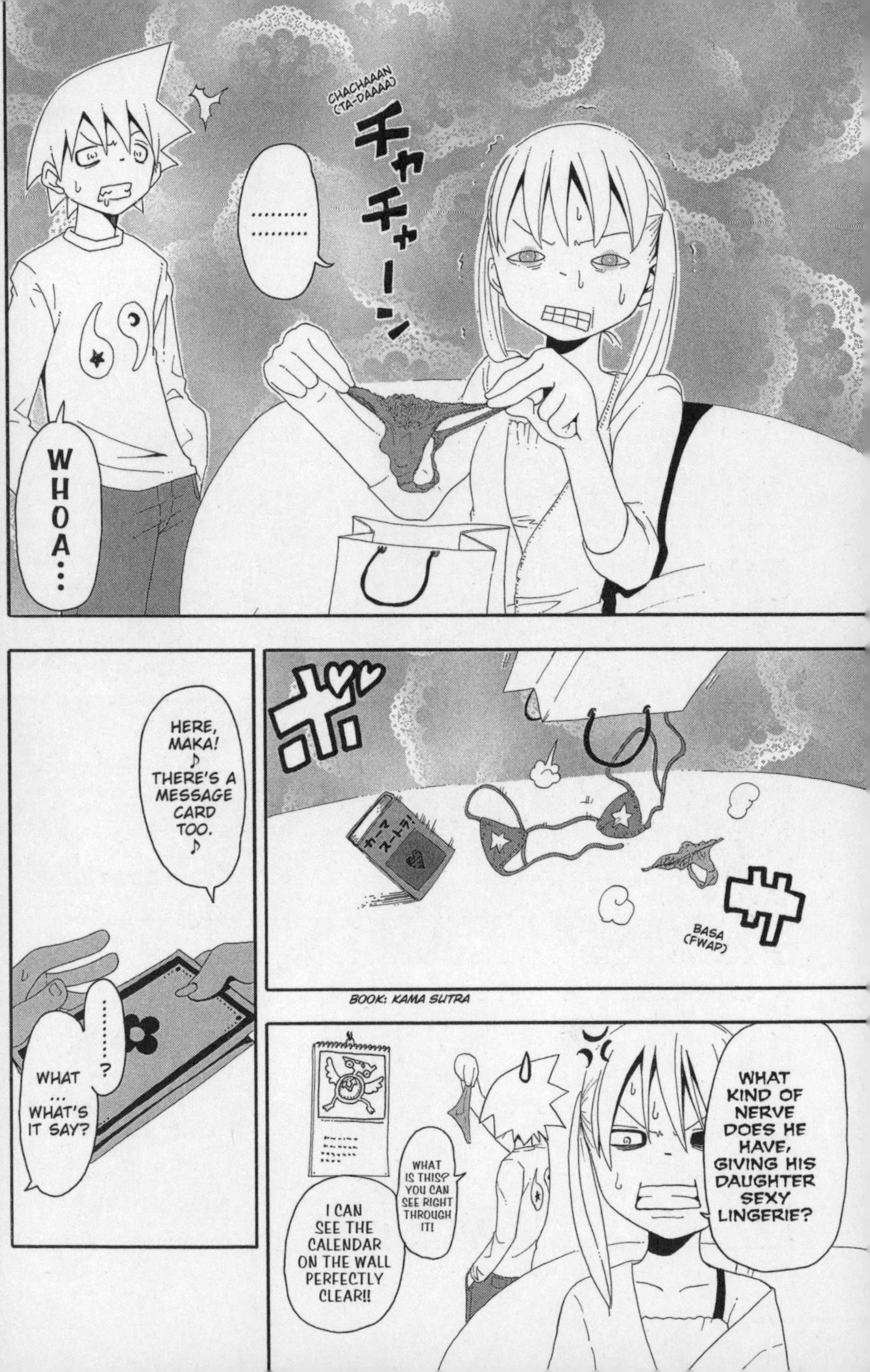
CHACHAAAN (TA-DAAAA)
チャチャーン
....
....
WHOA...
BASA (FWAP)
BOOK: KAMA SUTRA
WHAT KIND OF NERVE DOES HE HAVE, GIVING HIS DAUGHTER SEXY LINGERIE?
WHAT IS THIS? YOU CAN SEE RIGHT THROUGH IT!
I CAN SEE THE CALENDAR ON THE WALL PERFECTLY CLEAR!!
HERE, MAKA! ♪ THERE'S A MESSAGE CARD TOO. ♪
.........?
WHAT ... WHAT'S IT SAY?

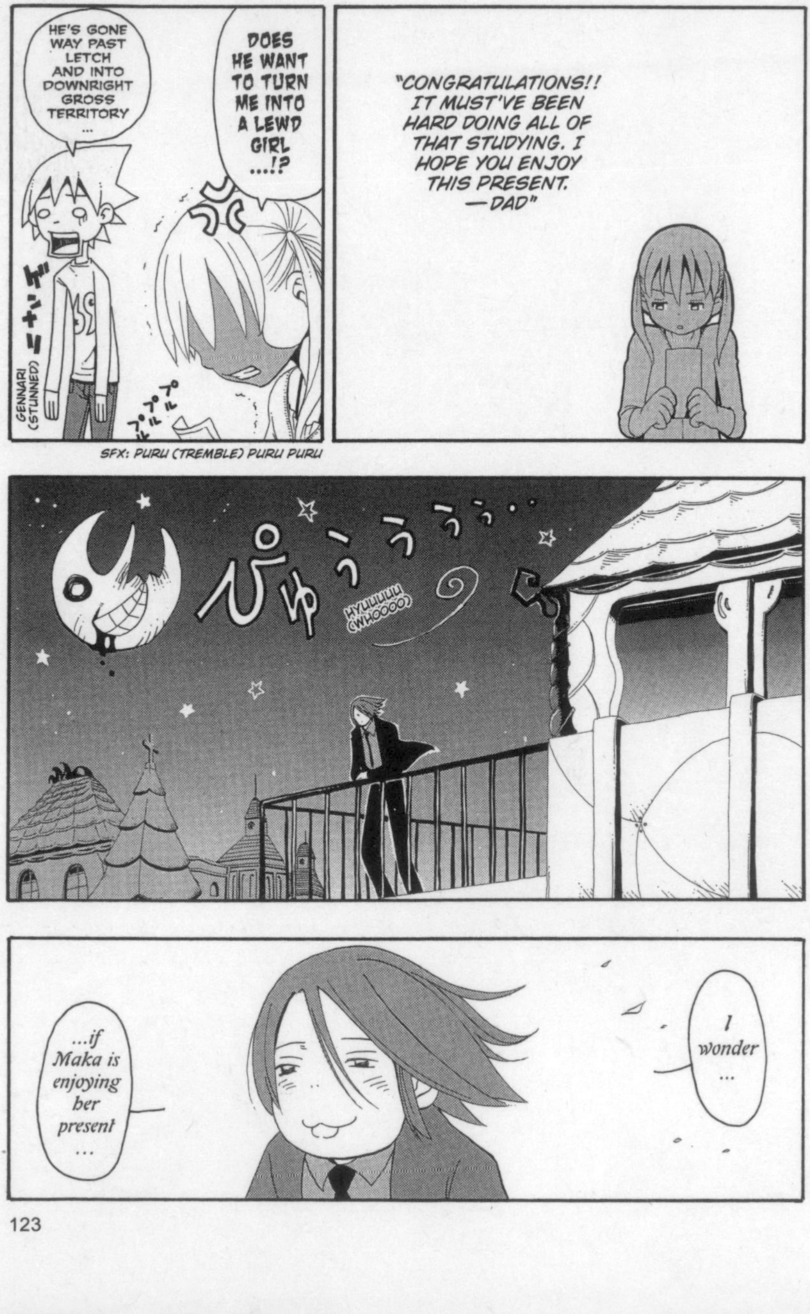
"CONGRATULATIONS!! IT MUST'VE BEEN HARD DOING ALL OF THAT STUDYING. I HOPE YOU ENJOY THIS PRESENT. —DAD"
DOES HE WANT TO TURN ME INTO A LEWD GIRL ...!?
HE'S GONE WAY PAST LETCH AND INTO DOWNRIGHT GROSS TERRITORY ...
GENNARI (STUNNED)
SFX: PURU (TREMBLE) PURU PURU
HYUUUUU (WHOOOO)
I wonder ...
...if Maka is enjoying her present ...

Maka ...

HE'S A REAL SCUM-BAG!!

I HATE HIM!!

THE RESULTS OF THE ULTIMATE WRITTEN EXAM ARE POSTED!!!

TOTAL OF 130 STUDENTS

1ST PLACE: MAKA   100 POINTS
2ND PLACE: OX-KUN   99 POINTS

....

27TH PLACE: TSUBAKI   81 POINTS

....

...

108TH PLACE: SOUL   35 POINTS

...

113TH PLACE: LIZ   28 POINTS

...

128TH PLACE: PATTY   2 POINTS
(THE PATTERN ON HER GIRAFFE WAS CORRECT IN PLACES.)

LEFT OUT OF CONSIDERATION:
    BLACK☆STAR
    KID   0 POINTS

EVERY-ONE BELOW SOUL WILL TAKE A MAKEUP EXAM!!

NO NONSENSE!

124

CHAPTER 13: BLACK DRAGON (PART 1)

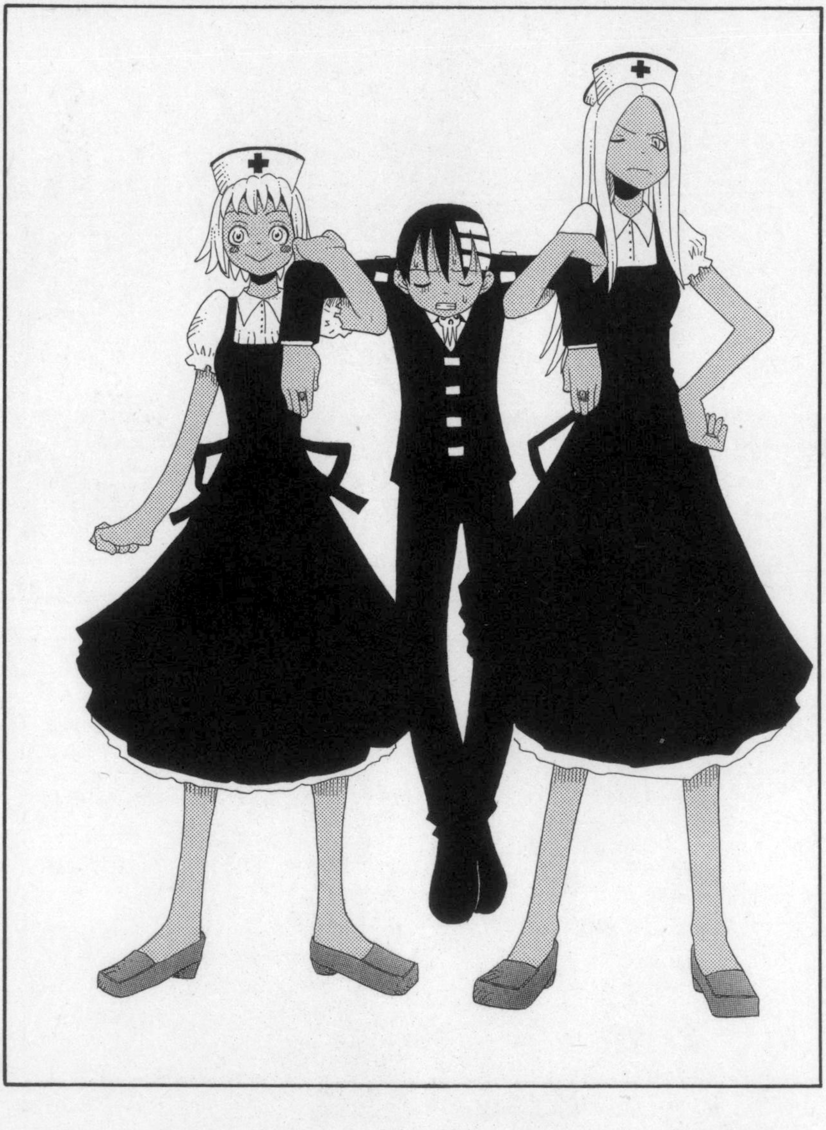

THE BALTIC COAST

RUUUN!

THE BLACK DRAGON HAS APPEARED!!

IT'S THE BLACK DRAGON!!

DO (DMM)

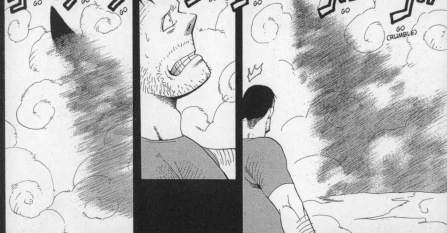

GO

GO

GO

GO

GO

GO

GO (RUMBLE)

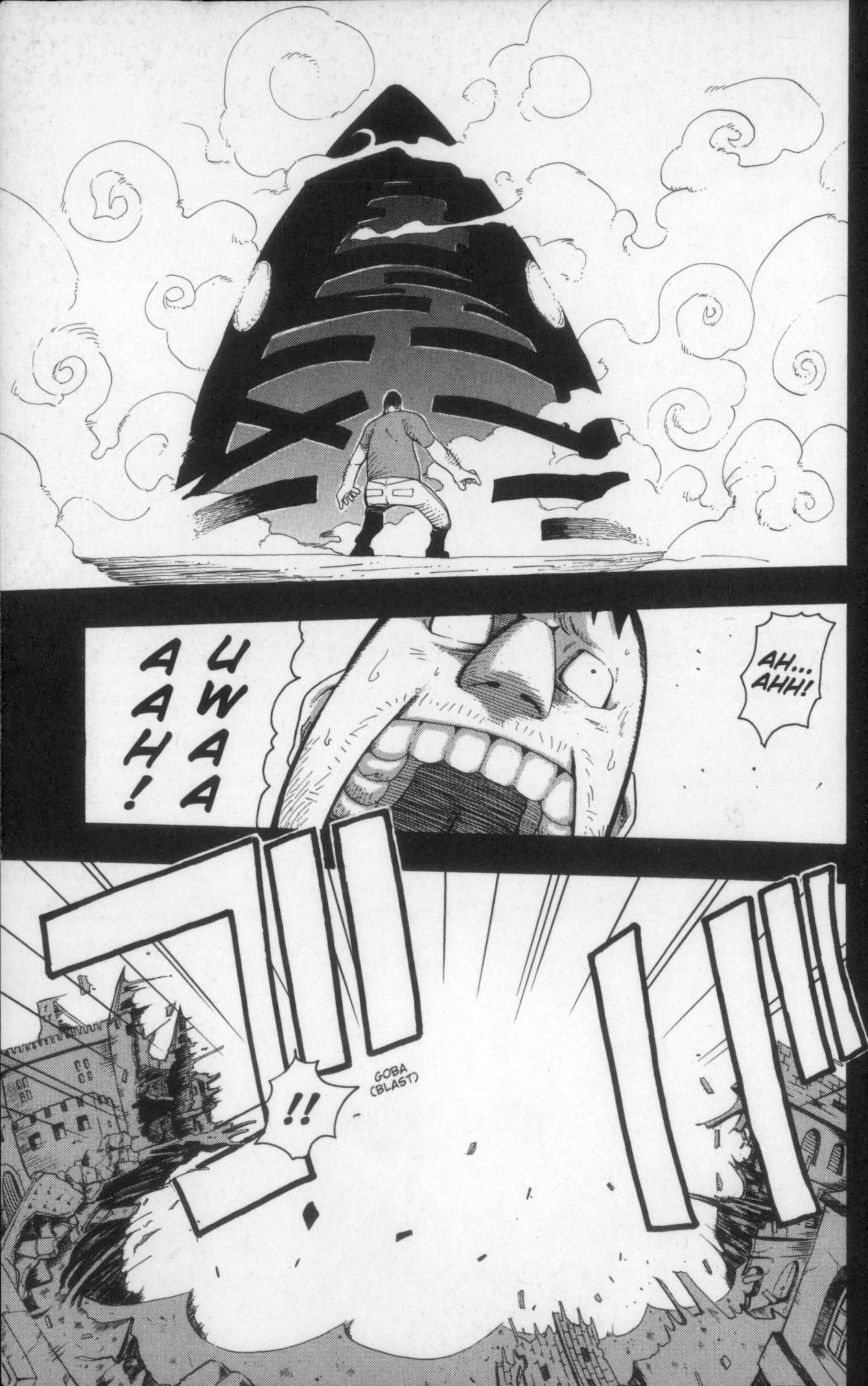
AH... AHH!
UWAAA
AAAH!
GOBA (BLAST)
!!

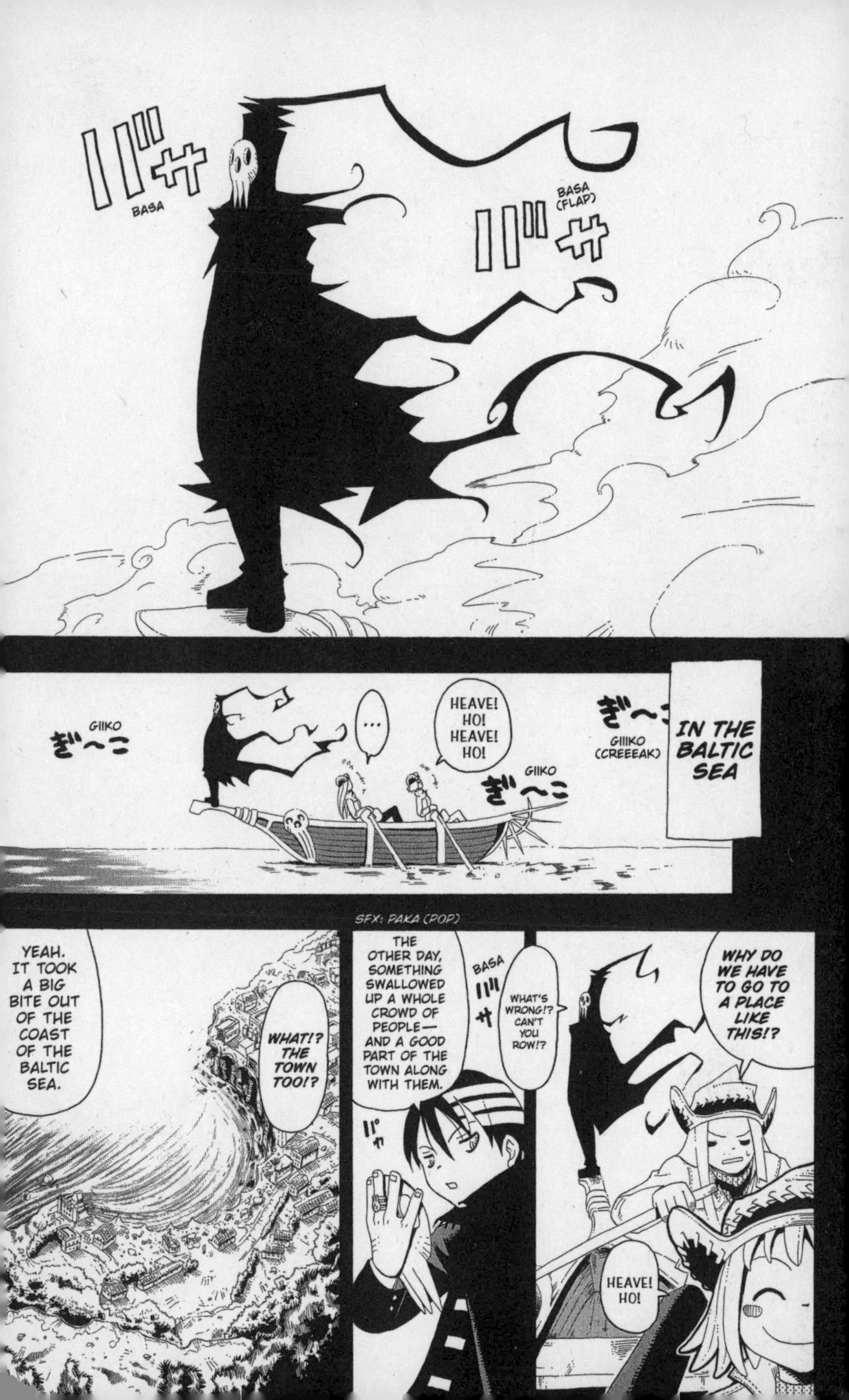
バサ
BASA (FLAP)
バサ
BASA
IN THE BALTIC SEA
ぎ〜こ
GIIKO (CREEEAK)
HEAVE! HO! HEAVE! HO!
ぎ〜こ
GIIKO
...
ぎ〜こ
GIIKO
SFX: PAKA (POP)
WHY DO WE HAVE TO GO TO A PLACE LIKE THIS!?
バサ
BASA
WHAT'S WRONG!? CAN'T YOU ROW!?
HEAVE! HO!
THE OTHER DAY, SOMETHING SWALLOWED UP A WHOLE CROWD OF PEOPLE— AND A GOOD PART OF THE TOWN ALONG WITH THEM.
パカ
WHAT!? THE TOWN TOO!?
YEAH. IT TOOK A BIG BITE OUT OF THE COAST OF THE BALTIC SEA.

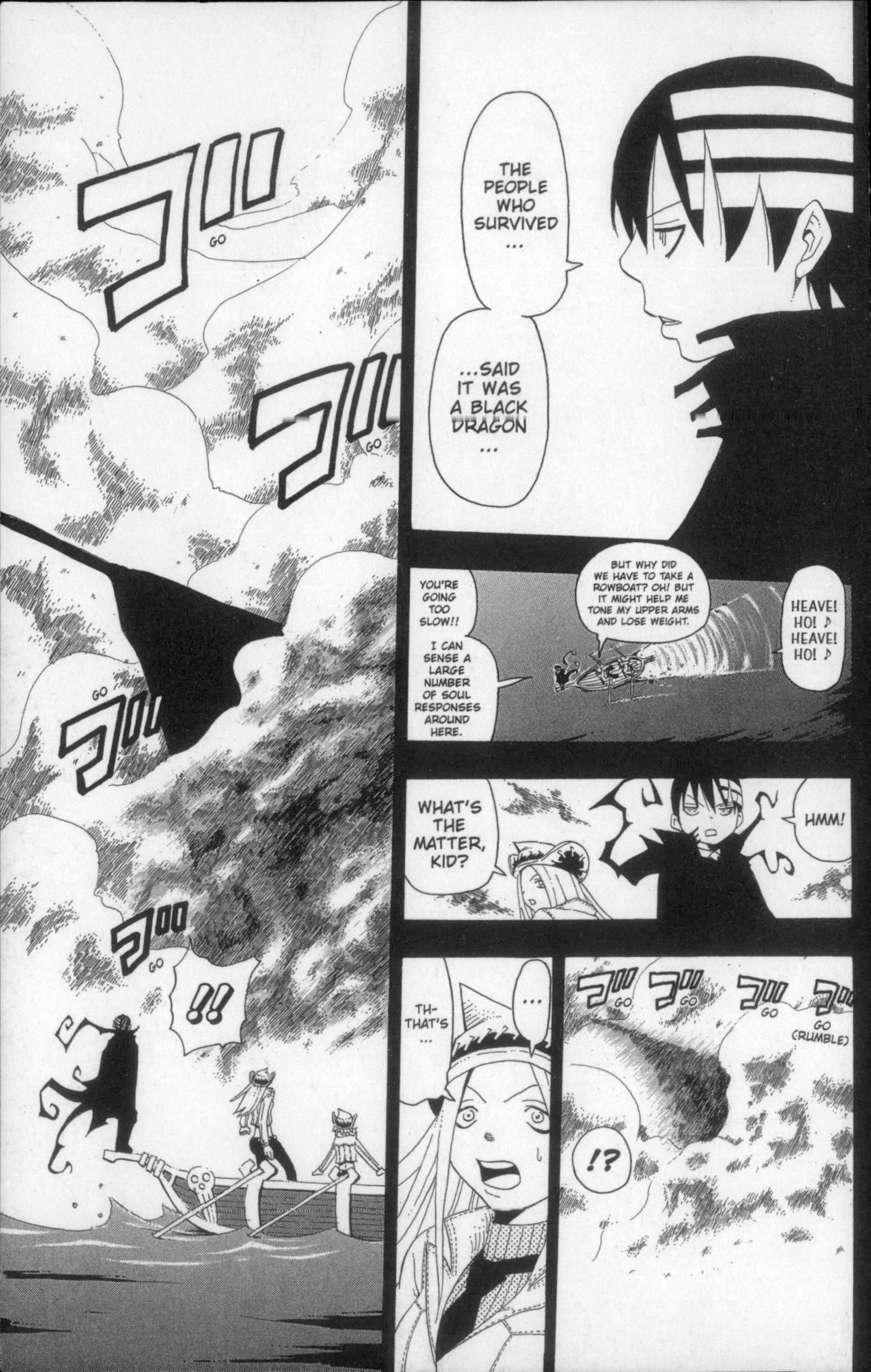
THE PEOPLE WHO SURVIVED ...
...SAID IT WAS A BLACK DRAGON ...
HEAVE! HO! ♪ HEAVE! HO! ♪
BUT WHY DID WE HAVE TO TAKE A ROWBOAT? OH! BUT IT MIGHT HELP ME TONE MY UPPER ARMS AND LOSE WEIGHT.
YOU'RE GOING TOO SLOW!!
I CAN SENSE A LARGE NUMBER OF SOUL RESPONSES AROUND HERE.
HMM!
WHAT'S THE MATTER, KID?
ゴゴ GO
ゴゴ GO
ゴゴ GO
ゴゴ GO (RUMBLE)
!?
...
TH-THAT'S ...
ゴゴ GO
ゴゴ GO
GO ゴゴ
ゴゴ GO
!!

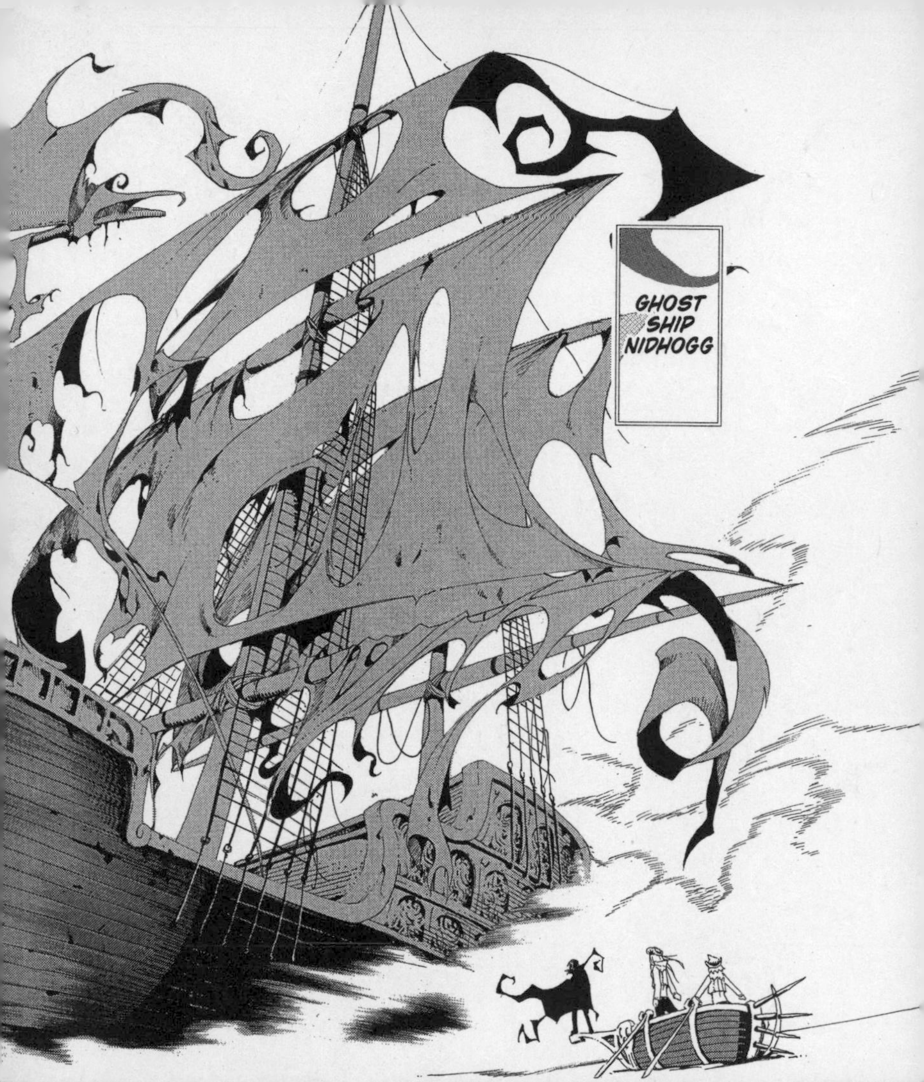
GHOST SHIP NIDHOGG

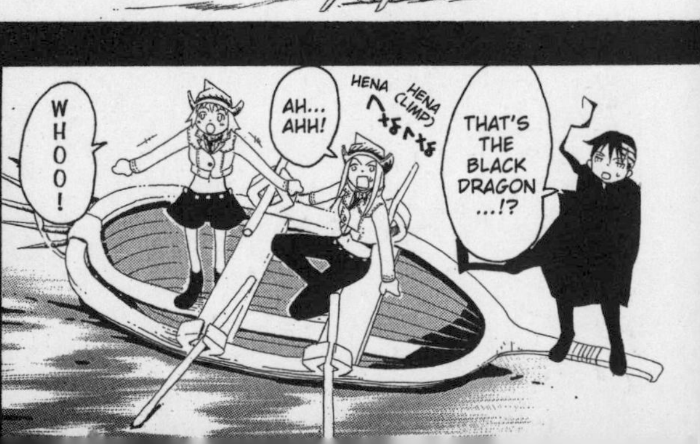
THAT'S THE BLACK DRAGON ...!?
HENA HENA (LIMP)
AH... AHH!
WHOO!

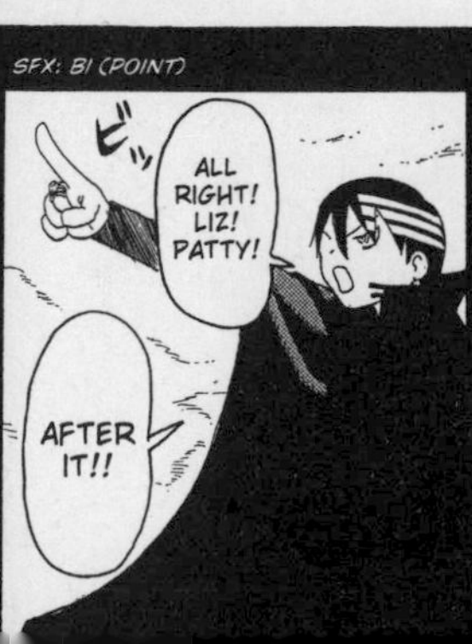
SFX: BI (POINT)
ALL RIGHT! LIZ! PATTY!
AFTER IT!!

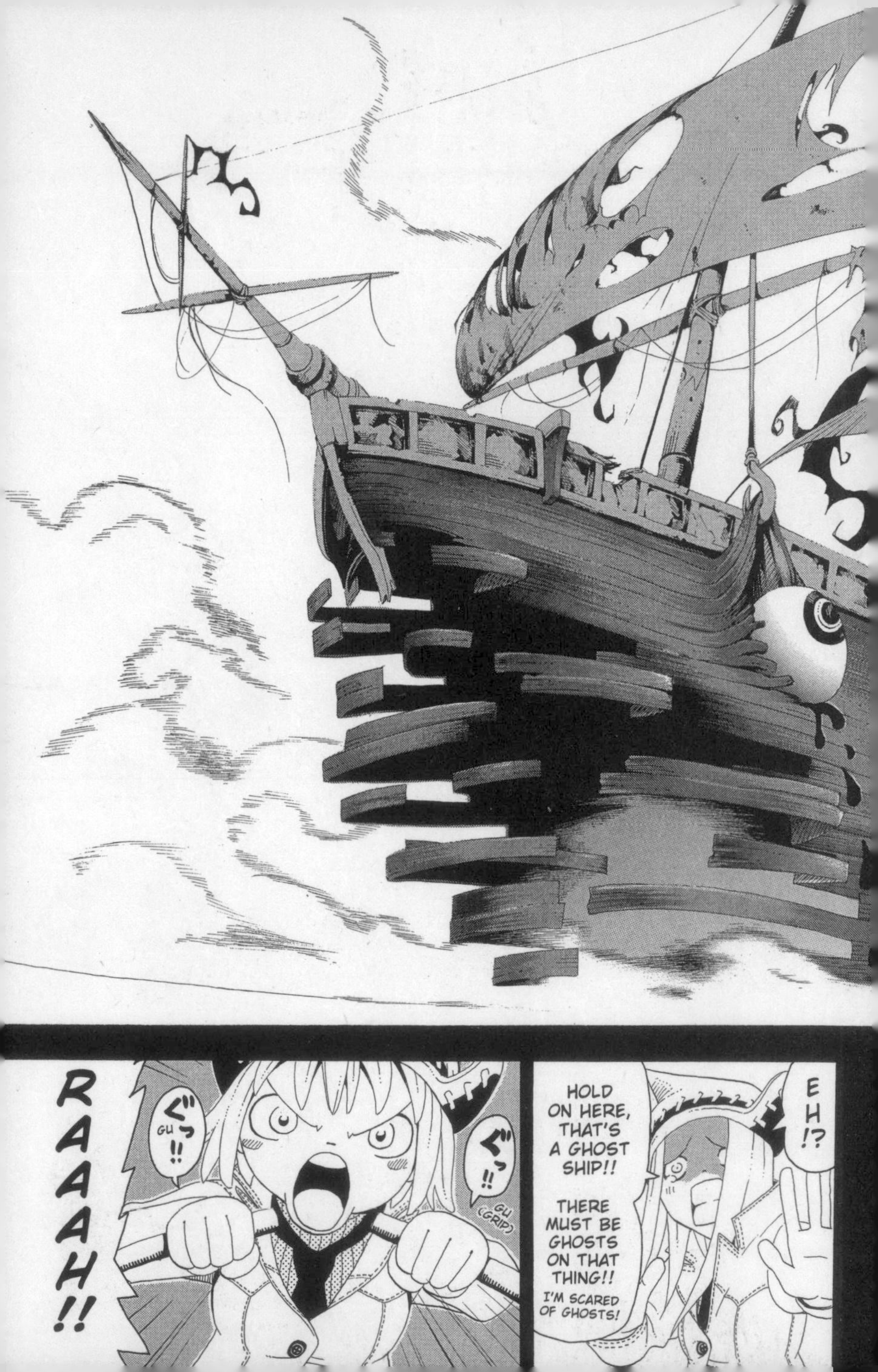
EH!?
HOLD ON HERE, THAT'S A GHOST SHIP!!
THERE MUST BE GHOSTS ON THAT THING!!
I'M SCARED OF GHOSTS!
ぐっ!!
GU (GRIP)
ぐっ GU!!
RAAAAH!!

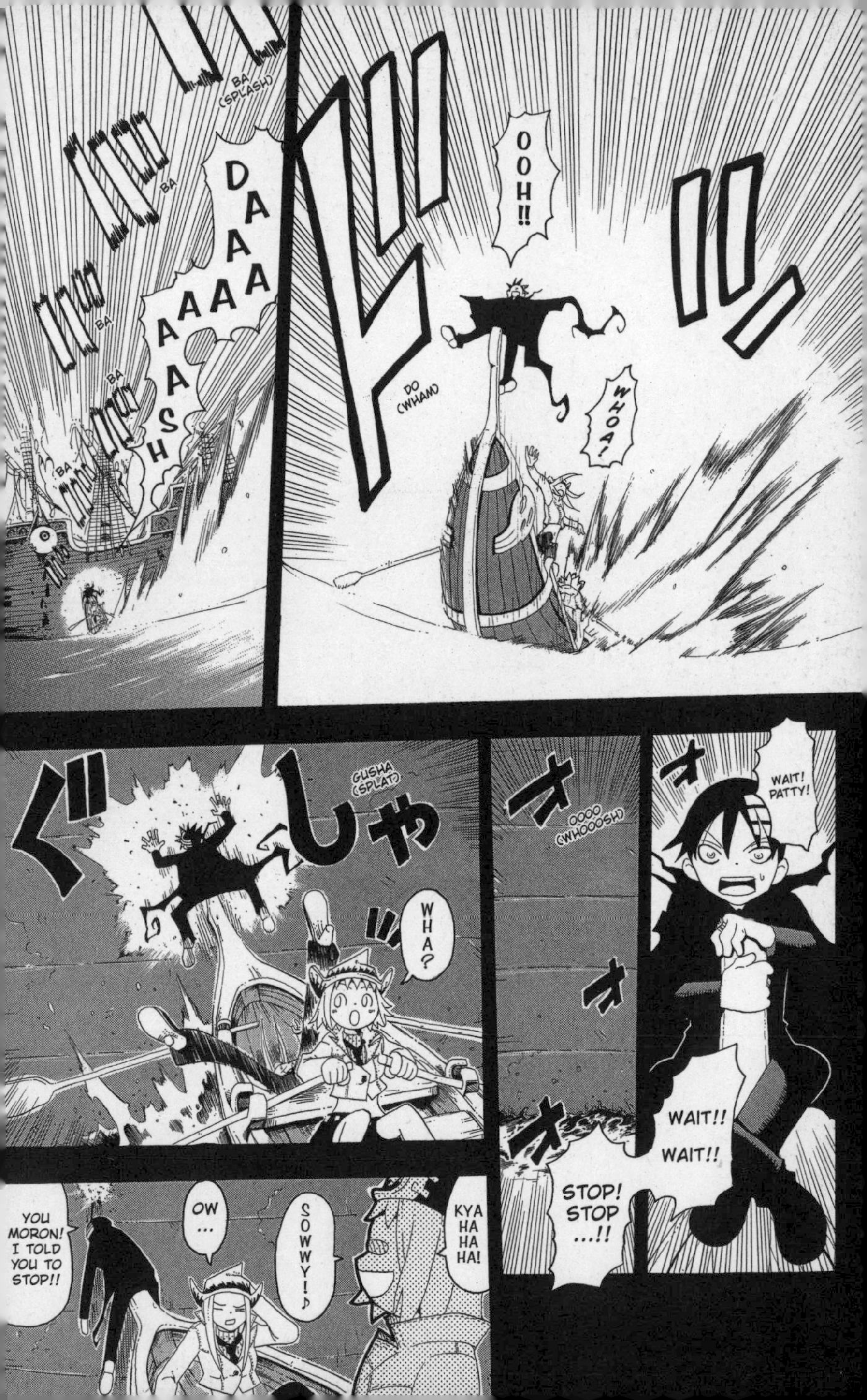
OOH!!
WHOA!
DO (WHAM)
BA (SPLASH)
BA
DAAAAAAASH
BA
BA
BA
WAIT! PATTY!
WAIT!!
WAIT!!
STOP! STOP ...!!
OOOO (WHOOOSH)
GUSHA (SPLAT)
WHA?
KYA HA HA HA!
SOWWY!♪
OW ...
YOU MORON! I TOLD YOU TO STOP!!

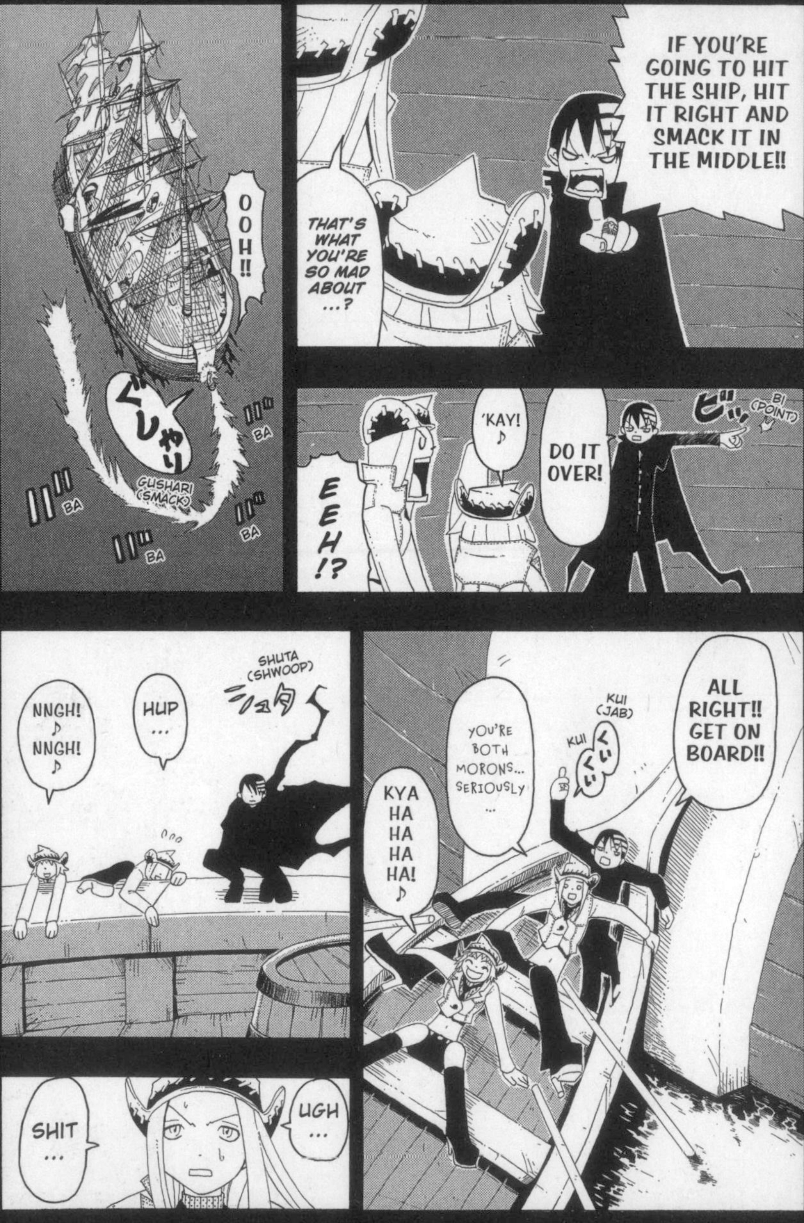

IF YOU'RE GOING TO HIT THE SHIP, HIT IT RIGHT AND SMACK IT IN THE MIDDLE!!
THAT'S WHAT YOU'RE SO MAD ABOUT ...?
BI (POINT)
DO IT OVER!
'KAY! ♪
EEEH!?
OOOH!!
GUSHARI (SMACK)
BA
BA
BA
BA
ALL RIGHT!! GET ON BOARD!!
KUI (JAB)
KUI
YOU'RE BOTH MORONS... SERIOUSLY ...
KYA HA HA HA HA! ♪
SHUTA (SHWOOP)
HUP ...
NNGH! ♪ NNGH! ♪
UGH ...
SHIT ...

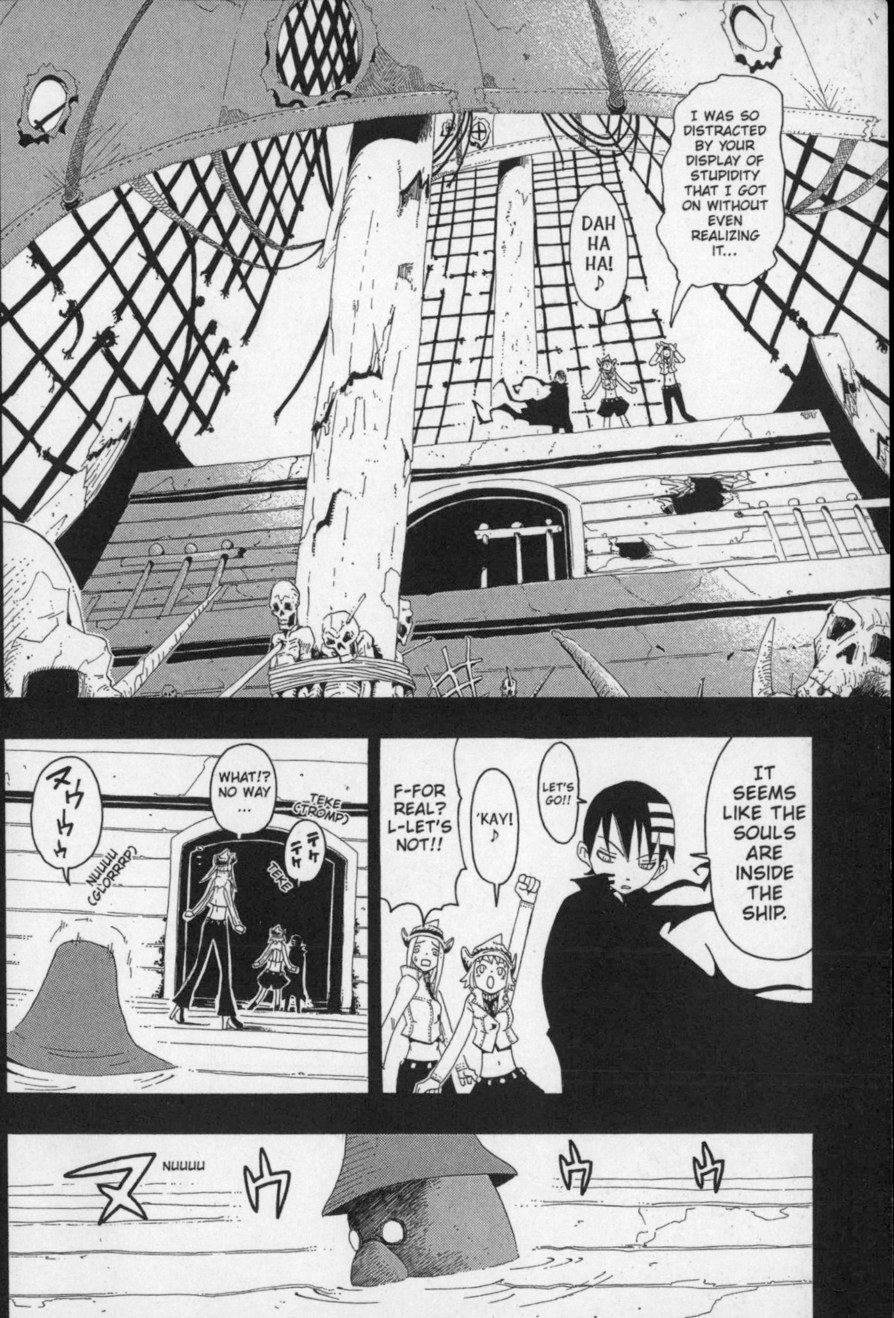

I WAS SO DISTRACTED BY YOUR DISPLAY OF STUPIDITY THAT I GOT ON WITHOUT EVEN REALIZING IT...
DAH HA HA! ♪
IT SEEMS LIKE THE SOULS ARE INSIDE THE SHIP.
LET'S GO!!
'KAY! ♪
F-FOR REAL? L-LET'S NOT!!
WHAT!? NO WAY ...
TEKE (TROMP)
TEKE
NUUUU (GLORRRP)
NUUUU

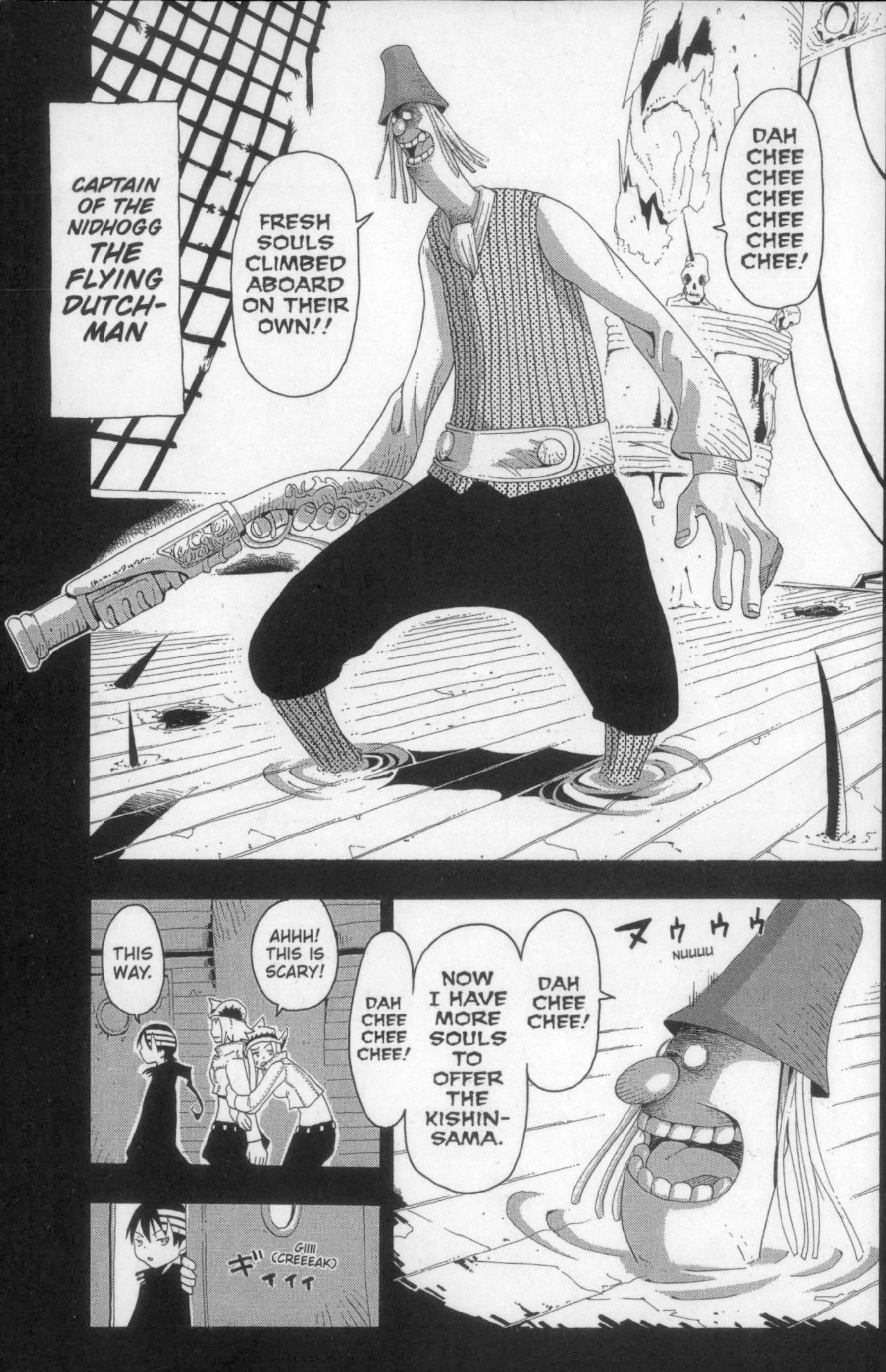
DAH CHEE CHEE CHEE CHEE CHEE CHEE!
FRESH SOULS CLIMBED ABOARD ON THEIR OWN!!
CAPTAIN OF THE NIDHOGG THE FLYING DUTCH-MAN
ヌウウウ
NUUUU
DAH CHEE CHEE!
NOW I HAVE MORE SOULS TO OFFER THE KISHIN-SAMA.
DAH CHEE CHEE CHEE!
AHHH! THIS IS SCARY!
THIS WAY.
ギィィィ
GIIII (CREEEAK)

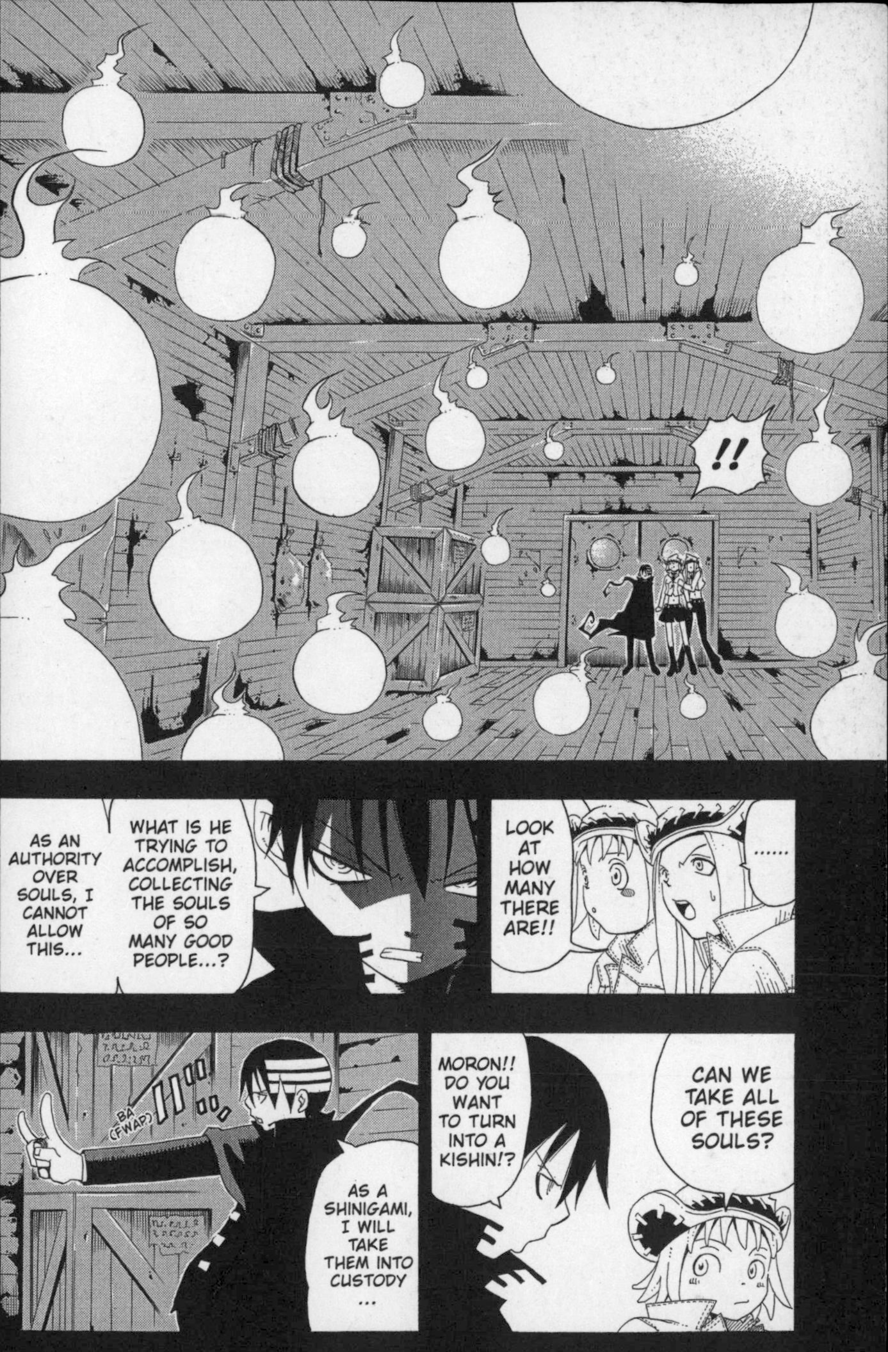
!!
......
LOOK AT HOW MANY THERE ARE!!
WHAT IS HE TRYING TO ACCOMPLISH, COLLECTING THE SOULS OF SO MANY GOOD PEOPLE...?
AS AN AUTHORITY OVER SOULS, I CANNOT ALLOW THIS...
CAN WE TAKE ALL OF THESE SOULS?
MORON!! DO YOU WANT TO TURN INTO A KISHIN!?
AS A SHINIGAMI, I WILL TAKE THEM INTO CUSTODY ...
BA (FWAP)

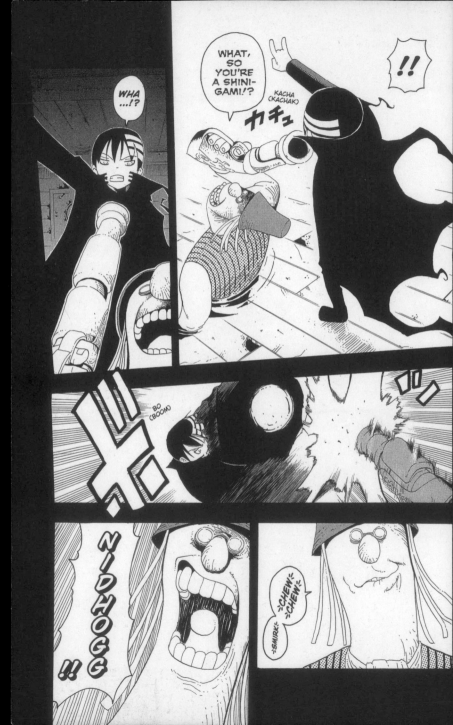

WHA...!?

WHAT, SO YOU'RE A SHINIGAMI!?

KACHA (KACHAK)

カチュ

!!

BO (BOOM)

NIDHOGG

!!

~CHEW~
~CHEW~

~SMIRK~

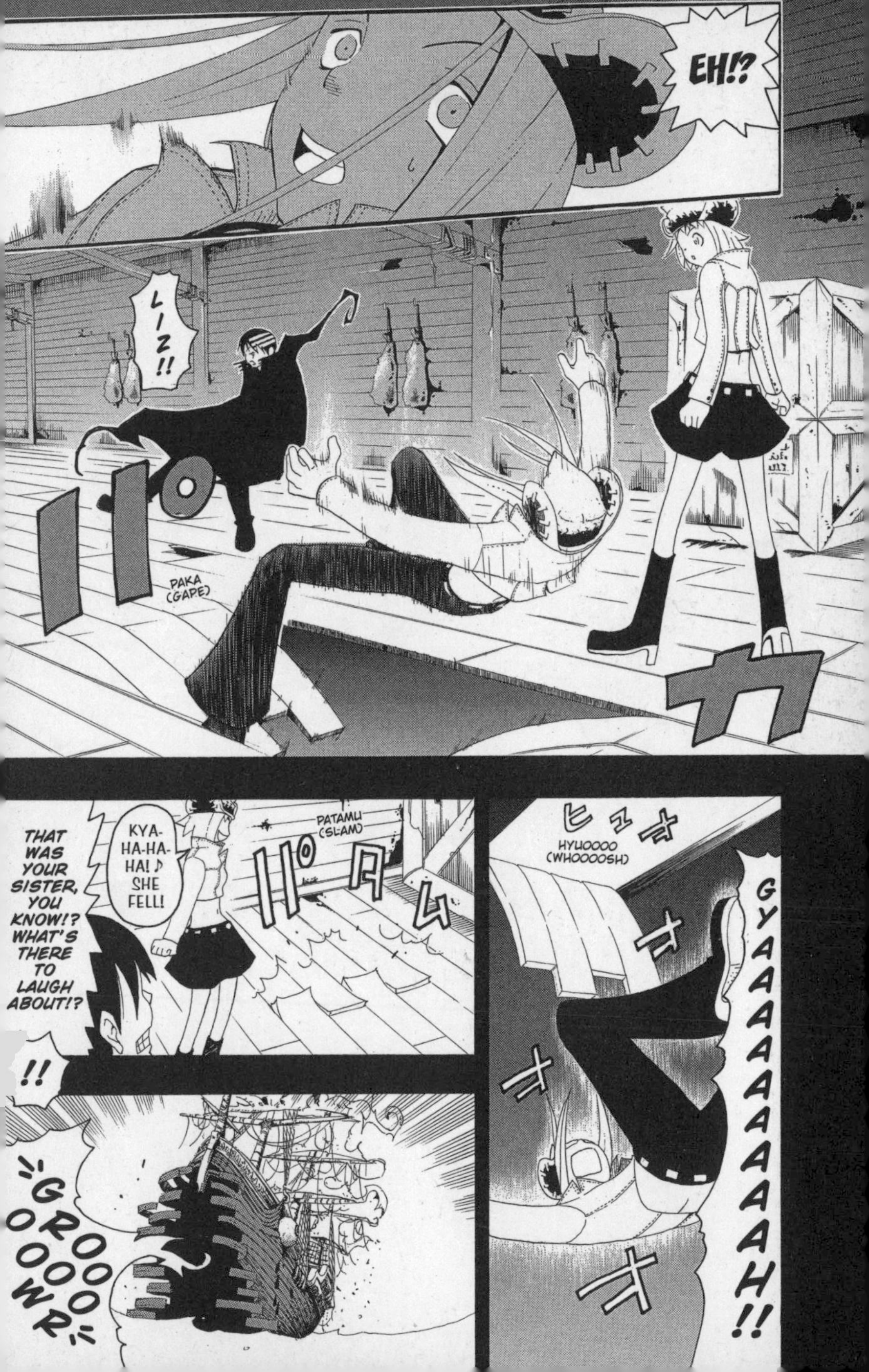
EH!?
LIZ!!
パカ
PAKA (GAPE)
ヒュオ
HYUOOO (WHOOOOSH)
GYAAAAAAAAAAH!!
パタム
PATAMU (SLAM)
KYA-HA-HA-HA! ♪ SHE FELL!
THAT WAS YOUR SISTER, YOU KNOW!? WHAT'S THERE TO LAUGH ABOUT!?
!!
GROOOOOOWR

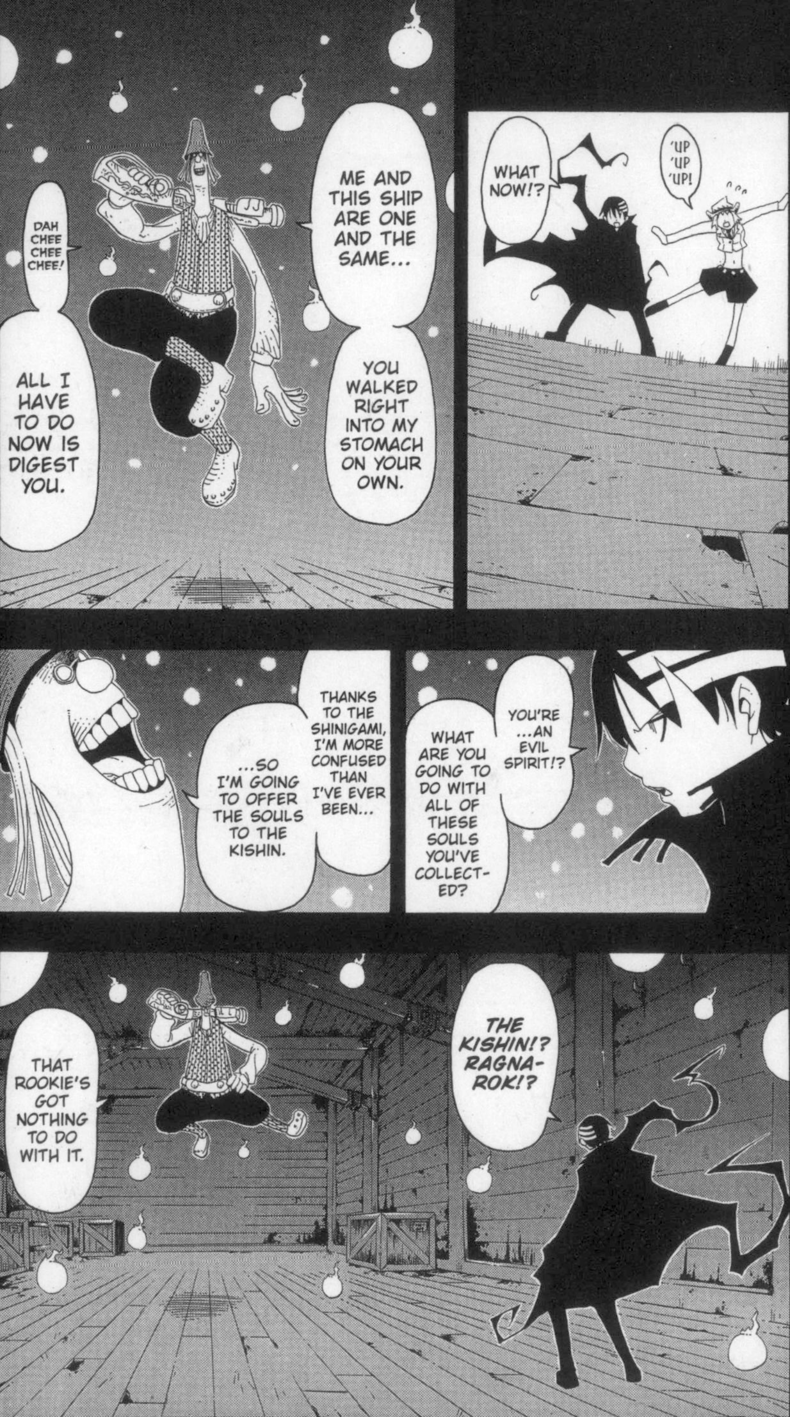
'UP 'UP 'UP!
WHAT NOW!?
ME AND THIS SHIP ARE ONE AND THE SAME...
YOU WALKED RIGHT INTO MY STOMACH ON YOUR OWN.
DAH CHEE CHEE CHEE!
ALL I HAVE TO DO NOW IS DIGEST YOU.
YOU'RE ...AN EVIL SPIRIT!?
WHAT ARE YOU GOING TO DO WITH ALL OF THESE SOULS YOU'VE COLLECTED?
THANKS TO THE SHINIGAMI, I'M MORE CONFUSED THAN I'VE EVER BEEN...
...SO I'M GOING TO OFFER THE SOULS TO THE KISHIN.
THE KISHIN!? RAGNAROK!?
THAT ROOKIE'S GOT NOTHING TO DO WITH IT.

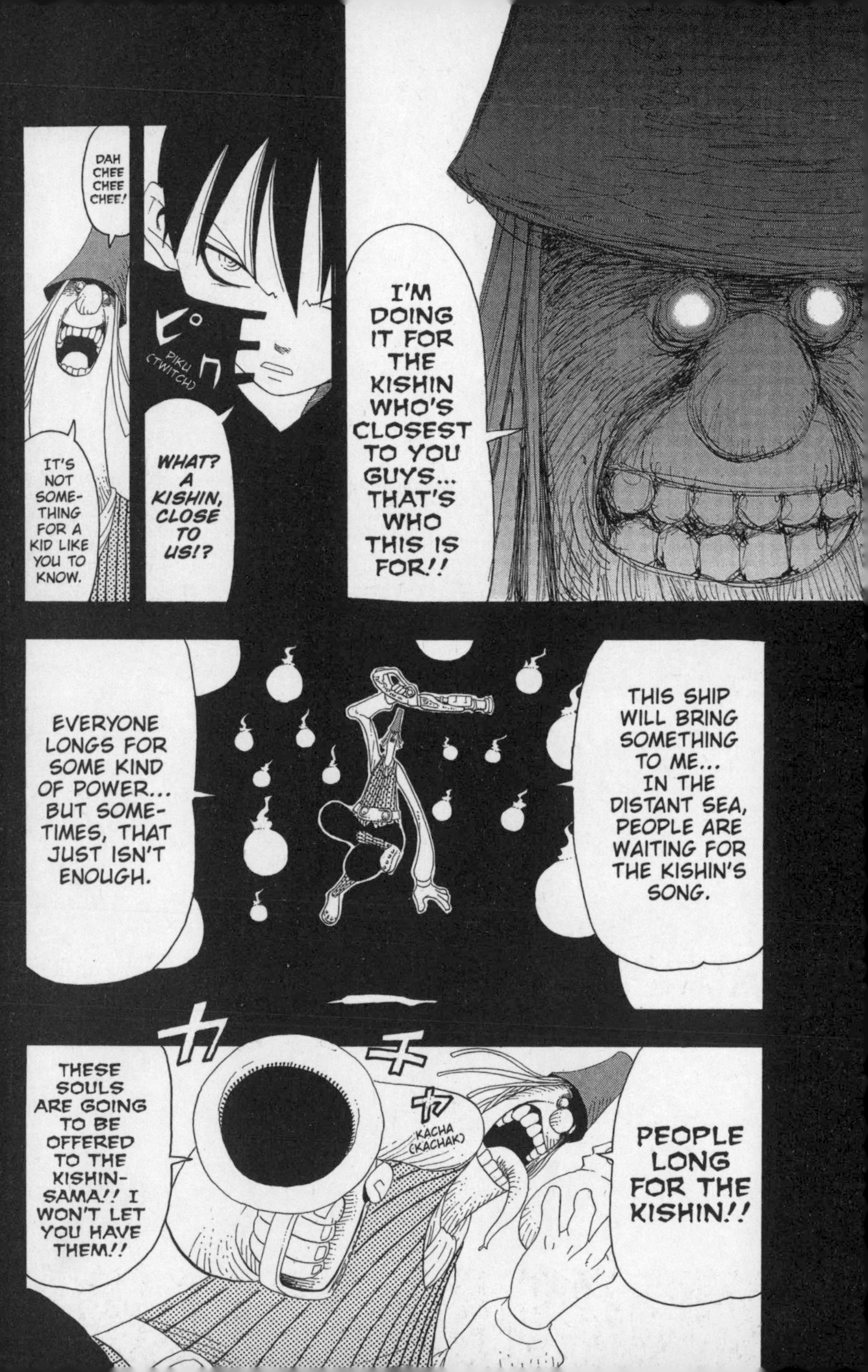
I'M DOING IT FOR THE KISHIN WHO'S CLOSEST TO YOU GUYS... THAT'S WHO THIS IS FOR!!
PIKU (TWITCH)
WHAT? A KISHIN, CLOSE TO US!?
DAH CHEE CHEE CHEE!
IT'S NOT SOMETHING FOR A KID LIKE YOU TO KNOW.
THIS SHIP WILL BRING SOMETHING TO ME... IN THE DISTANT SEA, PEOPLE ARE WAITING FOR THE KISHIN'S SONG.
EVERYONE LONGS FOR SOME KIND OF POWER... BUT SOMETIMES, THAT JUST ISN'T ENOUGH.
PEOPLE LONG FOR THE KISHIN!!
KACHA (KACHAK)
THESE SOULS ARE GOING TO BE OFFERED TO THE KISHIN-SAMA!! I WON'T LET YOU HAVE THEM!!

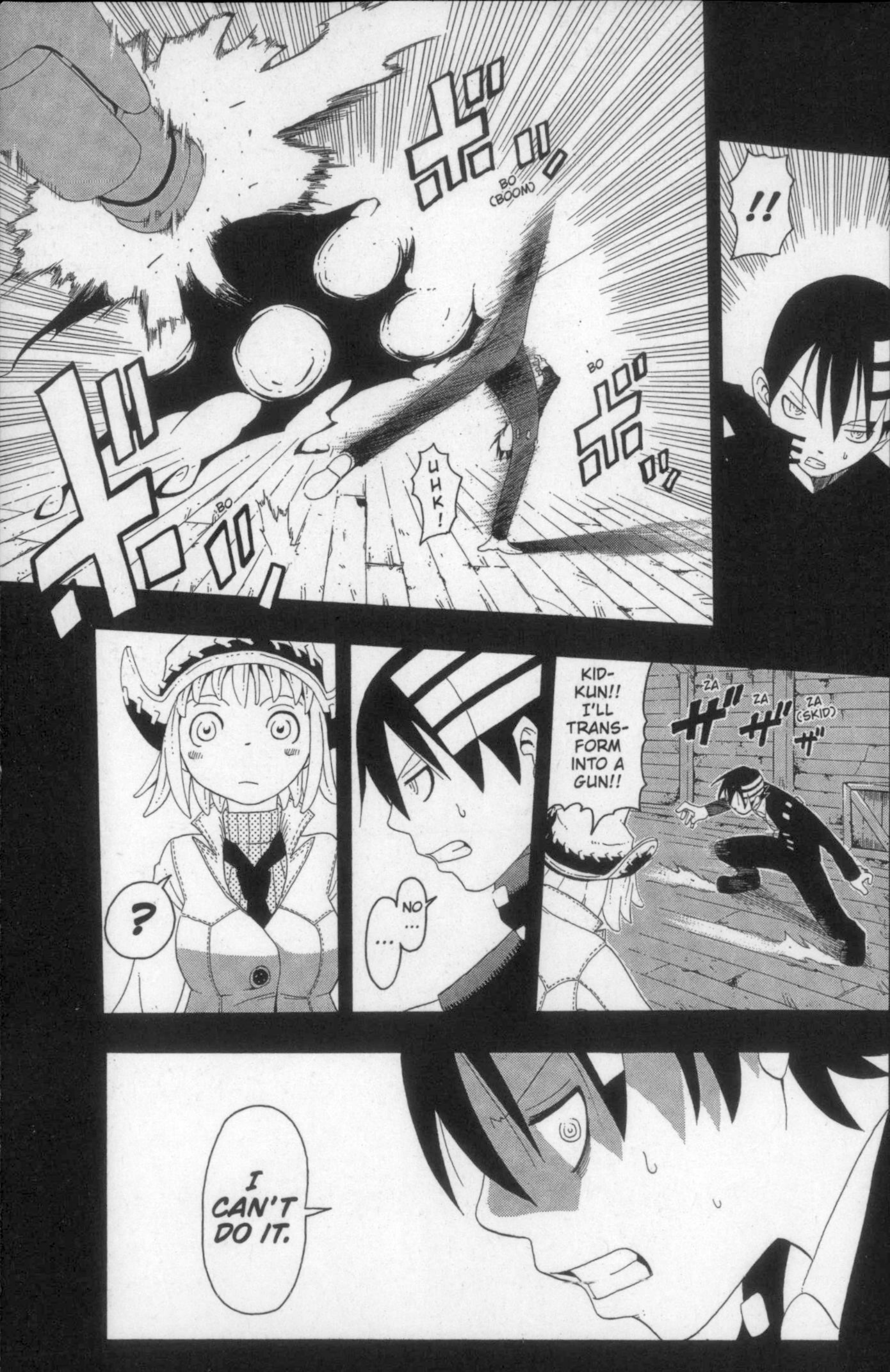

!!
BO (BOOM)
BO
UHK!
BO
KID-KUN!! I'LL TRANSFORM INTO A GUN!!
ZA
ZA
ZA (SKID)
NO... ...
?
I CAN'T DO IT.

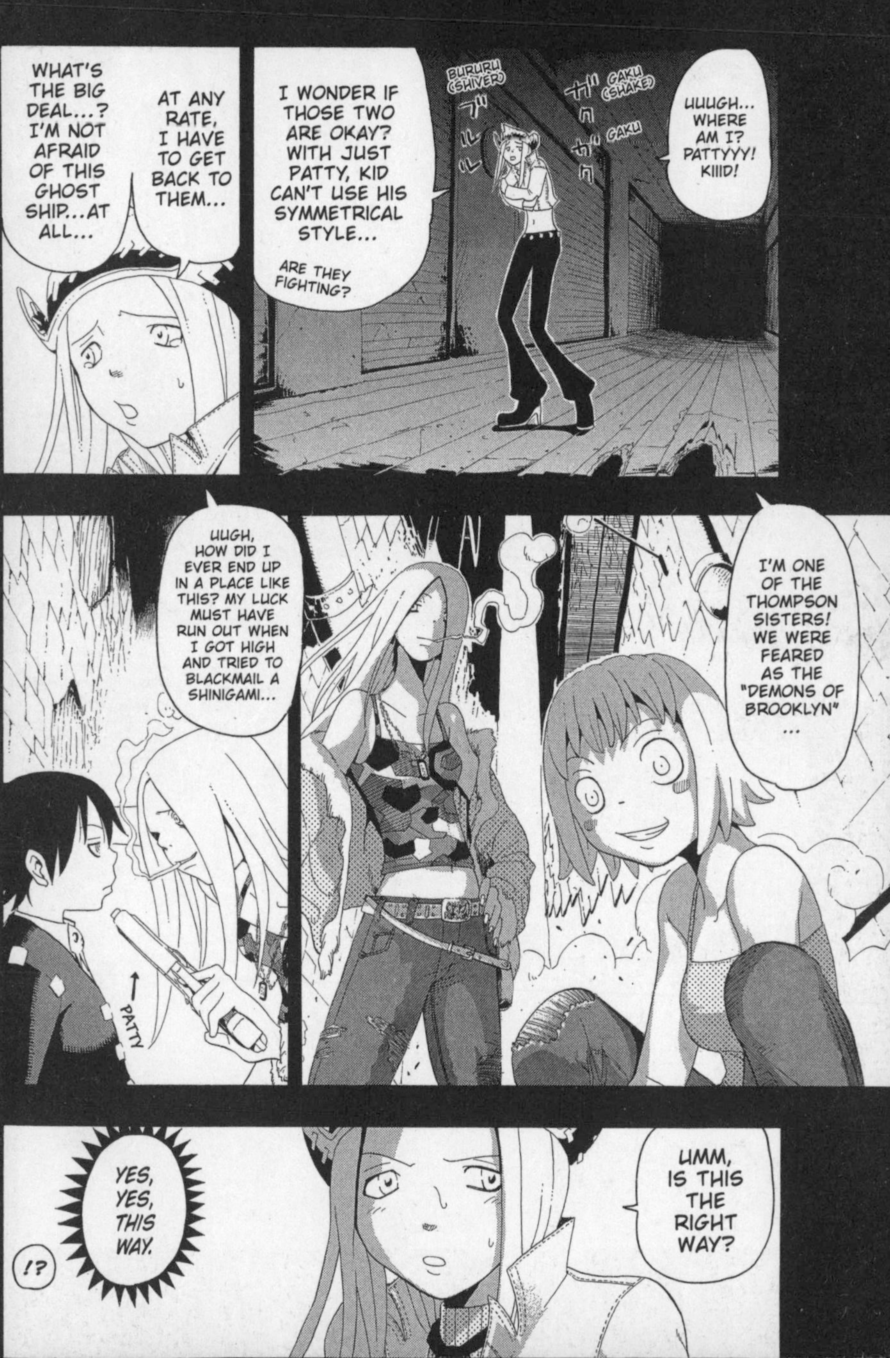
BURURU (SHIVER)
GAKU (SHAKE)
GAKU
UUUGH... WHERE AM I? PATTYYY! KIIID!
I WONDER IF THOSE TWO ARE OKAY? WITH JUST PATTY, KID CAN'T USE HIS SYMMETRICAL STYLE...
ARE THEY FIGHTING?
AT ANY RATE, I HAVE TO GET BACK TO THEM...
WHAT'S THE BIG DEAL...? I'M NOT AFRAID OF THIS GHOST SHIP...AT ALL...
I'M ONE OF THE THOMPSON SISTERS! WE WERE FEARED AS THE "DEMONS OF BROOKLYN"...
UUGH, HOW DID I EVER END UP IN A PLACE LIKE THIS? MY LUCK MUST HAVE RUN OUT WHEN I GOT HIGH AND TRIED TO BLACKMAIL A SHINIGAMI...
PATTY
UMM, IS THIS THE RIGHT WAY?
YES, YES, THIS WAY.
!?

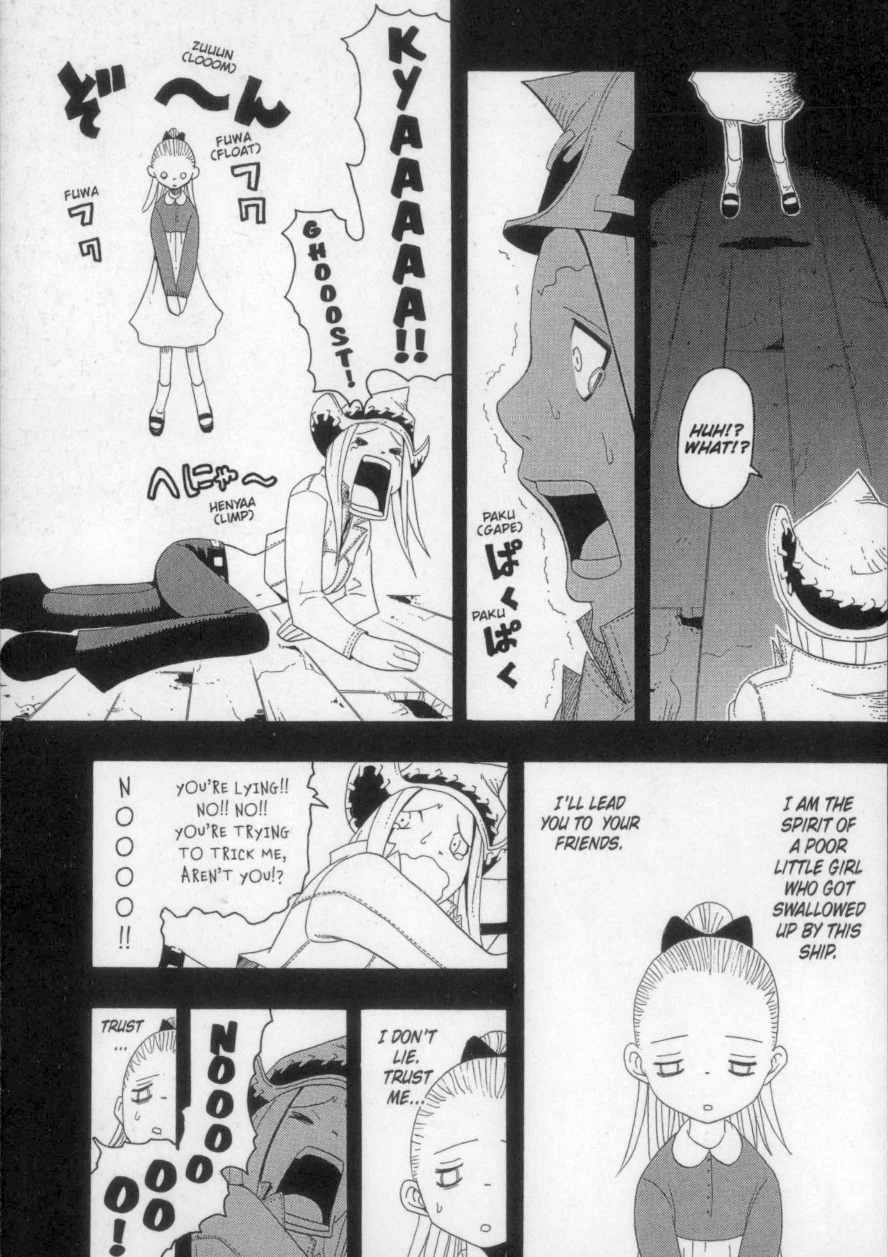
HUH!? WHAT!?
PAKU (GAPE) ぱく
PAKU ぱく
KYAAAAA!!
GHOOOST!
ZUUUN (LOOOM) ぞ〜ん
FUWA (FLOAT) フワ
FUWA フワ
へにゃ〜 HENYAA (LIMP)
I AM THE SPIRIT OF A POOR LITTLE GIRL WHO GOT SWALLOWED UP BY THIS SHIP.
I'LL LEAD YOU TO YOUR FRIENDS.
YOU'RE LYING!! NO!! NO!! YOU'RE TRYING TO TRICK ME, AREN'T YOU!?
NOOOOO!!
I DON'T LIE. TRUST ME...
NOOOOOOOO!
TRUST ...

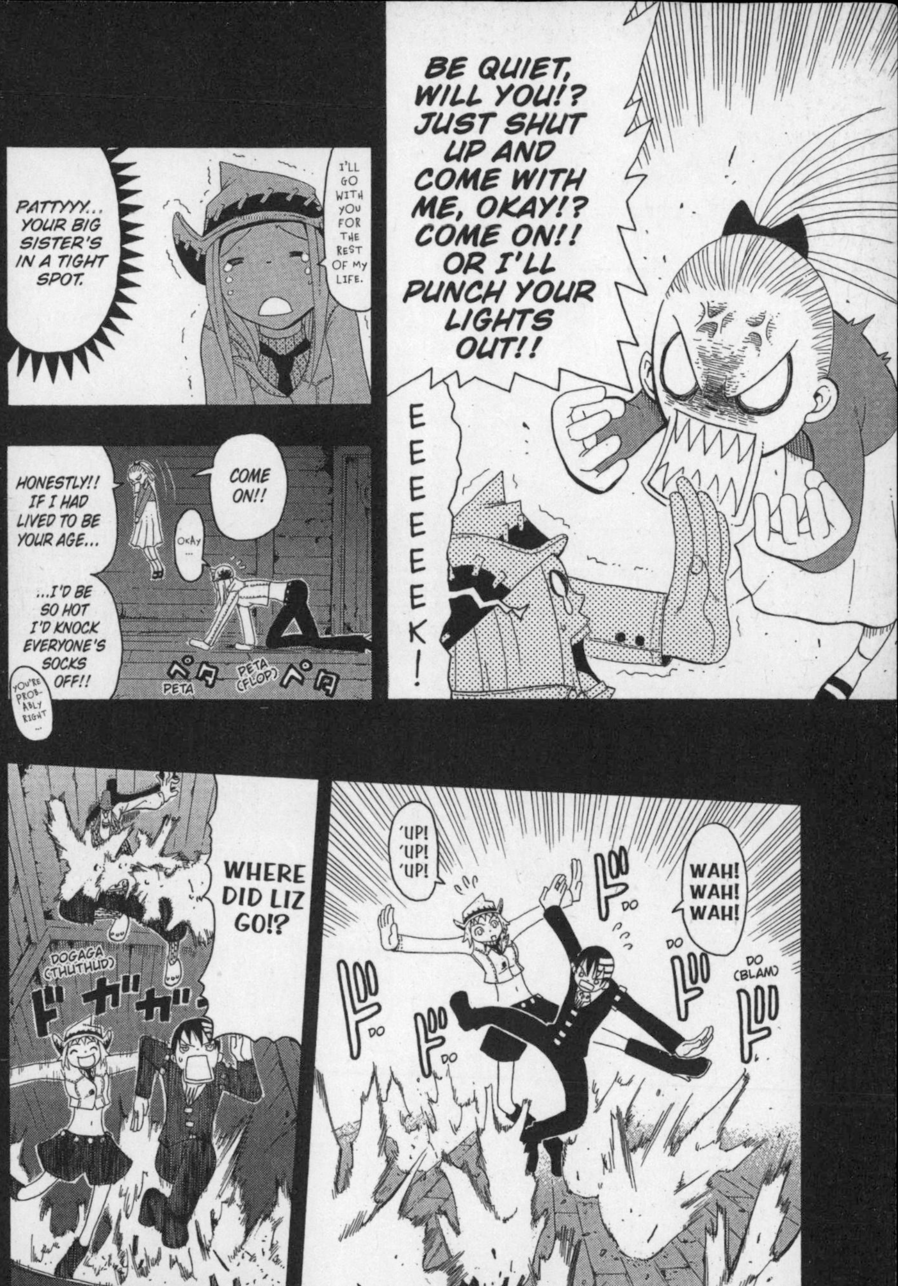

BE QUIET, WILL YOU!? JUST SHUT UP AND COME WITH ME, OKAY!? COME ON!! OR I'LL PUNCH YOUR LIGHTS OUT!!
EEEEEEEEK!
I'LL GO WITH YOU FOR THE REST OF MY LIFE.
PATTYYY... YOUR BIG SISTER'S IN A TIGHT SPOT.
COME ON!!
HONESTLY!! IF I HAD LIVED TO BE YOUR AGE...
OKAY...
...I'D BE SO HOT I'D KNOCK EVERYONE'S SOCKS OFF!!
PETA
PETA (FLOP)
YOU'RE PROBABLY RIGHT...
WAH! WAH! WAH!
'UP! 'UP! 'UP!
DO
DO
DO (BLAM)
DO
DO
WHERE DID LIZ GO!?
DOGAGA (THUTHUD)

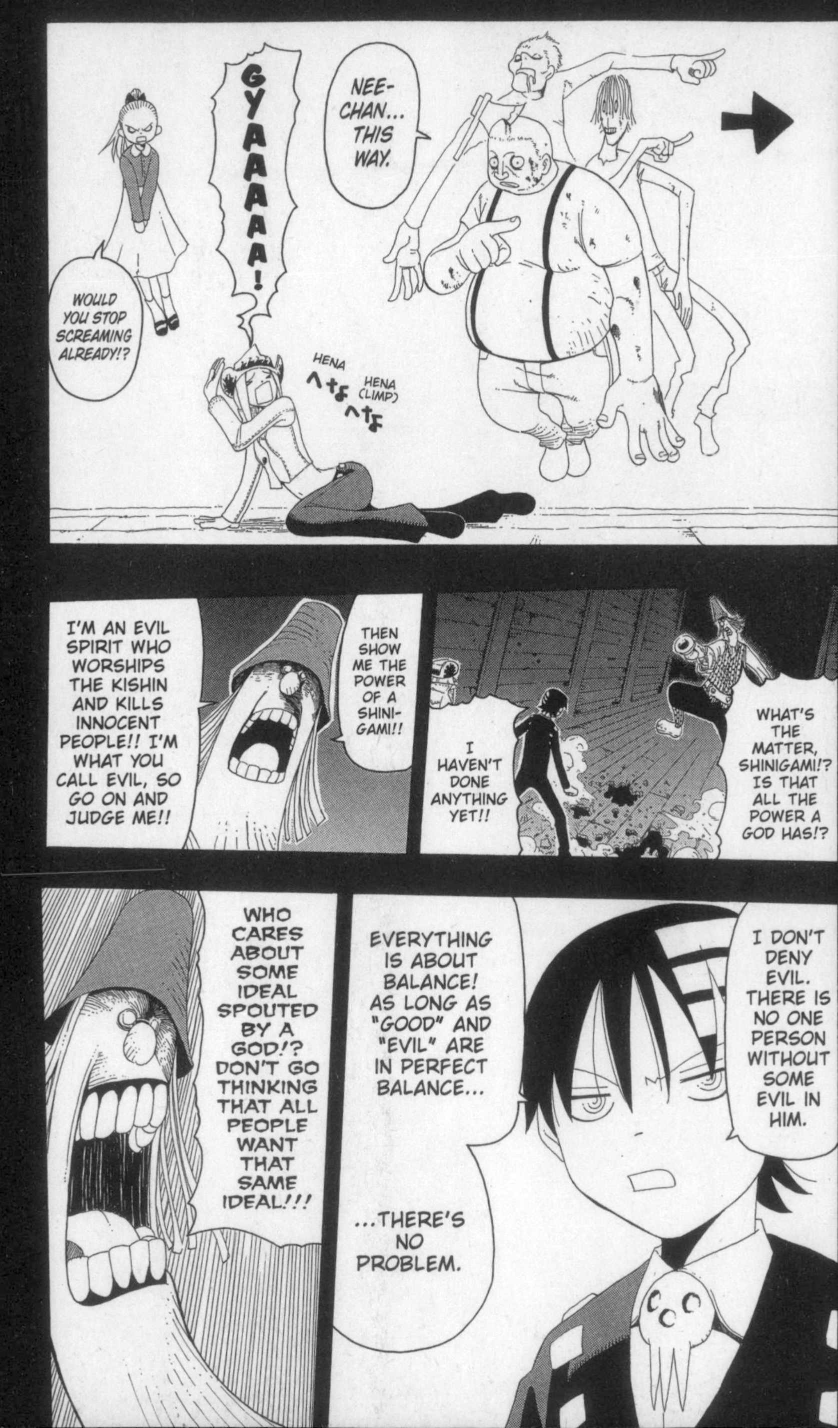
NEE-CHAN... THIS WAY.
GYAAAAAA!
WOULD YOU STOP SCREAMING ALREADY!?
へなへな
HENA HENA (LIMP)
WHAT'S THE MATTER, SHINIGAMI!? IS THAT ALL THE POWER A GOD HAS!?
I HAVEN'T DONE ANYTHING YET!!
THEN SHOW ME THE POWER OF A SHINIGAMI!!
I'M AN EVIL SPIRIT WHO WORSHIPS THE KISHIN AND KILLS INNOCENT PEOPLE!! I'M WHAT YOU CALL EVIL, SO GO ON AND JUDGE ME!!
I DON'T DENY EVIL. THERE IS NO ONE PERSON WITHOUT SOME EVIL IN HIM.
EVERYTHING IS ABOUT BALANCE! AS LONG AS "GOOD" AND "EVIL" ARE IN PERFECT BALANCE...
...THERE'S NO PROBLEM.
WHO CARES ABOUT SOME IDEAL SPOUTED BY A GOD!? DON'T GO THINKING THAT ALL PEOPLE WANT THAT SAME IDEAL!!!

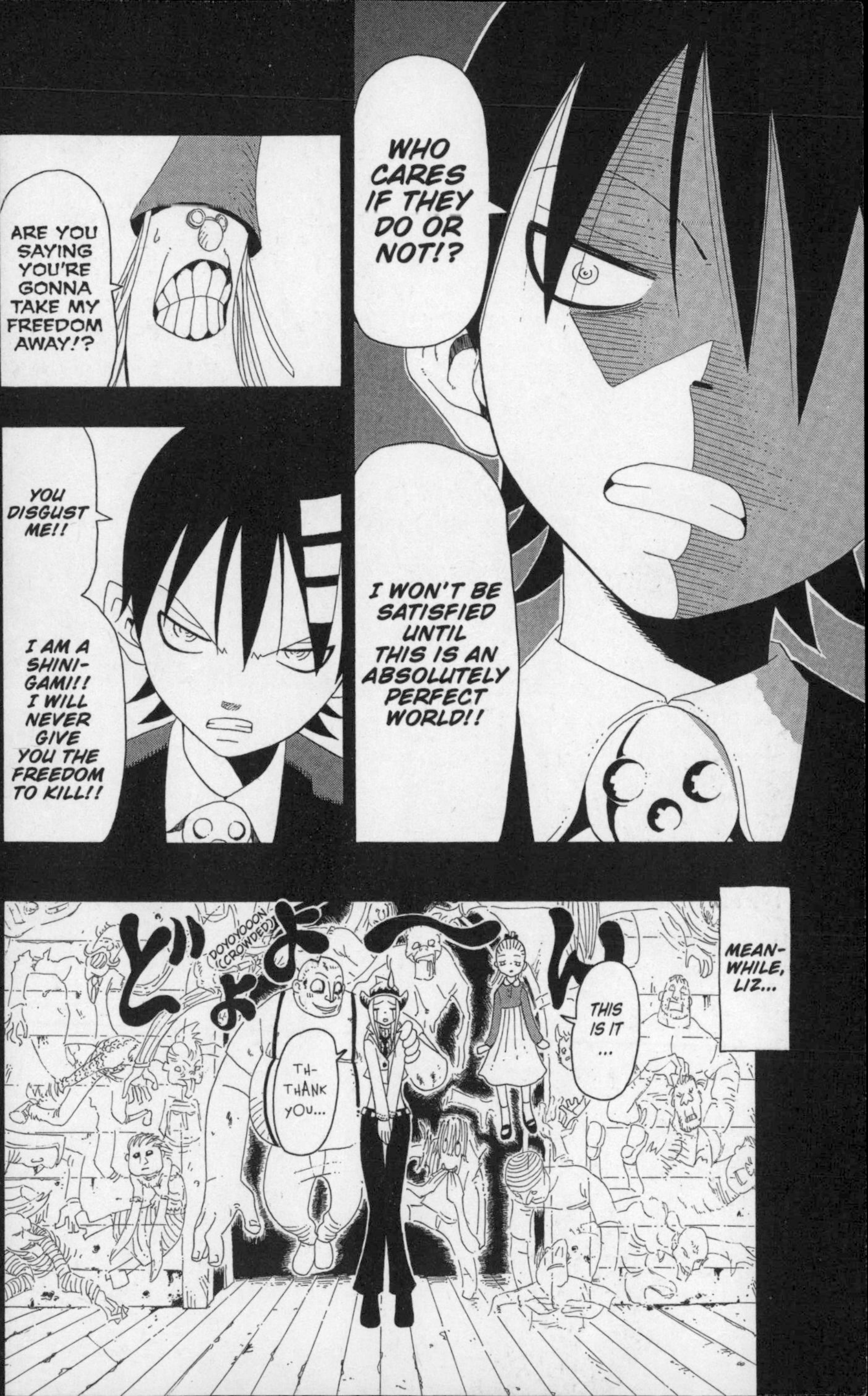
WHO CARES IF THEY DO OR NOT!?
I WON'T BE SATISFIED UNTIL THIS IS AN ABSOLUTELY PERFECT WORLD!!
ARE YOU SAYING YOU'RE GONNA TAKE MY FREEDOM AWAY!?
YOU DISGUST ME!!
I AM A SHINI-GAMI!! I WILL NEVER GIVE YOU THE FREEDOM TO KILL!!
MEAN-WHILE, LIZ...
どよ〜ん
DOYOYOOON (CROWDED)
THIS IS IT ...
TH-THANK YOU...

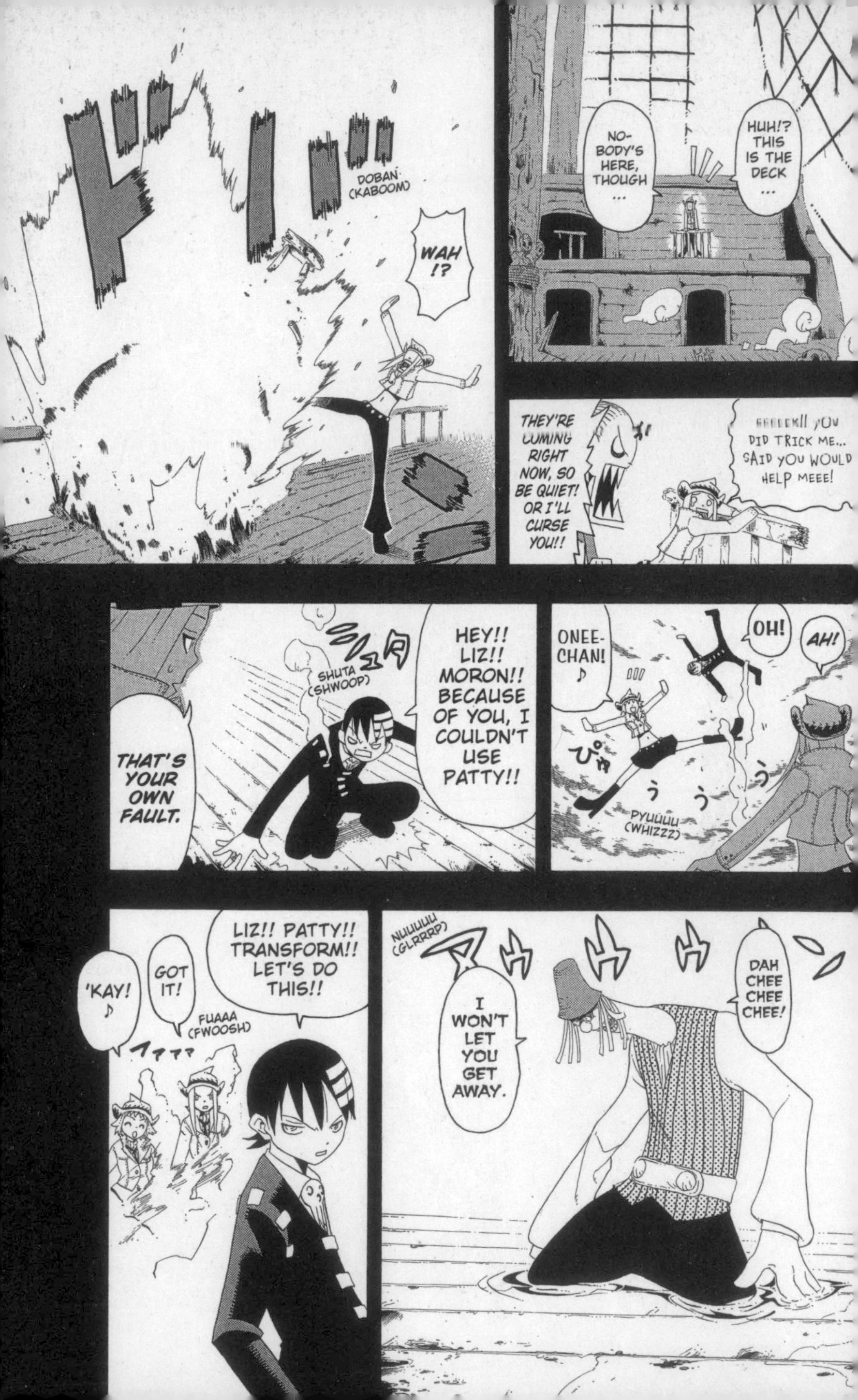
HUH!? THIS IS THE DECK...
NO-BODY'S HERE, THOUGH...
YOU DID TRICK ME... SAID YOU WOULD HELP MEEE!
THEY'RE COMING RIGHT NOW, SO BE QUIET! OR I'LL CURSE YOU!!
DOBAN (KABOOM)
WAH!?
OH!
AH!
ONEE-CHAN! ♪
PYUUUU (WHIZZZ)
HEY!! LIZ!! MORON!! BECAUSE OF YOU, I COULDN'T USE PATTY!!
SHUTA (SHWOOP)
THAT'S YOUR OWN FAULT.
DAH CHEE CHEE CHEE!
NUUUUU (GLRRRP)
I WON'T LET YOU GET AWAY.
LIZ!! PATTY!! TRANSFORM!! LET'S DO THIS!!
GOT IT!
'KAY! ♪
FUAAA (FWOOSH)

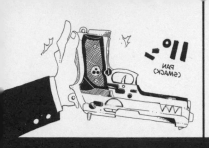

PAN
(SMACK)

PAN
(SMACK)

GASHIN
(GASHING)

(VWEEE)

DAH
CHEE
CHEE
CHEE
CHEE!

PRE-
PARE
YOUR-
SELF!

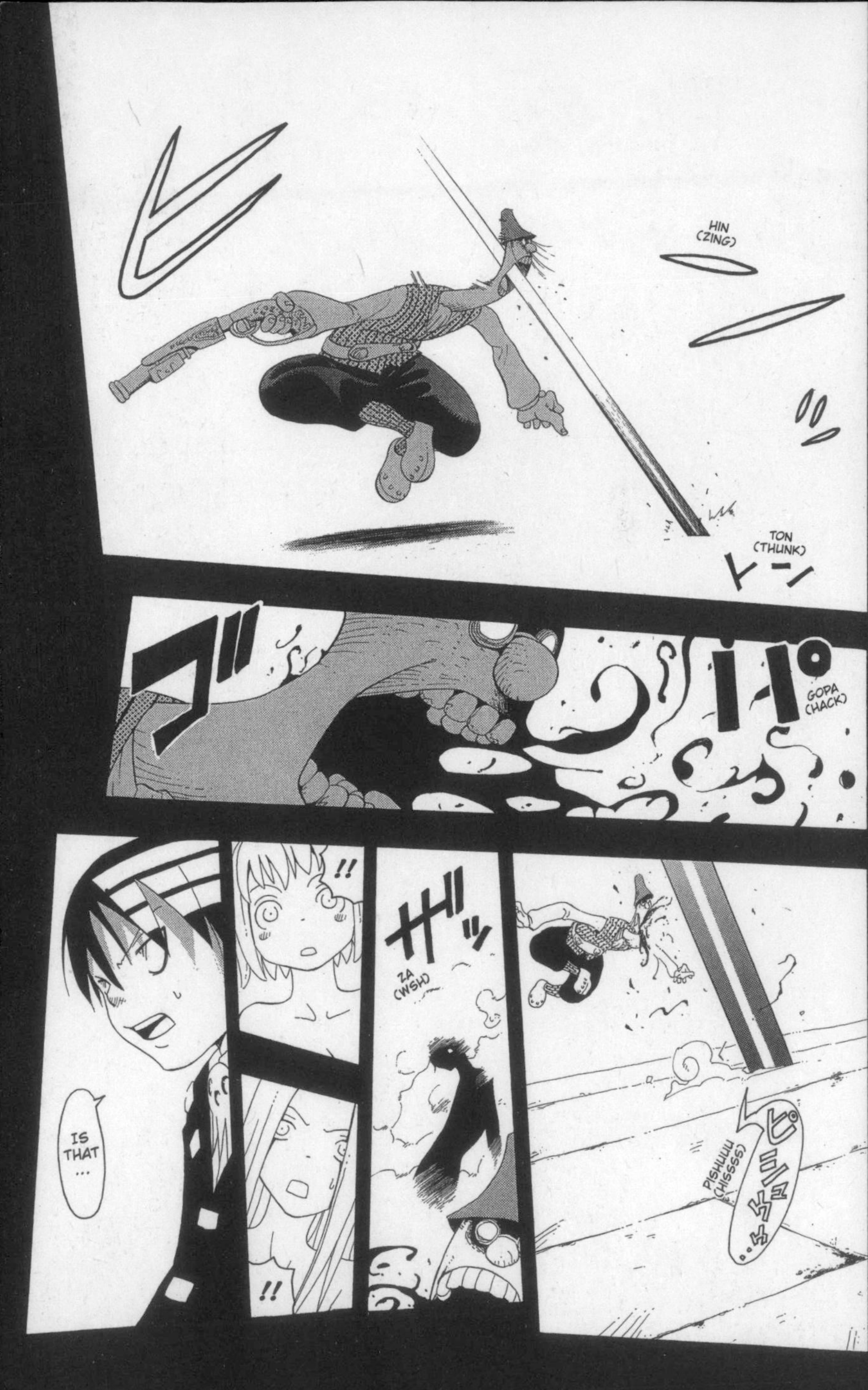
HIN (ZING)
TON (THUNK)
GOPA (HACK)
PISHUUU (CHISSSS)
ZA (WSH)
!!
!!
IS THAT ...

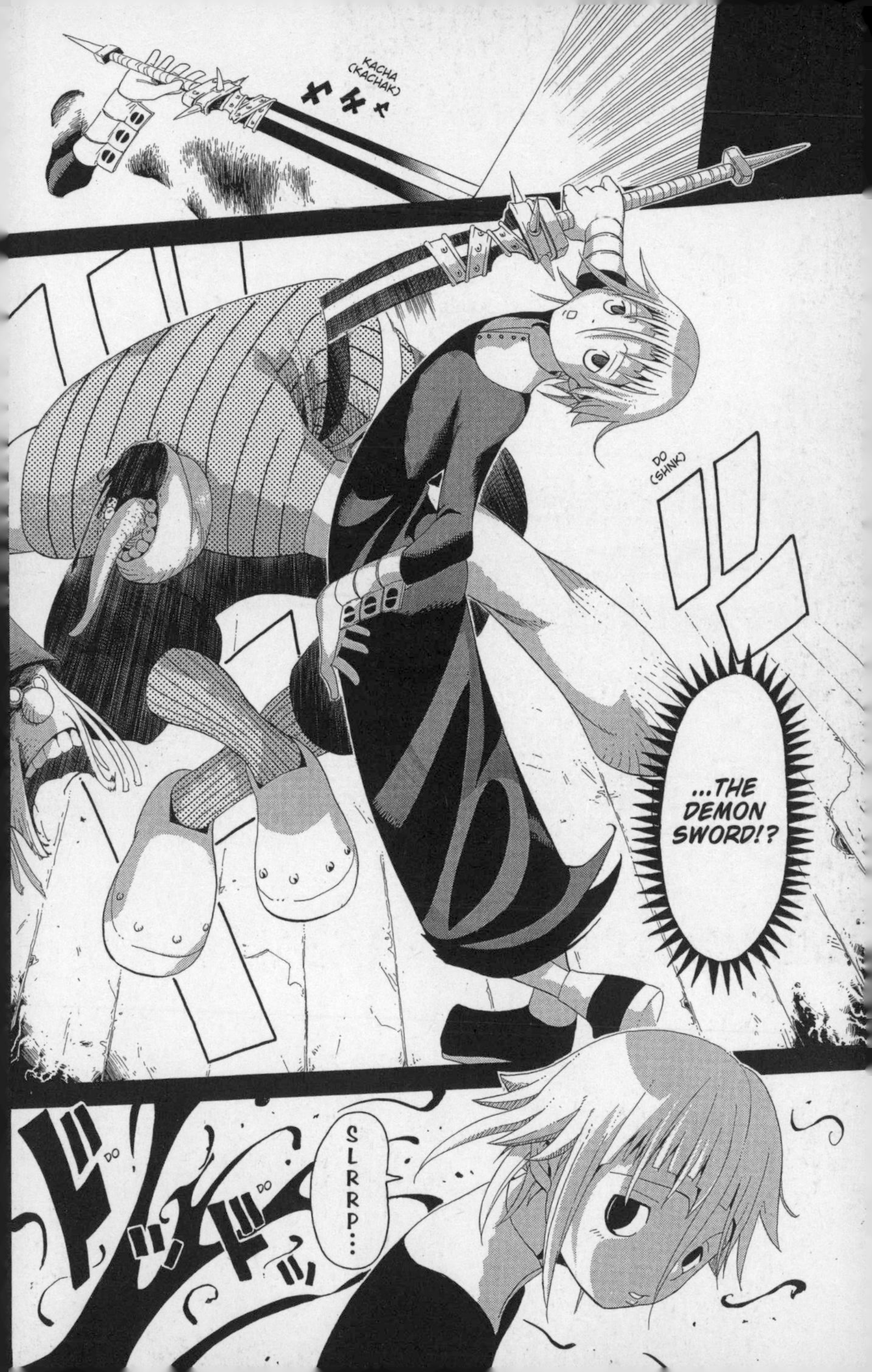
KACHA
(KACHAK)
DO
(SHNK)
...THE DEMON SWORD!?
SLRRP...
DO
DO

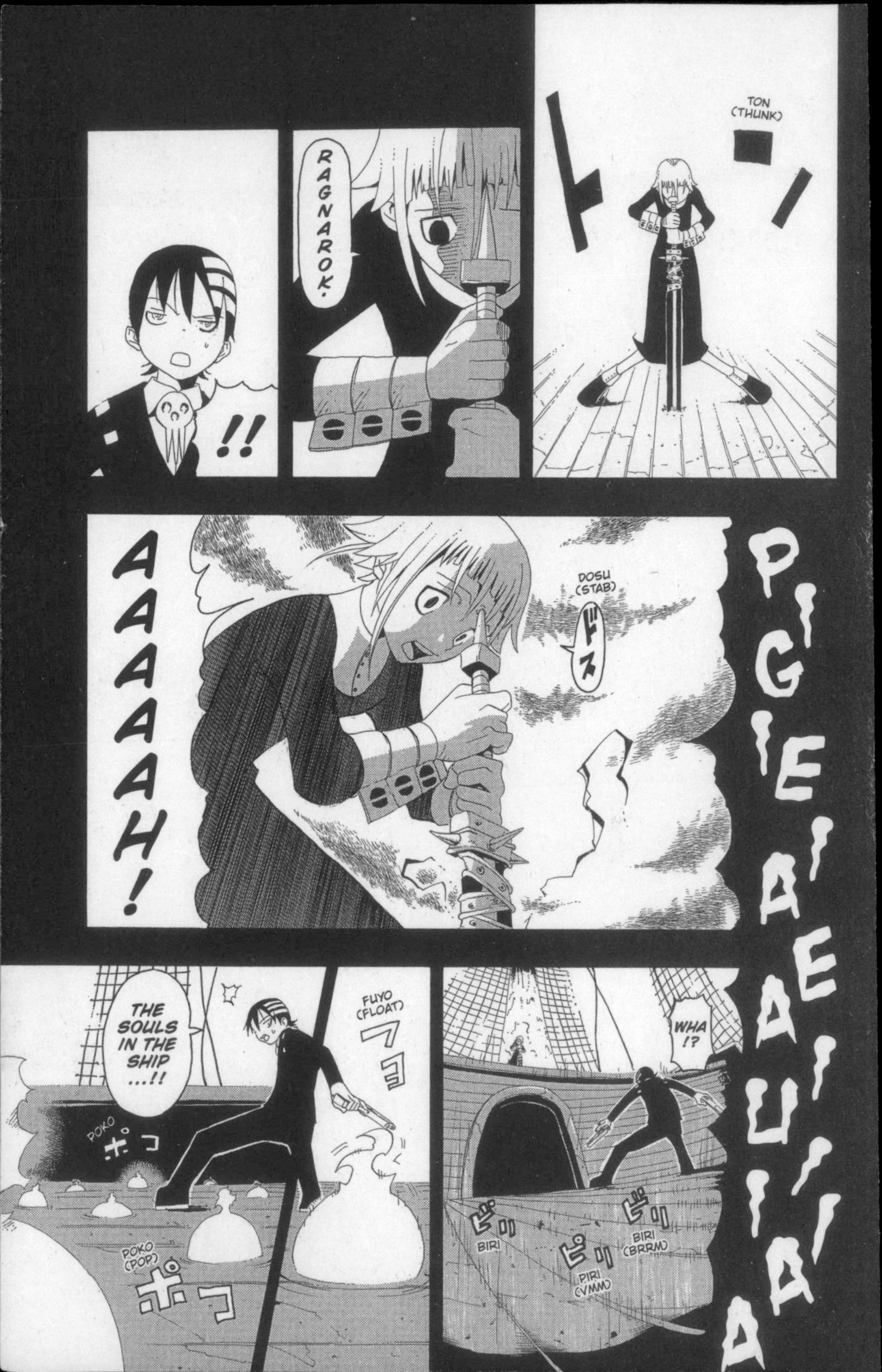
TON (THUNK)
トン
RAGNAROK.
!!
DOSU (STAB)
ドス
AAAAAAH!
PGEAEAUAA
WHA!?
BIRI (BRRM)
ビリ
PIRI (VMM)
ピリ
BIRI
ビリ
FUYO (FLOAT)
フヨ
THE SOULS IN THE SHIP ...!!
POKO
ポコ
POKO (POP)
ポコ

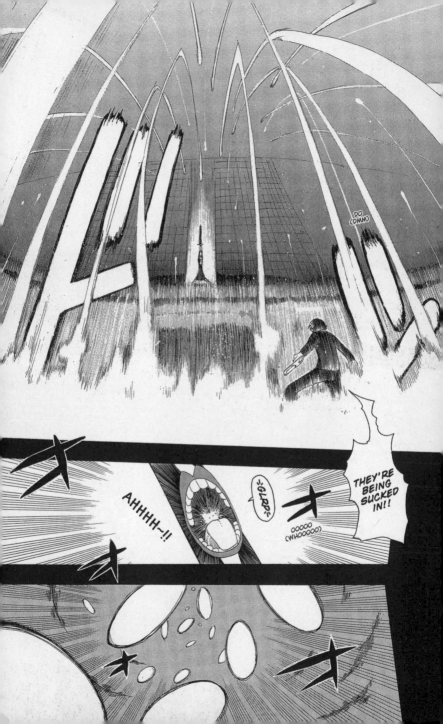

DO
(DMM)

AHHHH~!!

~GLRP~

OOOOO
(WHOOOOO)

THEY'RE BEING SUCKED IN!!

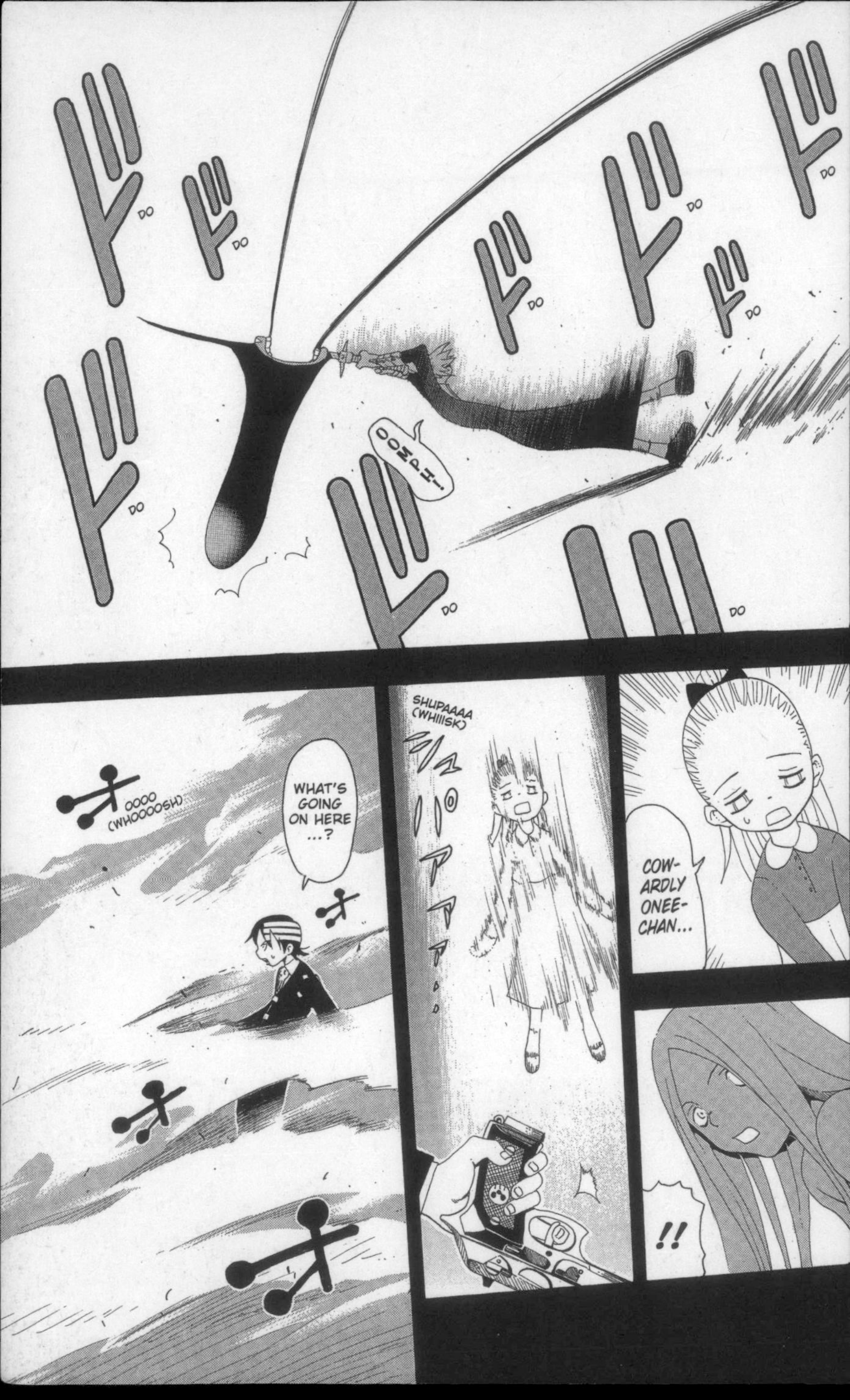
DO
DO
DO
DO
DO
DO
DO
OOMPH!
DO
DO
COW-ARDLY ONEE-CHAN...
!!
SHUPAAAA (WHIIISK)
OOOO (WHOOOOSH)
WHAT'S GOING ON HERE ...?

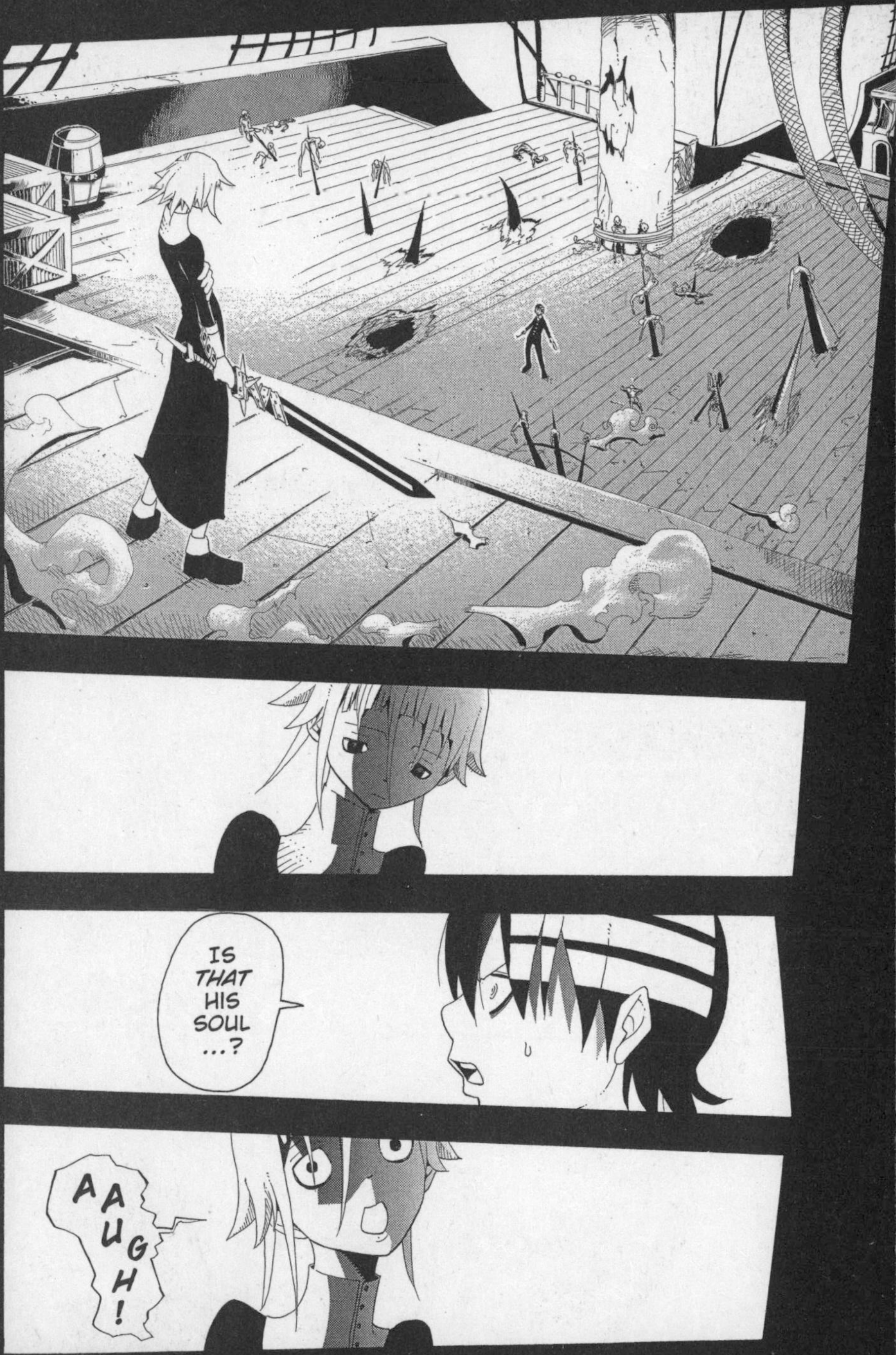
IS THAT HIS SOUL ...?
AAUGH!

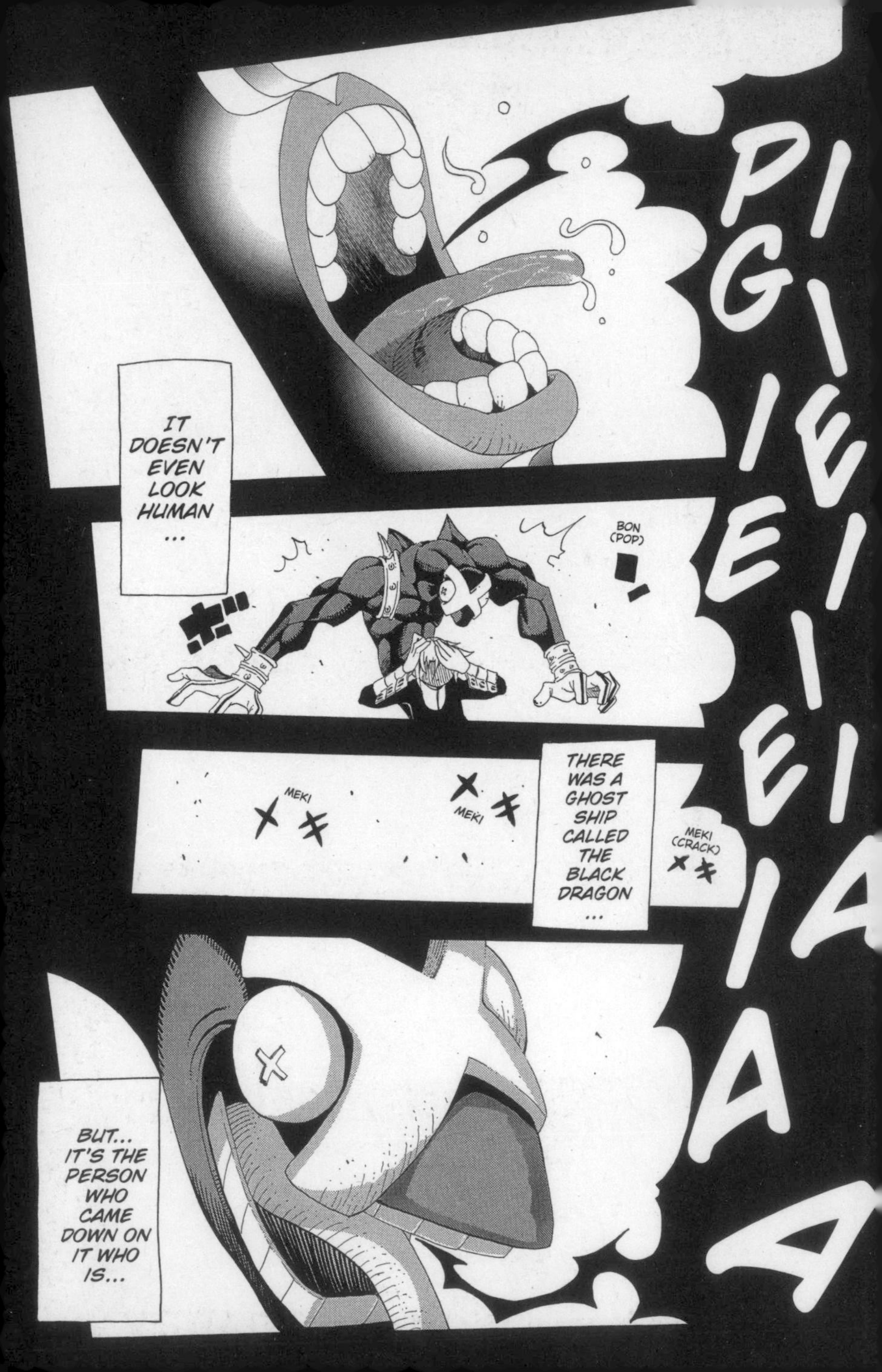

PIGIEEEEIAAA
IT DOESN'T EVEN LOOK HUMAN...
BON (POP)
THERE WAS A GHOST SHIP CALLED THE BLACK DRAGON...
MEKI (CRACK)
MEKI
MEKI
BUT... IT'S THE PERSON WHO CAME DOWN ON IT WHO IS...

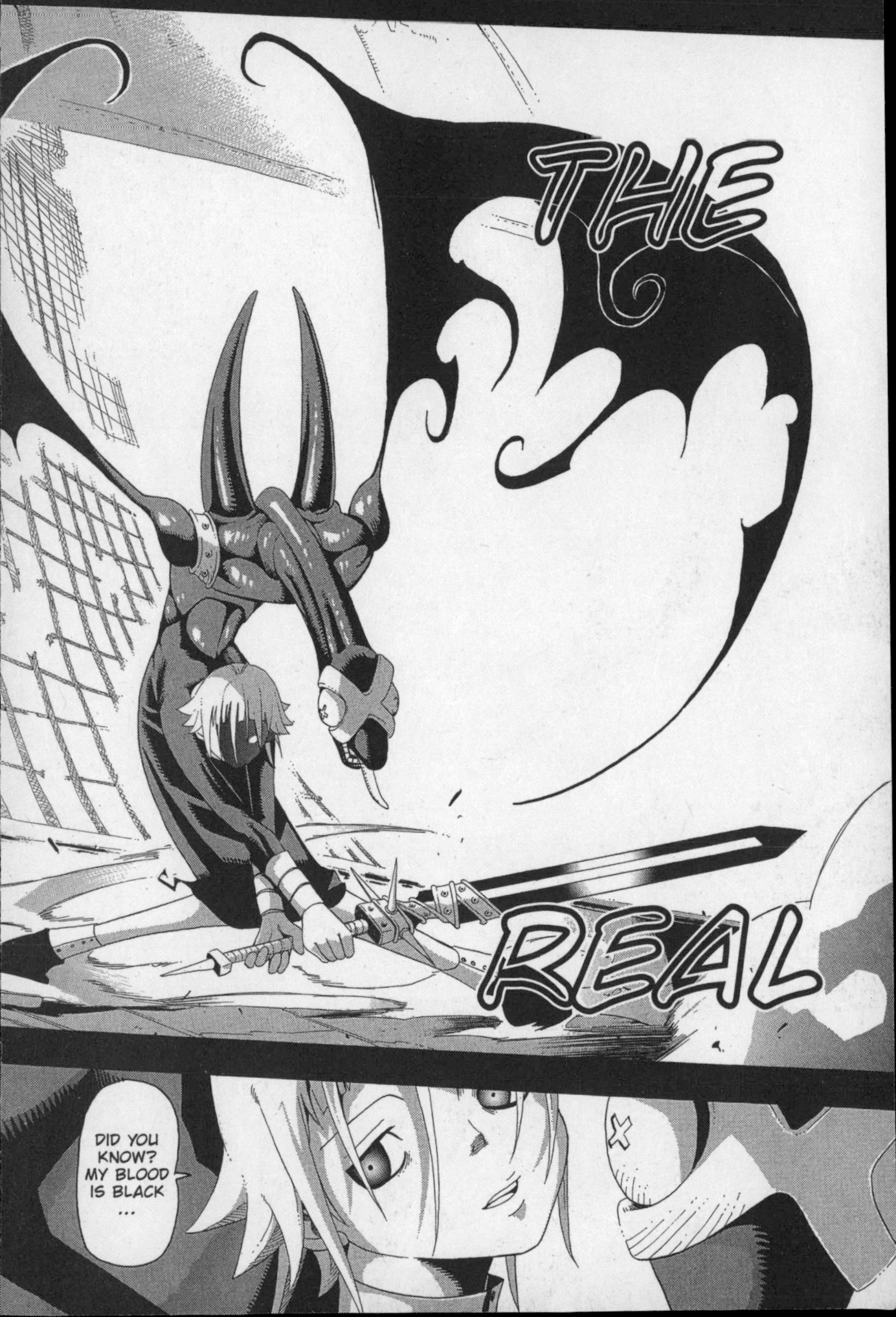
THE
REAL
DID YOU KNOW? MY BLOOD IS BLACK ...

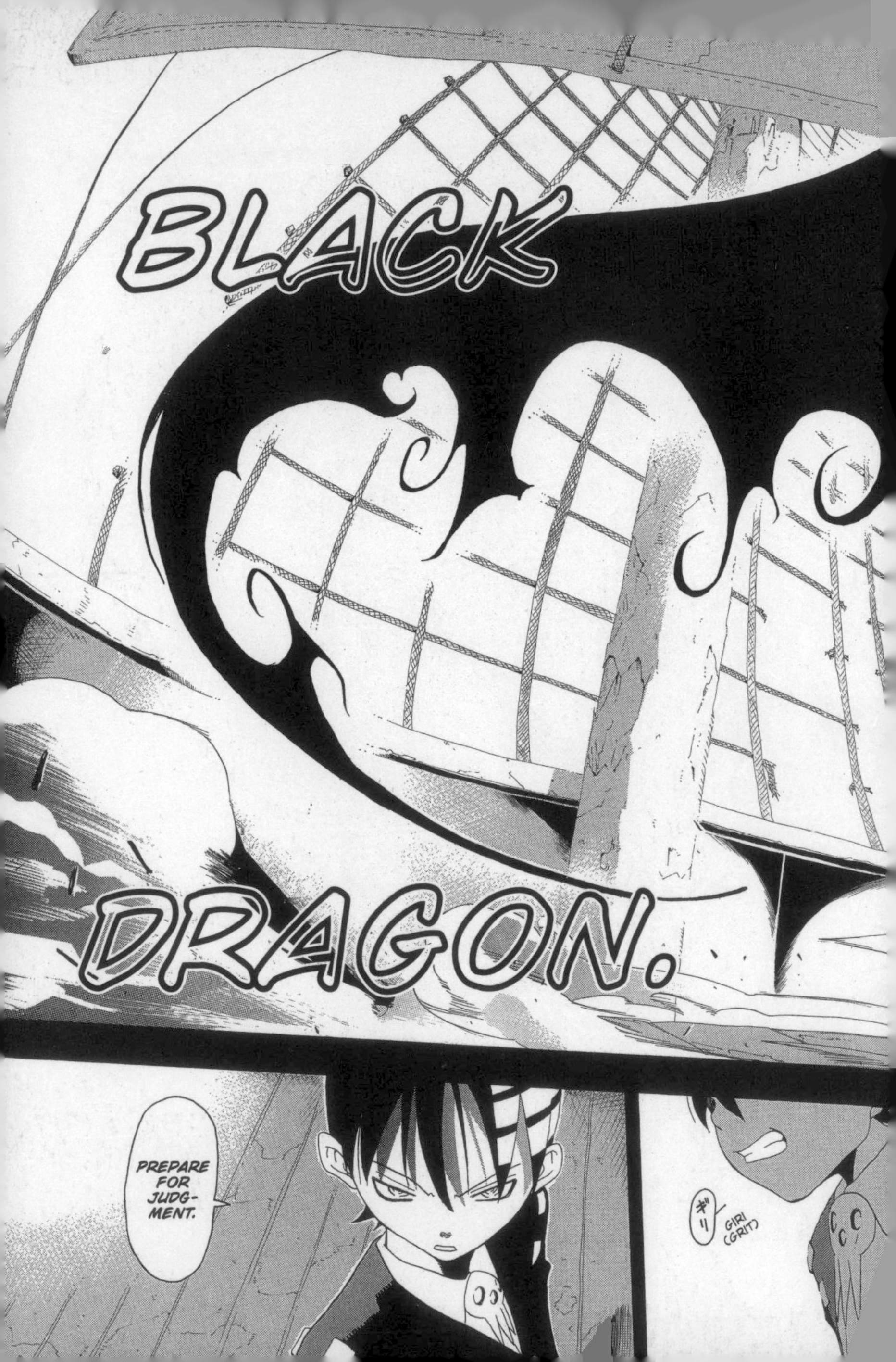
BLACK
DRAGON.
ギリ
GIRI (GRIT)
PREPARE FOR JUDG-MENT.

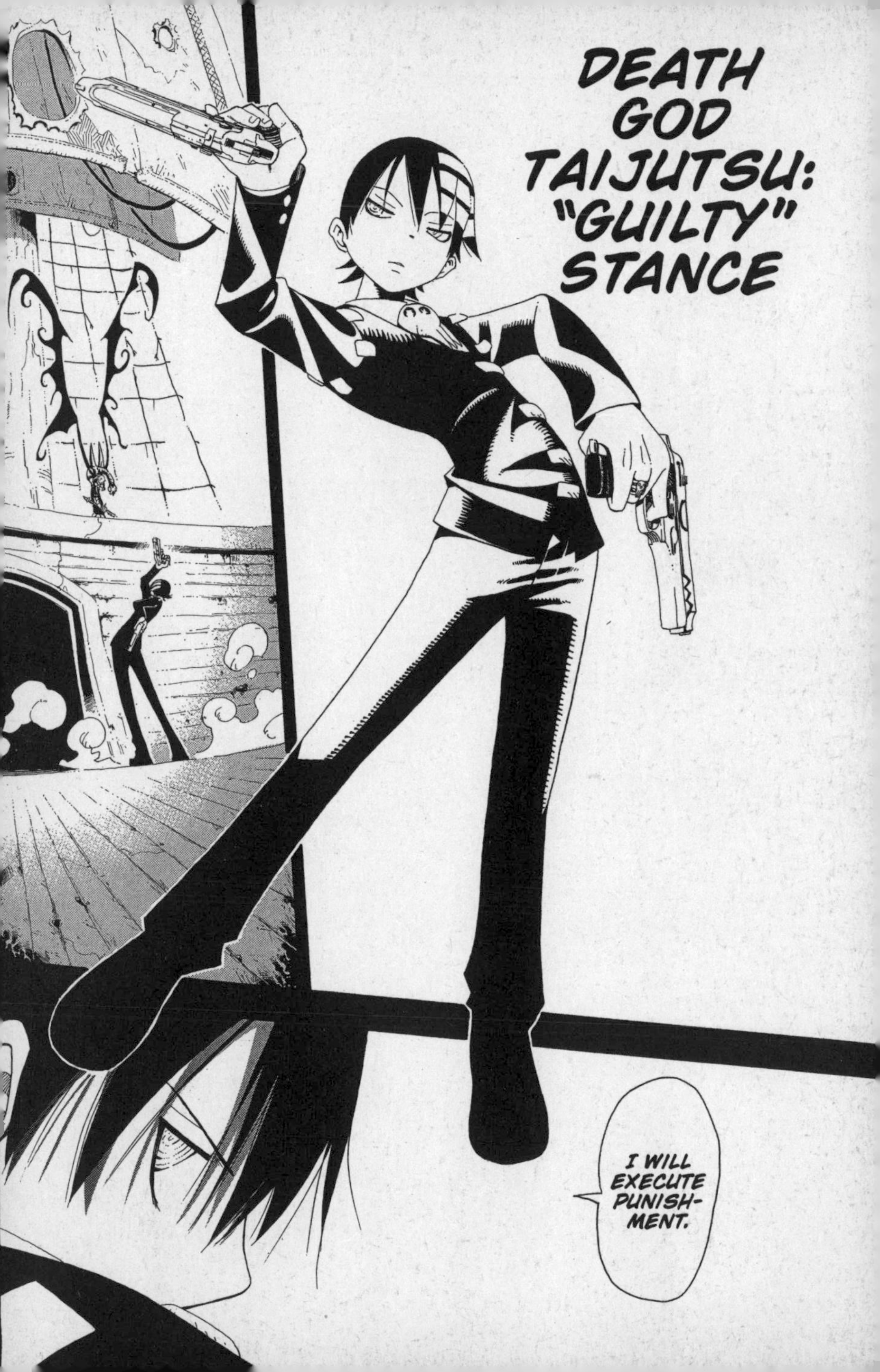
DEATH GOD TAIJUTSU: "GUILTY" STANCE
I WILL EXECUTE PUNISHMENT.

SOUL EATER

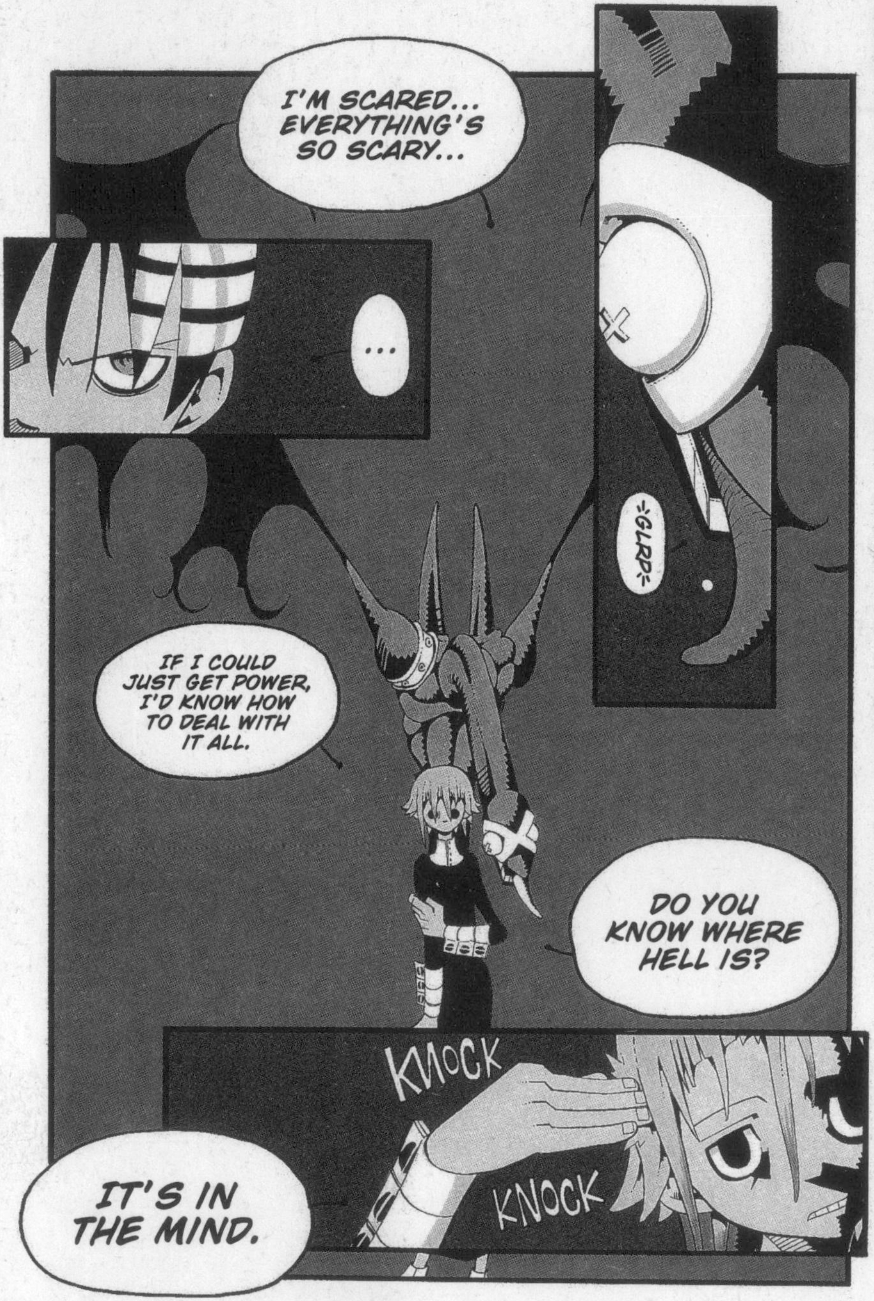
GLRP
I'M SCARED... EVERYTHING'S SO SCARY...
...
IF I COULD JUST GET POWER, I'D KNOW HOW TO DEAL WITH IT ALL.
DO YOU KNOW WHERE HELL IS?
KNOCK
KNOCK
IT'S IN THE MIND.

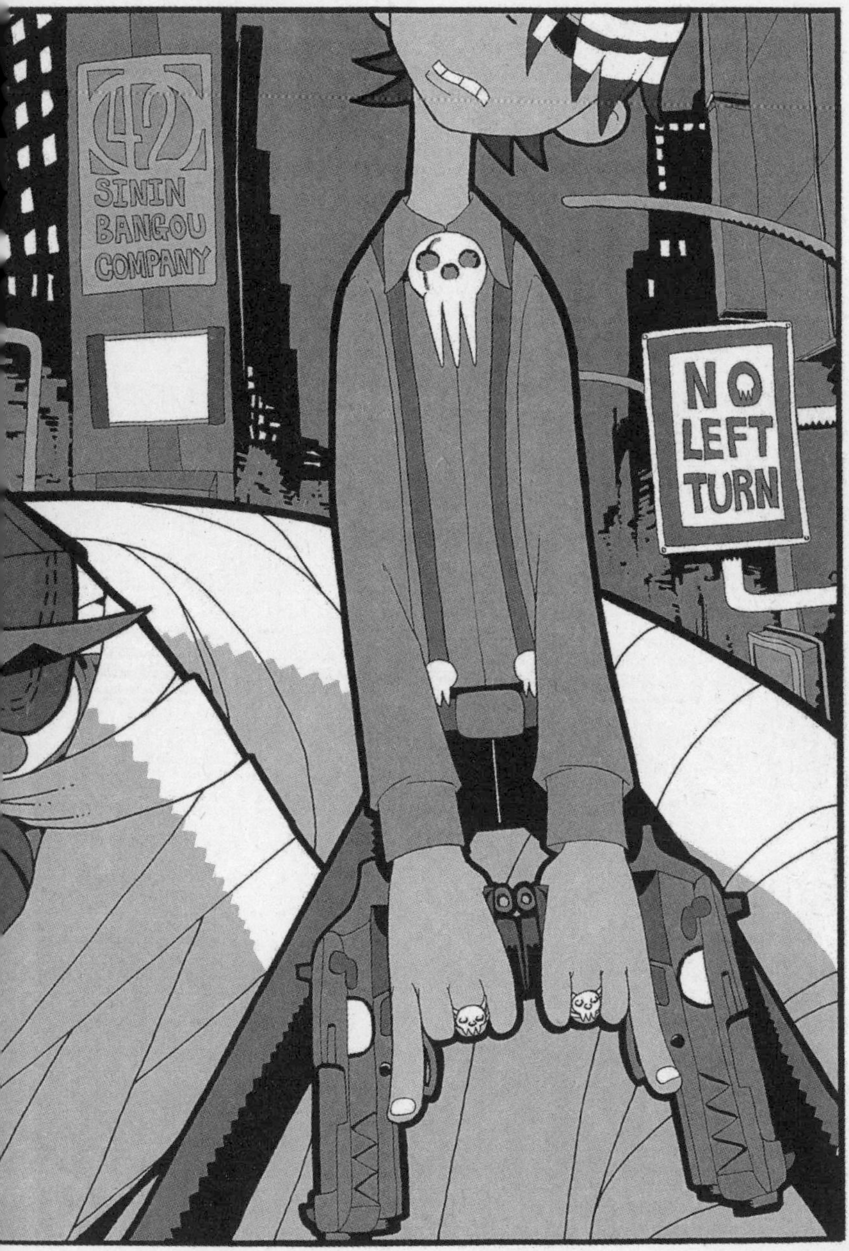

42
SININ
BANGOU
COMPANY
NO
LEFT
TURN

CHAPTER 14: BLACK DRAGON (PART 2)

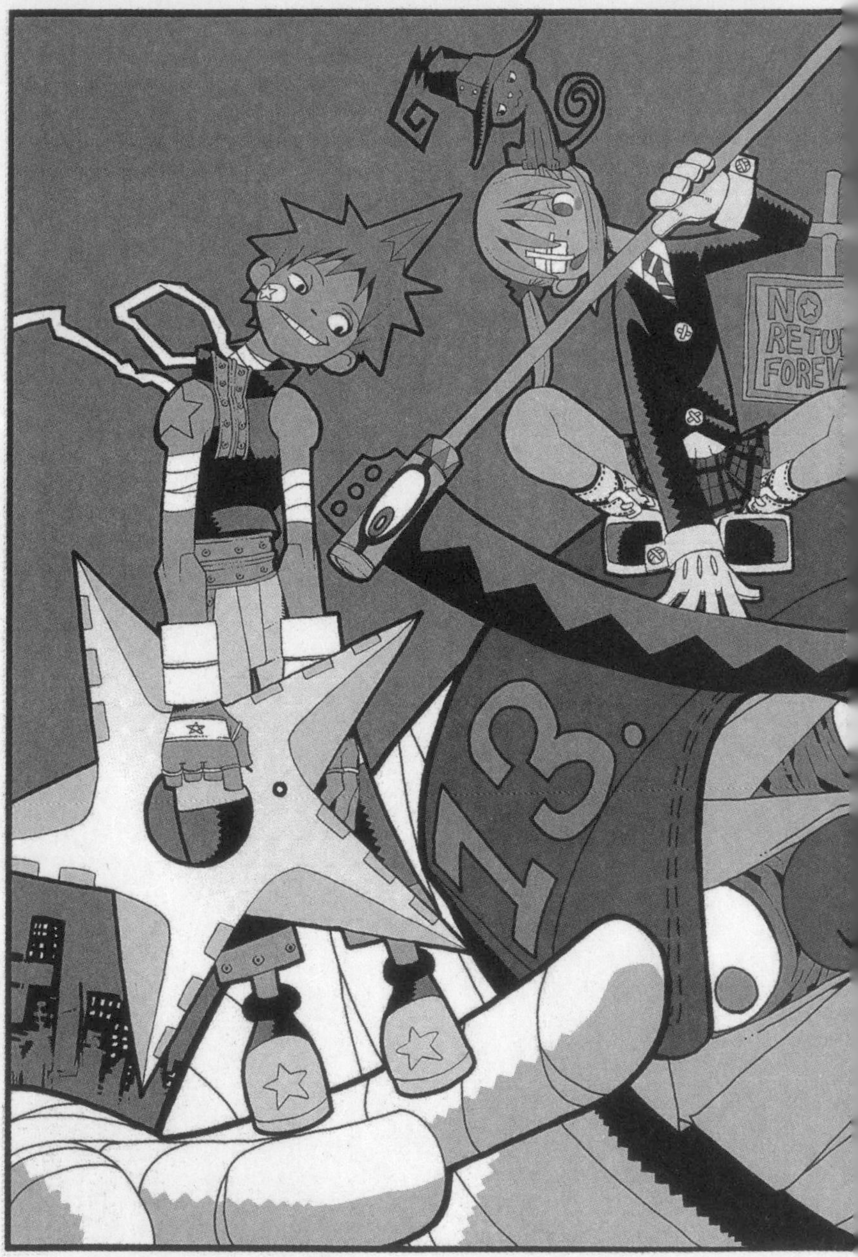
NO
RETU
FOREV

SOUL EATER

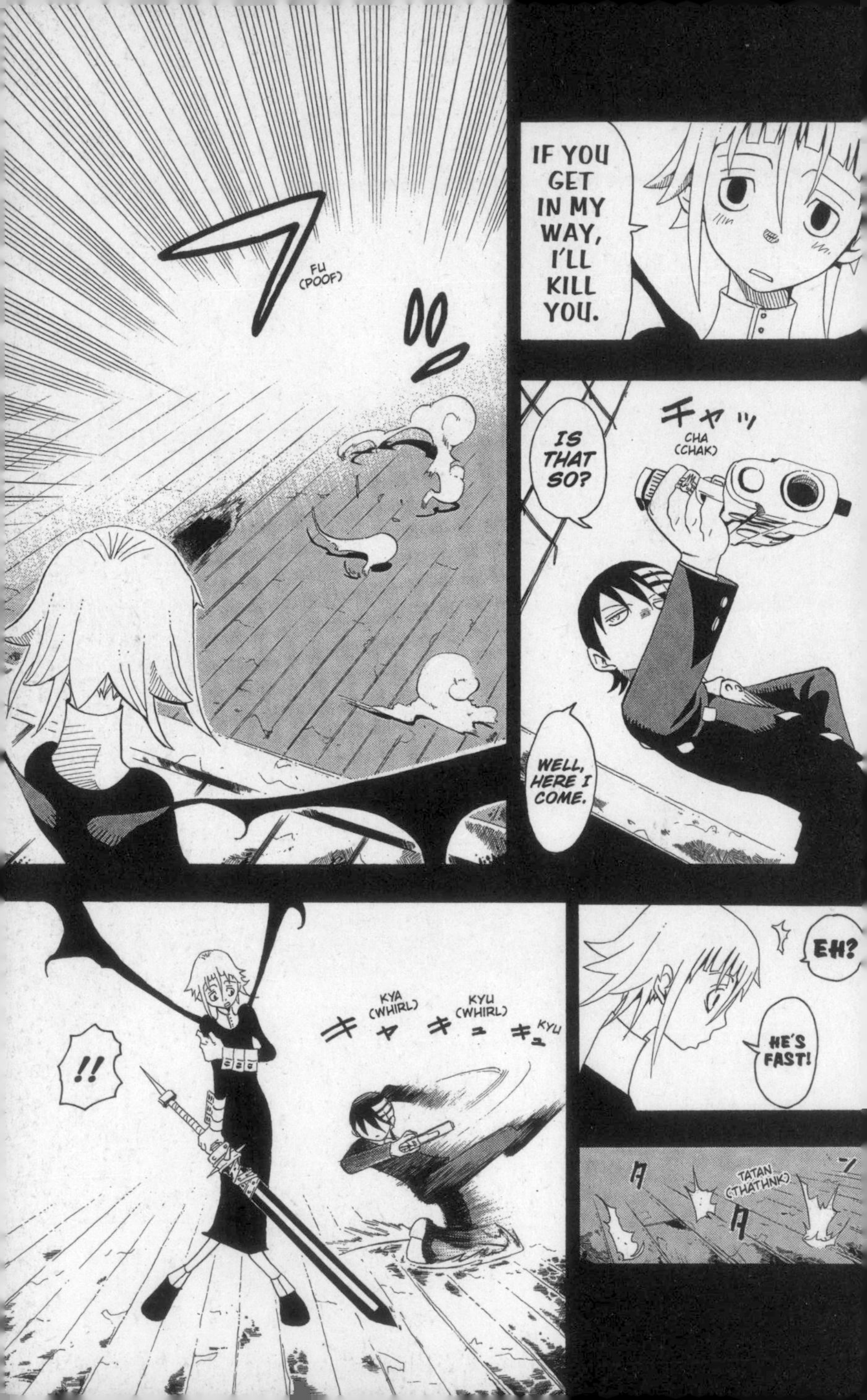
IF YOU GET IN MY WAY, I'LL KILL YOU.
IS THAT SO?
チャッ
CHA (CHAK)
WELL, HERE I COME.
FU (POOF)
EH?
HE'S FAST!
TATAN (THATHNK)
!!
キャ キュ キュ
KYA (WHIRL)
KYU (WHIRL)
KYU

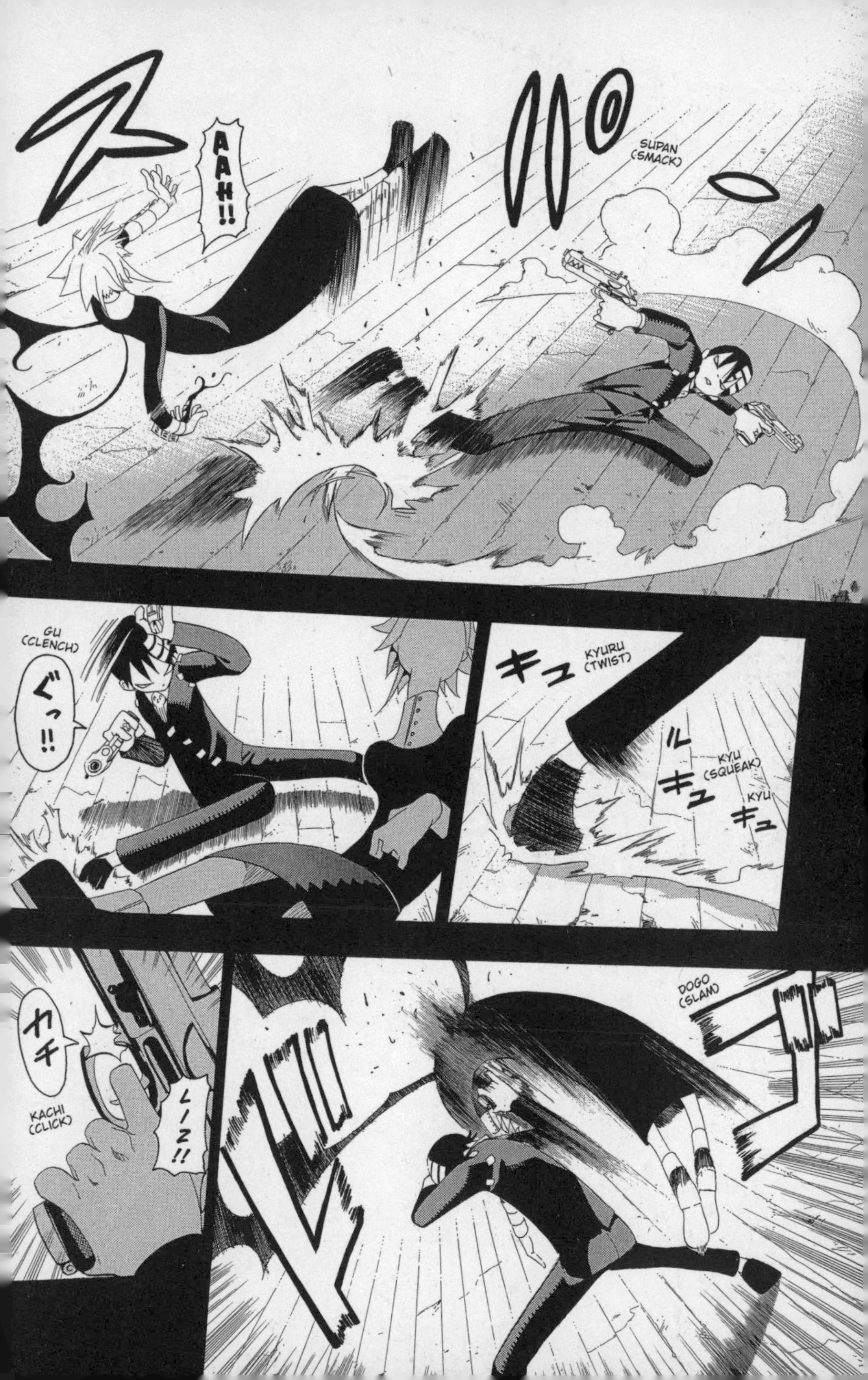
SUPAN (SMACK)
AAH!!
キュ
KYURU (TWIST)
ル
キュ
KYU (SQUEAK)
キュ
KYU
GU (CLENCH)
ぐっ!!
DOGO (SLAM)
カチ
KACHI (CLICK)
LIZ!!

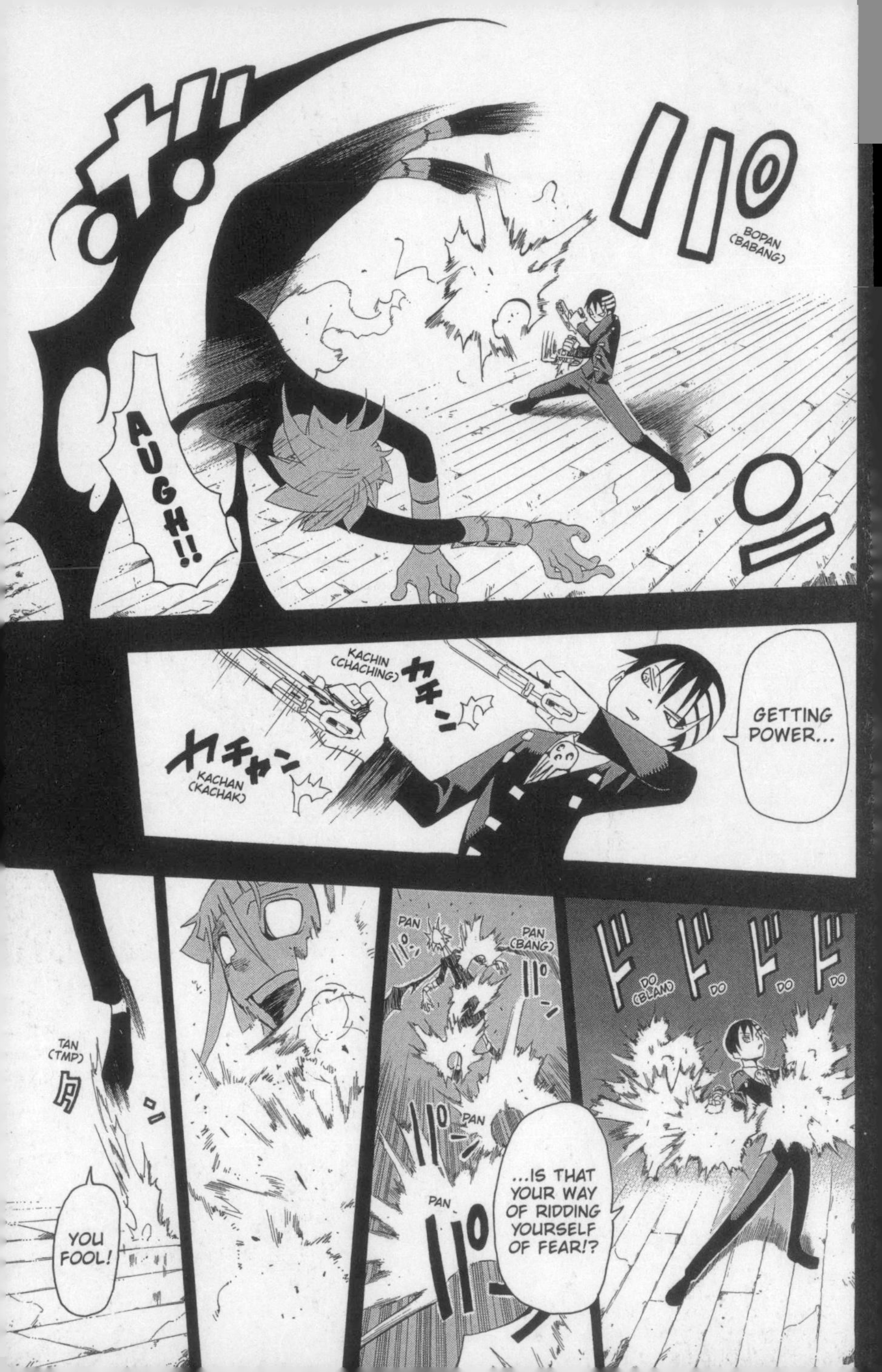
BOPAN (BABANG)
AUGH!!
GETTING POWER...
KACHIN (CHACHING)
KACHAN (KACHAK)
DO (BLAM)
DO
DO
DO
PAN (BANG)
PAN
PAN
PAN
...IS THAT YOUR WAY OF RIDDING YOURSELF OF FEAR!?
TAN (TMP)
YOU FOOL!

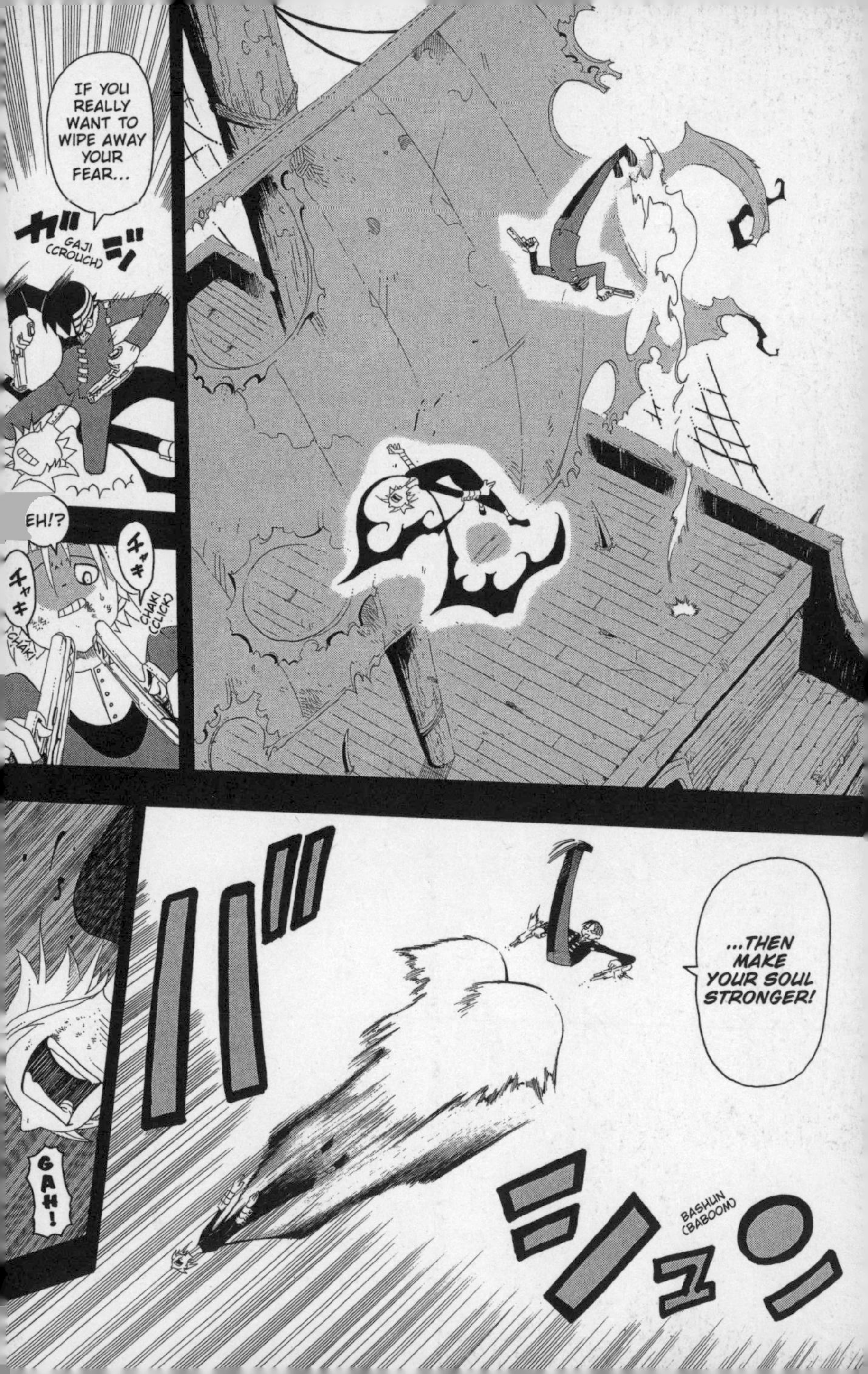
IF YOU REALLY WANT TO WIPE AWAY YOUR FEAR...
GAJI (CROUCH)
EH!?
CHAKI (CLICK)
CHAKI
...THEN MAKE YOUR SOUL STRONGER!
BASHUN (BABOOM)
GAH!

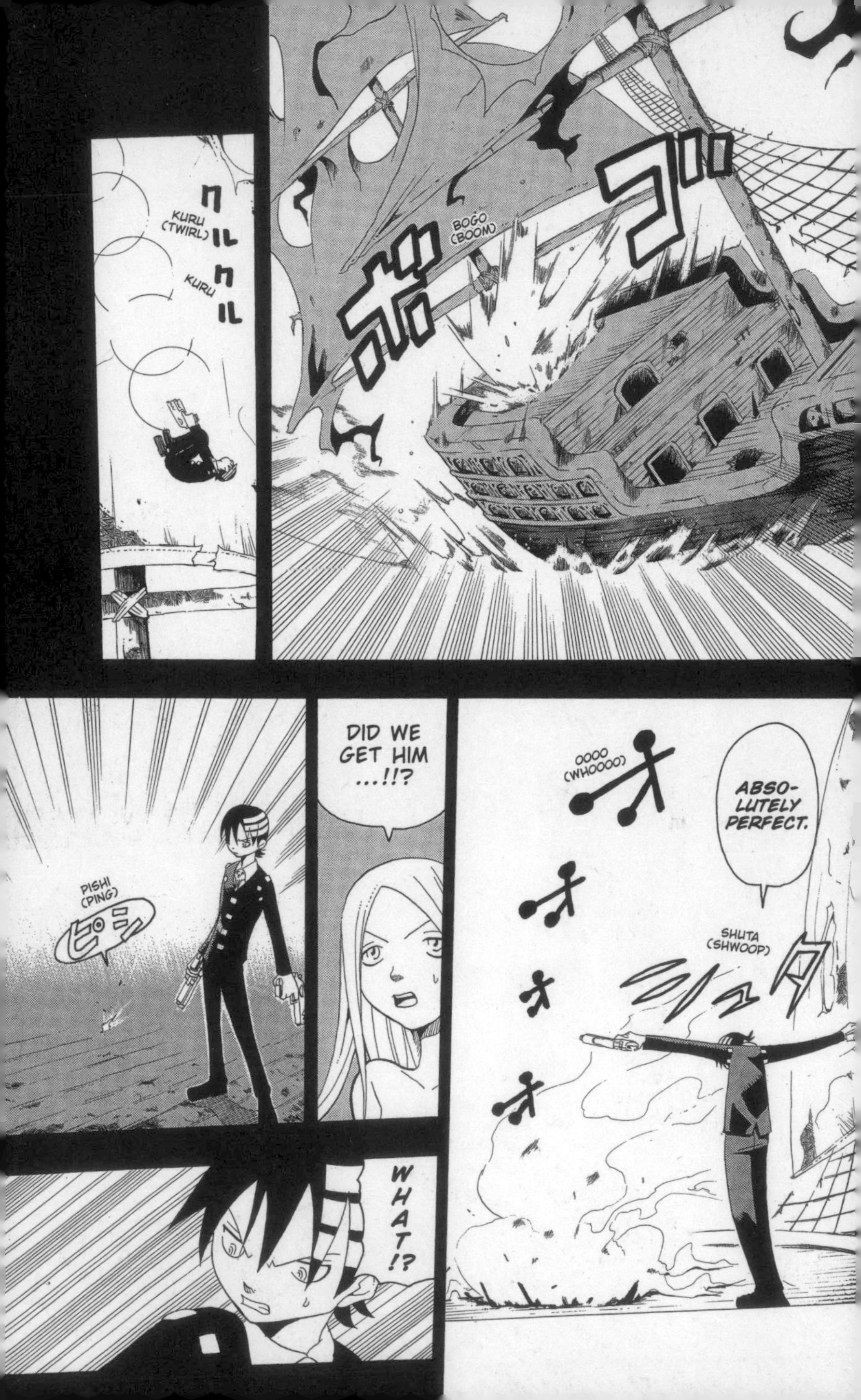
ボゴ
BOGO (BOOM)
クルクル
KURU (TWIRL) KURU
オオオオ
OOOO (WHOOOO)
ABSO-LUTELY PERFECT.
シュタ
SHUTA (SHWOOP)
DID WE GET HIM ...!!?
ピシ
PISHI (PING)
WHAT!?

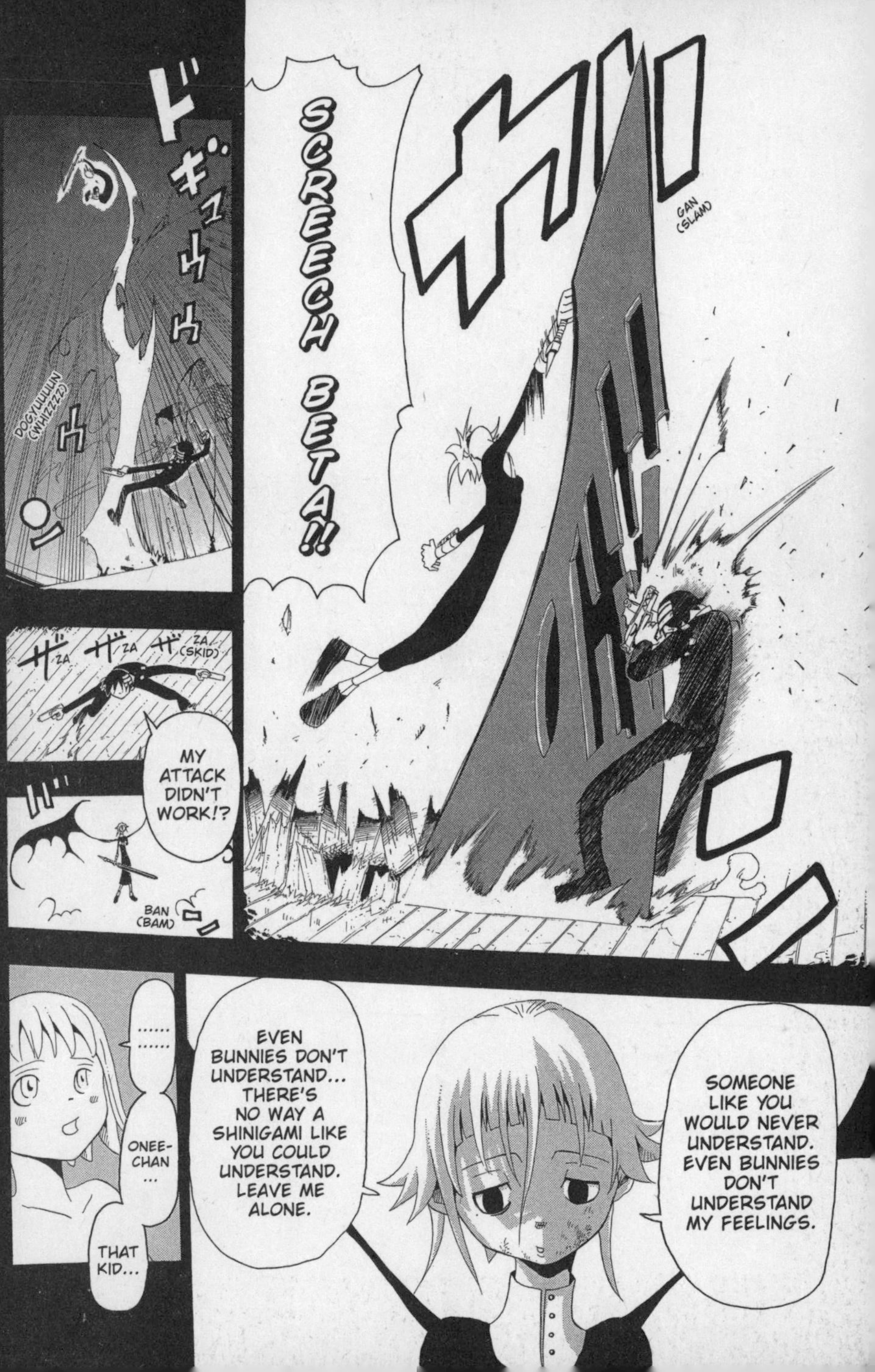
GAN (SLAM)
SCREECH BETA!!
DOGYUUUN (WHIZZZZ)
ZA ZA ZA (SKID)
MY ATTACK DIDN'T WORK!?
BAN (BAM)
SOMEONE LIKE YOU WOULD NEVER UNDERSTAND. EVEN BUNNIES DON'T UNDERSTAND MY FEELINGS.
EVEN BUNNIES DON'T UNDERSTAND... THERE'S NO WAY A SHINIGAMI LIKE YOU COULD UNDERSTAND. LEAVE ME ALONE.
......
......
ONEE-CHAN...
THAT KID...

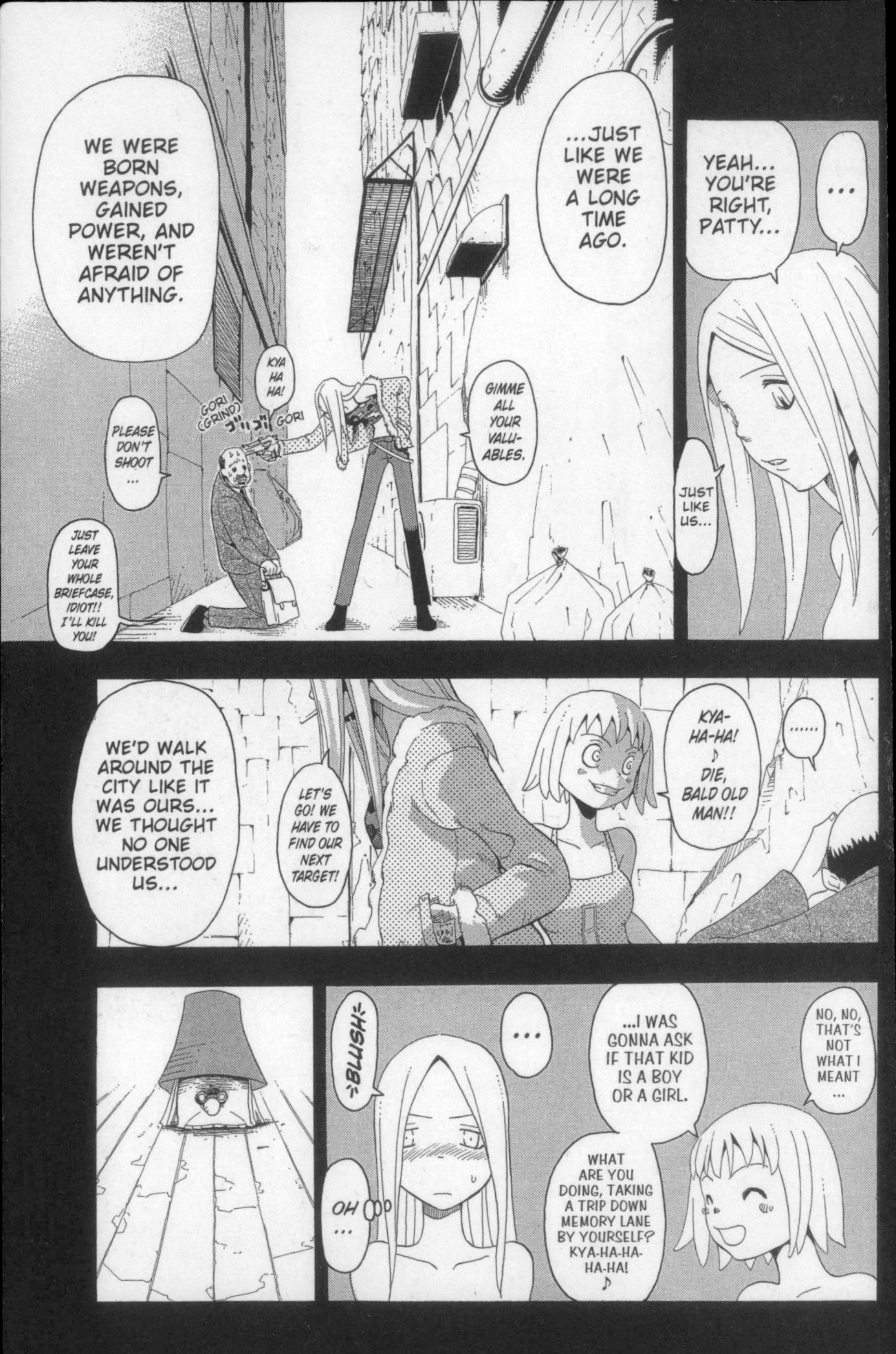
...
YEAH... YOU'RE RIGHT, PATTY...
JUST LIKE US...
...JUST LIKE WE WERE A LONG TIME AGO.
WE WERE BORN WEAPONS, GAINED POWER, AND WEREN'T AFRAID OF ANYTHING.
GIMME ALL YOUR VALU-ABLES.
KYA HA HA!
GORI (GRIND) GORI
PLEASE DON'T SHOOT ...
JUST LEAVE YOUR WHOLE BRIEFCASE, IDIOT!! I'LL KILL YOU!
......
KYA-HA-HA! ♪ DIE, BALD OLD MAN!!
LET'S GO! WE HAVE TO FIND OUR NEXT TARGET!
WE'D WALK AROUND THE CITY LIKE IT WAS OURS... WE THOUGHT NO ONE UNDERSTOOD US...
NO, NO, THAT'S NOT WHAT I MEANT ...
...I WAS GONNA ASK IF THAT KID IS A BOY OR A GIRL.
...
BLUSH
WHAT ARE YOU DOING, TAKING A TRIP DOWN MEMORY LANE BY YOURSELF? KYA-HA-HA-HA-HA! ♪
OH ...

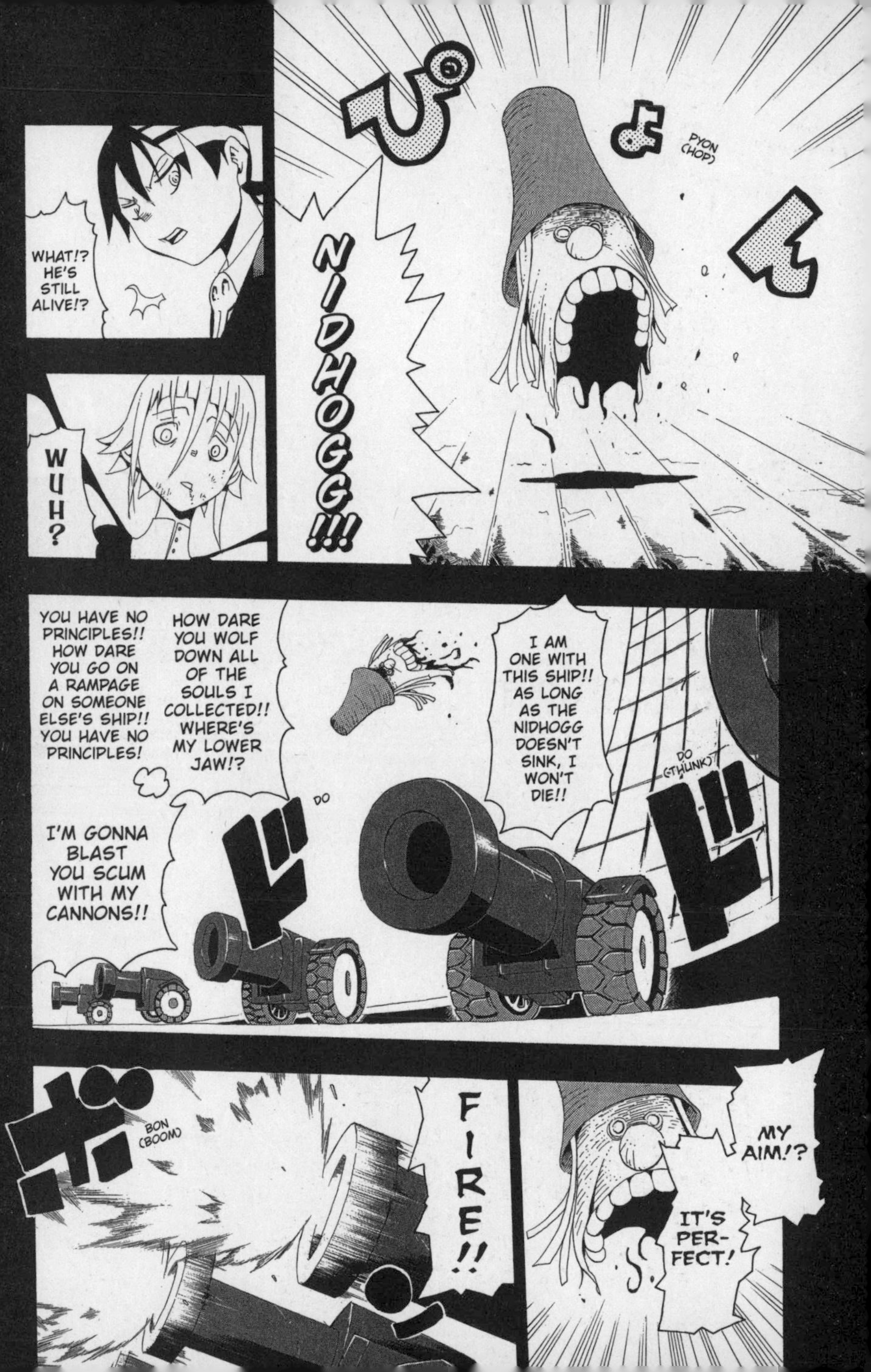

PYON (HOP)
NIDHOGG!!!
WHAT!? HE'S STILL ALIVE!?
WUH?
I AM ONE WITH THIS SHIP!! AS LONG AS THE NIDHOGG DOESN'T SINK, I WON'T DIE!!
DO (THUNK)
HOW DARE YOU WOLF DOWN ALL OF THE SOULS I COLLECTED!! WHERE'S MY LOWER JAW!?
YOU HAVE NO PRINCIPLES!! HOW DARE YOU GO ON A RAMPAGE ON SOMEONE ELSE'S SHIP!! YOU HAVE NO PRINCIPLES!
DO
I'M GONNA BLAST YOU SCUM WITH MY CANNONS!!
MY AIM!?
IT'S PER-FECT!
FIRE!!
BON (BOOM)

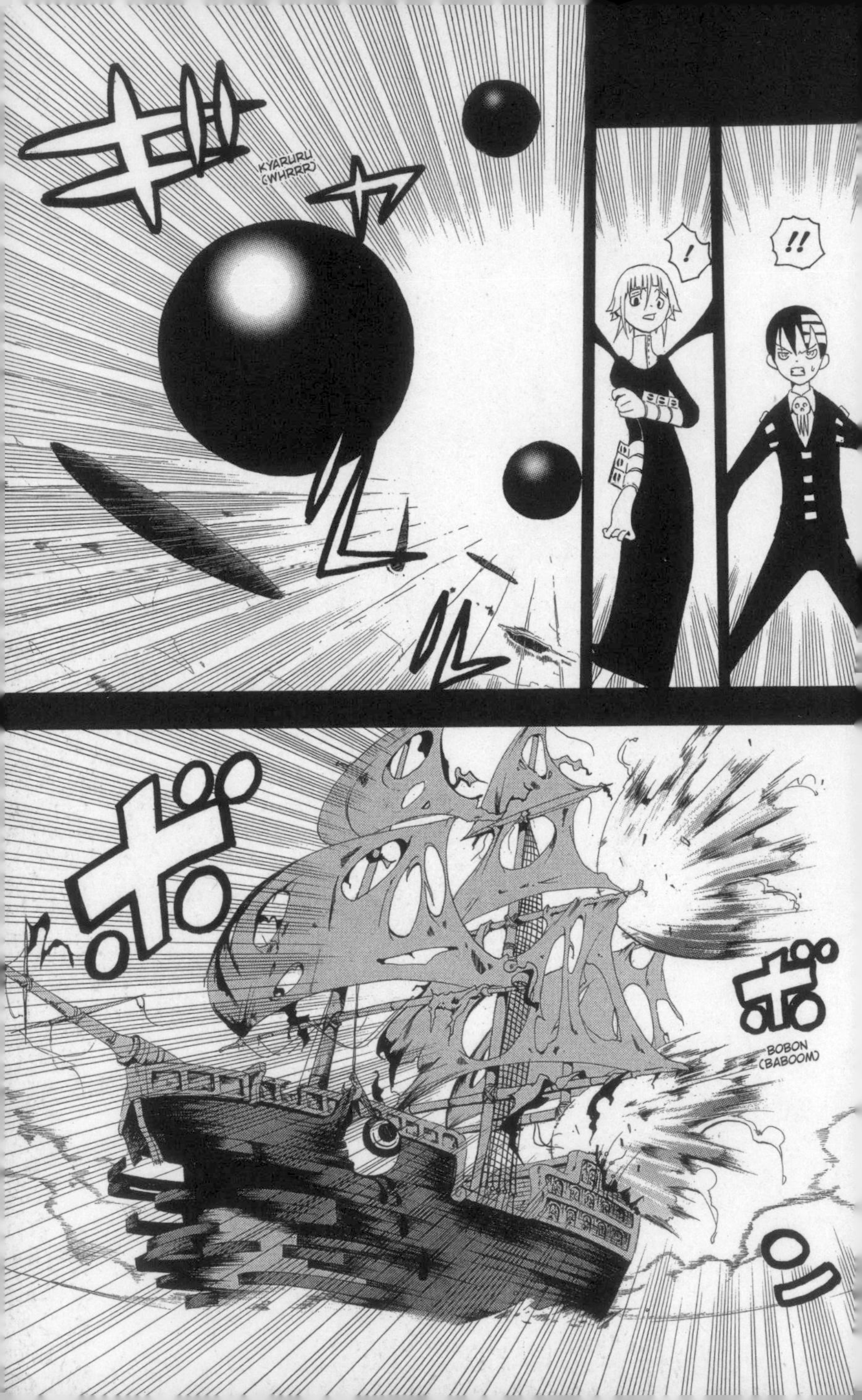
!!
!
KYARURU (WHRRR)
BOBON (BABOOM)

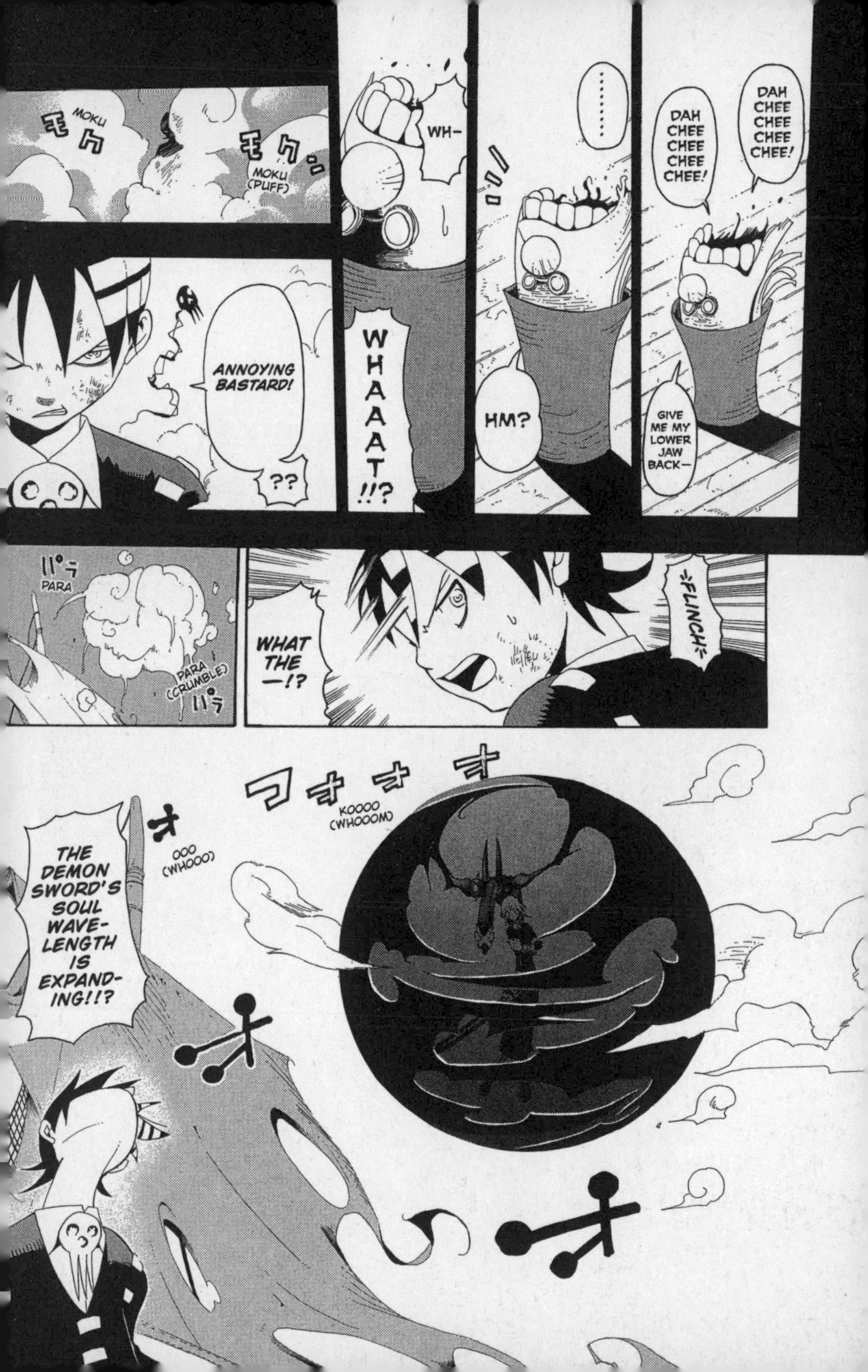
DAH CHEE CHEE CHEE CHEE!
DAH CHEE CHEE CHEE CHEE!
GIVE ME MY LOWER JAW BACK—
......
HM?
WH-
WHAAAT!!?
モク MOKU
モク。 MOKU (PUFF)
ANNOYING BASTARD!
??
FLINCH
WHAT THE —!?
パラ PARA
PARA (CRUMBLE) パラ
フォォォ KOOOO (WHOOOM)
オ OOO (WHOOO)
THE DEMON SWORD'S SOUL WAVE-LENGTH IS EXPANDING!!?

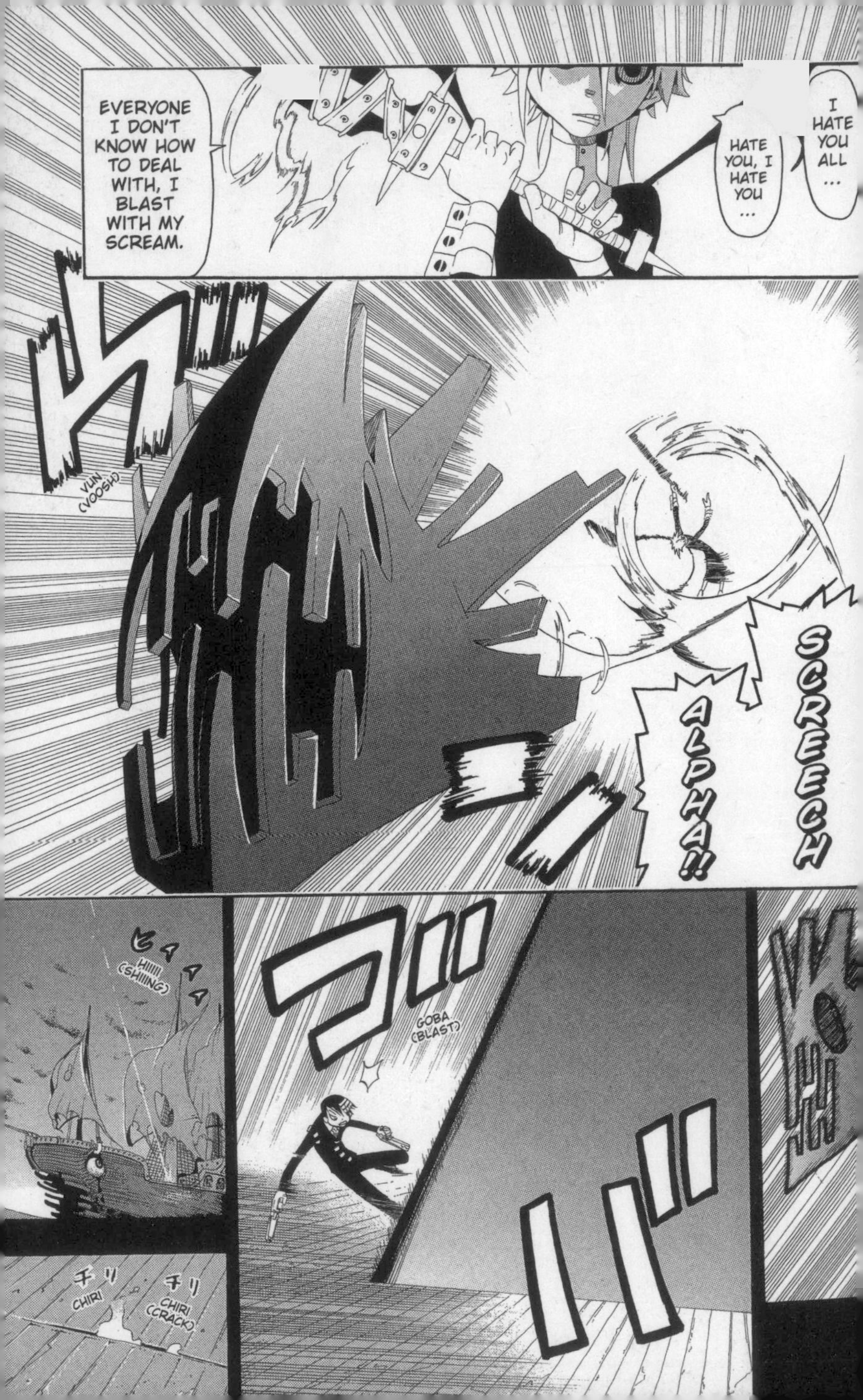
I HATE YOU ALL ...
HATE YOU, I HATE YOU ...
EVERYONE I DON'T KNOW HOW TO DEAL WITH, I BLAST WITH MY SCREAM.
SCREECH ALPHA!!
VUN (VOOSH)
GOBA (BLAST)
HIIIII (SHIING)
チリ チリ
CHIRI
CHIRI (CRACK)

ズ
(ZUBA) (SLASH)

GUH...

NGYAAAH!!

PGIEIEIIEIAA

びィィィィィ・|
(PIIIIN) (SHINING)

NN...

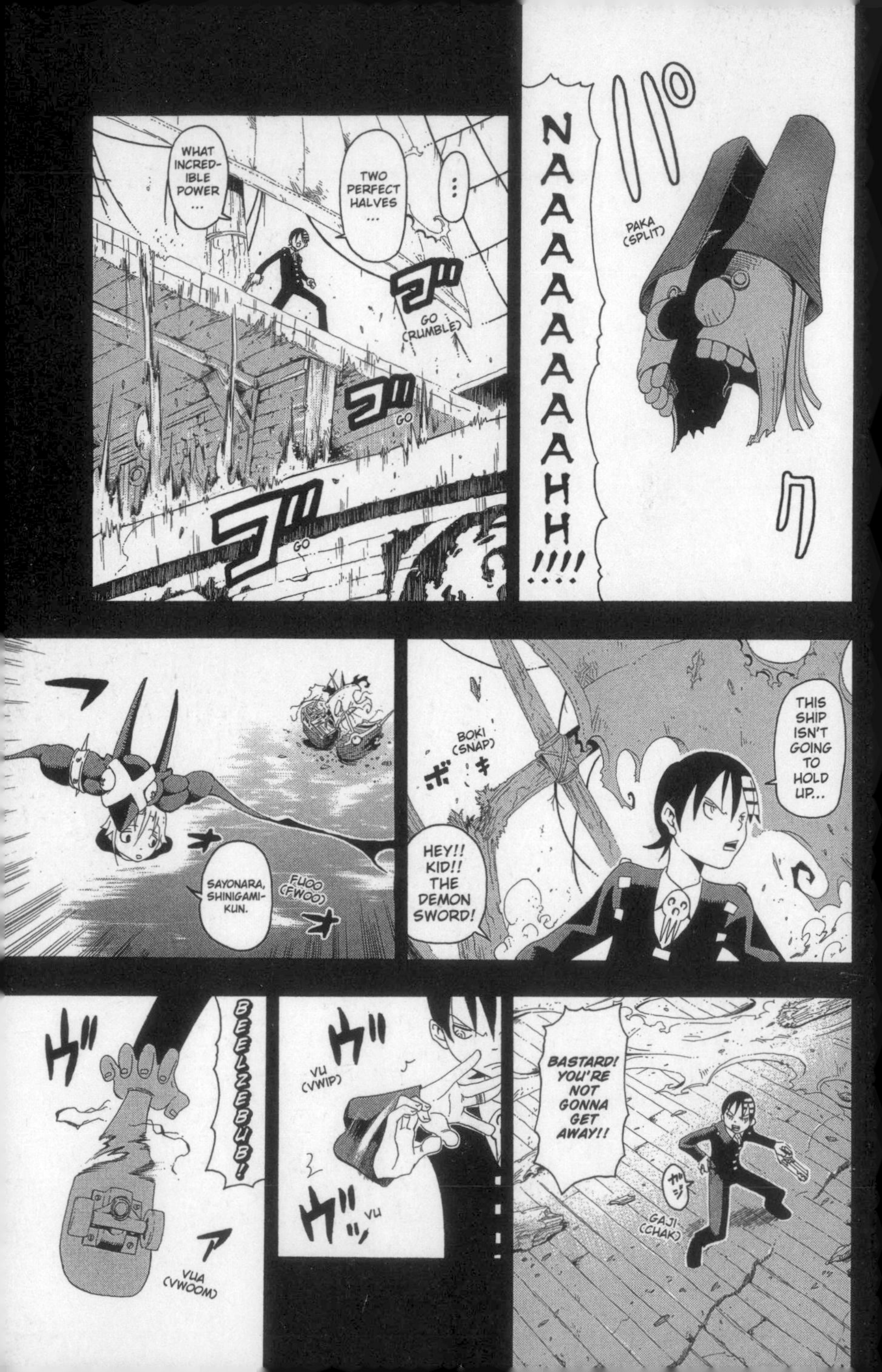
NAAAAAAAAAAAHH!!!!!
PAKA (SPLIT)
...
TWO PERFECT HALVES ...
WHAT INCREDIBLE POWER ...
GO (RUMBLE)
GO
GO
THIS SHIP ISN'T GOING TO HOLD UP...
BOKI (SNAP)
HEY!! KID!! THE DEMON SWORD!
FUOO (FWOO)
SAYONARA, SHINIGAMI-KUN.
BASTARD! YOU'RE NOT GONNA GET AWAY!!
GAJI (CHAK)
VU (VWIP)
VU
...
BEELZEBUB!
VUA (VWOOM)

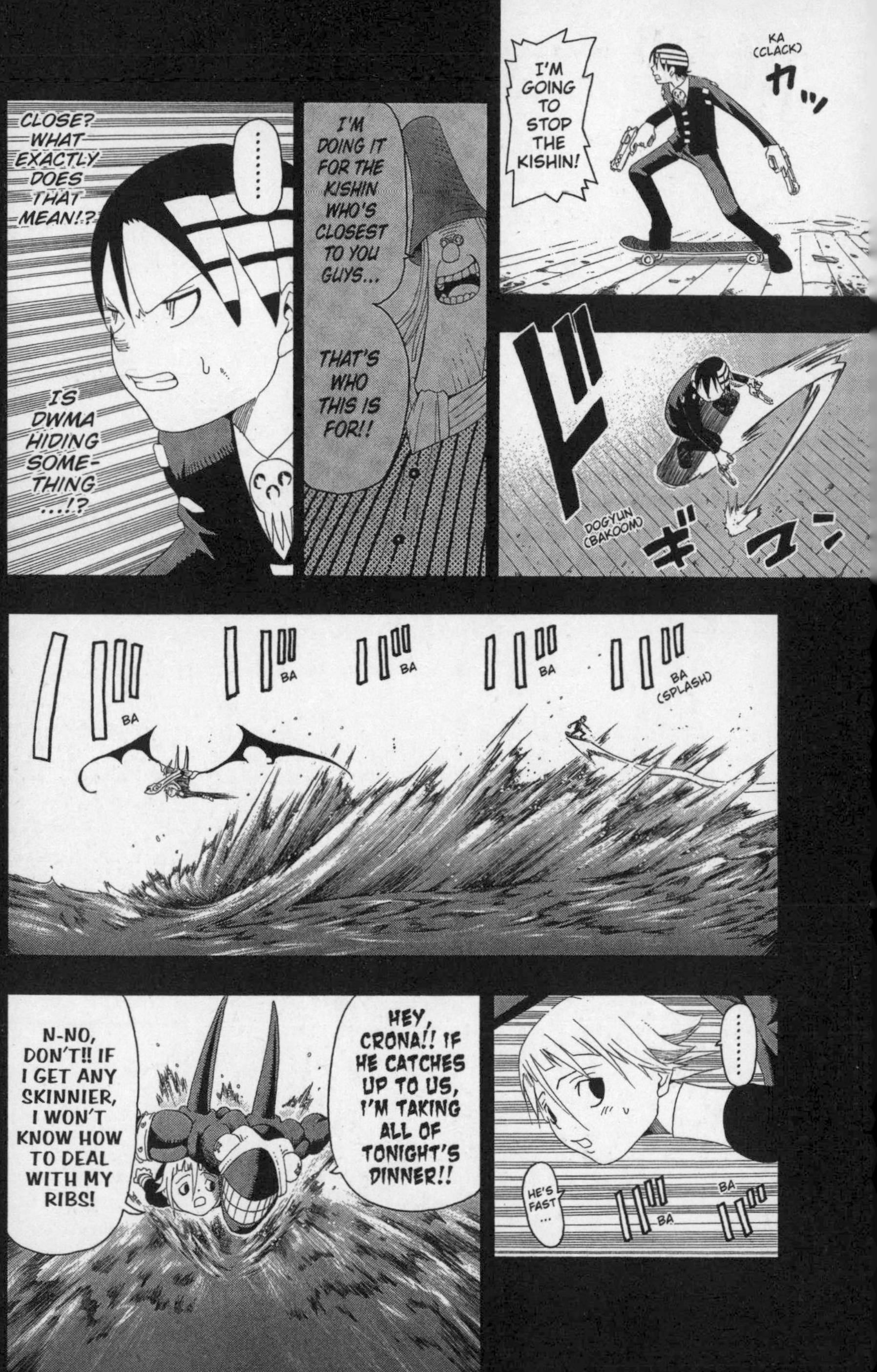I'M GOING TO STOP THE KISHIN!
KA (CLACK)
DOGYUN (BAKOOM)
I'M DOING IT FOR THE KISHIN WHO'S CLOSEST TO YOU GUYS...
THAT'S WHO THIS IS FOR!!
......
CLOSE? WHAT EXACTLY DOES THAT MEAN!?
IS DWMA HIDING SOME-THING ...!?
BA (SPLASH)
BA
BA
BA
BA
......
HE'S FAST ...
BA
BA
HEY, CRONA!! IF HE CATCHES UP TO US, I'M TAKING ALL OF TONIGHT'S DINNER!!
N-NO, DON'T!! IF I GET ANY SKINNIER, I WON'T KNOW HOW TO DEAL WITH MY RIBS!

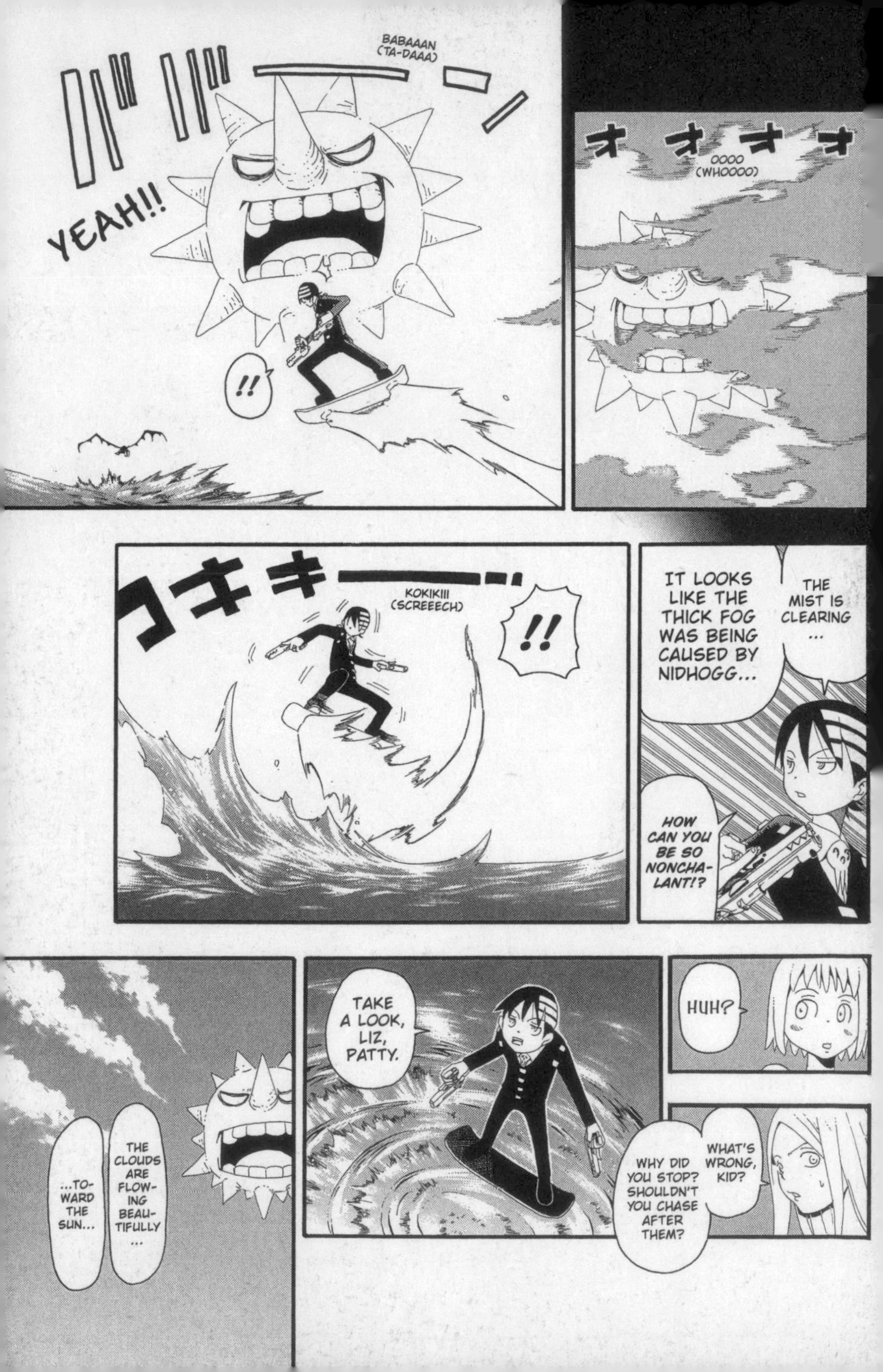
OOOO (WHOOOO)
BABAAAN (TA-DAAA)
YEAH!!
!!
THE MIST IS CLEARING...
IT LOOKS LIKE THE THICK FOG WAS BEING CAUSED BY NIDHOGG...
HOW CAN YOU BE SO NONCHALANT!?
KOKIKIII (SCREEECH)
!!
HUH?
WHAT'S WRONG, KID?
WHY DID YOU STOP? SHOULDN'T YOU CHASE AFTER THEM?
TAKE A LOOK, LIZ, PATTY.
THE CLOUDS ARE FLOWING BEAUTIFULLY...
...TOWARD THE SUN...

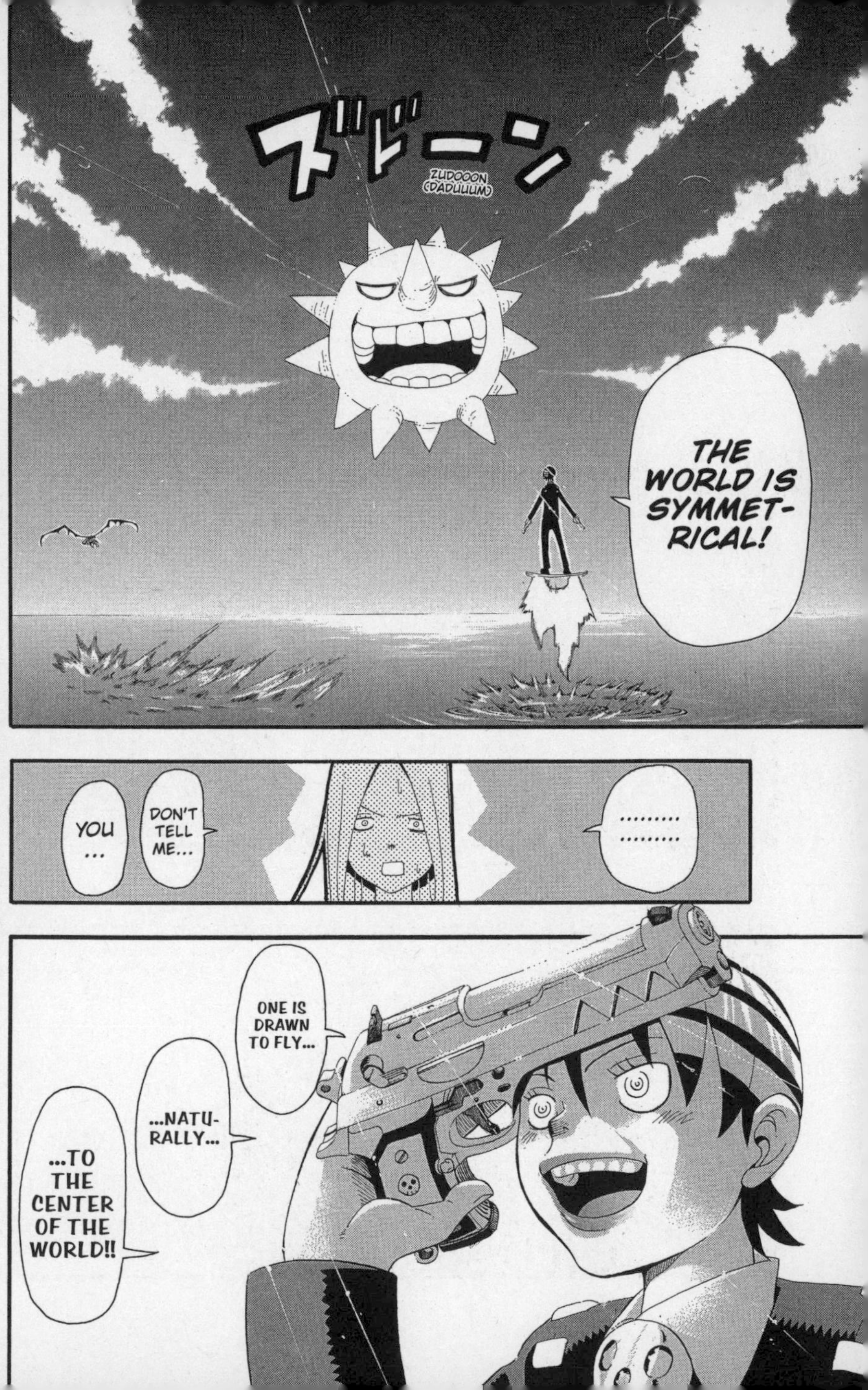
ズドーン
ZUDOOON (DADUUUM)
THE WORLD IS SYMMET-RICAL!
....
....
DON'T TELL ME...
YOU ...
ONE IS DRAWN TO FLY...
...NATU-RALLY...
...TO THE CENTER OF THE WORLD!!

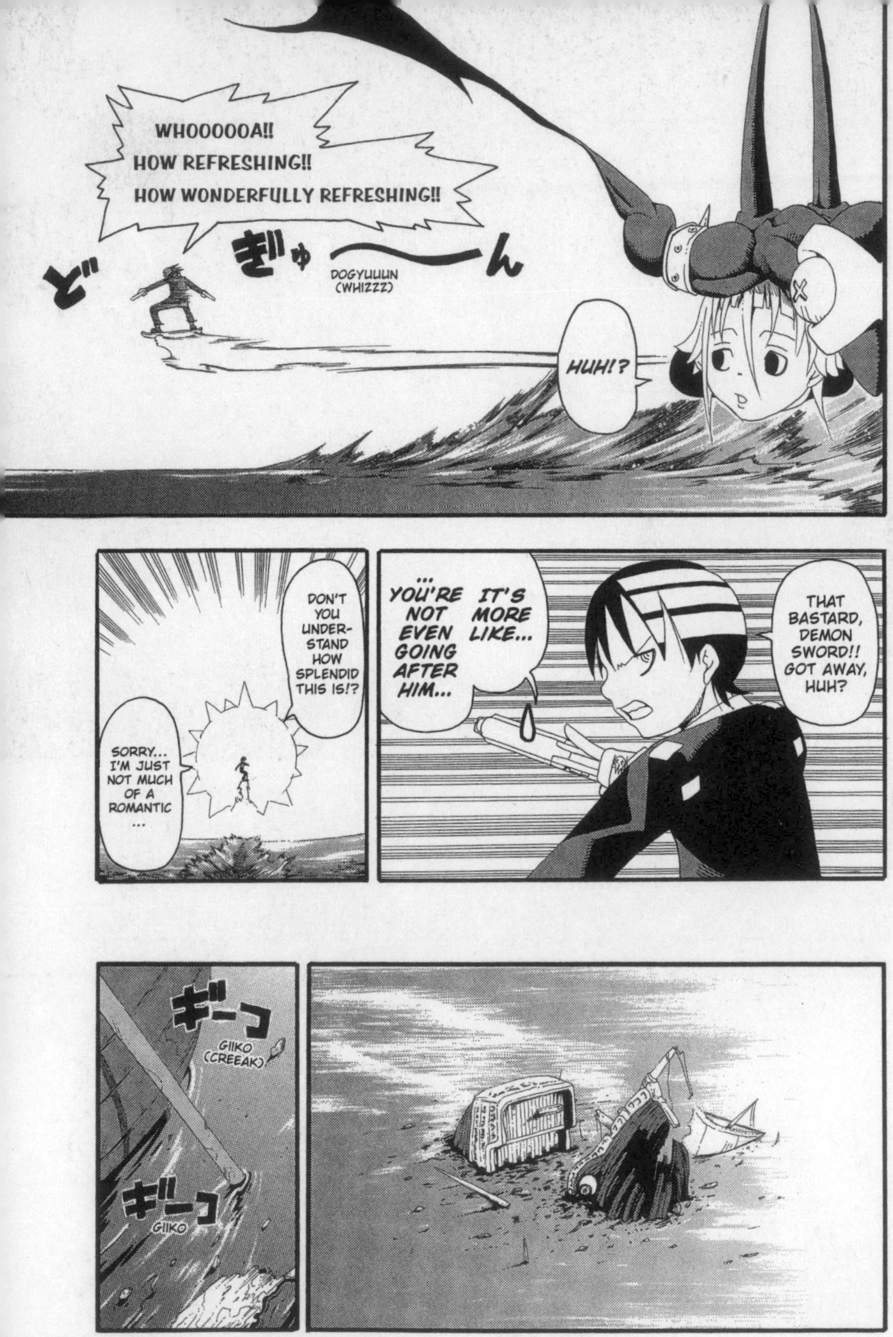
WHOOOOOA!! HOW REFRESHING!! HOW WONDERFULLY REFRESHING!!
どぎゅーーん
DOGYUUUN (WHIZZZ)
HUH!?
THAT BASTARD, DEMON SWORD!! GOT AWAY, HUH?
IT'S MORE LIKE...
...YOU'RE NOT EVEN GOING AFTER HIM...
DON'T YOU UNDER-STAND HOW SPLENDID THIS IS!?
SORRY... I'M JUST NOT MUCH OF A ROMANTIC ...
ギーコ
GIIKO (CREEAK)
ギーコ
GIIKO

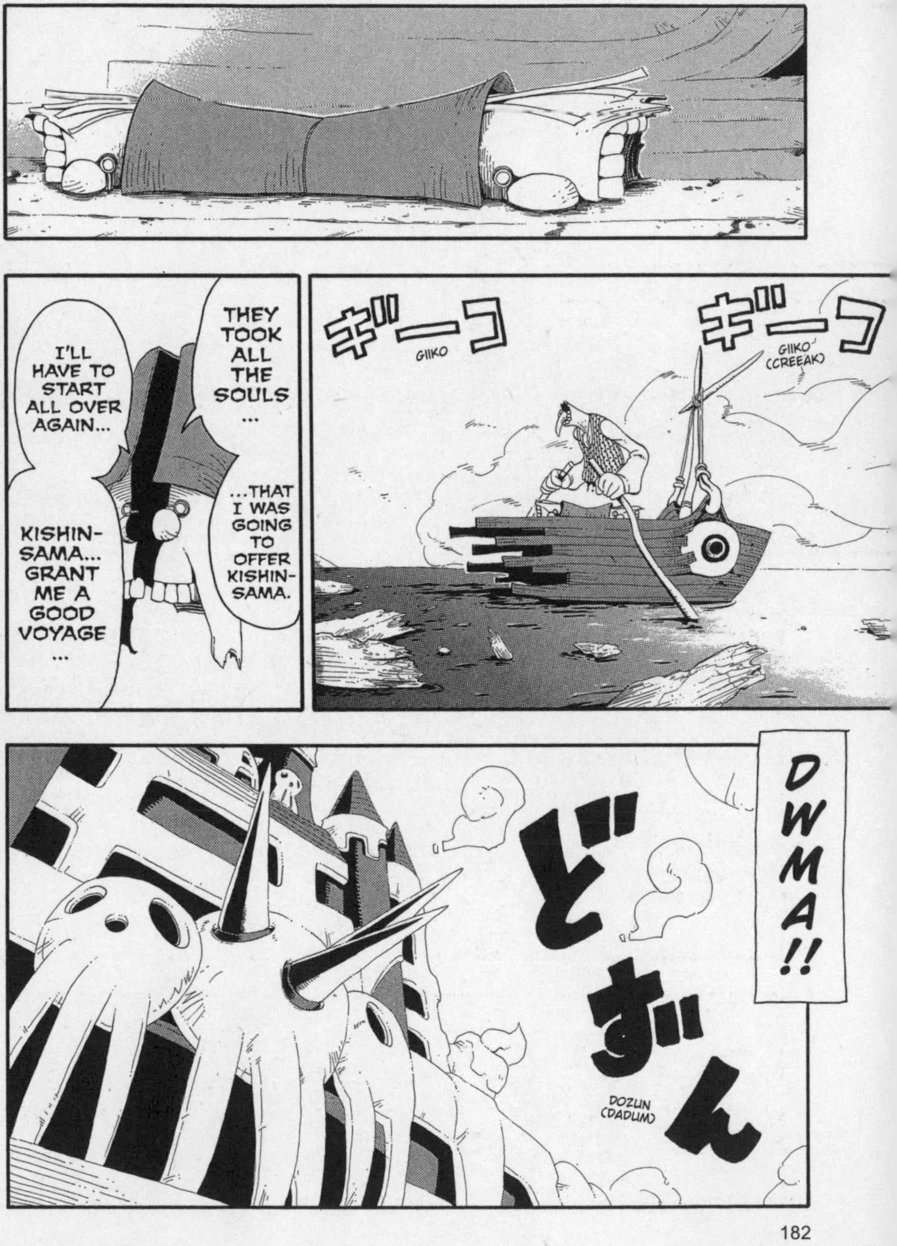
ギーコ
GIIKO (CREEAK)
ギーコ
GIIKO
THEY TOOK ALL THE SOULS...
...THAT I WAS GOING TO OFFER KISHIN-SAMA.
I'LL HAVE TO START ALL OVER AGAIN...
KISHIN-SAMA... GRANT ME A GOOD VOYAGE...
DWMA!!
どずん
DOZUN (DADUM)

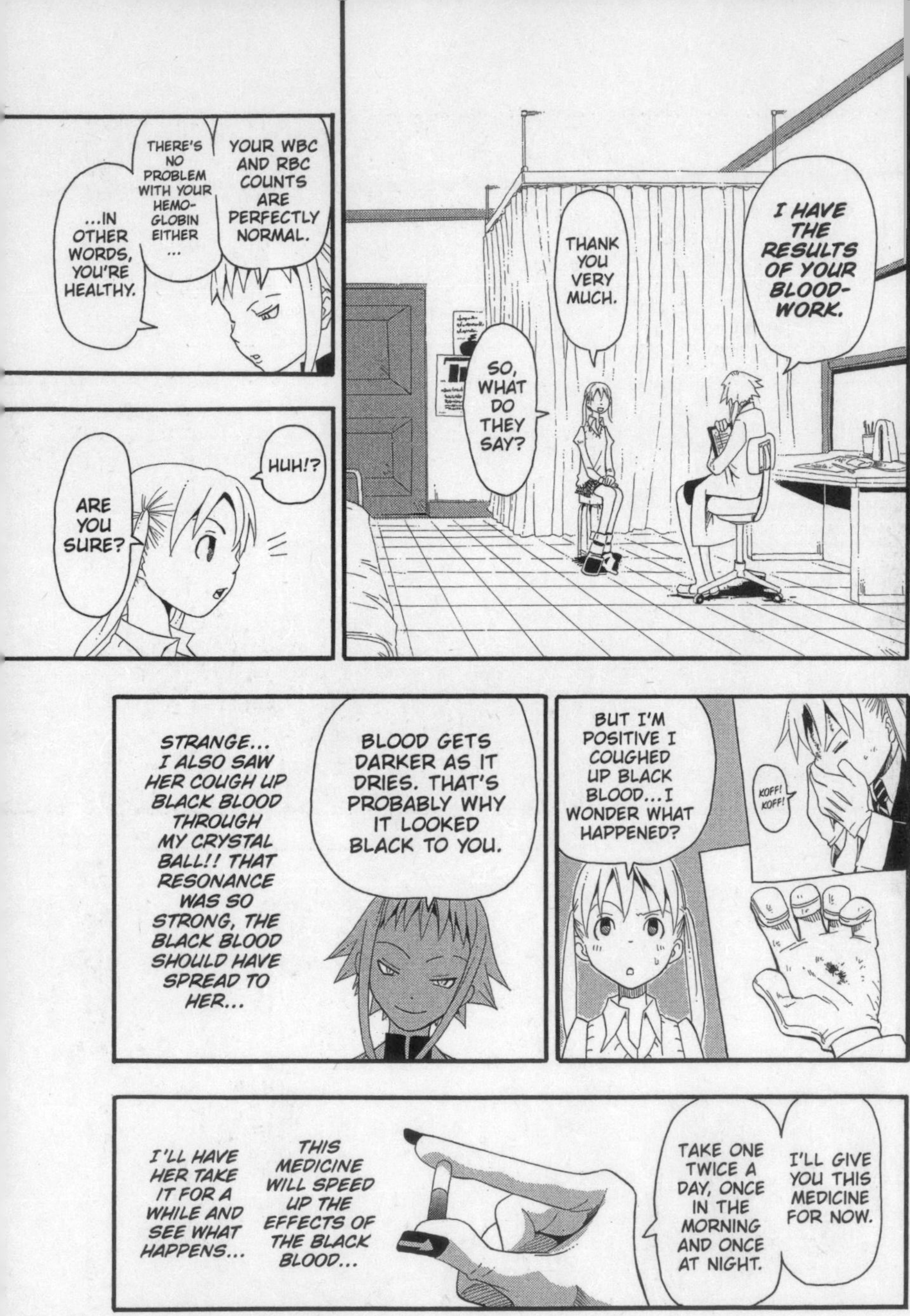
I HAVE THE RESULTS OF YOUR BLOOD-WORK.
THANK YOU VERY MUCH.
SO, WHAT DO THEY SAY?
YOUR WBC AND RBC COUNTS ARE PERFECTLY NORMAL.
THERE'S NO PROBLEM WITH YOUR HEMO-GLOBIN EITHER ...
...IN OTHER WORDS, YOU'RE HEALTHY.
HUH!?
ARE YOU SURE?
KOFF! KOFF!
BUT I'M POSITIVE I COUGHED UP BLACK BLOOD...I WONDER WHAT HAPPENED?
BLOOD GETS DARKER AS IT DRIES. THAT'S PROBABLY WHY IT LOOKED BLACK TO YOU.
STRANGE... I ALSO SAW HER COUGH UP BLACK BLOOD THROUGH MY CRYSTAL BALL!! THAT RESONANCE WAS SO STRONG, THE BLACK BLOOD SHOULD HAVE SPREAD TO HER...
I'LL GIVE YOU THIS MEDICINE FOR NOW.
TAKE ONE TWICE A DAY, ONCE IN THE MORNING AND ONCE AT NIGHT.
THIS MEDICINE WILL SPEED UP THE EFFECTS OF THE BLACK BLOOD...
I'LL HAVE HER TAKE IT FOR A WHILE AND SEE WHAT HAPPENS...

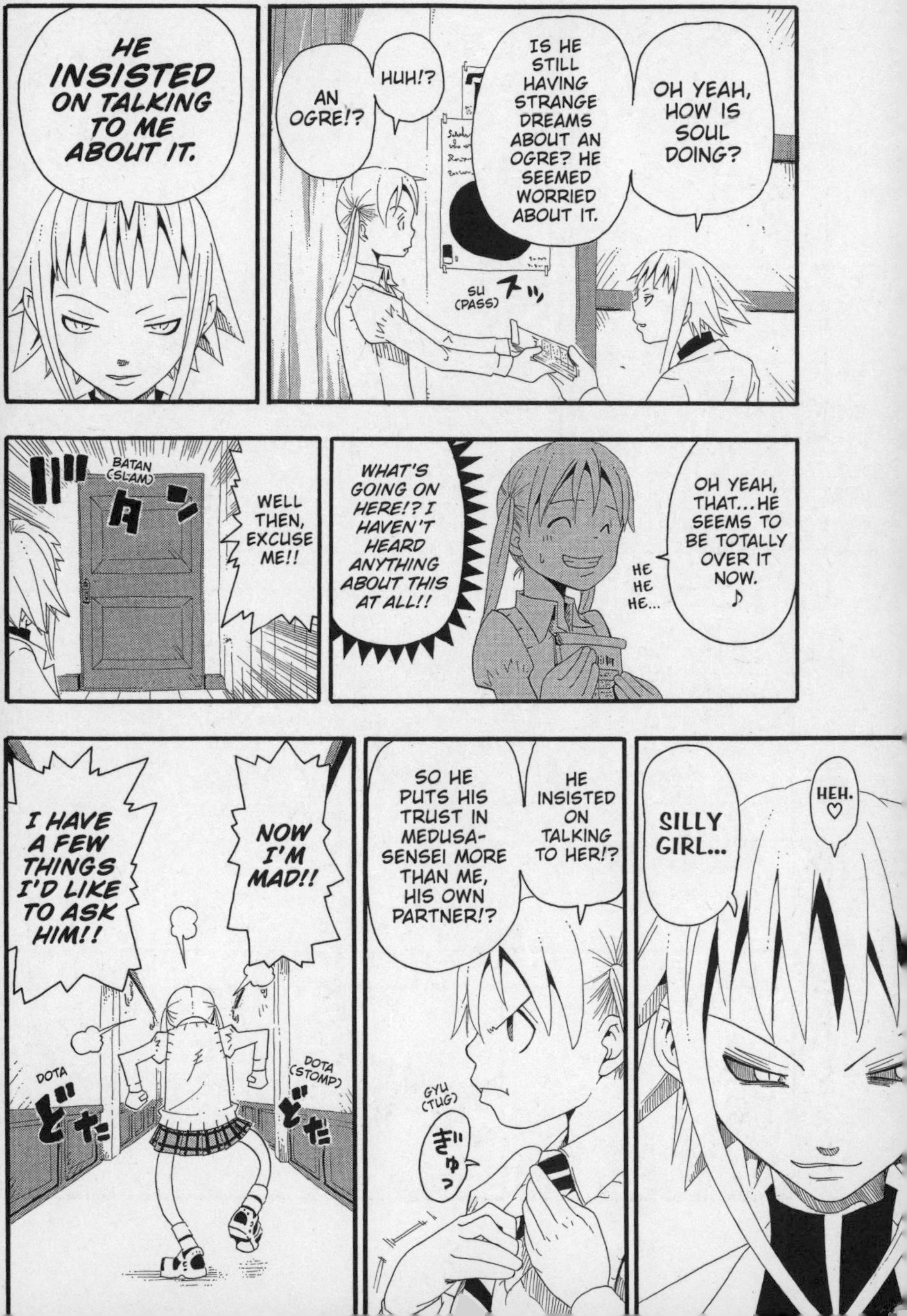
OH YEAH, HOW IS SOUL DOING?
IS HE STILL HAVING STRANGE DREAMS ABOUT AN OGRE? HE SEEMED WORRIED ABOUT IT.
HUH!?
AN OGRE!?
SU (PASS)
HE INSISTED ON TALKING TO ME ABOUT IT.
OH YEAH, THAT... HE SEEMS TO BE TOTALLY OVER IT NOW. ♪
HE HE HE...
WHAT'S GOING ON HERE!? I HAVEN'T HEARD ANYTHING ABOUT THIS AT ALL!!
WELL THEN, EXCUSE ME!!
BATAN (SLAM)
HEH. ♡
SILLY GIRL...
HE INSISTED ON TALKING TO HER!?
SO HE PUTS HIS TRUST IN MEDUSA-SENSEI MORE THAN ME, HIS OWN PARTNER!?
GYU (TUG)
ぎゅっ
NOW I'M MAD!!
DOTA (STOMP)
I HAVE A FEW THINGS I'D LIKE TO ASK HIM!!
DOTA

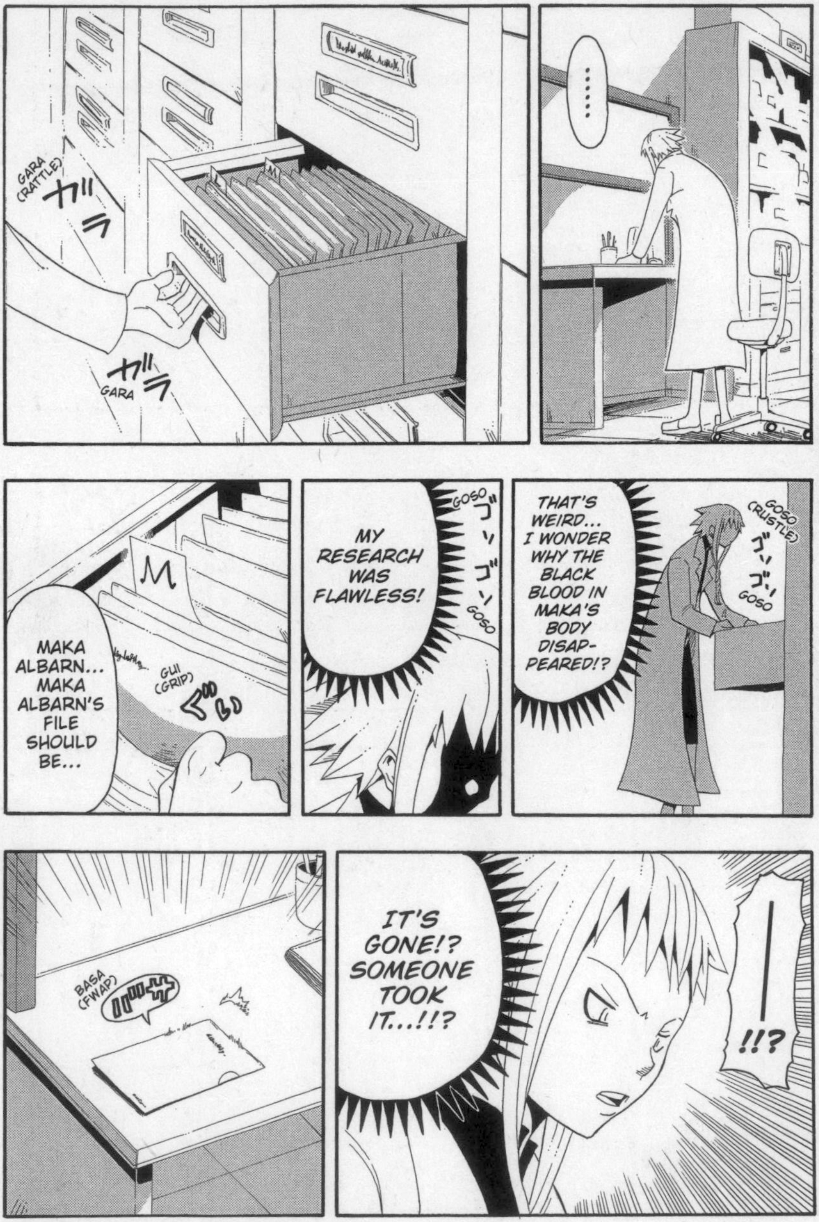
......
GARA (RATTLE)
GARA
THAT'S WEIRD... I WONDER WHY THE BLACK BLOOD IN MAKA'S BODY DISAPPEARED!?
GOSO (RUSTLE)
GOSO
GOSO
MY RESEARCH WAS FLAWLESS!
GOSO
MAKA ALBARN... MAKA ALBARN'S FILE SHOULD BE...
GUI (GRIP)
!!?
IT'S GONE!? SOMEONE TOOK IT...!!?
BASA (FWAP)

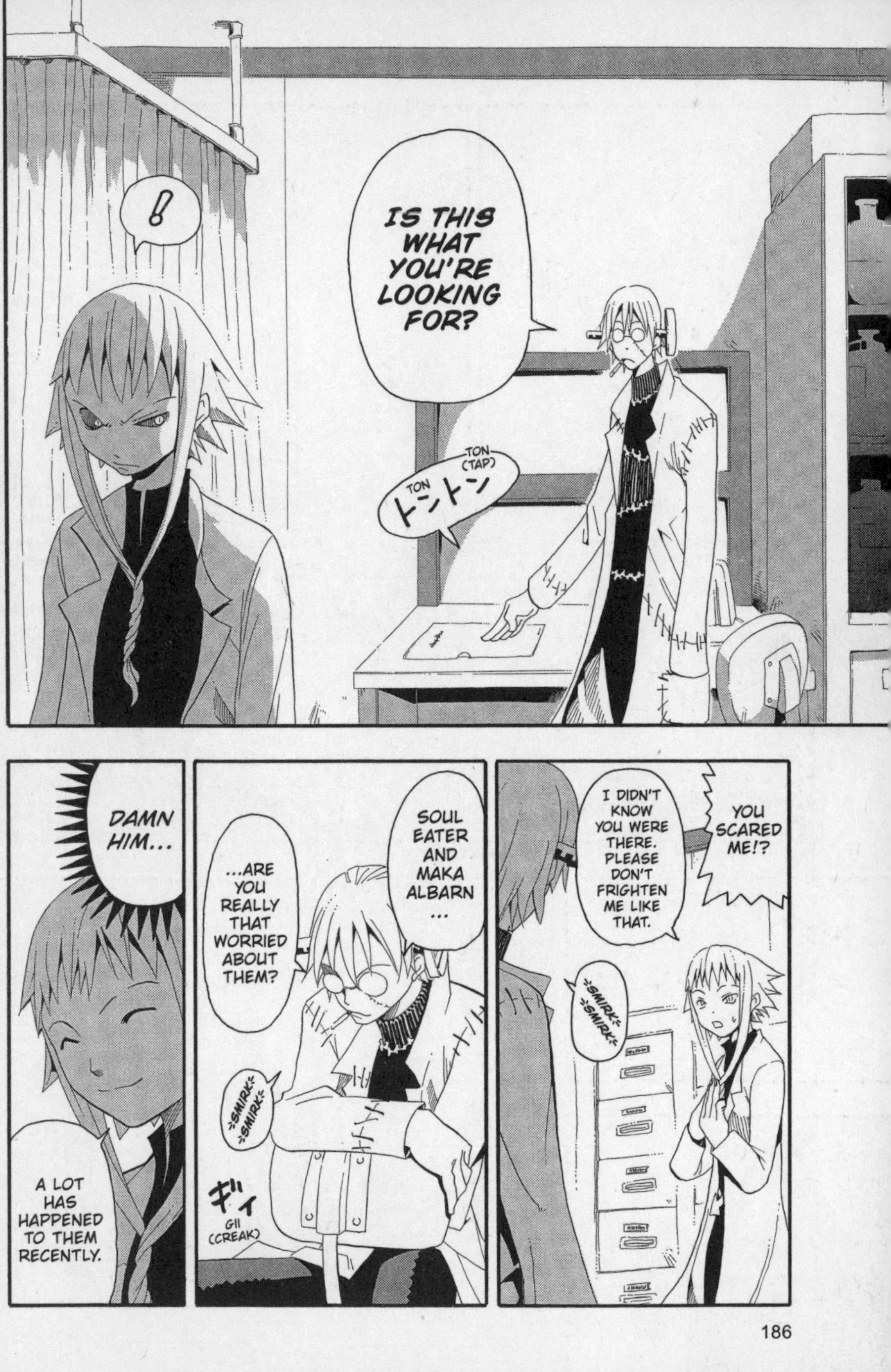
IS THIS WHAT YOU'RE LOOKING FOR?
TON TON (TAP) トントン
!
YOU SCARED ME!?
I DIDN'T KNOW YOU WERE THERE. PLEASE DON'T FRIGHTEN ME LIKE THAT.
SMIRK SMIRK
SOUL EATER AND MAKA ALBARN ...
...ARE YOU REALLY THAT WORRIED ABOUT THEM?
SMIRK SMIRK
ギィ GII (CREAK)
DAMN HIM...
A LOT HAS HAPPENED TO THEM RECENTLY.

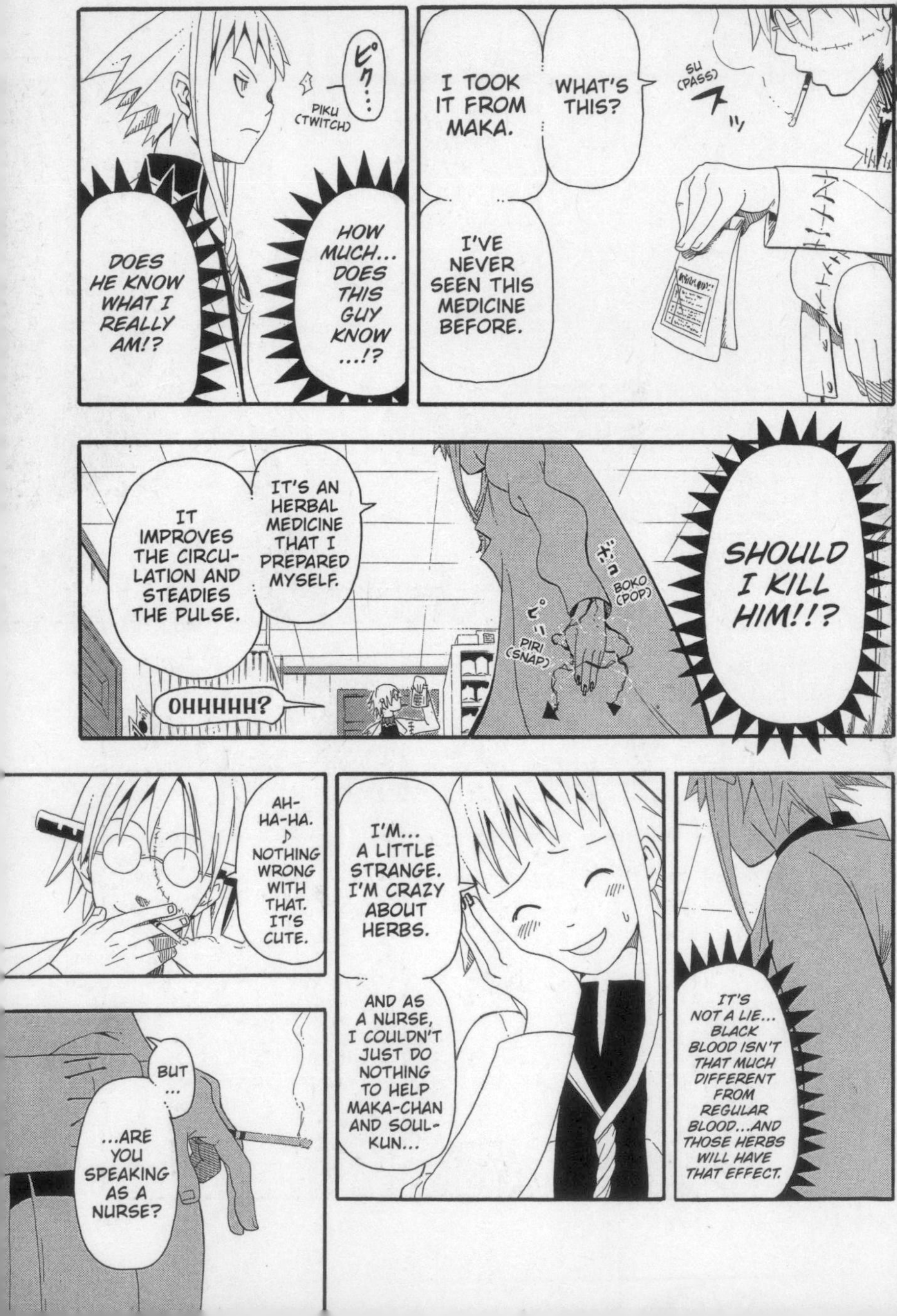

スッ
SU (PASS)
WHAT'S THIS?
I TOOK IT FROM MAKA.
I'VE NEVER SEEN THIS MEDICINE BEFORE.
ピク…
PIKU (TWITCH)
HOW MUCH... DOES THIS GUY KNOW ...!?
DOES HE KNOW WHAT I REALLY AM!?
SHOULD I KILL HIM!!?
ボコ
BOKO (POP)
ピリ
PIRI (SNAP)
IT'S AN HERBAL MEDICINE THAT I PREPARED MYSELF.
IT IMPROVES THE CIRCULATION AND STEADIES THE PULSE.
OHHHHH?
IT'S NOT A LIE... BLACK BLOOD ISN'T THAT MUCH DIFFERENT FROM REGULAR BLOOD...AND THOSE HERBS WILL HAVE THAT EFFECT.
I'M... A LITTLE STRANGE. I'M CRAZY ABOUT HERBS.
AND AS A NURSE, I COULDN'T JUST DO NOTHING TO HELP MAKA-CHAN AND SOUL-KUN...
AH-HA-HA. ♪ NOTHING WRONG WITH THAT. IT'S CUTE.
BUT ...
...ARE YOU SPEAKING AS A NURSE?

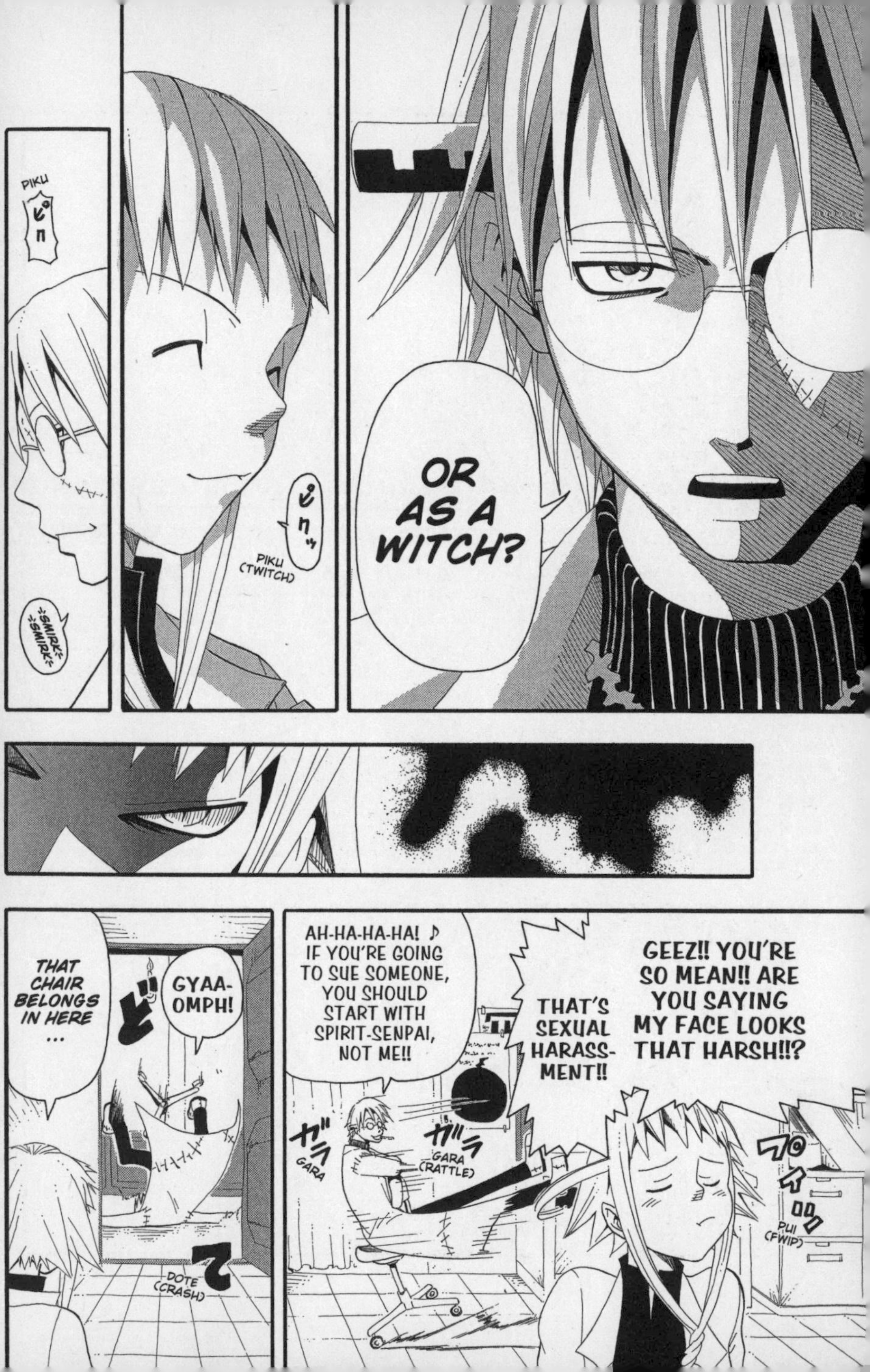
OR AS A WITCH?
PIKU (TWITCH)
PIKU
SMIRK SMIRK
GEEZ!! YOU'RE SO MEAN!! ARE YOU SAYING MY FACE LOOKS THAT HARSH!!?
THAT'S SEXUAL HARASS-MENT!!
PUI (FWIP)
AH-HA-HA-HA! ♪ IF YOU'RE GOING TO SUE SOMEONE, YOU SHOULD START WITH SPIRIT-SENPAI, NOT ME!!
GARA (RATTLE)
GARA
THAT CHAIR BELONGS IN HERE ...
GYAA-OMPH!
DOTE (CRASH)

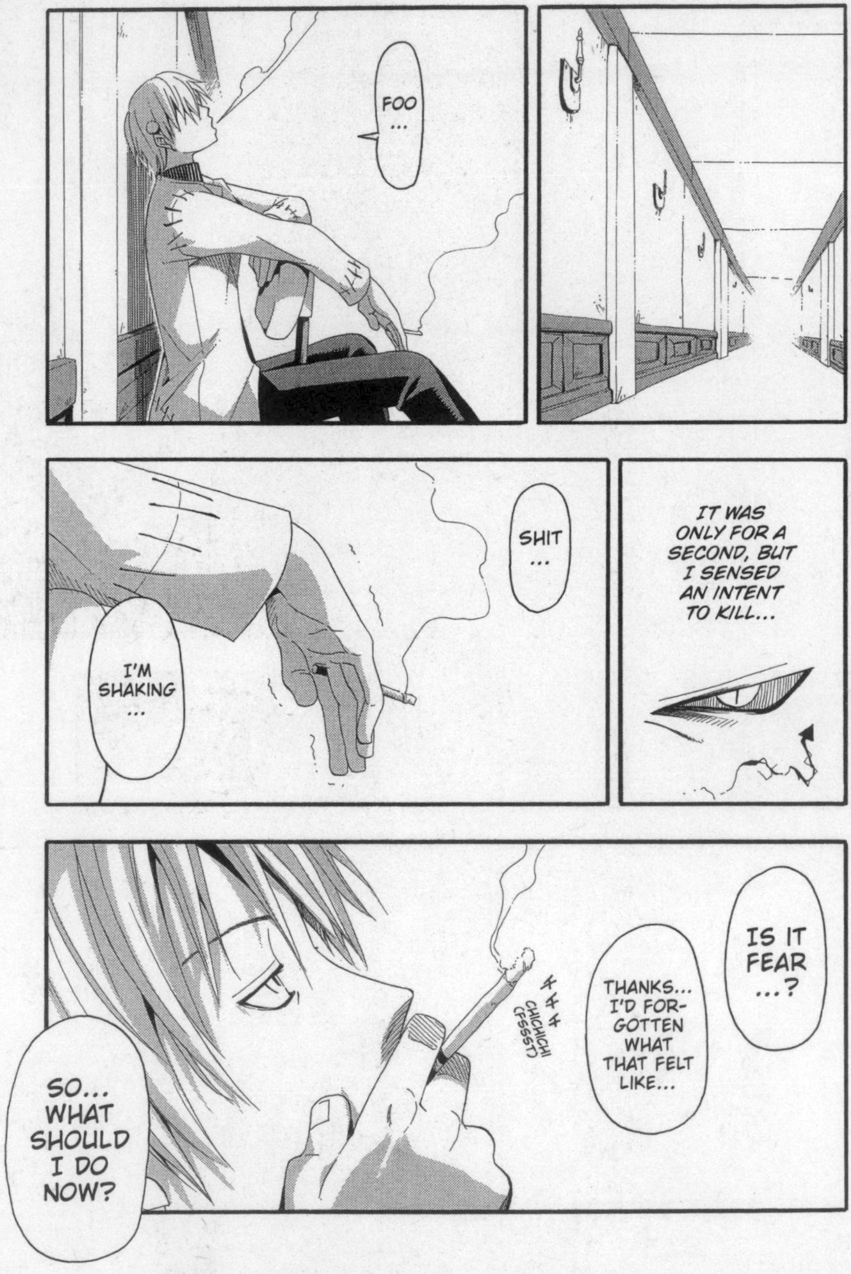
FOO ...
IT WAS ONLY FOR A SECOND, BUT I SENSED AN INTENT TO KILL...
SHIT ...
I'M SHAKING ...
IS IT FEAR ...?
THANKS... I'D FOR-GOTTEN WHAT THAT FELT LIKE...
CHICHICHI (FSSST)
SO... WHAT SHOULD I DO NOW?

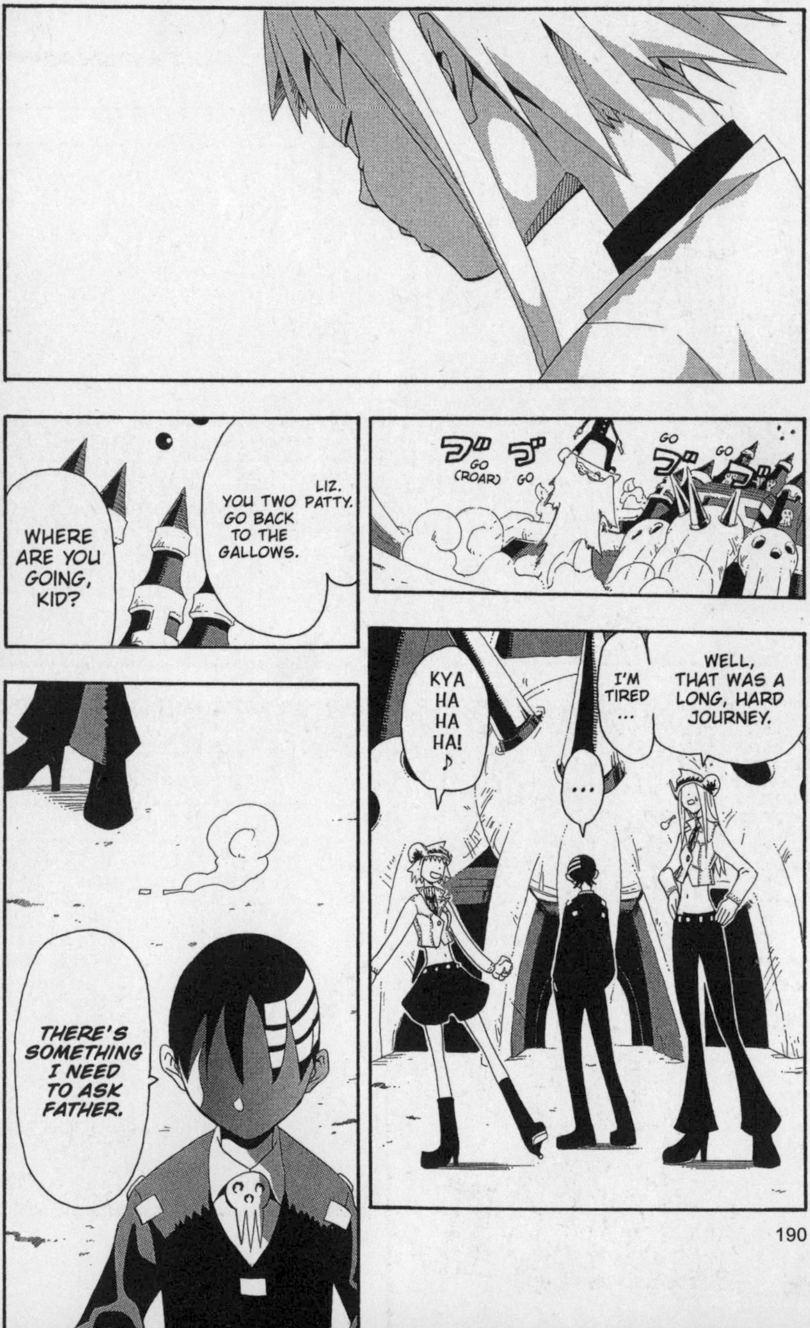
GO GO
GO (ROAR) GO
LIZ. PATTY. YOU TWO GO BACK TO THE GALLOWS.
WHERE ARE YOU GOING, KID?
WELL, THAT WAS A LONG, HARD JOURNEY.
I'M TIRED ...
...
KYA HA HA HA! ♪
THERE'S SOMETHING I NEED TO ASK FATHER.

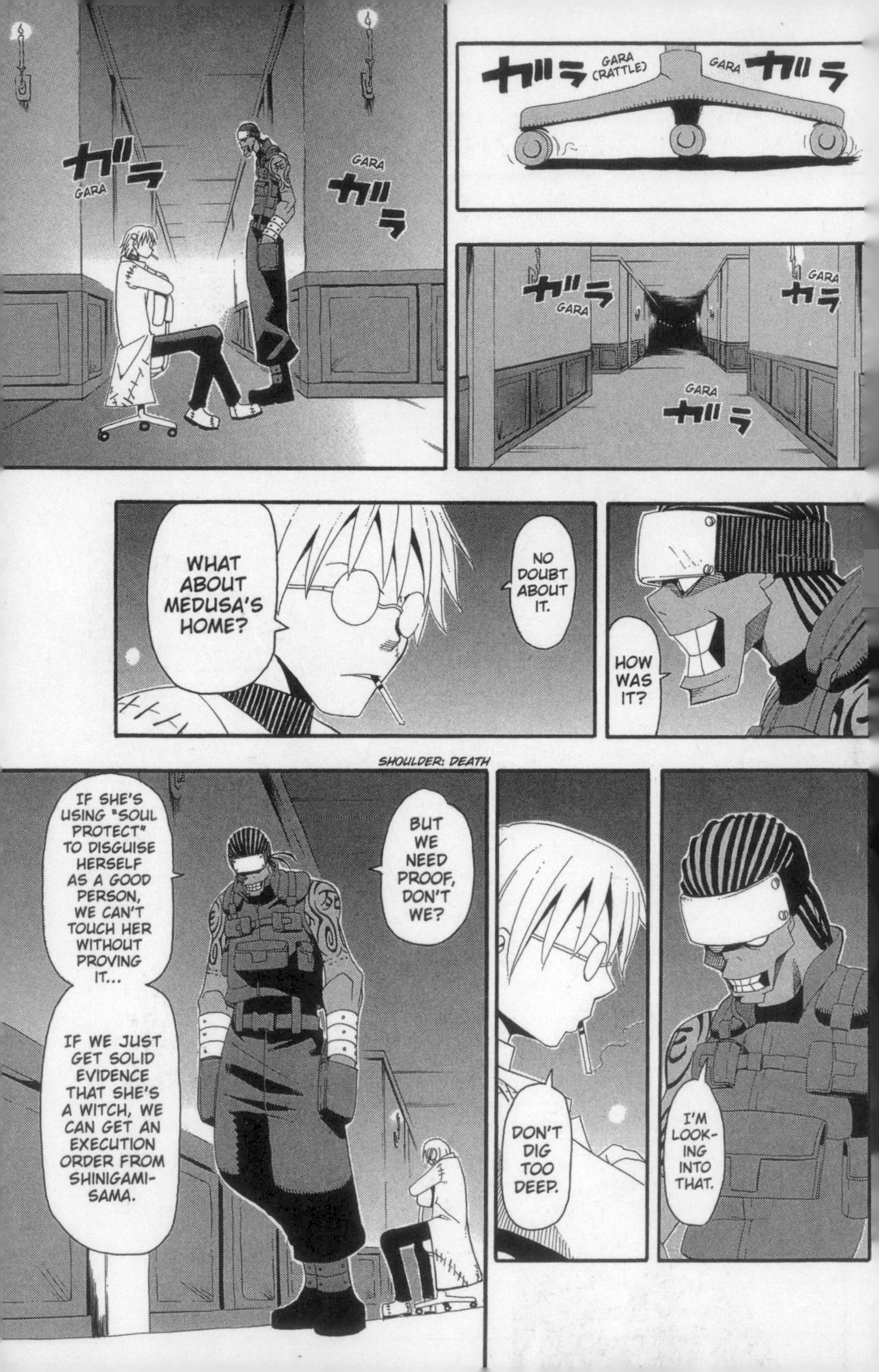
ガラ
GARA
ガラ
GARA (RATTLE)
GARA
カラ
ガラ
GARA
GARA
ガラ
GARA
ガラ
ガラ
GARA
HOW WAS IT?
NO DOUBT ABOUT IT.
WHAT ABOUT MEDUSA'S HOME?
SHOULDER: DEATH
I'M LOOKING INTO THAT.
DON'T DIG TOO DEEP.
BUT WE NEED PROOF, DON'T WE?
IF SHE'S USING "SOUL PROTECT" TO DISGUISE HERSELF AS A GOOD PERSON, WE CAN'T TOUCH HER WITHOUT PROVING IT...
IF WE JUST GET SOLID EVIDENCE THAT SHE'S A WITCH, WE CAN GET AN EXECUTION ORDER FROM SHINIGAMI-SAMA.

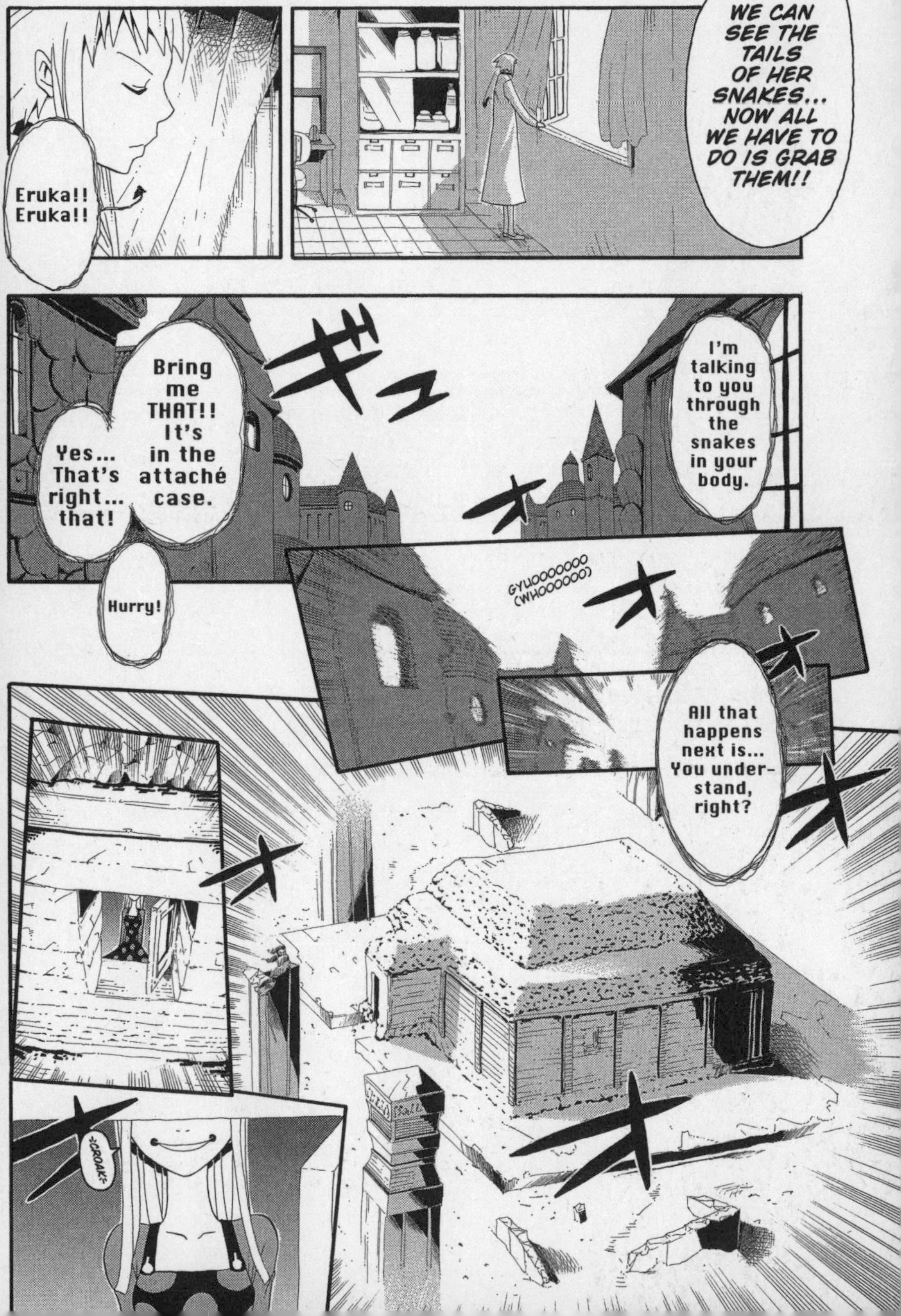
WE CAN SEE THE TAILS OF HER SNAKES... NOW ALL WE HAVE TO DO IS GRAB THEM!!
Eruka!! Eruka!!
I'm talking to you through the snakes in your body.
ギュ
Bring me THAT!! It's in the attaché case.
Yes... That's right... that!
Hurry!
GYUOOOOOOO (WHOOOOOOO)
All that happens next is... You understand, right?
CROAK

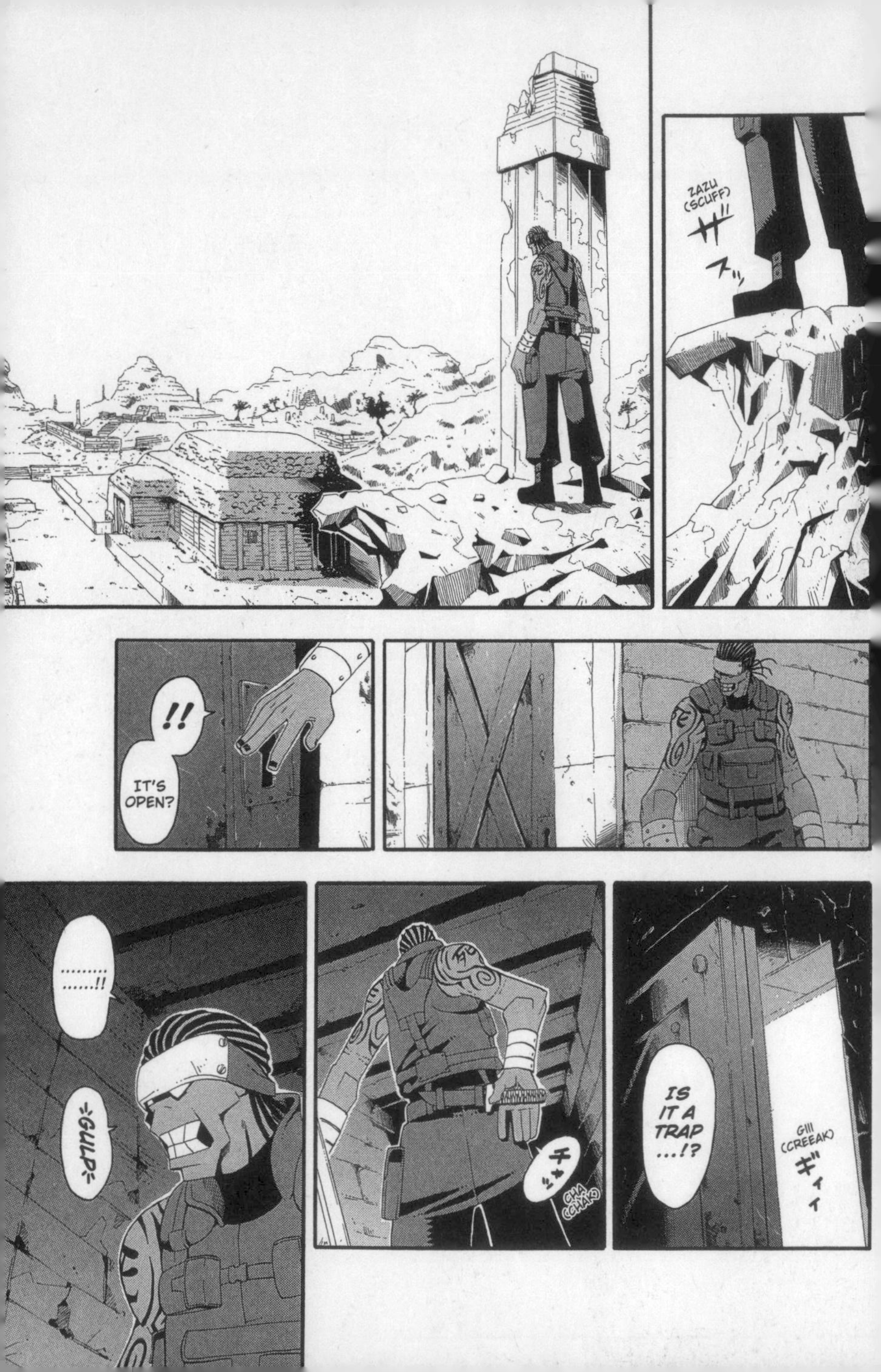
ZAZU (SCUFF)
!!
IT'S OPEN?
GIII (CREEAK)
ギィ
IS IT A TRAP ...!?
CHA (CHAK)
....
......!!
GULP

...THIS IS SUPPOSED TO BE A NURSE'S ROOM...?

HEY...

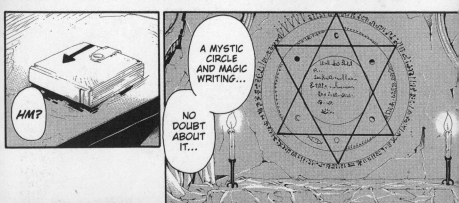

HM?

A MYSTIC CIRCLE AND MAGIC WRITING...

NO DOUBT ABOUT IT...

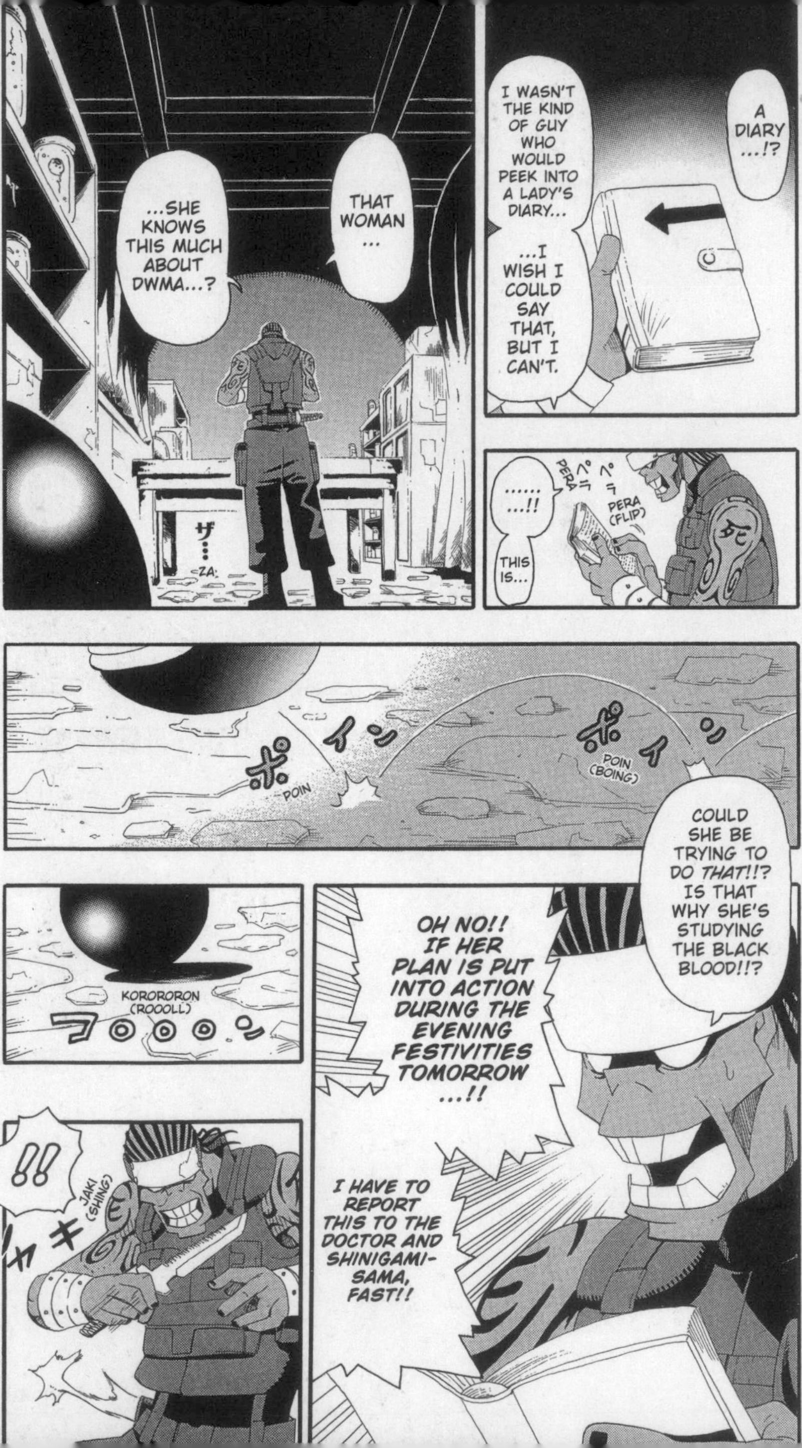
A DIARY ...!?
I WASN'T THE KIND OF GUY WHO WOULD PEEK INTO A LADY'S DIARY...
...I WISH I COULD SAY THAT, BUT I CAN'T.
PERA
PERA (FLIP)
......
...!!
THIS IS...
THAT WOMAN ...
...SHE KNOWS THIS MUCH ABOUT DWMA...?
ZA
POIN (BOING)
POIN
COULD SHE BE TRYING TO DO *THAT*!!? IS THAT WHY SHE'S STUDYING THE BLACK BLOOD!!?
OH NO!! IF HER PLAN IS PUT INTO ACTION DURING THE EVENING FESTIVITIES TOMORROW ...!!
I HAVE TO REPORT THIS TO THE DOCTOR AND SHINIGAMI-SAMA, FAST!!
KOROROROON (ROOOLL)
!!
JAKI (SHING)

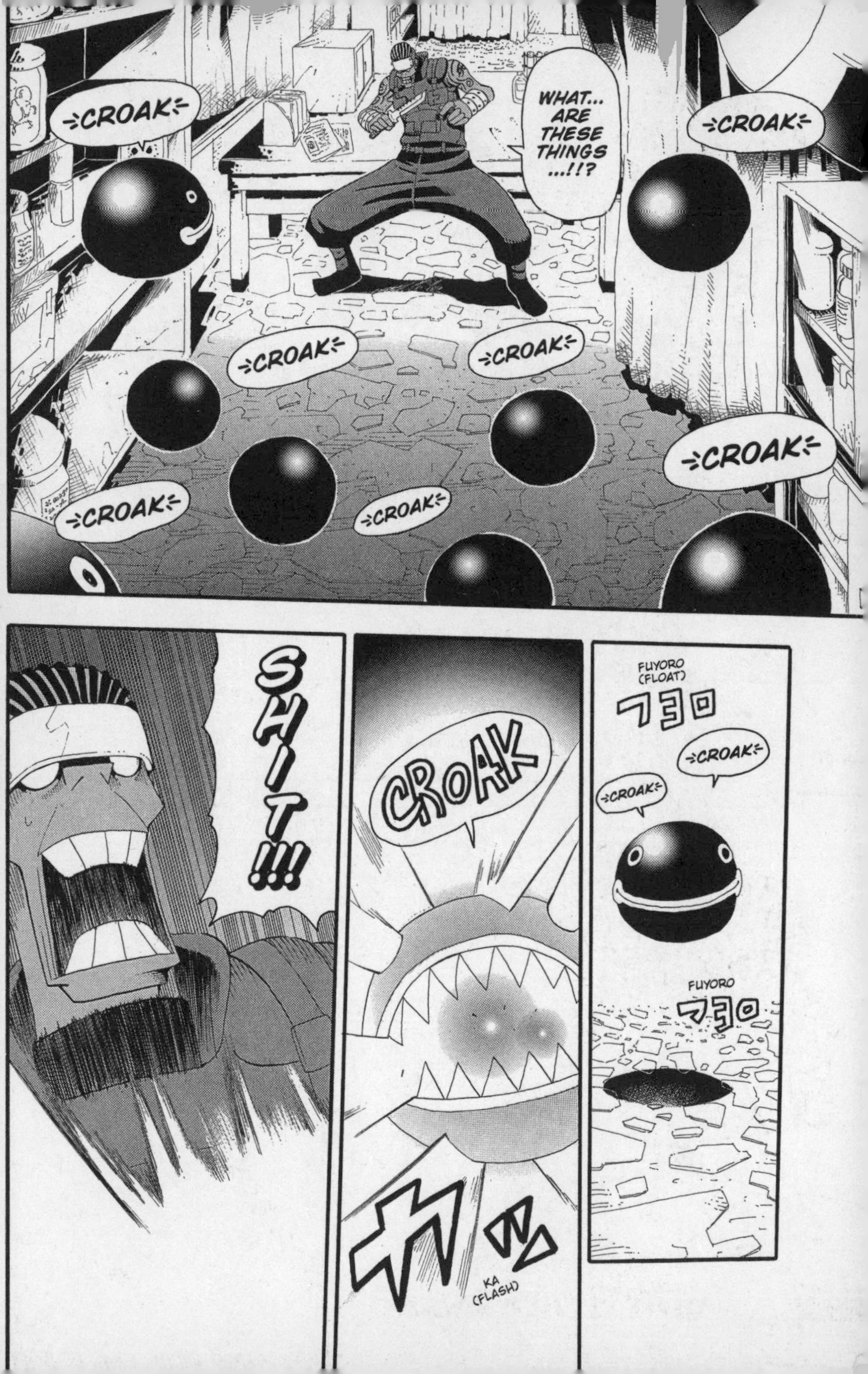CROAK
WHAT... ARE THESE THINGS ...!!?
CROAK
CROAK
CROAK
CROAK
CROAK
CROAK
FUYORO (FLOAT)
フヨロ
CROAK
CROAK
FUYORO
フヨロ
CROAK
カッ
KA (FLASH)
SHIT!!!

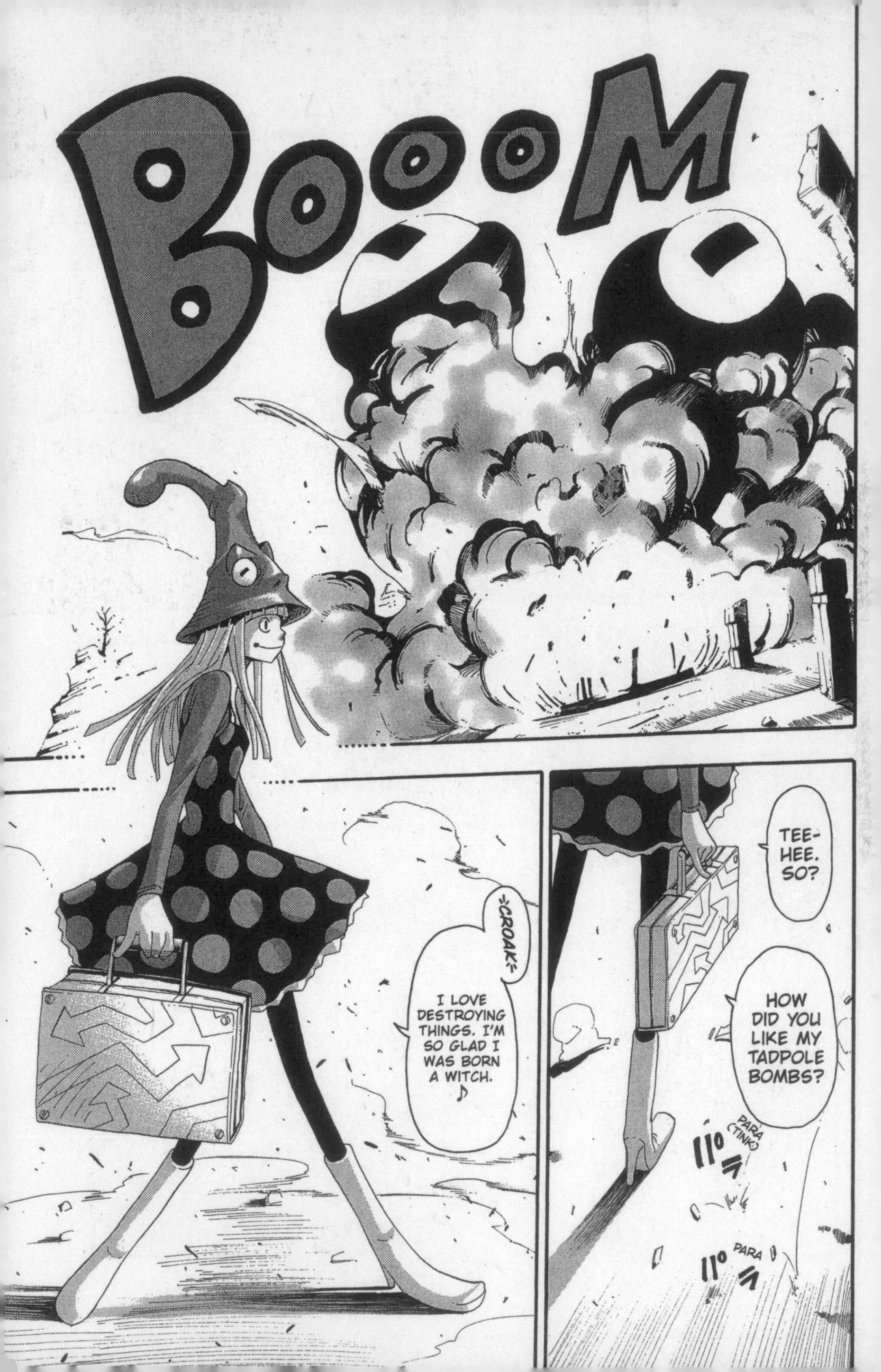
BOOOM
TEE-HEE. SO?
HOW DID YOU LIKE MY TADPOLE BOMBS?
PARA (TINK)
PARA
CROAK
I LOVE DESTROYING THINGS. I'M SO GLAD I WAS BORN A WITCH. ♪

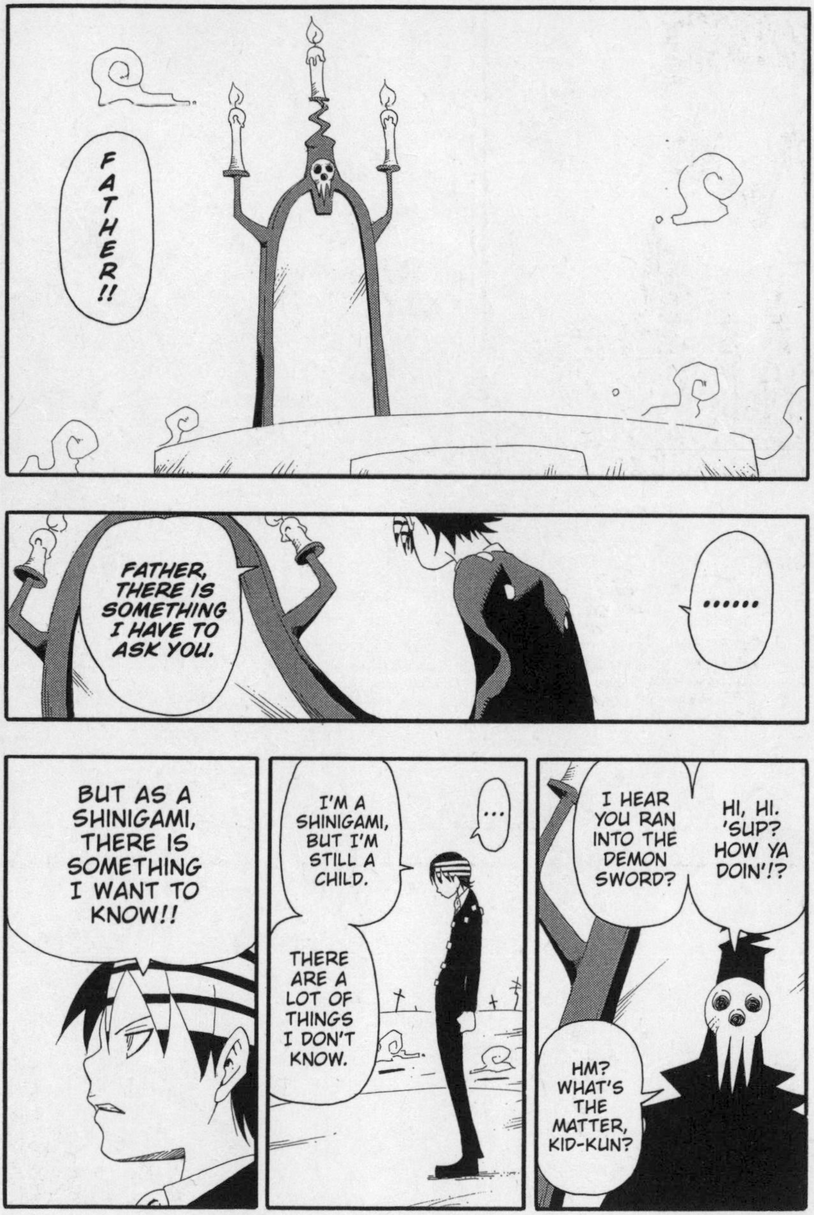
FATHER!!
......
FATHER, THERE IS SOMETHING I HAVE TO ASK YOU.
HI, HI. 'SUP? HOW YA DOIN'!?
I HEAR YOU RAN INTO THE DEMON SWORD?
HM? WHAT'S THE MATTER, KID-KUN?
...
I'M A SHINIGAMI, BUT I'M STILL A CHILD.
THERE ARE A LOT OF THINGS I DON'T KNOW.
BUT AS A SHINIGAMI, THERE IS SOMETHING I WANT TO KNOW!!

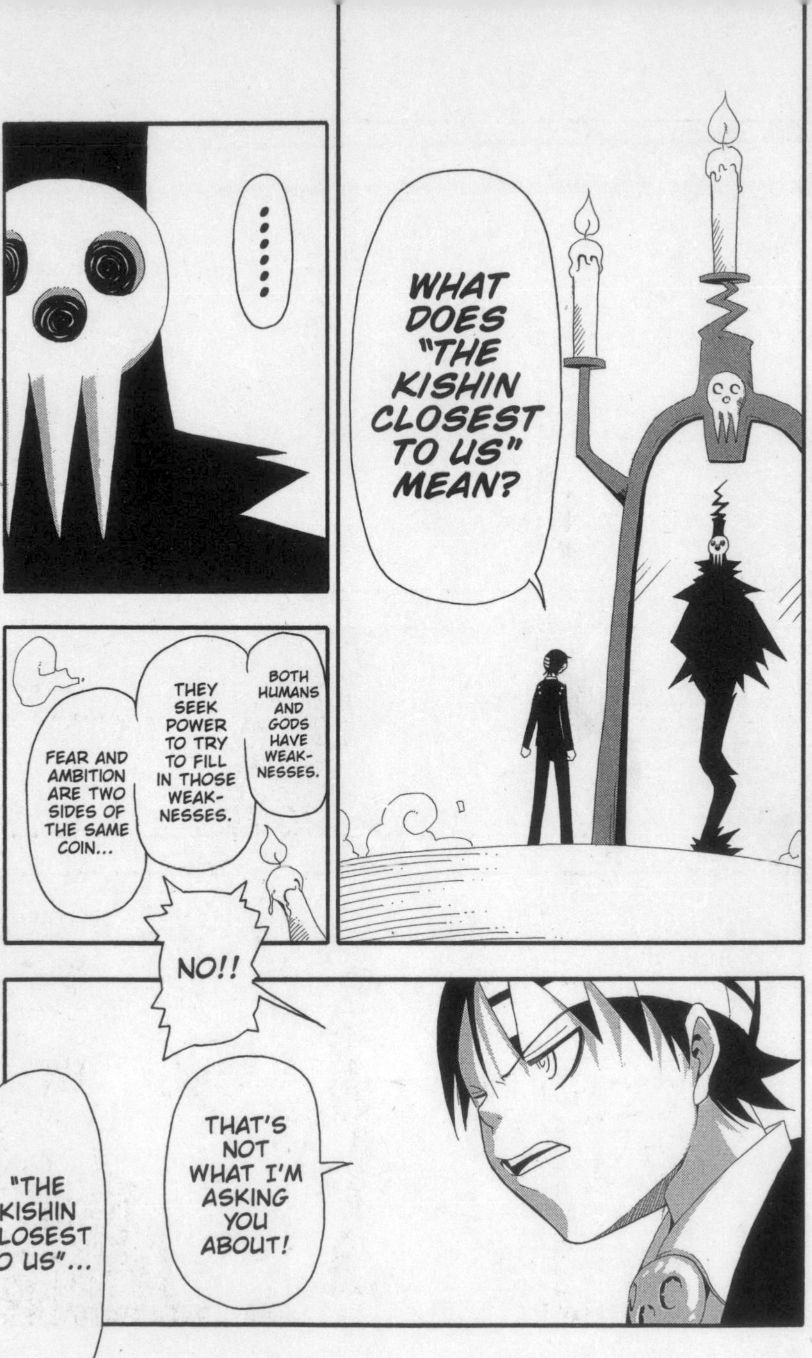
WHAT DOES "THE KISHIN CLOSEST TO US" MEAN?
......
BOTH HUMANS AND GODS HAVE WEAK-NESSES.
THEY SEEK POWER TO TRY TO FILL IN THOSE WEAK-NESSES.
FEAR AND AMBITION ARE TWO SIDES OF THE SAME COIN...
NO!!
THAT'S NOT WHAT I'M ASKING YOU ABOUT!
"THE KISHIN CLOSEST TO US"...

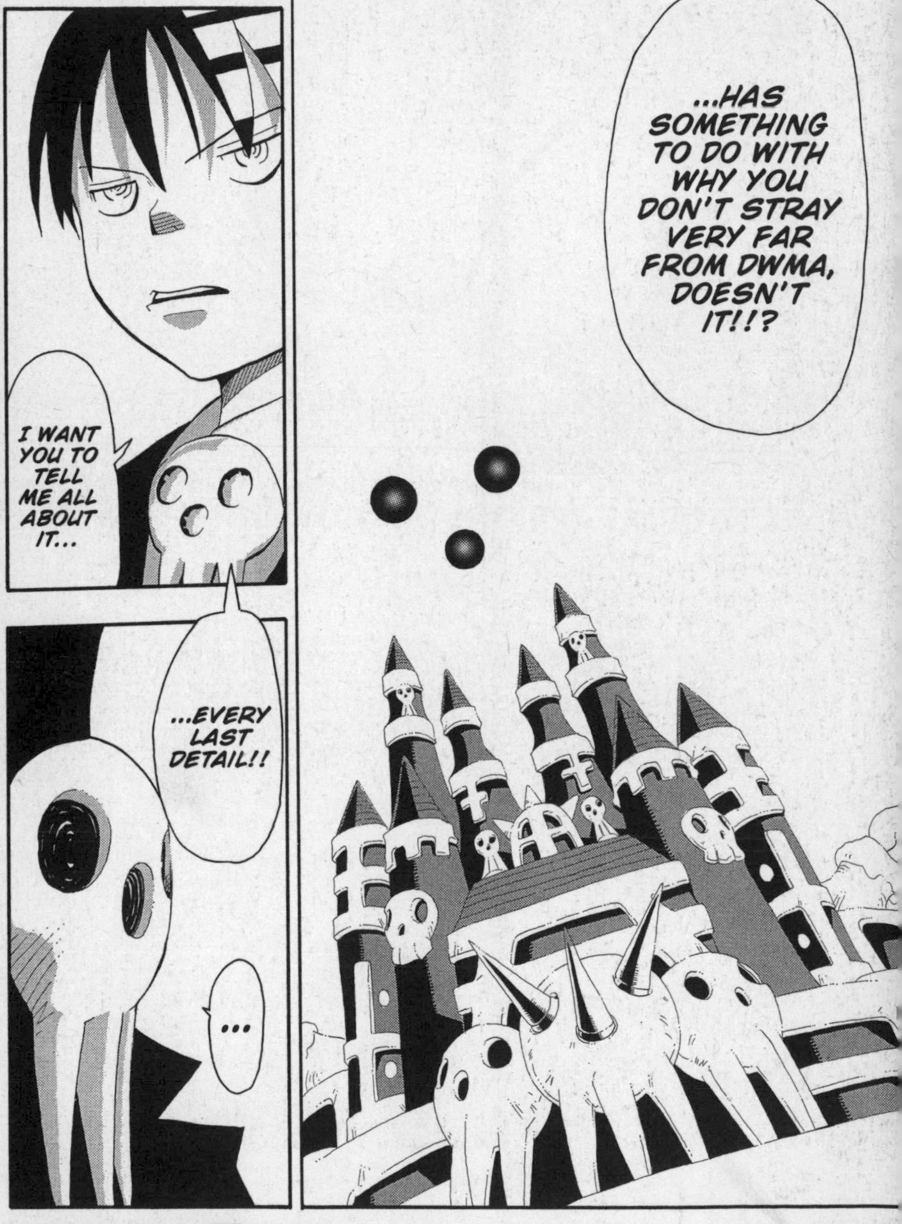
...HAS SOMETHING TO DO WITH WHY YOU DON'T STRAY VERY FAR FROM DWMA, DOESN'T IT!!?
I WANT YOU TO TELL ME ALL ABOUT IT...
...EVERY LAST DETAIL!!
...

SOUL EATER 4 END

SOUL EATER

PREVIEW

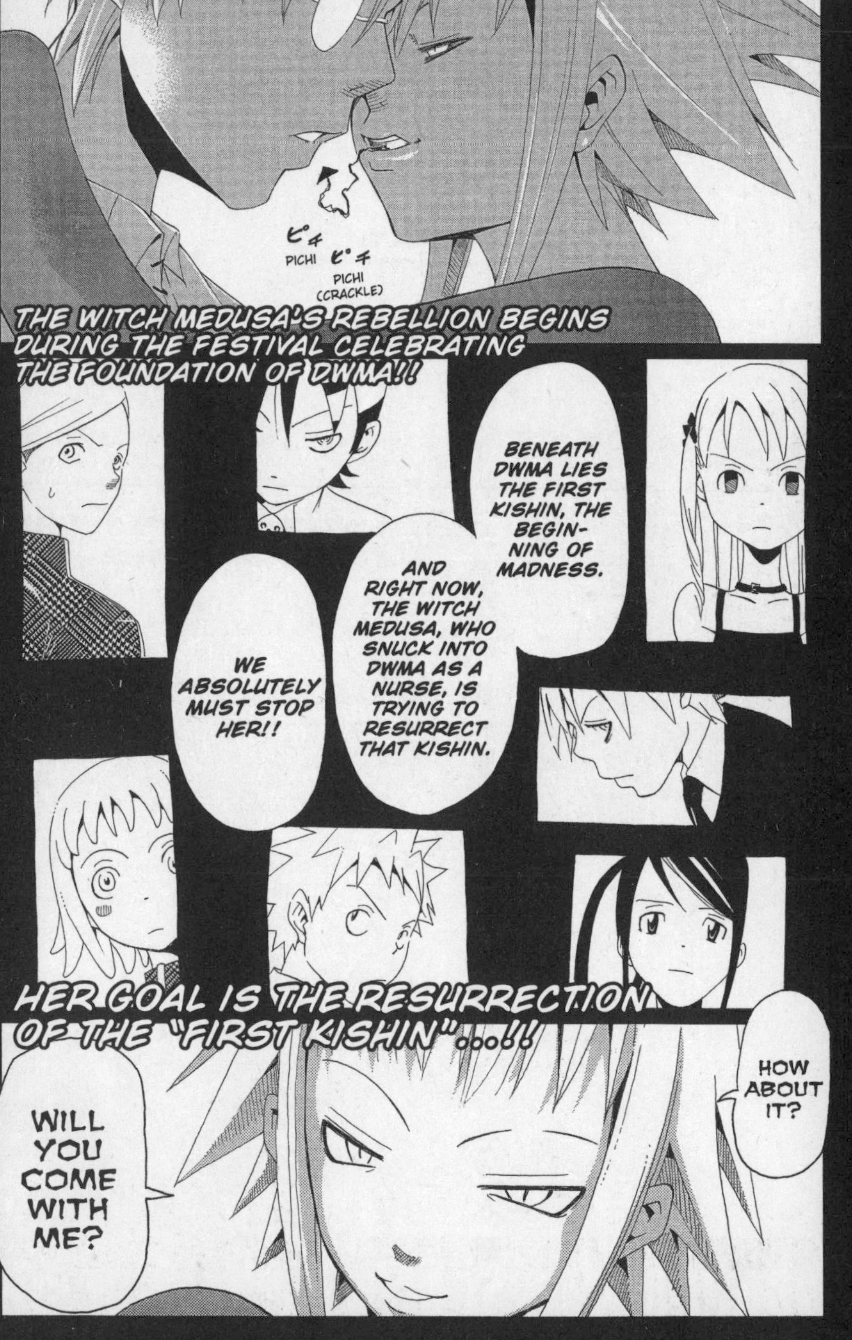
ピチ PICHI
ピチ PICHI (CRACKLE)
THE WITCH MEDUSA'S REBELLION BEGINS DURING THE FESTIVAL CELEBRATING THE FOUNDATION OF DWMA!!
BENEATH DWMA LIES THE FIRST KISHIN, THE BEGINNING OF MADNESS.
AND RIGHT NOW, THE WITCH MEDUSA, WHO SNUCK INTO DWMA AS A NURSE, IS TRYING TO RESURRECT THAT KISHIN.
WE ABSOLUTELY MUST STOP HER!!
HER GOAL IS THE RESURRECTION OF THE "FIRST KISHIN"...!!
HOW ABOUT IT?
WILL YOU COME WITH ME?

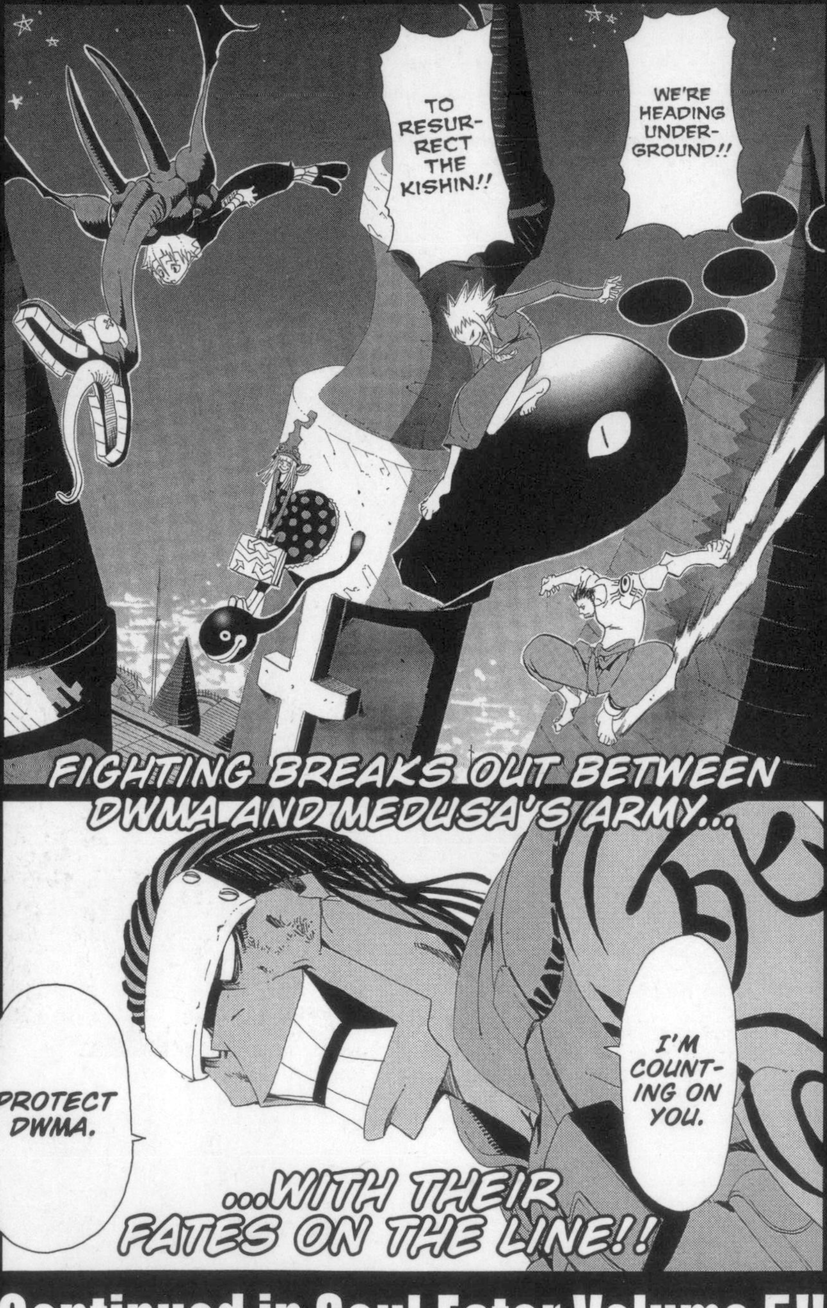
WE'RE HEADING UNDER-GROUND!!
TO RESUR-RECT THE KISHIN!!
FIGHTING BREAKS OUT BETWEEN DWMA AND MEDUSA'S ARMY...
I'M COUNT-ING ON YOU.
PROTECT DWMA.
...WITH THEIR FATES ON THE LINE!!

Continued in Soul Eater Volume 5!!

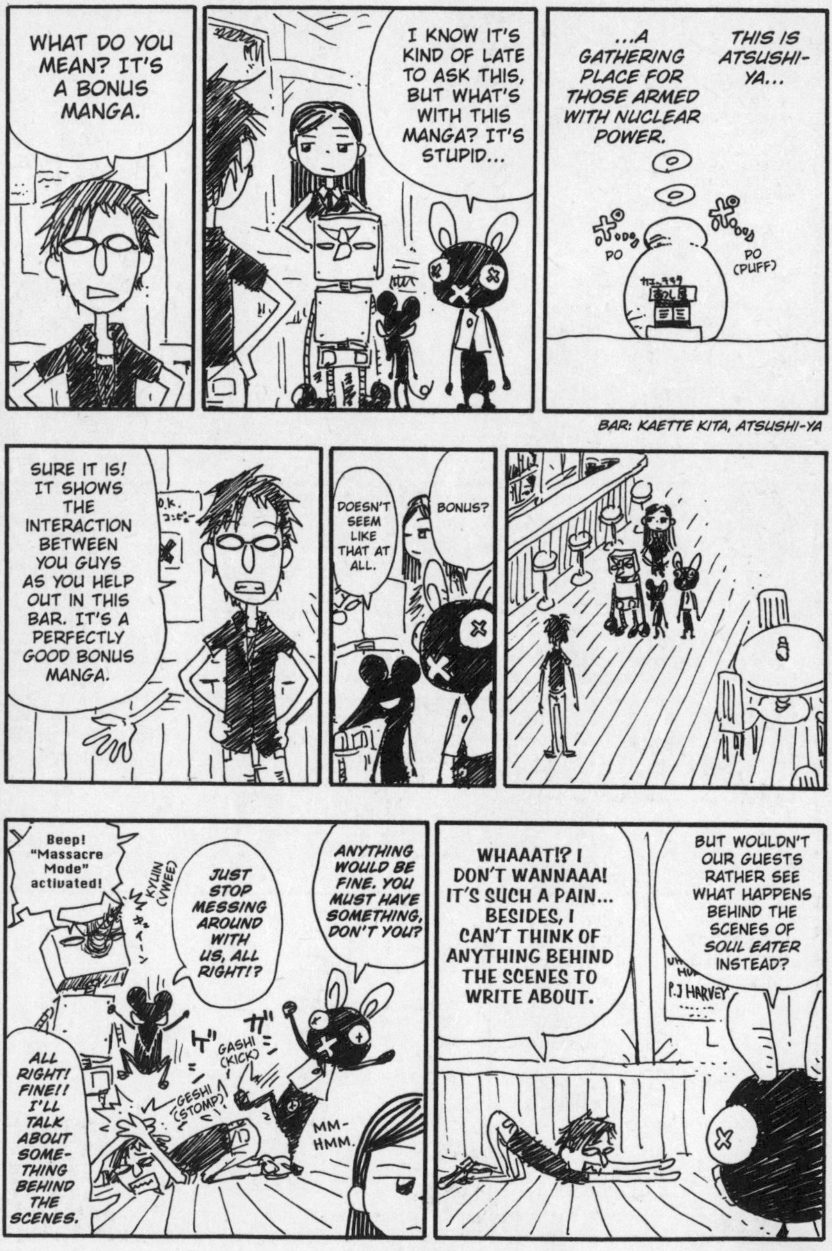
THIS IS ATSUSHI-YA...
...A GATHERING PLACE FOR THOSE ARMED WITH NUCLEAR POWER.
PO
PO (PUFF)
I KNOW IT'S KIND OF LATE TO ASK THIS, BUT WHAT'S WITH THIS MANGA? IT'S STUPID...
WHAT DO YOU MEAN? IT'S A BONUS MANGA.
BAR: KAETTE KITA, ATSUSHI-YA
BONUS?
DOESN'T SEEM LIKE THAT AT ALL.
SURE IT IS! IT SHOWS THE INTERACTION BETWEEN YOU GUYS AS YOU HELP OUT IN THIS BAR. IT'S A PERFECTLY GOOD BONUS MANGA.
BUT WOULDN'T OUR GUESTS RATHER SEE WHAT HAPPENS BEHIND THE SCENES OF SOUL EATER INSTEAD?
P.J HARVEY
WHAAAT!? I DON'T WANNAAA! IT'S SUCH A PAIN... BESIDES, I CAN'T THINK OF ANYTHING BEHIND THE SCENES TO WRITE ABOUT.
ANYTHING WOULD BE FINE. YOU MUST HAVE SOMETHING, DON'T YOU?
JUST STOP MESSING AROUND WITH US, ALL RIGHT!?
Beep! "Massacre Mode" activated!
KYUIIN (VWEE)
GASHI (KICK)
GESHI (STOMP)
MM-HMM.
ALL RIGHT! FINE!! I'LL TALK ABOUT SOMETHING BEHIND THE SCENES.

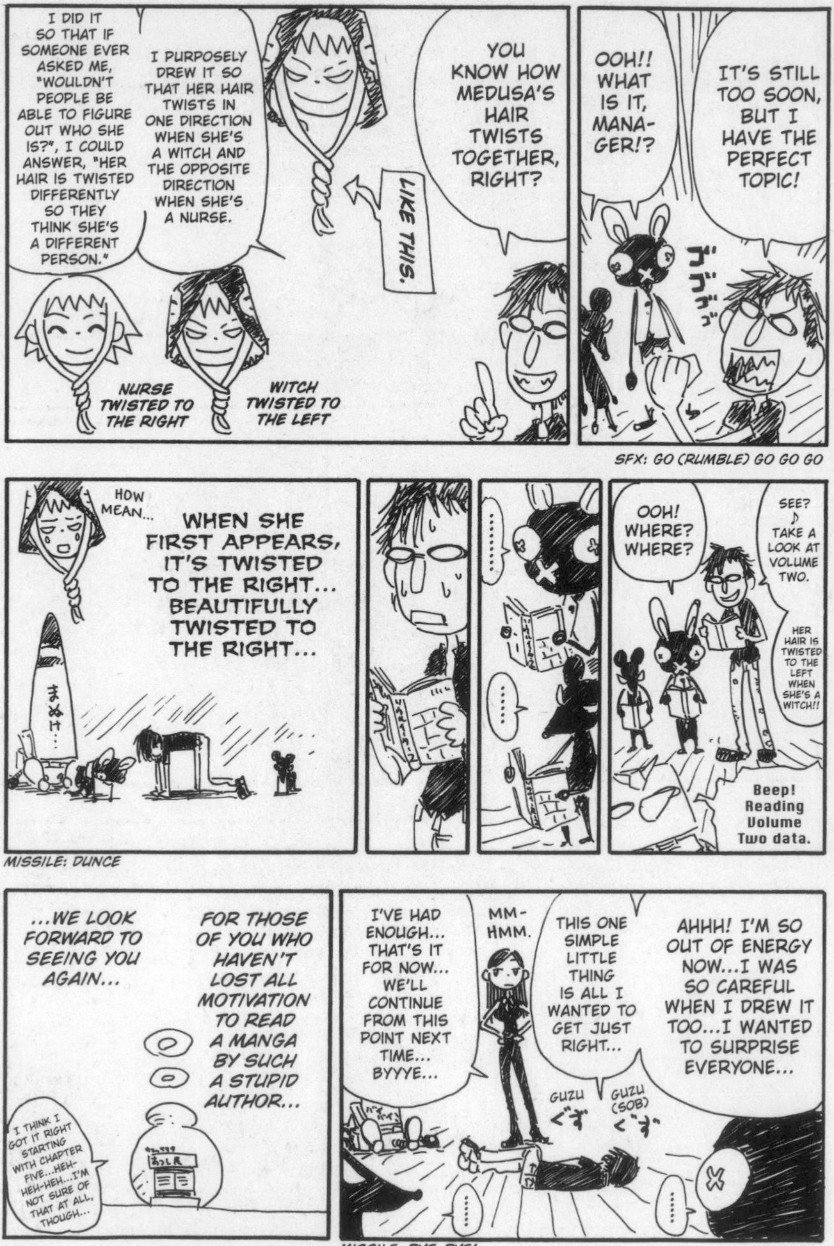
IT'S STILL TOO SOON, BUT I HAVE THE PERFECT TOPIC!
OOH!! WHAT IS IT, MANAGER!?
ゴゴゴゴ
YOU KNOW HOW MEDUSA'S HAIR TWISTS TOGETHER, RIGHT?
LIKE THIS.
I PURPOSELY DREW IT SO THAT HER HAIR TWISTS IN ONE DIRECTION WHEN SHE'S A WITCH AND THE OPPOSITE DIRECTION WHEN SHE'S A NURSE.
I DID IT SO THAT IF SOMEONE EVER ASKED ME, "WOULDN'T PEOPLE BE ABLE TO FIGURE OUT WHO SHE IS?", I COULD ANSWER, "HER HAIR IS TWISTED DIFFERENTLY SO THEY THINK SHE'S A DIFFERENT PERSON."
WITCH TWISTED TO THE LEFT
NURSE TWISTED TO THE RIGHT
SFX: GO (RUMBLE) GO GO GO
SEE? ♪ TAKE A LOOK AT VOLUME TWO.
OOH! WHERE? WHERE?
HER HAIR IS TWISTED TO THE LEFT WHEN SHE'S A WITCH!!
Beep! Reading Volume Two data.
....
......
WHEN SHE FIRST APPEARS, IT'S TWISTED TO THE RIGHT... BEAUTIFULLY TWISTED TO THE RIGHT...
HOW MEAN...
まぬけ…
MISSILE: DUNCE
AHHH! I'M SO OUT OF ENERGY NOW...I WAS SO CAREFUL WHEN I DREW IT TOO...I WANTED TO SURPRISE EVERYONE...
THIS ONE SIMPLE LITTLE THING IS ALL I WANTED TO GET JUST RIGHT...
MM-HMM.
I'VE HAD ENOUGH... THAT'S IT FOR NOW... WE'LL CONTINUE FROM THIS POINT NEXT TIME... BYYYE...
GUZU (SOB) ぐず
GUZU ぐず
......
......
FOR THOSE OF YOU WHO HAVEN'T LOST ALL MOTIVATION TO READ A MANGA BY SUCH A STUPID AUTHOR...
...WE LOOK FORWARD TO SEEING YOU AGAIN...
I THINK I GOT IT RIGHT STARTING WITH CHAPTER FIVE...HEH-HEH-HEH...I'M NOT SURE OF THAT AT ALL, THOUGH...
MISSILE: BYE-BYE!

Translation Notes

Common Honorifics

no honorific: Indicates familiarity or closeness; if used without permission or reason, addressing someone in this manner would constitute an insult.

-san: The Japanese equivalent of Mr./Mrs./Miss. If a situation calls for politeness, this is the fail-safe honorific.

-sama: Conveys great respect; may also indicate that the social status of the speaker is lower than that of the addressee.

-kun: Used most often when referring to boys, this indicates affection or familiarity. Occasionally used by older men among their peers, but it may also be used by anyone referring to a person of lower standing.

-chan: An affectionate honorific indicating familiarity used mostly in reference to girls; also used in reference to cute persons or animals of either gender.

-senpai: A suffix used to address upperclassmen or more experienced coworkers.

-sensei: A respectful term for teachers, artists, or high-level professionals.

Page 21
Nori refers to any one of several different kinds of seaweed used in cooking. *Nori* usually comes dried pressed into thin sheets. It is commonly used to wrap sushi rolls and *onigiri* (rice balls).

Page 22
"Imnyature"
Blair is trying to say the word "*otonagenai*," meaning "childish" or "immature," but when she says it, the "*nai*" part at the end turns into "*nyai*," making it sound cat-like. ("*Nya*" is how the Japanese represent a cat's "meow.")

Page 121
"I can't just keep it for myself."
The term Blair uses here is "*nekobaba*," which is rather fitting, given that the first part of the word, "*neko*," means "cat."

Page 130
In Norse mythology, Níðhöggr (often anglicized as **"Nidhogg"**) is the name of the dragon who gnaws at the roots of Yggdrasill, a great tree known as the "world tree."

Page 135
The name **"The Flying Dutchman"** comes from a legend about a ghost ship doomed to sail the sea forever, never to return home. In some versions of the tale, "The Flying Dutchman" refers to the ship itself, and in others it refers to the ship's captain. Some retellings have it that the captain is only allowed to go to port every certain number of years (the number varies in each version) to seek out a woman to share his fate. Seeing the ship is considered a bad omen.

Page 158
Taijutsu is a form of matial arts that focuses on physical skills and movement, as opposed to using weapons.

THE DEBUT SERIES FROM
ATSUSHI OHKUBO,
CREATOR OF
SOUL EATER

B.ICHI

THE POWER TO SOAR LIKE A BIRD
OR FIGHT LIKE A TIGER:
ALL IT TAKES IS A HANDFUL
OF BONES.

Complete Volumes 1-4
AVAILABLE NOW!

OLDER TEEN
OT

B. Ichi © Atsushi Ohkubo / SQUARE ENIX

SOUL EATER ④

ATSUSHI OHKUBO

Translation: Amy Forsyth

Lettering: Alexis Eckerman

SOUL EATER Vol. 4 © 2005 Atsushi Ohkubo / SQUARE ENIX. All rights reserved. First published in Japan in 2005 by SQUARE ENIX CO., LTD. English translation rights arranged with SQUARE ENIX CO., LTD. and Hachette Book Group through Tuttle-Mori Agency, Inc.

Translation © 2010 by SQUARE ENIX CO., LTD.

Yen Press
Hachette Book Group
1290 Avenue of the Americas, New York, NY 10104

www.HachetteBookGroup.com
www.YenPress.com

Yen Press is an imprint of Hachette Book Group, Inc. The Yen Press name and logo are trademarks of Hachette Book Group, Inc.

First Yen Press Edition: October 2010

ISBN: 978-0-7595-3127-7

20 19 18 17 16 15 14 13

BVG

Printed in the United States of America